Aeschines and Athenian Politics

AESCHINES AND ATHENIAN POLITICS

Edward M. Harris

New York   Oxford
OXFORD UNIVERSITY PRESS
1995

Oxford University Press

Oxford   New York
Athens   Auckland   Bangkok   Bombay
Calcutta   Cape Town   Dar es Salaam   Delhi
Florence   Hong Kong   Istanbul   Karachi
Kuala Lumpur   Madras   Madrid   Melbourne
Mexico City   Nairobi   Paris   Singapore
Taipei   Tokyo   Toronto

and associated companies in
Berlin   Ibadan

Copyright © 1995 Edward M. Harris

Published by Oxford University Press, Inc.,
200 Madison Avenue, New York, New York 10016

Library of Congress Cataloging-in-Publication Data
Harris, Edward Monroe.
Aeschines and Athenian politics / Edward M. Harris.
p.   cm.
Includes bibliographical references and index.
ISBN 0–19–508285–0
1. Greece—History—Macedonian Expansion, 359–323 B.C.   2. Athens
(Greece)—Politics and government.   3. Philip II, King of Macedonia,
382–336 B.C.   4. Aeschines.   5. Demosthenes.   6. Democracy—History.
I. Title
DF233.2.H37   1995
938′.07—dc20   94–4105

1 3 5 7 9 8 6 4 2

Printed in the United States of America
on acid-free paper

For Arielle Olney Harris,
Marion Stevens Harris,
and Edward Monroe Harris, Jr.

in angustiis fideles

Preface

This book has its origins in a Harvard dissertation entitled "The Political Career of Aeschines," which was submitted in the spring of 1983. Since then, it has been thoroughly revised with some parts completely rewritten. My main reasons for writing on Aeschines are that his speeches are a valuable source for a period that was a turning point in Greek history and that, aside from Ramming's brief dissertation, there has been no study devoted entirely to Aeschines' role in Athenian politics and diplomacy. I have therefore less to say about Aeschines' oratory except when it is relevant to his political career. There still remains much work to be done on Aeschines; I hope that this book will encourage others to study this relatively neglected author and to investigate those topics I have either passed over or not treated in sufficient depth.

One of the most pressing needs is for a new text of Aeschines' works. Schindel's recent Teubner edition is a reprint of Blass's 1908 edition, and the older Budé text of V. Martin and G. de Budé is inadequate. I am happy to report that my good friend and colleague Mervin Dilts, who recently edited the Aeschines scholia, will in the near future present a new edition of Aeschines' works based on a fresh reading of the primary manuscripts. In the absence of any more reliable edition, I had to rely for textual matters on the Arno reprint of F. Schultz's *Aeschinis Orationes* (Leipzig 1865).

My approach to the transliteration of Greek names is eclectic. For the better known names I tend to employ the Anglicized version ("Aeschines," not "Aiskhines," and "Eubulus," not "Euboulos"), but use the Greek form for less familiar names.

I have received much assistance over the years while working on Aeschines, but my main debt is to my dissertation adviser, Ernst Badian. He first suggested to me in a graduate seminar that Aeschines' speeches might be a promising field of inquiry. He was a superb adviser, demanding and rigorous, yet also helpful and encouraging. Though he has not been involved closely with the revision of the dissertation, the training I received from him has proven invaluable. I would also like to thank Albert Henrichs and Thomas Martin, who served as readers on the dissertation committee. Mogens Hansen and Peter Rhodes read the dissertation after it was completed and offered many good suggestions for revision. Finally, I would like to express my gratitude to my colleagues at Brooklyn College—Dee Clayman and Roger Dunkle, who were kind enough to read earlier drafts of the first two chapters, and to my graduate students, Maria Schönhammer and Martha Rowen, who read the entire manuscript at different stages to check for errors.

The book is dedicated to my daughter, Arielle Olney Harris, and to my parents, Edward M. Harris, Jr., and Marion Stevens Harris. Arielle was born just about the time I began work on Aeschines. Her cheerful presence often helped to keep my spirits up during the lonely and difficult process of revision. My parents generously contributed toward my rather prolonged education and later provided crucial support at a moment of crisis. Without their help, I could never have completed this book. I deeply appreciate the patience and loyalty all three have shown over the past decade.

Darien, Connecticut   E. H.
July 1994

Contents

Aeschines and Athenian Politics

Introduction

The decade that began in 348 B.C. with the fall of Olynthus and climaxed in 338 B.C. in the Battle of Chaeronea marked a decisive turning point in Greek history. Before 348, the Macedonians played only a marginal role in the world of the Greek poleis of central and southern Greece. The kings of Macedon, when not fighting off dangerous pretenders, were forced to devote most of their efforts to securing the kingdom's vulnerable borders against neighboring tribes. Their few attempts at territorial expansion were checked first by the Athenian Empire in the fifth century, then by the Spartans and the Thebans in the fourth century. But the stalemate of the major Greek powers after the Battle of Mantinea in 362 removed the barriers to Macedonian ambitions. When Philip ascended the throne in 359, he quickly put the affairs of the kingdom in order, developed his military resources, and took advantage of the new opportunity. By 348 he had already made remarkable progress. The neighboring tribes of Paeonia and Illyria had been defeated, the Chalcidian League destroyed, and its leading city Olynthus sacked. Philip had also extended his power southward, leading the Macedonians and his Thessalian allies to victory over the Phocians. Yet these achievements were only a prelude. In the next decade his military victories and diplomatic triumphs established Philip as the undisputed leader of the Greeks. Although Philip did not live to see his army win its greatest victories in Asia, his legacy proved to be long-lasting: Macedon remained the leading power in Greece until the Roman conquest.

Philip's achievement was as stunning as it was unexpected. Certainly no Athenian would have predicted in 350 that only a dozen years hence his city would be compelled to heed the commands of a king who ruled over a distant barbarian tribe. How was Philip able to gain hegemony for Macedon so quickly? Was it the inevitable outcome of Macedonian military strength? How much of his success was the result of astute diplomacy—or bribery? Or did the divided Greeks yield to Philip because he promised peace and unity?

Demosthenes had no doubt about the real answer: it was the venality of Greek traitors such as Thrasylochus of Messene, Daochus of Thessaly, and Aeschines of Athens, all of whom betrayed the freedom of the Greeks. Demosthenes forcefully promoted his view in several brilliant speeches, which provide us with much of our information (and disinformation) about Philip II. But not everyone in antiquity concurred with his opinion. Polybius, for one, argued that all the men Demosthenes denounced as traitors were in fact true patriots who had their communities' best interests at heart. Far from betraying the liberty of the Greeks, the men who supported Philip brought their fellow citizens the benefits of peace and freedom. In Polybius' view it was Demosthenes who almost brought ruin on Athens through his disastrous policies.

Scholars have written a great deal about Demosthenes' actions during Philip's rise to power, but have paid much less attention to the politicians in the Greek cities who supported Macedonian aims and opposed Demosthenes. If the men who favored Philip are discussed at all, scholars tend to lump them together into one pro-Macedonian party, a sort of fifth column for Philip's plans. To some extent, scholars have taken their cue from Demosthenes, who makes no distinctions among those who supported Philip, accusing them all of being willing instruments of Macedonian tyranny. Since scholars are indebted to Demosthenes for much of their evidence about the period, many have repaid him by adopting his view of his opponents. In most cases we have very little evidence with which to test Demosthenes' statements about Philip's friends among the Greeks. There is one significant exception: the Athenian politician Aeschines.

Aeschines, though far less eloquent and prolific an orator than his rival Demosthenes, wrote three long speeches that have survived from antiquity. Nine letters have also come down to us under his name, but they are recognized to be later forgeries. Aeschines' speeches are extremely valuable for the historian since they present us with an account of events in the years from 348 to 338 that differs markedly from that of Demosthenes. While most of the other Greek politicians who tried to cooperate with Philip are mere names on the lips of their detractors, Aeschines gives a detailed account of his dealings with Philip and a lengthy explanation of his policies. The only other contemporary orator who spoke in favor of Philip and whose work has survived is Isocrates, but he was never active in the Athenian Assembly and furnishes us with few details about specific events.

A study of Aeschines' political career therefore offers us the opportunity to examine why one Athenian politician chose to disagree with Demosthenes' estimate of Macedonian aims and to advise the Assembly to side with Philip. Was Aeschines bribed by Philip to support his cause? Did Philip deceive Aeschines about his aims? Did Aeschines show concern for the interests of Athens or act only to advance his own career? Was he a member of a well-organized group of pro-Macedonian politicians? These are questions that have stirred less interest among modern historians of Classical Greece, who have concentrated mainly on the goals and actions of Philip and Demosthenes.

There are other good reasons for taking a closer look at Aeschines' career. In recent years there has been much valuable work done by historians, in particular Peter Rhodes and Mogens Hansen, on the political institutions of Athenian democracy. Yet most of this work has focused on the rules and procedures of democratic institutions. Aeschines' speeches, on the other hand, provide us with a rare glimpse of the Athenian democracy at work. In fact, his narrative of the negotiations surrounding the Peace of Philocrates is one of the most detailed accounts we have of Athenian diplomacy and policy-making in action. It gives us a chance to observe how Athenian ambassadors attempted to carry out the wishes of the Assembly and reach agreements with foreign leaders. Aeschines is also unusual insofar as he was able to be active in Athenian politics without being a member of the liturgical class. Although there must have been other politicians in Athens who lacked substantial wealth, Aeschines is the only one about whom we have enough information to give us some idea of the path he followed to reach his position of influence in the Assembly. A study of his career thus has much to teach us about the relationship between wealth and talent in Athenian politics.

While there is much to learn from Aeschines' speeches, there are two important considerations to keep in mind when using them as historical evidence. First, Aeschines delivered his speeches at political trials in a highly charged atmosphere. Both he and his opponent Demosthenes each portray his own actions in the best possible light and his adversary's in the worst. Unlike modern courts where professionally trained judges enforce strict rules of procedure and evidence, the courts of Classical Athens had no rules restraining litigants from resorting to all manner of prevarication and rhetorical subterfuge. Naturally, each speaker had to be careful about preserving his credibility and could not be too reckless in embroidering the truth. Yet the members of the court were not omniscient, and it would have been difficult for them to detect artful cases of *suppressio veri* and to distinguish fact from plausible fiction.

Second, we must not lose sight of two crucial facts: both Aeschines and Demosthenes were Athenians, and Athens was only one of the Greek cities with which Philip dealt. Aeschines and Demosthenes were very proud of the fact that they were Athenians, but often neglected to remember that Athens was not Philip's sole concern. As a result, both politicians were in the habit of interpreting Philip's actions solely in terms of their effects on Athens. It would be unrealistic, however, to assume that Philip fashioned all his plans with only Athens in mind. Philip owed his power and influence among the Greeks to his good relations with many communities. Above all, he could not afford to ignore the tribes of northern Greece that posed an immediate threat to his kingdom. Thus we should always be prepared to question any interpretation of Philip's motives and aims put forward by Aeschines or Demosthenes. Demosthenes was certain Philip's main goal was to destroy Athens; Aeschines frequently maintained that Philip really intended to help Athens. And if we discover that one of these views is unlikely to be correct, that does not prove that the other is necessarily right. There is always the possibility that both men misunderstood Philip's intentions.

Since most of the information we have for Aeschines' career is drawn from his speeches and those of Demosthenes, our first task is to determine how reliable these sources are as historical evidence. In chapter 1, therefore, I will discuss the nature of forensic speeches as historical evidence and establish a set of criteria for evaluating the reliability of statements made by the two orators. In chapter 2, I will apply these criteria to the evidence for Aeschines' family background, early career, and entry into politics. After some introductory remarks about wealth, social status, and civic duties, this chapter examines the social status of Aeschines' family, the reasons for his late entry into politics, and the path he took to enter his public career.

The next three chapters treat the Peace of Philocrates. Since an understanding of Philip's aims and diplomatic methods are essential for a study of the treaty, chapter 3 surveys Philip's relations with Athens to 348 and his initial attempts to begin negotiations. The rest of the chapter looks into the reasons why the Athenians decided to accept Philip's invitation to discuss peace and alliance, and Aeschines' participation in the First Embassy to Macedon. The chapter also considers Aeschines' shift in policy between 348 and 346 and probes the motives behind it. Chapter 4 gives an account of the ratification of the Peace of Philocrates and Aeschines' decision to support the treaty. Chapter 5 covers events from the Second Embassy to the trial of Timarchus. The chapter begins with an analysis of the dispute between Aeschines and Demosthenes during the Second Embassy and the policy Aeschines urged Philip to pursue. The chapter then goes on to discuss the continuation of the conflict between Aeschines and Demosthenes after their return to Athens and the reasons why Philip did not adopt the proposals Aeschines made to him. The chapter concludes with a discussion of the trial of Timarchus and its implications for Aeschines' position in Athenian politics after the surrender of Phocis.

Chapters 6 and 7 chart the decline of Aeschines' influence and his repeated attempts to regain a leading position in the Assembly. Chapter 6 analyzes the causes of Aeschines' loss of political influence during the years 345–341. It investigates Aeschines' motives for his continued support for Philip, Philip's response to his critics in Athens, and the shift in Aeschines' attitude toward Athenian relations with Philip. Chapter 7 covers Aeschines' career from the outbreak of war with Philip in 340 to the trial of Ctesiphon in 330. The first part of the chapter examines Aeschines' actions during the war with Philip and his role in the declaration of the Fourth Sacred War. The second part looks at this attempt to attack Demosthenes by his prosecution of Ctesiphon and considers why he delayed his prosecution for so long before bringing it to court. Chapter 8 summarizes the main points that have emerged in this study of Aeschines' career and attempts to answer the questions posed in this introduction.

1

Whom to Believe?

When setting out to write a study of the political career of Aeschines, one is immediately confronted with the problem of how to use the sources. The problem is not an unusual one for modern historians of Classical Greece, who often have to rely on accounts written long after the event or on a single contemporary account composed by an author whose bias and unreliability are readily apparent. In one regard, however, the career of Aeschines presents unique problems with sources: virtually all of our information about him has to be extracted from his own speeches and those of his most bitter enemy, Demosthenes. Although there are numerous sources for the period in which he lived—Plutarch's *Lives,* in particular those of Demosthenes, Phocion, and Alexander; Books 16 and 17 of Diodorus' *Universal History;* Justin's summaries of Books 7 through 12 of Pompeius Trogus' *Philippic Histories;* fragments from the lost histories of authors such as Anaximenes, Androtion, Demetrius of Phaleron, Douris of Samos, Hermippus, Idomeneus, Marsyas, Philochorus, and Theopompus; and dozens of inscriptions from Attica and elsewhere—few mention Aeschines, and not one provides us with information about him that cannot be found either in his own orations or in those of Demosthenes.[1]

We are admittedly fortunate to possess information from speeches that represent opposing points of view, but this piece of luck turns out to be a mixed blessing. If Aeschines and Demosthenes agreed about the facts of the events in which they were involved and differed only in their interpretations of these events, we would have no trouble when trying to determine what actually happened. In that case, our task would be relatively simple: all we would have to do is to separate out fact from interpretation and then analyze the remaining information to construct an account of Aeschines' career. But that is not the task we are confronted with. In the speeches that constitute our main sources, Aeschines and Demosthenes rarely agree on the facts of the case and not infrequently contradict each other about what took place.

This is hardly surprising. Unlike the historian, who stood to gain little by distorting the facts, the Athenian politician who was speaking in court had a great deal at stake. Aeschines and Demosthenes delivered the speeches that provide us with most of our information about Aeschines' career at three trials: the first occurred in 346, the second in 343, and the third in 330. At the first, Aeschines accused Timarchus, a political ally of Demosthenes, of addressing the Assembly after prostituting himself; at the second, Demosthenes charged Aeschines with treason; and at the third, Aeschines prosecuted Ctesiphon for passing an illegal decree of praise for Demosthenes. Each case was not just a legal dispute; all three trials were major political battles. In Classical Athens victory in court was a powerful means of achieving political success. Defeat could be costly: conviction might mean death, exile, or the confiscation of a defendant's property. The accuser who failed to gain one fifth of the votes cast by the court in a public case had to pay a fine of a thousand drachmai and lost his right to bring any public prosecutions in the future. With so much at stake, a politician would use any means at his disposal to win his case. If lies, deception, and innuendoes might improve his chances for victory, these means would not be shunned. We should also keep in mind that the Athenian law code possessed no set of rules of evidence and that the magistrates who presided at trials in Athens never intervened to rule statements inadmissible or to exclude evidence. Thus litigants could use hearsay, repeat rumors, or appeal to testimony and documents that were irrelevant to the case without fear of being interrupted by the presiding magistrate. In short, nothing aside from the knowledge of the men sitting in judgment and the limits of plausibility restrained the litigant from inventing falsehoods and distorting the truth.[2]

How, then, are we to decide which of the statements made by Aeschines and Demosthenes to trust? Clearly we have to establish a set of criteria by which to judge the conflicting accounts presented by the two orators. Although many scholars have studied the period, none has attempted to formulate a system of rules by which to evaluate their statements. Arnold Schaefer has been one of the few to make some useful comments on the subject, but his own method was marred by using "consistency" as one of his criteria. By this term he did not mean "internal consistency," which can be a reliable criterion for judging the veracity of an account, but something rather different. Schaefer thought that if one speaker gave one version of an event on one occasion and another version at another time, this speaker could not be trusted, not only for this particular incident, but in general. Schaefer found Aeschines guilty of inconsistency in his two accounts of the Peace of Philocrates. In 346 Aeschines boasted about his cooperation with Philocrates during the negotiations with Philip earlier in that year, but in 343 he denied that he had ever had anything to do with him. As a result, Schaefer concluded that Aeschines was not reliable as a source and saw fit to discard much of the information found in his speeches. But the same charge of "inconsistency" can be leveled at Demosthenes. In 343 Demosthenes claimed that in Elaphebolion 346 Aeschines had spoken in the Assembly before ambassadors whom the Athenians had summoned from the Greek cities to participate in the negotiations with the Macedonian ambassadors. In 330, however, Demosthenes denied that any such embassies had been summoned by the Athenians in Elaphebolion 346. Thus, if we were to follow Schaefer's principle impartially, we would have to distrust all the statements made by Demosthenes as well. This would place us in the awkward position of being unable to trust any statement made by either orator.[3]

But this is not the main reason for rejecting this kind of "consistency" as a criterion for judging the trustworthiness of statements found in our sources. If a speaker gives two different accounts of the same event, it is possible that both of these accounts are false, but it is equally possible that one is true and the other false.

If a speaker is inconsistent in this way, it only indicates that we cannot accept as true everything he says. It does not imply that everything he says is false. When we come upon a case where a speaker gives two different versions of the same event, therefore, we should not reject them both, but instead try to determine on other grounds which statements in each account are true and which are false.

One method of approach might be to decide which speaker is more trustworthy by considering the judgment of the court: if the verdict was guilty, we should accept the account given by the prosecutor; if innocent, that given by the defendant. But anyone who is familiar with the legal system of Classical Athens will quickly recognize the shortcomings of this approach. We know from several incidents that the members of an Athenian court might occasionally be influenced more by a dazzling speech than by the arguments presented. Following a defeat in war or some other misfortune, a defendant might be convicted merely out of a desire to find a scapegoat. Or the court might be swayed by its mood that day. We should keep in mind that trials in Athens were completed within the space of a day and consequently the members of the court had little chance to consider over an extended period of time the merits of the cases presented by the two sides. The swiftness of the proceedings made the court far more susceptible to act on the passion of the moment. An anecdote recounted by Aristotle provides an illustration of what could happen in such a legal system. Aristotle tells us that the Athenians were more angry at the general Ergophilus than they were at the general Callistratus, but they nevertheless acquitted the former because they had condemned the latter to death on the previous day.

Yet, even if we knew that a court had attempted to evaluate impartially the arguments it had heard, we could still not be certain that the members of the court had made up their minds on the basis of all the arguments and all the evidence that had been presented in court. Unlike a modern jury, which during its deliberations can ask to review the evidence submitted by both sides, the Athenian court had no written record of the speeches and could not review the evidence it had heard before casting its vote. Consequently, the court arrived at its decision not on the basis of all the evidence and all the arguments presented, but only on what it happened to remember. Since we have no means of knowing what the court might remember or forget, it is impossible to know in any given case what an Athenian court took into consideration when it decided to condemn or acquit. It is therefore inadvisable to rely on the verdict of the court as a means of evaluating the reliability of the statements made in a forensic oration.[4]

What method should we employ? The most straightforward one would be to examine the evidence each speaker uses to prove his assertions. If a speaker calls witnesses or cites a document to verify his account of an event, we should accept what he says; if he provides no evidence, we have a right to question his statements. But this approach encounters an immediate objection: although the texts of the speeches of Aeschines and Demosthenes contain many references to the testimony of witnesses and the evidence of documents, how can we be certain that they actually called these witnesses and cited these documents on the day they delivered their speeches in court? What if they made substantial changes and added extensive new material to the published versions of their speeches?[5]

Although there is much evidence that the written versions of the speeches of Aeschines and Demosthenes were very close to the versions delivered in court, there are also some indications that certain revisions were made in the written versions. The evidence for such revision can be found by comparing the speeches delivered by Aeschines and Demosthenes at the same trial. If the defendant's speech states that a charge was made by the accuser, but the accuser's speech does not contain the charge, it is possible to conclude that the accuser actually made the charge, at the trial, but deleted it from the version of the speech he later committed to papyrus. We must bear in mind, however, that the court did not have a text of the accuser's speech when listening to the defendant's speech. The court probably remembered the main points the accuser made, but they would not be able to recall each individual detail and nuance of his speech. The defendant might, therefore, add or alter small details without fear of the court noticing these slight changes. The defendant might also state that the accuser had said something that he had actually only implied. For instance, in the beginning of the speech he delivered at his trial in 343, Aeschines recalls an argument employed by his opponent. Demosthenes, he says, argued that since Philocrates was condemned, the court should likewise condemn Aeschines. Although this argument is not found in the text we have of the speech, Demosthenes does often stress that Aeschines collaborated with Philocrates, and the court knew of course that Philocrates had been condemned to death in absentia shortly before. Even though the argument attributed to him by Aeschines does not appear *expressis verbis* in his speech, Demosthenes was obviously trying to drive this point home so that if he did not actually say what Aeschines said he did, the court might well have had the impression that Demosthenes had made this argument. Thus, only when the defendant refers to a statement made by the accuser that the court would have remembered because it was striking or important, and when this statement is not found in the text of the accuser's speech, can we conclude that the accuser deleted this statement from the written version of his speech.[6]

On this criterion there are only two cases where we have evidence of revision. Both are found in the speech Aeschines delivered as defendant in 343. In the beginning of his speech Aeschines tells how his accuser compared him to Dionysius the tyrant of Syracuse and described the dream of a Sicilian priestess. Nothing corresponding to this can be found in the version of Demosthenes' speech that has come down to us. In this case it is clear that the revision was made solely for stylistic reasons. In the only other case where there is clear-cut evidence for revision, it appears that the change was made for other reasons. This is a charge made by Demosthenes that Aeschines drove away from the sacrifices Critobulus, the representative of Cersebleptes, in the presence of the allies and the Athenian generals. Aeschines states that Demosthenes made the charge, but it does not appear in our text of his speech. In this case only is it likely that Demosthenes omitted from his written version a charge that he made in the speech he delivered in court. Demosthenes probably neglected to include the charge in his written version because it was a weak one that was easily refuted by Aeschines. But this one minor deletion is hardly evidence for extensive revision. And it does not impugn the use of documents and the testimony of witnesses as a criterion for evaluating the reliability of the information found in the speeches of Aeschines and Demosthenes.[7]

The kinds of revisions that would give us cause for concern would be those relating to documents and witnesses. But there is no evidence that indicates an orator ever stated in the written version of his speech that for a certain event he had witnesses whom he did not have in court on the day when he delivered his speech, or that in the written version of his speech an orator altered the text of a document or referred to a document that did not exist. If such revisions were made, we would have expected that at least occasionally in the versions of the speeches we now have, Aeschines and Demosthenes would give us markedly different accounts of the same event and that both of these accounts would be supported by equally good evidence or that the two orators would make contradictory statements about the same document. But that never occurs. If each orator gives a different account of the same event, one tends to have good evidence to support his account while the other always has either only irrelevant evidence or no evidence at all. In 343, for example, Demosthenes claimed that Aeschines had spoken in favor of Philocrates' proposal for peace with Philip in the Assembly on the second day of the debate, that is, on Elaphebolion 19, but provides no evidence to prove his assertion. Aeschines replied by arguing that he could not have spoken on that day since the debate about the treaty with Philip was limited to the previous day, Elaphebolion 18, and no further discussion was allowed on Elaphebolion 19. He then cited as evidence the decree that regulated the procedure at these two meetings of the Assembly.

At the same trial in 343, Aeschines said that on the Second Embassy Demosthenes carried with him only one talent, an amount that would have been sufficient to pay the ransom of just one man who was not very wealthy. This clearly implies that Demosthenes did not ransom more than one Athenian prisoner during the Second Embassy. Demosthenes, on the other hand, stated that he had loaned several men the money to pay their ransom and later made a gift of this money to them. Aeschines provided no evidence to support his version while Demosthenes called on the men to whom he had loaned money to verify his statements. Twice Aeschines and Demosthenes use the same document as evidence, but in neither case do they disagree with each other about the contents of these documents. In short, there is no evidence that in the written versions of their speeches Aeschines and Demosthenes ever refer to the testimony of witnesses or the evidence of documents that they did not present in court when they delivered their speeches.[8]

But how reliable was the testimony of the witnesses they called and the documents they cited? There is no reason to question the trustworthiness of public documents. Official copies of all public documents were kept in the archives and guarded. At the trial, it was the clerk, not the litigant, who read out the document to the court. There was no opportunity to tamper with or to misquote documents at the trial.[9] Yet, while documents could not lie, witnesses could. Indeed, several orators claimed that the bribery of witnesses was widespread. We know that at the end of the fifth century at least, Athenian politicians often belonged to *hetaireiai,* or clubs, that were organized in part, as Thucydides tells us, for the purpose of aiding members in court. One of the services the members of these clubs might render was to offer perjured testimony on behalf of another member.

On the other hand, there were severe penalties for perjury. If either party at a trial considered that a witness had given false testimony, he might declare before the court cast its vote that he objected to the testimony of that witness. He would then prosecute this witness by means of a *dike pseudomartyrion,* a charge of presenting false testimony. We do not know what the penalty was for one conviction on this charge, but if a man was condemned three times for this offense, he lost his citizen rights. Even one conviction on this charge would have been very damaging since it would have stamped the convicted man as a certified liar. With such a reputation he would be less likely to be called upon by his friends in the future to serve as a witness for them in court. That would have put him at a serious disadvantage since one of the most valuable favors one could do for a friend was to testify on his behalf in court. A conviction for lying would make a man's testimony useless and thus deprive him of one of the best ways of helping his friends, and we might add, harming his enemies, always a weighty consideration for an ancient Greek. For these reasons, we have strong grounds for accepting any statement made by an orator that is supported by the evidence of witnesses.[10]

Yet even if an orator calls witnesses or cites a document to corroborate his statements, we must also determine whether or not this evidence would actually have supported his statements. Athenian orators were quite capable of providing irrelevant evidence and then claiming that this "evidence" proved that their assertions were true. This problem is compounded by the fact that the testimony of the witnesses who were called and the contents of the documents that were cited have not survived in the texts of the speeches that have come down to us. In the case of witnesses a speaker normally indicates the facts about which they testified. Nevertheless, we must try to determine as closely as possible what are the limits of the evidence provided by witnesses. For instance, Demosthenes in 343 accused Aeschines of having taken bribes from Philip. He refers to two different occasions on which Philip attempted to bribe the Athenian ambassadors. The first time, Philip communicated with each of the ambassadors separately and offered them money, which all of them except one or two accepted. On the other occasion, Philip tried to offer all the ambassadors one collective bribe, which he called a guest-gift. Demosthenes refused this gift on behalf of the ambassadors and bid Philip use the money to pay the ransom for the Athenians held prisoner in Macedon. Philip complied with his request and promised to send the prisoners to Athens before the Panathenaea festival. After describing the second attempt to bribe the ambassadors, Demosthenes called Apollophanes and several others who had been present to testify. It is obvious that these witnesses were present only when Philip tried to present his guest-gift to all the ambassadors together. Their evidence is thus not relevant to Demosthenes' allegation that Philip communicated with the ambassadors individually and succeeded in bribing several of them. That part of his story is unsupported by evidence and may well be malicious invention.[11]

The same caution is necessary when we deal with the documents. Although we cannot be certain about the contents of a document cited by a speaker aside from what he reveals to us about it, we do in certain cases know from general principles concerning Athenian public records what a given document could *not* have contained. In 343, for example, Aeschines attempted to prove that Demosthenes was a close associate of Philocrates and said that Philocrates nominated Demosthenes to serve on the First Embassy. To support his assertion, Aeschines instructed the clerk to read out the decree of Philocrates that called for the election of ten ambassadors to be sent to negotiate with Philip. We know, however, that this decree could not have proven Aeschines' claim that it was Philocrates who nominated Demosthenes to serve on the embassy. We have several copies of decrees that provide the names of the men elected to serve as ambassadors, but none of these ever records the names of those who nominated them.[12]

When evaluating documents as evidence, we must also be especially careful in separating what the speaker says the document contained from his interpretation of its contents. The best illustration of this can be found in Demosthenes' statements about the *probouleuma* passed by the Council in Skirophorion 346. Demosthenes says that this measure did not include the customary vote of praise for the members of the Second Embassy. He interprets this omission as an expression of the Council's disapproval of the actions of the Second Embassy. While we must accept Demosthenes' statement that the decree did not contain a vote of praise for the Second Embassy, we are still entitled to question his interpretation of the Council's motion.[13]

So far we have seen that it is not enough for a speaker merely to furnish some evidence if we are to believe his account of an event. For us to regard his account as trustworthy his evidence must be relevant. Nor should we believe every statement a speaker makes about a certain event when only some of his statements are backed up with evidence, but others are not. And even if the account given by a speaker is corroborated by relevant evidence, we still are not compelled to accept the interpretation he puts on those events. On the other hand, all statements that are supported by relevant evidence should be regarded as essentially reliable.

A corollary to this principle immediately follows. This is that we should suspect any important statement made by a speaker that is not supported by evidence. There was no excuse for a speaker who failed to cite the evidence of documents or the testimony of witnesses when making a charge. Anyone who spoke in court had at his disposal a large collection of public documents, any of which he could have read out by the clerk to prove the truth of his assertions. We know that all decrees passed by the Council and Assembly were kept by the Secretary of the Council. These decrees were the main records for all business transacted by the Athenian democracy since all important public business had first to be introduced to the Council and then gain the approval of the Assembly. Letters sent to the Assembly from Athenian magistrates abroad or from foreign communities were also kept in the archives. Records were kept of trials, but these carried only the names of the prosecutor and the defendant, the nature of the charge, the verdict, and the judgment imposed by the court. The Athenians, however, did not keep minutes at their meetings. Moreover, their decrees recorded only the name of the man who had proposed a measure and not the names of all those who had spoken for or against it. Thus, when Aeschines wished to prove that Demosthenes, while serving as one of the *proedroi* at a meeting of the Assembly of Elaphebolion 25, 346, spoke out against a proposal regarding Cersebleptes, the king of Thrace, he had to call on the other *proedroi* to testify. Nor were copies of reports made by ambassadors to the Council and Assembly kept in the archives. When Aeschines in 343 wished to have the reports given by the members of the First Embassy submitted as evidence, he had to call on the ambassadors themselves to testify. We should also note that since copies were kept only of those motions that were passed, there was no record of proposals that were not approved by the Council or the Assembly.[14]

In cases where there was no document available that could be read to verify some statement about public business, it was still possible, as we have seen in the two cases above, to call on witnesses to testify. Athenian citizens were not the only ones who could give testimony; foreigners, too, could testify. In 343 Aeschines had representatives from Phocis testify about his actions in Delphi in the summer of 346. Thirty years before, in 373, Jason of Pherae came all the way from Thessaly to serve as a witness for his friend Timotheus. If a man was going abroad and would be unable to attend a trial, he could leave a sworn statement, which was witnessed by several citizens, before he left on his trip. His statement could be read out in court, where those who had witnessed it would then testify they had been present when the statement was recorded. Nor was it possible to use the excuse that those who had witnessed the event in question refused to come forward. If a witness was reluctant to testify, the litigant could ask the herald to issue a summons. The witness who failed to heed the summons was fined a sum of one thousand drachmai. The only free Athenians who could not testify were those who had lost their citizen rights or were in exile. Given these procedures, there was no reason why a litigant could not bring forward some kind of evidence to back up his main assertions.[15]

Are there any charges that are unsubstantiated by evidence, which we might just the same take seriously? What about a charge made by the accuser which the defendant does not refute? Is it not natural to interpret the defendant's silence as a sign of his inability to answer the charge? The silence of a defendant may be a sign of his inability to disprove an accusation, but there may be other reasons for his failure to respond. It is necessary to recall that both Aeschines and Demosthenes, when acting as prosecutors, utter dozens of slanders about their opponents, many of which are not directly relevant to the case. Few of these slanders are supported by any evidence at all. These insults are so numerous that it would have been impossible for the defendant to reply to all of them in detail. The defendant had only a limited amount of time in which to speak and had to make sure he replied to all the serious charges. If he spent too much time disproving unsubstantiated slanders, he would never be able to cover his main points before the water ran out of the clepsydra. For instance, in 330 Aeschines accused Demosthenes of having obtained his seat on the Council in 347 through bribery, but offered no evidence in support of this charge. In his reply to Aeschines, Demosthenes does not as much as allude to the slander. There are good reasons to suspect the charge since if it were true, we would have expected to find it in the speech Aeschines delivered against Demosthenes in 343. On that occasion, Demosthenes was prosecutor and would not have had a chance to respond to it. Yet Aeschines omitted the charge from his speech in 343, presumably because the event in question was relatively recent at the time, and Aeschines therefore felt less confident in his ability to deceive the court.[16]

On the other hand, when a speaker makes a statement that is not supported by evidence about his opponent, who then alludes to this statement without refuting it, there is a greater likelihood that the statement is true. Two examples will illustrate this principle. In his speech as prosecutor in 343, Demosthenes said that Aeschines had at one time been a *tritagonistes,* an actor who is confined to playing lesser roles because of his inferior talents. Aeschines alludes to the charge, but does not refute it. In much the same fashion, Aeschines twice sneers at Demosthenes for having been a *logographos,* a professional speech writer. Demosthenes refers to this charge, but does not deny it. Nor could he have, since we know from other sources that he had indeed written speeches for other Athenians.[17]

The only other exception to our rule that all statements not supported by relevant evidence ought to be regarded with suspicion is the case of statements made about public events from the very recent past. We need only look at the statements made by Aeschines about his association with Philocrates. When prosecuting Timarchus in 346, Aeschines boasted about his cooperation with Philocrates during the negotiations that led to the peace treaty with Philip earlier in that year. Three years later in 343, after Philocrates had been condemned to death in absentia for having betrayed Athens, Aeschines denied that he had ever had anything to do with Philocrates. Here it is clear that we should accept the earlier statement and not the one made three years after the events in question. By the same token, we should place more trust in the statements made by Demosthenes about the events of 346 in his speech *On the Peace,* which he delivered during the same year, than in those found in his speech of 343.[18]

When applying these criteria to the statements of Aeschines and Demosthenes, we must be as impartial as possible. What we should not do is to examine the statements of one orator, then, upon finding several of them unreliable, assume that the account given of the same event by his opponent is ipso facto trustworthy. When we discover that one man is a liar, there is a strong temptation to believe that his opponent must be honest, but that temptation must be resisted. It is especially important to bear this point in mind when comparing the accounts given by the two orators about the outbreak of the Fourth Sacred War. Demosthenes charges that Aeschines had conspired with Philip to start the war, but supplies no evidence to prove his accusation, which, as we will see, is also extremely implausible. Aeschines presents a narrative of the war's outbreak that is not fully supported by the evidence he adduces, yet is far more plausible than that of his rival. But plausibility does not guarantee reliability. Even though Aeschines presents a credible account, we must still remain skeptical about any of his statements that he does not support with documents or witnesses. In cases such as this one, we simply have to suspend judgment on the issues about which the two men disagree.[19]

We can now sum up our guidelines for evaluating the evidence found in the speeches.

1. Statements that are supported by relevant evidence can be regarded as reliable.
2. It is important to determine whether the evidence cited by the speaker could actually have proven the truth of his statement.
3. While we can trust a statement of fact that is corroborated by relevant evidence, nothing compels us to accept the speaker's interpretation of that fact.
4. All statements not supported by evidence should be regarded with suspicion.
5. The only kinds of unsubstantiated assertions that can be trusted are those

made about public events in the recent past and charges made by the prosecutor that are mentioned by the defendant without being refuted.
6. The failure of the defendant to respond to a charge made by his accuser is not strong grounds for considering the charge to be true.

The rigorous application of these principles will obviously force us to reject many of the statements made by Aeschines and Demosthenes as historical evidence.[20] As a result, we will discover that out of the wealth of information found in their speeches only a small amount can be trusted and used to construct an account of Aeschines' political career. But it is better to build on a rock that is small yet firm than on a broad plain filled with quicksand.

2

Family, Early Career, and Start in Politics

Even in the case of the most important figures in antiquity, the information we possess about their early lives is scant at best. We do not know the year of birth for many famous people, and little is told to us about their education and early activities. Occasionally we are fortunate enough to have a few anecdotes about the childhood and youth of a prominent figure, but these too must be treated with great caution. Anecdotes are often transmitted orally for several generations before being written down and are thus subject to all the changes that this kind of source works on its material. The ancient historians themselves took little or no interest in the early lives of great men and tended instead to direct their attention primarily to battles and political events, which they felt to be the true subject matter of history. Biographies were written about remarkable individuals, but these were almost invariably composed many years after the deaths of their subjects by writers who often had much the same sources as scholars today have. Consequently, these biographies rarely add much to our meager stock of information. When they do contain matter that is not found in other sources, it is unlikely to be the product of painstaking research. Rather, it is most probably a fiction invented by an imaginative biographer, who, frustrated by the paucity and dullness of the sources available to him, took the liberty of inventing sensational details.[1]

In the case of Aeschines we are relatively lucky to have a number of statements drawn from his own speeches and those of his opponent Demosthenes about his family background and his activities prior to his entry into politics. Although it is impossible to draw any conclusions about the formative influences on his personality from these few scraps of information, we can still look at his social background and consider how wealthy his family was and what advantages or liabilities this background gave him. This in turn will help us to understand why he took the route he did to enter politics in Athens and also to explain why he entered politics relatively late in his life. Yet before we can discuss the position of Aeschines and his family in Athenian society, it is first necessary to examine briefly certain aspects of the social structure of that society. As with any community, the population of Athens could be divided into numerous sets of groups according to various criteria. Since we are concerned, however, primarily with the impact that wealth and social status had on the chances of an Athenian citizen for political success, the most important sets of groups for our purposes will be, first, the liturgical and military classes, and second, the status-groups designated by various labels, but best known by the terms *kaloi kagathoi* and *poneroi*.[2]

Although legal and political rights were for the most part shared equally by all citizens in the fourth century, military and financial burdens were still distributed according to wealth. The most affluent men in Athens formed the liturgical class, those who served in the cavalry as young men and when older acted as captains of the triremes of the Athenian fleet. These men were also called on to finance the approximately one hundred annual festival liturgies. Of these the most famous were those for the dramatic contests. Each man who volunteered or was selected by the archon for this task was assigned to produce the plays of one of the authors whose work had been selected for performance that year. Such a peson was called a *choregos* and paid the wages of the chorus and bought the costumes for the entire troupe. Prizes were awarded for the best plays at these festivals and as a result the *choregoi* could become quite competitive, spending as much as two thousand drachmai in their efforts to outdo each other. As trierarch, the member of the liturgical class would be assigned a trireme on which he would serve as captain for a year and be expected to make sure that his ship was fully equipped. The public treasury normally provided the equipment for the trireme, including sails, tackle, and oars, in addition to the funds needed to buy rations and to pay the crew; the trierarch himself was obligated to make some contribution toward the upkeep of the ship. This amount appears to have been somewhere between forty and sixty *mnai*, but those who wished to impress their fellow citizens with their devotion to the city might spend much more. About twelve hundred men formed the liturgical class in the fourth century. No set qualification existed for inclusion in this class, but it has been calculated that "during the fourth century men whose property was worth less than 3 *tal.* were free from liturgical obligations, while men whose property was worth over 4 *tal.* were very unlikely to escape such obligations in the long run."[3]

A slightly larger group than the twelve hundred called on to serve as trierarchs and to pay for the festival liturgies was made up of those who were required to pay the *eisphora*, an extraordinary levy on property for war purposes. In 378 those who were subject to this levy were grouped into one hundred symmories, and each one of the symmories was headed by three men who were called respectively the *hegemon* (leader), *deuteros* (second man), and *tritos* (third man). These men would advance to the fleet the entire sum to be contributed by the entire symmory and then collect this sum, minus what they themselves owed, from the other members of the symmory. The "Three Hundred" who acted as the leaders, second men, and third men of the symmories were the wealthiest men in Attica. They had to be; the payments they had to advance to the navy were quite substantial and must have created strains on even the very largest fortunes.[4]

Those who did not have enough money to perform liturgies might become hoplites in the army provided their property was above a certain minimum. Everyone who met this property qualification was enrolled as an ephebe as soon as he reached the age of eighteen and was registered as a citizen in his deme. All those ephebes who were enrolled in the same year formed an age class and had their names recorded together on a tablet placed in the archives. As ephebes, these young men received military training for two years in outposts scattered throughout the Attic countryside. Every hoplite who graduated from this training was liable for duty up to age sixty unless disabled for some reason, but the older men appear to have been called up only in emergencies. The number of Athenian hoplites reached a high of 18,000 to 25,000 in 431, then must have fallen sharply in the following decades as the losses from the plague and the Peloponnesian War took their toll. By 400 there may have been as few as 10,000, but their numbers rose throughout the fourth century and appear to have reached 14,500 by 322. Citizens who possessed less than the minimum needed for hoplite service were generally free from military duties and financial burdens, yet might row in the fleet for a wage if they wished to. These were the poorest citizens in Athens and were called thetes. We have no reliable figures for the number of thetes in any period, but it seems reasonable to infer that their total was roughly equivalent to that of the hoplites.[5]

When attempting to determine the financial resources of an Athenian citizen, it is obviously useful to know what duties he was asked to perform for the community. Even in the absence of any firm knowledge of a man's holdings, we can still get some idea of the relative size of his fortune if we can find out whether he served as a hoplite or as a trierarch. This is important information for, as we will see, a large income gave one a distinct advantage in Athenian politics. At the same time, we should bear in mind that the possession of wealth did not automatically win a man respect in Athenian society. Money and property may have been a necessary condition for social prestige, but they were not a sufficient condition. The Athenian who owned several farms and workshops staffed by slaves might still not be deemed worthy of the hand of a girl whose father prided himself on being one of the *kaloi kagathoi*. There is likewise no reason to think that someone who did not have quite enough property to perfrom liturgies would be ipso facto banned from polite society.[6]

This brings us to the topic of status-groups, the other aspect of Athenian social structure we need to examine. Despite the fact that all Athenians were equal in most regards when it came to legal and political rights, they nonetheless tended to divide themselves roughly into two status-groups. In one of these groups were the *kaloi kagathoi* (gentlemen), *chrestoi* (good people), *gnorimoi* (well-known), *beltistoi* (best people), in short, those who were considered respectable. In the other group were the *poneroi* (wretched), *kakoi* (bad), and *banausoi* (laborers), those who were unable to meet the criteria for inclusion in respectable society. We should be careful to refrain from regarding the *kaloi kagathoi* as nobles or aristocrats since those words conjure up visions of a class whose members enjoy hereditary privileges, own large ancestral estates, and possess formal titles such as "duke," "marquis," and "earl." This kind of class never existed in Classical Athens. These status groups were purely informal—the *kaloi kagathoi* did not keep a list of those whom they thought socially acceptable. Anyone could claim to be a *kalos kagathos,* imitate their life-style, and try to join their company in the gymnasium. But the members of polite society were also free to shun anyone who in their opinion was déclassé.[7]

The *kaloi kagathoi* were united not so much by common material interests as by a common life-style. These gentlemen aspired to be both independent and generous. In daily life they pursued those activities that they considered to be conducive to moral and intellectual refinement. Independence meant economic self-sufficiency, freedom from the need to work for another man. One of the greatest misfortunes that could befall an Athenian citizen was the necessity of having to hire oneself out to someone else. This placed an Athenian in the position of a slave who had to take orders from his master. Aside from the humiliation, the physical work performed by hired hands was viewed as demeaning; it made one coarse and unfit for more dignified pursuits. The ideal was to have enough property to live off the income provided by farms or workshops staffed by slaves. This kind of arrangement gave one the leisure to participate in activities like exercise in the gymnasium, racing horses, attending fashionable symposia, and pursuing a career in politics. The *kalos kagathos* revealed his noble and generous nature by helping his friends and by performing liturgies for the community.[8]

The life of a *kalos kagathos* required a substantial amount of property. It is therefore no wonder that the *kaloi kagathoi* were often referred to as *hoi plousioi* (the rich). Those who served in the cavalry and performed liturgies surely had enough to afford the necessary life-style, but those further down the economic scale might also be able to qualify. In fact, several authors imply that many of the hoplites could be considered *kaloi kagathoi*. But it was not enough to be affluent and lead the life of a *kalos kagathos;* it was also necessary to have parents who were thought to be respectable. Hence the gentleman was often described as *eugenes* or *gennaios* (well-born). One did not have to have a long line of ancestors stretching all the way back to Solon and beyond, but it could help. Certainly those who were so favored did not hesitate to remind others of their distinguished lineages and naturally expected respect and deference in return. And just as old wealth could be a source of prestige, nouveaux riches met with resentment. Aristotle, for example, advises the prospective orator that it is far more easy to stir up indignation against a man whose wealth has been recently acquired than one who has received his property through inheritance. Cratinus put the newly rich in the same category as slaves and other undesirables. The social prejudice against those whose parents did not make it into the ranks of the *kaloi kagathoi* can be seen in the case of Iphicrates. Despite his entry into the liturgical class and his election to the generalship, Iphicrates was nevertheless insulted for his humble origins. Phormion and Pasion were among the wealthiest men in Athens, yet they could still be taunted for their servile birth.[9]

If one was to aspire to the life-style of a *kalos kagathos,* one of the prerequisites was a good education. This meant the traditional schooling, which consisted of learning the works of the poets, especially Homer, exercise in the gymnasium, and training in music. All this gave one discipline, character, social grace, and a good physique. Knowledge of the poets and musical skill was a sine qua non for the gentleman who wished to make a good impression at a symposium. Exercise out of doors in the gymnasium made it possible to distinguish the bodies of the *kaloi kagathoi* from those of the *banausoi*. Gentlemen were well tanned with broad shoulders and muscular thighs and buttocks. The *banausos* had a pale complexion and a body deformed from toiling indoors all day and from bending over his work. The *banausos* had neither the time nor the money to spend on education; he would barely know how to read and write.[10]

Since many Athenians could fulfill some, but not all, of the criteria for inclusion among the *kaloi kagathoi,* there was no clear dividing line between the *kaloi ka-*

gathoi and the *poneroi,* between the social elite and the mass of citizens. For example, the independent farmer who owned and worked his fields did not fit neatly into either group. Farming was more respectable than most of the manual trades, and it was not considered undignified for a gentleman to spend time in the country directing the work on his estate. But the farmer who was not wealthy enough to buy many slaves or hire free men to do most of his work and thus had to perform many of the tasks required in sowing and harvesting his crops could not imitate the life-style of the *kalos kagathos.* He would have little time to gain an education or exercise in the gymnasium. Although he could boast of a certain degree of self-sufficiency and did not have to work for another man, he lacked the leisure to acquire the refinement of a gentleman and remained rustic and unsophisticated, an *agroikos.* The independent farmer occupied a sort of middle ground between the two extremes represented by the *kaloi kagathoi* and the *poneroi.* This group was by no means insignificant, but probably made up a large proportion of the entire citizen population of Attica.[11]

Family Background

With these considerations in mind, we can now study the social position of Aeschines and his family. All the information we have about Aeschines' family is derived from two main sources, Aeschines himself and his opponent Demosthenes. Not surprisingly their respective portraits of his parents differ markedly. The difficulties of reconciling these two portraits are aggravated by the fact that neither orator provides any evidence to prove his claims. Yet although all of Demosthenes' wilder allegations can be dismissed as slander and many of Aeschines' inflated claims to respectability can easily be punctured, we will find there remains a small residue of fact on which both men tacitly agree. From these few facts significant conclusions about the social status of Aeschines' family can be drawn.[12]

When we scrutinize the statements of the two men, we need to look at each one in the context in which it was delivered. For instance, we should first consider the statements made by Demosthenes as prosecutor in 343 so that when we come to the information in the speech Aeschines delivered at the same trial, we will know what attacks he was responding to. As we turn to the comments made by Demosthenes at the trial of Ctesiphon in 330, we must likewise remember that on that occasion Aeschines had no chance to reply to anything his opponent said about his parents.

We begin therefore with the speech Demosthenes made as prosecutor in 343. In this speech Demosthenes makes only a few isolated remarks about Aeschines' parents. In one place he describes how Aeschines' mother made money carrying out religious purifications and how his father earned his living by teaching reading and writing. Elsewhere in the speech Demosthenes calls the father, Atrometus, a *grammatistes,* "schoolteacher," and relates how the mother, Glaucothea, gathered together bands of worshippers for some degenerate purpose. He does not specify what this scandalous activity was, but by assuring the court that another priestess was condemned to death for performing the same act, implies that it was very sacrilegious. After this abuse, he challenges his opponent to name any benefits he and his father have brought the city and suggests several possible answers, such as service in the cavalry or as a hoplite, performance of a trierarchy, financing a chorus or some other liturgy, or payment of the *eisphora*.[13]

It is difficult to evaluate any of these statements before we look at Aeschines' reply to them. We should however note his challenge to Aeschines to list any services he and his family have performed for the city. Numerous court speeches reveal that it was normal for the defendant to provide proof of his patriotism and good will toward the community by citing all the duties he had performed on its behalf. This was done not only with the intention of demonstrating one's good character, but also in hope that the members of the court would feel grateful for all the favors he had bestowed upon them. Yet, although it was customary for the defendant to remind the court of his generosity, it was unusual for the accuser to challenge him to do so, and the fact that Demosthenes invites Aeschines to list his services to the Athenians strongly suggests that he is confident that his opponent will have a hard time complying with his request.[14]

Aeschines begins the reply he delivered in 343 to Demosthenes' insults about his parents with an account of his father Atrometus, who was born in 437/36 or 436/35. It is perhaps significant that Aeschines never mentions here or elsewhere any ancestors before his father. There is no reason to go so far as to infer from his silence that they were slaves or freedmen, but we are safe in assuming that they were probably undistinguished and performed no memorable deeds. Aeschines attempts to give the impression that his father was associated with some of the older, more respectable families in Athens when he says that Atrometus belongs to the same phratry as the Eteobutadai, who held the priesthood of Athena Polias. This means very little, however, since many Athenians were enrolled in a phratry, many of which were headed by well-known *gene* such as the Eteobutadai. Aeschines then recounts how his father spent his youth competing in athletic contests. The aim of this should be obvious: Aeschines is trying to show that his father, at least as a young man, was free from the need to work for a living and pursed the life-style of a *kalos kagathos,* exercising regularly in the gymnasium.[15]

Aeschines continues by telling how Atrometus was prevented from practicing as an athlete by the loss of property during the Peloponnesian War. Aeschines is probably referring to the damage inflicted by the Spartans after they occupied Dekeleia in 413 and not to the incursions made by the Peloponnesian army in the early years of the war. The latter began in 431 when Atrometus was only six or seven years old, thus well before he could have begun his athletic career. Besides, it is unlikely that Atrometus and his family would have suffered very much from the early invasions even if the bulk of their property lay in or near their deme of Kothokidai, which happened to lie right in the path of the Peloponnesian army. Thucydides reports that these incursions were of short duration, did not cause much damage, and left the fields to be worked the rest of the year.[16]

Aeschines passes over what his father did between the time he lost his property and the time he was forced into exile by the Thirty, but he does say something about his activities during the reign of the Thirty. His motive for this should be transparent—he had no wish to dwell on his father's poverty in these years. Aeschines understandably prefers to say that Atrometus was banished by the Thirty and helped to restore the democracy. Aeschines' description of his father's heroic actions against the Thirty is clearly aimed at refuting Demosthenes' charge that his family had never rendered the city any major services.[17]

Aeschines' account of these events invites scrutiny. He tells us that his father was exiled, accompanied his wife to Corinth, then went to Asia where he served as a soldier and took part in some battles, and ultimately returned to Athens in time to aid in the overthrow of the oligarchy. The chronology of these actions presents difficulties. The precise date on which the Thirty came into power is unknown, but they seized control of Athens by the summer of 404 and were out of power by the late summer of 403. Aeschines nevertheless claims that his father traveled to Corinth, then went to Asia, fought in several battles there, and returned to Athens all within this space of time. Moreover, Atrometus could not have arrived in Asia until the late summer of 404 at the earliest, too late for the campaigning season of 404. And he must have left in the early spring of 403 to make it back to join Thrasybulus and the other exiles in restoring the democracy, and therefore too early to fight in the campaigning season of 403 in Asia. A scholium on this passage states that Atrometus was hired by a Persian satrap, but this is probably a guess, for the author of the scholium cites no authority and is apparently unable to name the satrap. We certainly do not hear of any band of Greek mercenaries serving in Asia in this year. The only mercenaries fighting in Asia during this period whom we hear about in our sources are those recruited by Clearchus in 403 to march with Cyrus in his campaign against the Persian king.[18]

Aeschines' brief account of Atrometus' activity during the reign of the Thirty clearly cannot be accepted as it stands. Aeschines may possibly have gone so far as to invent the story of his father's exile and participation in the restoration of the democracy. As we have already seen, Aeschines had a strong motive for doing this, but in the absence of conclusive proof all we can do is to express doubt. Yet Aeschines had no reason to invent the story of his father's military service in Asia since this was not especially praiseworthy. Everyone would have assumed that fighting in Asia meant service as a mercenary, and that was nothing to boast about since mercenary service was often the sign of poverty. Given these considerations, the safest conclusion is to move Atrometus' service as mercenary down to the 390s when our sources tell us many Greeks were hiring themselves out as soldiers to Persian satraps. Aeschines may then have placed his father's mercenary service after his exile under the Thirty to give the impression that Atrometus had been forced to take service in Asia for political reasons and not because of his poverty, as was in fact the case.[19]

In the same passage where he recounts the exploits of his father, Aeschines also mentions that Atrometus took his wife to Corinth before he set out for Asia. There she presumably remained until his return. Unlike Demosthenes, Aeschines does not refer to his mother by her name Glaucothea, but calls her ''my mother.'' This is due to the Athenian sense of propriety which forbade a man to utter in public the name of a respectable woman and constrained him to refer to her only with a periphrasis such as ''the wife of Atrometus.'' It is thanks only to the contempt of Demosthenes, who did not feel these scruples about his opponent's mother, that we possess our knowledge of her name. In the other passage from this speech where he refers to his mother, Aeschines uses another periphrasis, this time calling her the sister of

Cleobulus, the son of Glaucus of Acharnai, who along with Demaenetus, a member of the *genos* of the Bouzygai, defeated Chilon, the commander of the Spartan fleet. It is curious how Aeschines slips in the name of the famous *genos* to which Demaenetus belongs. Unable to show that his own ancestors were members of the more celebrated *gene*, Aeschines tries to create the impression that his relatives were closely associated with men from these *gene*, just as he linked his father with the Eteobutadai. Unlike the case with his father, however, Aeschines names his mother's father and says that her brother achieved renown in a naval battle.[20]

Which naval battle was this? At first glance it might appear to be identical to an incident recounted in the *Hellenica Oxyrhynchia*. According to this work, a certain Demaenetus in the year 397/96 commandeered a trireme from the dockyard of the Athenian fleet in the Piraeus. With the consent of the Council, but without the approval of the Assembly, Demaenetus sailed away with the intention of joining Conon. As soon as word of Demaenetus' action got out, there was an uproar, and the leaders of the city were accused of dragging Athens into war with Sparta. The members of the Council then decided to convoke a meeting of the Assembly. At the meeting a decision was made to inform Milon, the Spartan harmost on Aegina, that Demaenetus had sailed without the permission of the Athenian people. Immediately after receiving the message, Milon sailed off in pursuit and caught up with Demaenetus off Thorikos on the east coast of Attica. Just as the story reaches its climax, the papyrus becomes very fragmentary, but the tattered remains seem to indicate the Demaenetus abandoned his ship and then was able to obtain another in which he resumed his journey to Conon. Milon seized the ship Demaenetus had abandoned, but did not pursue him further and returned to Aegina.[21]

There are of course discrepancies between this account and what Aeschines says about the battle his uncle took part in, but they may be the product of Aeschines' imperfect knowledge of events that had taken place before his birth. Aeschines is elsewhere rather careless about details of Athenian history and could easily have substituted the name ''Chilon'' for ''Milon.'' Nor should we discount the possibility that Aeschines, who has a noticeable tendency to exaggerate his family's prestige, transformed what had been a small skirmish with the Spartan harmost on Aegina into a full-scale naval battle with the commander of the entire Spartan fleet. Thus if the naval battle alluded to by Aeschines is indeed identical with the incident involving Demaenetus described in the *Hellenica Oxyrhynchia*, we can see that fighting in this action could hardly have brought Cleobulus much renown. Alternatively, Aeschines may be referring to some other battle that was so insignificant that it failed to attract the notice of the historians whose narratives of this period survive.[22]

What Aeschines fails to say about his family in these passages from his speech of 343 is equally as significant as what he does say. In response to Demosthenes' challenge to list all his public services, Aeschines has very little to offer: his father was one of several hundred who helped restore the democracy in 403, and his uncle took part in some obscure naval engagement against the Spartans. One thing is quite clear: no one in his family could boast of having attained major public office, served as trierarch, or performed festival liturgies. Notable also is the fact that Aeschines does not deny that his father was a schoolteacher. He even admits Atrometus was not affluent, having lost his property during the Peloponnesian War and then being forced to earn money as a mercenary in Asia. For the moment we will leave aside the question of just how poor Atrometus was, but at this point we can safely conclude that he was not in the liturgical class. This probably held true for Glaucothea's family as well.

At the trial of Ctesiphon in 330 Demosthenes once more attacked Aeschines' parents. This time his insults grew more vicious. Demosthenes charges Atrometus was originally a slave named Tromes, "Trembler," and used to work for a certain Elpias, who taught school near the temple of Theseus. His mother was formerly a prostitute and was rescued from this "excellent profession" by the aid of the boatswain Phormio, the slave of Dion of Phrearroi. Her disgusting conduct earned her the nickname Empousa, "Hobgobblin." In another passage from the same speech, Demosthenes recounts with great sarcasm and unconcealed glee how Aeschines spent his youth doing chores for his parents. As a child, he ground ink and washed down the benches for the students at this father's school. When he was older, he assisted his mother while she performed initiations. He read to her from holy books, then at night donned a fawnskin, held the cup from which libations were poured, purified the initiates with mud and bran, and led them in a chant that went "I have escaped the bad, I have found the good." By day he marched bands of initiates crowned with fennel and white poplar through the streets of Athens, handled snakes, and carried ivy and the winnowing fan, all the while shouting "Hyes, attes! Attes, hyes!"[23]

We do not need to search far to find a reason for the higher degree of insult in this speech: at the trial of Ctesiphon, Demosthenes was speaking last and knew that his opponent would have no opportunity to reply to his slanders. The allegations about Atrometus being a slave and Glaucothea being a prostitute can be discarded. If there was any truth to these charges, Demosthenes ought to have uttered them in his earlier speech. In other respects, however, Demosthenes is rather consistent: he calls Atrometus a schoolteacher and says that Glaucothea was a priestess in both speeches. In the later speech he goes into far greater detail in his description of her priestly duties, but it is difficult to identify the rites that Demosthenes is talking about. Of the several candidates proposed, none has won general acceptance. The mysteries of Dionysus have been suggested, and so have those of Sabazius. Yet the reading of holy books and the emphasis on purification seem to point in the direction of Orphic practices. I doubt that Demosthenes is portraying these rites with clinical accuracy. The uncertainty about their precise identity is most likely due to the orator's indiscriminate jumbling of practices drawn from different types of exotic ceremonies, all thrown together for the sake of humorous effect by a process of comic syncretism. The most we can say with some certainty is that Glaucothea conducted some kind of private purification ritual for the benefit of anyone who wished to participate.[24]

What can we conclude about Aeschines' parents from this material? The statements of Aeschines and Demosthenes concur insofar as they both represent Atrometus as not belonging to the wealthier stratum of Athenian society. But if Atrometus, at least after his losses in the Peloponnesian War, was not wealthy, how poor was he? Something can be inferred from his profession as schoolteacher. The fact that he had to work for a living indicates that he is not likely to have had a large amount of property, but given the absence of any details about his assets it is impossible to tell whether he was a thete or not. The best evidence for Atrometus' economic position is the fact that his son Aeschines was able to serve as a hoplite. Service as a hoplite, though not one of the most expensive duties demanded of a citizen, did nevertheless require some expenditure. In fact, some who met the property qualification could not afford the expenses of a military campaign. Since it is unlikely that Aeschines and his brothers could have acquired enough money by themselves before reaching the age of majority at eighteen to afford the necessary equipment, it is safe to conclude that Atrometus must have had enough property to qualify as a hoplite. Atrometus was thus by no means poverty-stricken, although he may have appeared so to Demosthenes, whose fortune was one of the largest in Attica.[25]

As for social status, Atrometus was hardly a *kalos kagathos*. The need to work for a living robbed him of the leisure to pursue the life of a gentleman. Nor was the profession of schoolmaster highly respected. For instance, one of the many insults directed at Epicurus by his rivals was that his father taught school for a pitiful fee. Yet this profession must have been more respectable than the manual crafts. After all, the children whom Atrometus taught must have come from those families that could afford to give their sons a good education. This enabled Aeschines and his brothers to grow up in the company of the young *kaloi kagathoi* and thereby to become acquainted with those who would serve in the cavalry and become trierarchs in later life. Their familiarity with the young *kaloi kagathoi* made it easier for them to mingle with the members of respectable society in the gymnasia, where Aeschines claimed, not without plausibility, he and his brothers passed their leisure hours. Yet, despite these advantages, it was still an embarrassment for Aeschines to have had a father who had been a schoolteacher, a fact that Demosthenes never permitted him to forget.[26]

Before moving on to discuss the family of Aeschines' mother, there is an additional piece of evidence to consider, one not found in the speeches. This is the tombstone of Aeschines' maternal uncle Cleobulus. The tombstone consists of a stele, which carries an inscription in which Cleobulus is praised as a seer and as a soldier who was crowned for his valor in battle. Above the inscription is a sculpted relief depicting an eagle grasping a snake in its talons. The relief must represent the kind of portent that a seer was trained to interpret and thus symbolizes Cleobulus' profession. It is ill-advised to draw any conclusions about the social position of Cleobulus from the fact that he was honored with such a memorial. This type of stele could not have cost much more than thirty drachmai at the very most, not a large sum, one that was certainly within the reach of a man who had served as hoplite. And Cleobulus' tombstone is far less elaborate than many of the more lavish funeral monuments of the period. We also know that the custom of paying such honors to the dead was not confined to a small elite, but was fairly widespread. Yet his military service still indicates that Cleobulus like his brother-in-law Atrometus was of hoplite status.[27]

Nor should we conclude that Cleobulus' profession as seer and Glaucothea's priesthood reveal that they both came from an old priestly family and were thus far more respectable than the slanders of Demosthenes would permit us to believe. Such a conclusion would be mistaken for two reasons. First, it is clear that Glaucothea was not a priestess in one of the famous state cults that alone conferred a large measure of prestige. Far otherwise; she appears to have held private ceremonies for which she may have charged a fee, if we can believe Demosthenes. There was nothing especially dishonorable about such religious practices, however ridiculous Demosthenes tries to make them appear. Second, it is necessary to distinguish between a seer and a priest. The priest was one who performed sacrifices on behalf of a group of people who formed a religious association. These associations might be public or private. Priests and priestesses derived their prestige from the importance of the cults they administered. A cult like that of Athena Polias was obviously a source of great pride to the Eteobutadai, whose daughters held its priesthood. Yet if the cult were a minor one, it would bring little renown to those who conducted its rites. The priesthoods of public cults were official positions, and some were elective just like the magistracies. On the other hand, the magistrates of the city might themselves act as priests and perform sacrifices on behalf of the entire city.

The seer was very different from a priest. The seer did not inherit his position, nor was he appointed or elected to it. Instead he learned the skill of prophecy. Although this skill, like many others in Archaic and Classical Greece, was often passed down from father to son, it could theoretically be learned and practiced by anyone in the community. The skill of prophecy consisted of ascertaining the will of the gods by a variety of means, the most traditional one being the interpretation of omens such as the flight of birds. The seer was normally called on by individual clients to give advice about what sacrifices they should perform in order to assuage the anger of the gods or to improve their lot in life. The seer was generally consulted about sacrifices on private matters, but might also offer his advice from time to time at public meetings. Unlike the priest, the seer did nor perform sacrifices on behalf of others; rather he acted as a religious expert who used his knowledge to counsel his clients. Despite the fact that anyone who wished to could try to prophesy, not everyone was equally good at it. Some, such as the seer who correctly suggested to Xenophon that a sacrifice to Zeus Meilichios would put an end to his run of back luck, were very gifted. But others who were not so successful at producing positive results were often regarded as charlatans and quacks. In contrast to the priest, whose prestige derived from the renown of the cult he administered, the seer owed his prestige to the success and reliability of his prophecies. The best ones were naturally in high demand and might gain widespread fame. One thinks immediately of Lampon, who attained prominence in the fifth century and earned the friendship of Pericles. Sthorys, a seer from Thrace, was awarded citizenship by the Athenian people for his accurate prophecy of Conon's naval victory over the Spartans. Talented seers could command impressive fees. A seer named Thrasyllus retired to his native Aegina with a large fortune after a lucrative career making prophecies.[28]

We can now see there is no reason to believe that Glaucothea and Cleobulus belonged to a prominent priestly family. Cleobulus was not even a priest, and Glaucothea was only a priestess in a small private cult. Given our ignorance about Cleobulus' record as a seer, we have no way of knowing how much prestige he enjoyed. Indeed, Aeschines' complete silence about his uncle's profession suggests that Cleobulus never made any stunning prophecies and remained just an obscure seer, certainly not in the class of a Lampon or a Thrasyllus.

The picture that emerges from the information provided by Aeschines and Demosthenes is of a family that was not poor, but without the advantages of birth and wealth that would have enabled Aeschines and his brothers to gain easy acceptance into the circle of respectable society. Just the same, Atrometus was able to give his sons one social advantage: a traditional education. Among his claims to be included among the *kaloi kagathoi,* this certainly proved to be Aeschines' strong suit, and he put it to good use in his court speeches, where by his extensive quotations from the poets he portrays himself as a cultured gentleman. This helps to explain why of all the Attic orators Aeschines is the one who is most addicted to reciting long passages of poetry. Unable to point to any famous ancestors or to numerous public services performed by his family, Aeschines could only use what he had learned from his education to show that he merited the respect to which a *kalos kagathos* was entitled. His obvious pride in his education made him a bit of a snob. In all three of his speeches he often berates his enemies for their lack of knowledge and refinement.[29]

But Atrometus was not affluent enough to pay for the lessons given by the professional teachers of rhetoric such as Isocrates, who charged one thousand drachmai for his entire course. Yet the lack of this kind of training was not considered a social handicap; study with the professional teachers of rhetoric or the Sophists was not a prerequisite for becoming a *kalos kagathos.* If anything, their influence was often seen as pernicious. The hostility of Pheidippides toward Socrates and his ilk at the beginning of Aristophanes' *Clouds* was no doubt characteristic of the attitude held by many *kaloi kagathoi* toward the Sophists and teachers of rhetoric. When his father Strepsiades insists that Socrates and his associates in the Thinkery are *kaloi kagathoi,* Pheidippides strenuously denies his claim. They are *poneroi,* he asseverates, men who go barefoot and are as pale as *banausoi.* If he studies with them, he will lose his sun-tanned complexion gained while racing horses and exercising in the gymnasium. Once he has become as pale as these eggheads, he will never be able to show his face to the young men who serve with him in the cavalry. The attitude of Pheidippides is similar to that of several other *kaloi kagathoi* whom we meet in the dialogues of Plato. In the *Meno* Anytus says he has had his own son educated in the traditional manner, but has a horror of Sophists. Callicles, who figures so prominently in the *Gorgias,* calls them worthless fellows. And in the dialogue named after him, Laches declares that quibbling over words is suitable for a Sophist, but not for a man who wishes to lead the city. Cleon appealed to this widespread prejudice when he compared those who opposed his drastic measures for Mytilene to Sophists.[30]

Oddly enough, the social position of Atrometus' family is best characterized by no one other than Demosthenes. When speaking about the professions of Aeschines and his brothers, Demosthenes admits condescendingly that they were not entirely blameworthy, but goes on to assert that they are not deserving of the generalship either. Despite his hostility, Demosthenes does not place Atrometus and his family at the bottom of the Athenian social scale, but was equally certain that they did not belong to the upper crust, that segment of society that in his opinion was alone worthy of election to the generalship. His lack of social advantages did not ultimately prevent Aeschines and his brothers from entering politics and achieving a modest degree of success. Whatever Demosthenes may have thought about his family's social status, Aeschines' brother Philochares was elected general at least three times. Nonetheless, his modest means forced him to work for a living for several years before he was able to attract the attention of two powerful men who helped him to get started on a political career.[31]

Early Career

Aeschines has little to say about his life in the years before he entered politics. The only information he provides comes from his speech of 343 where he lists the military campaigns he has served on to demonstrate his patriotism. There he recounts that he fought at Nemea (366), at Mantinea (362), and in the two campaigns on Euboea (357 and 348). In the second campaign on Euboea his conduct was so valorous that he received two crowns, one at the battle site and another in the Assembly. His omission of his activities in this period is not a sign of embarrassment on his part; they were simply not relevant to his aim of proving to the court that he was a loyal Athenian citizen who had risked his life for his community and thus deserved their gratitude.[32]

Where Aeschines is silent, Demosthenes gleefully fills in. To be sure, we must scrutinize his evidence with care. Yet amid the torrent of reckless slander, Demosthenes provides us with some reliable information that sheds light on Aeschines' activities prior to his entry into politics. Aeschines had to work for a living during these years, but the jobs he took were good training for his public career. And despite the scorn heaped on them by Demosthenes, they did not cripple Aeschines with serious social handicaps.

In his speech of 343, Demosthenes relates that Aeschines and his brother Aphobetus first served as undersecretaries, earning two or three drachmas a day. In another passage from the same speech, he reminds Aeschines that he should not be ignorant of the curse pronounced by the herald since it was his duty when he served as assistant to the Council and Assembly to read the law about the curse to the herald. His comments in this speech are merely scornful, but his invective grows more bitter in the speech delivered for Ctesiphon. There he declares that Aeschines began to work for the community as a public secretary upon reaching the age of majority, but left that profession after having committed the kind of crimes he now charges others with. Demosthenes characteristically fails to specify his opponent's crimes, and we should also bear in mind that Aeschines had no chance to reply to these remarks since Demosthenes was speaking last on this occasion. Not that Aeschines would have bothered to rebut them, had he had the opportunity. This sort of vague abuse was all too common and easily ignored.[33]

To judge from Demosthenes' statements, Aeschines appears to have started out as an undersecretary to various magistrates. These secretaries were drawn from a pool and were prohibited from serving the same magistracy for two years in a row. The restriction was probably enacted to prevent them from becoming too powerful by learning more about the duties of the magistracies than those who held the positions each year. The office to which Demosthenes says Aeschines was later elected must be that of the secretary who read documents to the Council and Assembly. This office was always elective, unlike the Secretary for the Laws, which was always selected by lot, and the Secretary for the Council, which was elective at first, then after 368/67 selected by lot. Since Demosthenes implies that Aeschines spent several years serving as undersecretary before his election to the post of public secretary, it is unlikely he would have been able to stand for election to the post of Secretary for the Council before it ceased to be elective. Furthermore, the other two secretaries appear to have been responsible only to the Council whereas Demosthenes reveals that Aeschines served both the Council and Assembly simultaneously. Finally, Demosthenes' statement that Aeschines read out the law about the curse to the herald certainly fits the office of the secretary who read documents to the Council and Assembly better than the other two posts.[34]

Aeschines was eminently well suited for the position because of his remarkable voice. His service in the post must have been a valuable education, for it appears to have given him a good knowledge of laws and decrees, one which he drew on heavily during his prosecutions of Timarchus and Ctesiphon. The position of undersecretary was not a dishonorable one, as even Demosthenes admits, but the fact that Aeschines had to accept a paid position indicates that he did not have enough wealth to support himself without working for a living. This was clearly something of an embarrassment for him later. On the other hand, it was an honor to win election to the post of public secretary and to take one's meals in the *tholos* along with the *prytanes*.[35]

Demosthenes says that after finishing his service as a public secretary, Aeschines became an actor. In his speech of 343 he describes how Aeschines was a member of a troupe that included Theodorus and Aristodemus. Unlike his more distinguished colleagues, who took the better parts, Aeschines always performed the third, or less important, roles. Demosthenes takes obvious pleasure in reminding the court how it was customary for the third actor (*tritagonistes*) to perform the part of tyrant, such as Creon in Sophocles' *Antigone*. Elsewhere in the same speech Demosthenes recounts how Aeschines, despite his remarkable voice, was driven from the stage by the jeers of the audience and forced to quit the profession. In his speech of 330 Demosthenes again refers to Aeschines as *tritagonistes*, but instead of making him an associate of the renowned Theodorus and Aristodemus, places him in the company of Simylus and Socrates, otherwise known as "The Growlers." As we noted before, Demosthenes' invective becomes more biting in the later speech. Here he says that it was not hisses and catcalls that drove Aeschines from the stage, but figs, olives, and grapes. Demosthenes adds sarcastically that these vegetables provided him with more sustenance than the meager fees he collected for his wretched acting. Since Demosthenes spoke at the trial of Ctesiphon without fear of rebuttal, we should accordingly place more weight on the remarks made in his earlier speech.[36]

It is important to note that Demosthenes taunts Aeschines not for having been an actor, but for being an incompetent actor. When insulting Aeschines, he never calls him *hypocrites* (actor), but *tritagonistes*, the one who is confined to lesser roles because of his mediocre skills. Aeschines alludes to these comments about his acting, but never attempts to refute them point by point. In accordance with the principles we have laid down, we should accept the essential point of Demosthenes' remarks, that is, that Aeschines was at one time an actor. Yet at the same time, we have a right to be skeptical about the details provided by Demosthenes, especially the more insulting ones found in his later speech.[37]

Was Aeschines ashamed of the fact that he had once been an actor? One might well come to that conclusion after reading a work entitled *Problems* attributed to Aristotle. There the question is raised "Why are the artists of Dionysus in the majority of cases bad men?" and the answer given is that they are depraved because they have no time to spend in pursuit of wisdom and are either profligate or in need all of the time. Yet this is only the opinion of a philosopher and not the only evidence available to us. A better indication of social attitudes toward actors are the activities of some contemporary actors. Neoptolemus, highly prized for his voice by Philip II of Macedon and several others, served as ambassador for the king on a mission to Athens and was instrumental in persuading the Athenians to begin negotiations with the king in 346. Another actor, Aristodemus, was elected by the Athenians to go as ambassador to Philip in 347 and later to Thessaly and Magnesia. According to Aeschines, Demosthenes himself proposed a crown for Aristodemus as a reward for his services on the last two missions. In short, there is no reason to believe that actors were generally despised. On the contrary, some of them enjoyed so much respect that they were entrusted with positions of honor and responsibility. Their ability to speak effectively was highly valued in a society where oratory was important in both politics and diplomacy and made them attractive candidates to act as ambassadors to speak on behalf of their cities abroad. This was certainly true for Aeschines, who soon after entering his political career put his trained voice to use on embassies to the Peloponnese, Macedon, and Delphi.[38]

If Aeschines failed to respond to Demosthenes' attacks on his acting, it was not because he was ashamed to have followed that profession at one time. As for his talent as an actor, we have no means of judging. Demosthenes, our principal informant on this matter, is not an impartial drama critic. The fact that Aeschines shared the stage with two of the most famous actors of his day would appear to indicate he had some talent, though not enough to place him in the first rank. Nor do we have any idea how much Aeschines would have earned as an actor. The most successful could reap impressive rewards for their performances, but Aeschines was probably not among their number.[39]

Demosthenes' claim that Aeschines left the stage because hostile audiences made it dangerous for him to remain there does not inspire confidence in its veracity. Aeschines is far more likely to have given up acting because he was able to better his position in society by means of marriage and thus no longer found it necessary to work for a living. The date of his marriage is not known, but in 343 he introduced his wife and three small children to beg the court for mercy at his trial. The very young age of his children appears to point to a recent marriage, probably around 348, just around the time he entered the political arena.[40]

The father of Aeschines' bride was a man named Philodemus. He seems to have been influential in his deme of Paiania, because Aeschines says that he was called upon to vouch for Demosthenes when the latter was enrolled on the list of citizens upon coming of age. Demosthenes' allegation made in 330 that Aeschines inherited five talents from Philodemus' son Philon also gives the impression that the family was rather wealthy. This impression is strengthened by the fact that Philodemus' uncle was a member of the Thousand, a group of property owners who were liable for the trierarchy and for liturgies. Whether we should believe Demosthenes' allegation, however, is another question. Demosthenes provides this information when accusing Aeschines of failing to perform liturgies despite his ability to do so. Since Demosthenes was speaking for the defendant when he made the charge, it is impossible to know how Aeschines would have responded to it. Demosthenes may have invented the legacy or inflated its value to make Aeschines' failure to perform liturgies appear to be the result of lack of public spirit and not his lack of means. Yet Philon's ability to bequeath such a large amount must have appeared plausible. Certainly Demosthenes could not have told this story unless Philon's wealth was common knowledge.[41]

Even if Aeschines never inherited any money from Philon, he must have received a sizable dowry from his father-in-law Philodemus. As a rich man, Philodemus may have presented his son-in-law with up to a talent. Whatever the exact sum, it seems to have been enough to allow Aeschines to stop working for a living. By the time Demosthenes prosecuted him in 343, Aeschines could no longer be ridiculed for having to labor for wages. But the dowry did not lift Aeschines into the liturgical class. If it had, the ambitious Aeschines ought to have undertaken one or more liturgies before his trial in 343 and to have boasted about them in the speech he delivered then as was traditional for a defendant to do. Yet if Aeschines had been in the liturgical class and had failed to perform any liturgies by 343, Demosthenes would definitely have made an issue of it in his speech of that year just as he did later in 330. Instead Demosthenes in 343 attributed the failure of Aeschines' family to undertake liturgies to poverty, not to lack of patriotism.[42]

Looking back over Aeschines' early career, one cannot help but be struck by the contrast it forms with that of Demosthenes. Demosthenes was fortunate enough to have a father whose property of almost fourteen talents made him one of the wealthiest men in Attica. He was less lucky in his father's choice of guardians, who embezzled most of the assets he inherited. Despite the dishonesty of his guardians, Demosthenes was able to recover much of his property and to acquire not only a traditional education, but also training with Isaeus. Before the age of thirty, Demosthenes had completed four trierarchies, either on his own or in conjunction with another. By age thirty-six he had acted as *choregos* for the Panathenaea and had voluntarily produced a dithyrambic performance at the Dionysia as well as provided a feast for his entire tribe. While still in his twenties, he may have prosecuted Cephisodotus, if we can trust Aeschines on this point. After this legal battle, he refrained from prosecuting others until Meidias' outrageous behavior prompted him to seek revenge in court. He did keep active in the courts indirectly, however, by writing speeches for other politicians. Demosthenes gave his first speech in the Assembly at around age thirty and spoke frequently thereafter.[43]

Demosthenes was not unique in getting such an early start. Timarchus, who was about the same age as Aeschines, was active as a member of the Council at roughly age thirty or shortly after; a few years later he served as a magistrate on Andros. By the time of his trial in 346 Timarchus had served on numerous embassies. Nausicles, another contemporary of Aeschines, had already been elected general at least once by the time he reached his late thirties in 353/52, the year in which he won acclaim for defending the pass at Thermopylai against Philip of Macedon. In comparison with these men, Aeschines was a late starter: he gave his maiden speech in the Assembly in 348 when he was about forty-two.[44]

When both men were elected to serve on the First Embassy to Philip in 346, Demosthenes, who was about six years younger than Aeschines, had far more experience in politics and had accomplished far greater services for the city. It is therefore not surprising to find him looking down on Aeschines as an upstart who was usurping honors and privileges to which his social background did not entitle him. Next we need to examine how Aeschines managed to rise so swiftly to prominence in the Assembly despite his lack of those advantages that had enabled Demosthenes to begin his public career at a much earlier age.

Aeschines' Entry into Politics

To understand what it meant to be a politician and how one started on a political career in Classical Athens, a brief look at the political institutions of the city is necessary. The most powerful political institution in Athens was the Assembly, where all major decisions regarding important issues, both foreign and domestic, were voted on by the citizens of Athens. The Athenians of the Classical period did not elect officials to make crucial political decisions for them. They met at least forty times a year to listen to debates and make collective decisions directly. The Council of Five Hundred and the magistrates only reported to the Assembly and carried out its policies. Not only could every citizen vote in the Assembly; anyone who wished to could also make a proposal and submit it to the Athenian people for consideration. If the proposal gained a majority of the votes cast by the Assembly, it became official policy. One did not need to be elected to office to exert a decisive influence on the affairs of the city. All one had to do was to stand up at a meeting of the Assembly and speak one's mind.[45]

Although the Assembly was open to all Athenians who wished to address it, few actually took full advantage of the opportunity. Out of the thousands of Athenian citizens, only a handful appear to have regularly spoken on public issues and made proposals concerning foreign and domestic matters. The Athenians called these men *rhetores*—orators—and that is precisely what they were, men who exercised an influence in politics not by virtue of holding an office, but solely through their ability to speak persuasively to a large gathering of men. Although *rhetores* might be elected to minor offices or selected by lot to serve in the Council, these activities were secondary to their main role, which was to give advice to the Athenian people on public matters. They measured their success not so much by the importance of the positions they held as by the number of proposals they convinced the Assembly to ratify that brought benefits to the Athenian people. The highest honor a *rhetor* could aspire to was to be awarded a gold crown and to have a motion of praise for his accomplishments read out in the Assembly and the Theater of Dionysus.[46]

The most powerful official post a *rhetor* might hold was to serve as ambassador for his city during negotiations with a foreign state. Since the Athenians did not maintain a professional diplomatic corps, they elected those *rhetores* who advised them about foreign affairs as ambassadors and sent them abroad to negotiate treaties and alliances. But these appointments usually lasted just a short time, not longer than it took to travel abroad, conduct the negotiations, and return to Athens. After delivering their reports about their embassies, they relinquished their posts and returned to their customary role as *rhetores*.[47]

The only magistrates who held much power in Athens were the ten gnerals who were elected annually by the Assembly to lead the army and navy. Theirs was the most prestigious office an Athenian could aspire to. For the ambitious it afforded the chance to win lasting fame by winning victories over the enemies of Athens. Yet no matter how successful a general might be, he still had to submit to the will of the Assembly and carry out its orders. The prestige his office conferred on him made it easier for the general to gain a favorable hearing, but the office did not grant him any special privileges in the Assembly. If he wished to influence public decisions, the general had to submit a proposal to the Assembly in the same way as any other Athenian citizen.[48]

The traditional way to get started in politics was to demonstrate one's good will toward the Athenian people by a conspicuous display of generosity. This could be done in several ways, perhaps the most effective one being to spend lavishly on a chorus for one of the dramatic festivals. Such an effort not only helped to bring victory to one's tribe, but provided entertainment for all who attended the performance. Another way of winning favor was to provide a sumptuous meal for one's tribe when called to finance one of the official feasts that accompanied the City Dionysia and the Great Panathenaea. According to an anecdote recounted by Plutarch, Alcibiades made his debut in the Assembly by making a voluntary contribution (*epidosis*) when an appeal was made to the wealthy for financial assistance. The anecdote may be fictional, but it aptly illustrates how important such generosity was for establishing one's reputation. Nor did one have to distribute largesse only through public channels; it was equally possible to do private favors for one's fellow citizens. Cimon used his enormous wealth to make gifts of food and clothing to poor Athenians. Mantitheus boasted to a court that he had given thirty drachmai apiece to poor men of his deme to cover their personal expenses during a military campaign. Demosthenes donated money to pay the ransom of several Athenians held prisoner in Macedon. After his victory in the chariot races at the Pythian games, Chabrias invited many to celebrate his achievement at a feast at Colias.[49]

The gratitude and recognition gained from this generosity came in handy at meetings of the Assembly. The Athenians were not ones to forget a favor and often repaid their benefactors by casting votes for them when they were candidates for public office. Xenophon describes how a certain Nicomachides complained to Socrates about losing to the wealthy Antisthenes in his bid to be elected general. Antisthenes had fewer qualifications for the post than Nicomachides, but had courted popularity by winning first place at many dramatic competitions. It is perhaps no accident that the first public activity of Pericles we know about is his victory as *choregos* for Aeschylus' dramatic trilogy of 472. Nicias was able to maintain public favor by his unstinting generosity, most notably by his benefactions to the sanctuary of Apollo on Delos. The situation did not change in the fourth century: Demosthenes tells us how Meidias was in the habit of citing his many liturgies when speaking in the Assembly.[50]

Another way to start on a political career was through the courts. Since there was no public prosecutor in Athens, it was possible for anyone to prosecute someone whom he suspected of a public crime. Several ambitious men took advantage of this opportunity to accuse prominent politicians of various crimes against the community, such as treason or embezzlement. Because these cases were tried before courts staffed by hundreds of citizens and often drew large crowds of spectators, they might serve as a means of drawing attention to the aspiring politician intent on gaining a reputation for protecting the public interest. The first person to pursue this path with notable success was Cleon; all the other prominent politicians before him chose to make their way in politics by means of liturgies, private generoisty, and military service. Several men in the fourth century, such as Hyperides, Aristogeiton, Aristophon, and Lycurgus, followed Cleon's example with varying degrees of success. This path, however, involved certain risks. A man who prosecuted too frequently might acquire a reputation for being a *sykophantes,* one who prosecuted for private gain or slandered the rich and powerful out of envy at their good fortune. Success in the courts might thrust one suddenly into the political spotlight, but a humiliating defeat could plunge a man into permanent ignominy. Even success in court was not without danger. Every man whom a politician brought into court would become his sworn enemy. The more one prosecuted, the more numerous one's enemies became. Each one of these enemies, not to mention their many relatives and friends, would be eager to retaliate by launching prosecutions of their own. Nothing demonstrates this better than the example of Timarchus. Together with Demosthenes, Timarchus accused Aeschines of betraying Athenian interests as ambassador to Philip in 346. Before the case came to court, however, Aeschines struck back by accusing Timarchus of having violated the law that forbid male prostitutes to address the Assembly. Aeschines was able to bring his case to court first and obtained a conviction, which cost Timarchus his citizen rights.[51]

When embarking on a political career, it is always advantageous to have powerful friends and relatives. In democratic Athens, where all offices were filled by election or lot, it was not possible to gain appointment merely on the strength of one's connections. The Athenians still felt that they could tell a great deal about a man from his parents and from the company he kept. They were naturally more inclined to trust those who were descended from, or associated with, men who had proven to be reliable in the past. When it came to electing ambassadors, the Assembly often picked men whose ancestors had maintained ties with the community to which the embassy was being sent. In the fifth century, the political scene was dominated by men such as Miltiades, Cimon, Thucydides (the son of Melesias), Pericles, and Alcibiades, who belonged to old and well-established families. But the turmoil at the end of the fifth century decimated the ranks of these families. As a result, Athenian politics in the fourth century was full of politicians and generals whose family trees were quite barren when it came to illustrious ancestors. Some men, such as Callistratus, whose uncle Agyrrhius had been active in politics, and

Timotheus, whose father Conon had won the battle of Cnidus over the Spartan fleet in 394, did not have to struggle up from obscurity, but they tended to be the exception to the rule of *novi homines*. Although the majority of those who served as generals or spoke in the Assembly did not have prestigious families to help them get started, they could still attach themselves to prominent figures and hope their endorsements would boost their chances for advancement. Phocion, for example, fought several campaigns with Chabrias and became his protégé. Chabrias in return promoted Phocion's career and assigned him to missions that helped to build his reputation.[52]

The path that Aeschines took when entering politics was partly dictated by circumstances and partly the result of personal choice. Given his limited resources, the possibility of gaining popularity by performing expensive liturgies was automatically ruled out. Yet the same could not be said for the possibility of making his mark as a prosecutor in the courts. Though not blessed with a large inheritance, Aeschines was endowed with an excellent voice and some talent as an actor. These qualities clearly stood him in good stead when he brought Timarchus to trial in 346, but by then Aeschines had already become prominent, having addressed the Assembly many times and having served on four important embassies. And when he prosecuted Timarchus, it was only in self-defense. Had Timarchus and Demosthenes not charged him at his *euthynai* with betraying Athenian interests, Aeschines would never have brought his suit at all. So reluctant was Aeschines to resort to the courts when attacking opponents that he did not bring charges against another person until ten years later when in 336 he accused Ctesiphon of proposing an illegal decree. He then waited another six years before he felt confident enough to allow the case to be heard. His unwillingness to use the courts to further his career is all the more surprising considering how well he did against Timarchus.[53]

One of the reasons why Aeschines did not choose to make his reputation in the court is that he was able to get his start by other means. As we will soon see, Aeschines was lucky enough to gain the friendship of two men whose opinions and abilities were highly esteemed in the Assembly. Their friendship helped him to achieve prominence without creating risks and incurring opprobrium. The Athenians regarded the courts as a place for sordid wrangling, not the sort of area the members of polite society spent much time in. In fact, one of the most effective ways of winning a court's favor was to claim that one had never before been involved in a legal dispute. Aeschines, like anyone who aspired to be a *kalos kagathos,* did not prosecute unless he absolutely had to. There may have been another consideration that deterred him. Prosecutions gained a man enemies who would seek to retaliate by bringing charges against him. That was less of a threat to a rich man, who, when accused of wrongdoing, could always cite his numerous benefactions and expect to win acquittal from a grateful court. But Aeschines could not rely on such a method of defense. Speaking on his own behalf in 343, Aeschines had little to boast about in terms of public service. The best he could do was to mention the campaigns he had fought and a crown won for bravery in battle. That was not very impressive when placed next to Demosthenes' list of liturgies and may in part account for the narrow margin by which he was acquitted of charges for which there was no solid evidence. Considering his vulnerability to judicial attack, it is not surprising Aeschines did not go out of his way to make enemies of prominent men by prosecuting them.[54]

The lack of a large fortune was not the only disadvantage Aeschines inherited from his family. Since his mother and father do not appear to have been related to any of the powerful families in Attica, Aeschines had no relatives who could have helped him launch his political career. His father had never participated in politics beyond performing his normal duties as citizen and had enjoyed no close friendship with any famous general or politician. Despite his father's membership in the phratry to which the Eteobutadai belonged, Aeschines never appears to have been connected with Lycurgus, the most distinguished member of that *genos* during his lifetime. Although his uncle Cleobulus won a crown for valor in battle, he may have been dead by the time his nephew was ready to speak in the Assembly. The only man to our knowledge associated with Cleobulus was Demaenetus, but no evidence indicates he ever lent Aeschines support. Aeschines' older brother Philochares was a general during the years 345/44, 344/43, and 343/42, but his tenure began after Aeschines had served on several embassies. If anything, Philochares may have owed his rise to his brother's success. Iphicrates, to whom Philochares had attached himself earlier in his career, was dead by 352. His son Menestheus, though married to the daughter of the renowned Timotheus, never appears to have come near to equaling his father's reputation and influence. Nor could Menetheus' father-in-law Timotheus have helped Aeschines: after his trial in 354/53 Timotheus went into exile. His son Conon remained in Athens, but never rose to prominence. Thus all the influential men whom Aeschines could have met through family connections were either dead or in no position to assist him getting started in politics.[55]

Aeschines made one valuable friend while training as an ephebe. This was Nausicles, who later nominated him for election as ambassador in 346. Nausicles also served on the same embassy and later testified on Aeschines' behalf at his trial in 343. Nausicles became a national hero when he commanded the Athenian expedition that prevented Philip from seizing Thermopylai in 352 and won a gold crown in recognition of his achievement. Yet despite his support at a crucial juncture, it was not Nausicles who was responsible for starting Aeschines on his political career.[56]

The political patron who launched Aeschines on his career in the Assembly appears to have been Phocion. Aeschines came to the attention of Phocion during the Athenian campaign on Euboea in 348. In that year, Plutarch of Eretria asked the Athenians to ward off the threat of his neighbor Callias of Chalcis. The Assembly granted his request and sent a force of hoplite and cavalry to Euboea under the command of Phocion. Aeschines joined the expedition, possibly as a volunteer. He was about forty-two at the time, and men thirty-five and older were usually called up only in emergencies. It was not Aeschines' first campaign. He had previously fought with distinction on an expedition to bring supplies to Phleious in 366, at the Battle of Mantinea in 362, and on an earlier campaign in Euboea in 357. After landing his troops on Euboea, Phocion led the force inland until he reached the territory around Tamynai, where he was ambushed and cut off by Callias' troops. During the ensuing battle, Aeschines fought as a member of a company of picked troops that played a decisive role in securing the Athenian victory. His bravery in action was so great that he was awarded a crown of honor on the battlefield. As a further honor, he was selected to accompany the taxiarch Temenides to announce the victory to the Assembly. During his report to the Assembly, Temenides spoke about Aeschines' valor with such enthusiasm that the Athenians rewarded him with another crown of honor.[57]

The campaign on Euboea was the beginning of a long friendship between Aeschines and Phocion. When Aeschines was charged with treason by Demosthenes, Phocion stepped forward in court to testify on his behalf. In 338 after the Athenian defeat at Chaeronea, the two men went as ambassadors to negotiate peace with Philip. It may have been through Phocion that Aeschines struck up an association with Eubulus. Shortly after his awards for bravery, Aeschines made his debut in the Assembly speaking in support of a proposal made by Eubulus. After the Assembly ratified the proposal, Aeschines was elected as one of the ambassadors sent to carry out Eubulus' decree. In subsequent years Aeschines continued to champion Eubulus' policies. In 346 the two men advocated peace with Philip in the Assembly during the meeting of Elaphebolion 18. When Aeschines was prosecuted by Demosthenes in 343 for his role in negotiating the peace, Aeschines claimed it was not himself, but the policy of Eubulus that was being attacked. Eubulus agreed with Aeschines' assessment of Demosthenes' motive for he appeared on his friend's behalf at the trial. Eubulus may have introduced Aeschines to several prominent men in his circle, who were later seen in his company. The most notorious of these was Meidias, who feuded with Demosthenes and punched him during the festival of Dionysus in 348. When Demosthenes brought Meidias to trial in 346, Eubulus declared he would testify for him presumably out of friendship. Meidias accompanied Aeschines to Delphi as *pylagoros* in 339 and died shortly after. The warmth with which Aeschines refers to Meidias in his speech against Ctesiphon strongly suggests they were close friends. The Stephanus who accompanied Aeschines on the Third Embassy to Philip in 346 may be identical with Stephanus of Eroiadai with whom Eubulus socialized. Aeschines and Stephanus may have had a common friend in Phaedrus, the son of Callias of Sphettos, which would lend some support to the identification.[58]

Phocion may have also assisted Aeschines in finding a wife. Philodemus, the father of Aeschines' bride, had two sons, one of whom, Philon, had served under Chabrias in Egypt. Phocion had been Chabrias' protégé, and after his mentor's death, looked after his incorrigible son Ctesippus. Since there are no other known links between the families of Aeschines and Philodemus, it is possible that Phocion, who may have made the acquaintance of Philon through their common friend Chabrias, may have introduced Aeschines to Philon and recommended him as a suitable candidate for the hand of his sister. Admittedly this is only speculation, but such a hypothesis would explain how Aeschines was able to marry a woman from a family which was socially above his own station.[59]

Eubulus and Phocion were very useful friends for a novice politician to have. Eubulus exercised great influence in public through his control of the Theoric Fund. This fund was ostensibly created for the inauspicious purpose of making small grants to citizens to enable them to attend major religious festivals. Sometime in the 350s, however, Eubulus and Diophantus persuaded the Athenians to have all the surplus revenues from the public budget paid into this fund, a move which gave those in control of the fund the power to initiate expensive construction projects. There was probably little money in the fund during the lean years after the Social War when Athenian revenues dropped to 130 talents a year. In the next decade the financial picture brightened, and revenues rose to 400 talents a year, enabling Eubulus to build dockyards, an arsenal, and roads. All of these projects must have greatly enhanced his prestige in the Assembly. The appointment of Aeschines' younger brother Aphobetus to a position supervising Athenian revenues may have been the result of Eubulus' recommendation.[60]

While Eubulus gained a reputation for financial expertise, Phocion won his laurels on the battlefield. Phocion first gained distinction at the Battle of Naxos in 376 where he commanded the left wing of the Athenian fleet and contributed to Chabrias' victory over the Spartans. We know nothing of his exploits in the next three decades aside from his command at Chios in 356 during the Social War and his victory at Tamynai in 348, but the silence of our sources should not lead us to conclude he was otherwise inactive during the period. The Athenians clearly trusted his ability and judgment for they elected him general forty-five times before his death in 318.[61]

What probably made Aeschines attractive to these men was his ability to speak. Neither Phocion nor Eubulus seems to have had much talent as an orator. According to Plutarch, Phocion attempted to serve Athens both as a general on the battlefield and as a speaker in the Assembly. His aspiration to excel in both arenas defied a contemporary trend. In Phocion's day, the *bema* or rostrum of the Assembly was monopolized by *rhetores*, not generals. Despite his unfashionable ambition, Phocion's accomplishments as a speaker never equaled those he achieved on campaign. In fact, none of our sources record an event when a speech of Phocion had a major impact on Athenian policy during Aeschines' years in the Assembly. His eloquence seems to have been more laconic than Attic: all he left behind was a set of blunt epigrams, which delighted Plutarch, but do not appear to have endeared him to his fellow citizens. Phocion and Eubulus therefore needed someone to express their views on the Assembly. Aeschines' strong voice and dramatic training made him eminently well qualified for the task.[62]

We must not make the mistake of viewing Aeschines as merely the mouthpiece of a political party headed by Phocion and Eubulus. Aeschines may have claimed in 343 that he was being prosecuted for the policies of Eubulus, but it would be unwise to rule out the possibility that Aeschines was incapable of exercising his own judgment or influencing his more experienced associates. Second, there never existed in Classical Athens the kind of political parties we are familiar with. The modern political party, with its elaborate organizational structure, elected and appointed officials, regular meetings, mass membership, ideological commitments, and access to mass media, was unknown in antiquity. Politics was on a much smaller scale. In place of parties, there were loose-knit groups of *rhetores* and generals, individuals joined by the bonds of friendship or expedience, who aided each other in pursuit of success in the courts and the Assembly. It would be misleading to label these groups "parties" for that would give the erroneous impression that they were more stable and organized than they actually were. Aeschines, Eubulus, Phocion, and their friends did not constitute a party. Rather, they saw eye to eye on important issues and cooperated to further their common goals and their individual careers.[63]

Despite his late start in politics, Aeschines rose to prominence relatively quickly. While Demosthenes was not elected to an important embassy until eight years after his first speech in the Assembly, Aeschines earned this honor almost immediately. Lack of wealth delayed his entry into politics, but it did not slow him down once he was started. Had he been born a thete, however, he might not have been able to get started at all: he would never have qualified to go on campaign as a hoplite, and his marriage to the daughter of Philodemus would have been out of the question. His father's modest amount of property made the difference between a late start and no start at all. Yet what is most interesting about Aeschines' early career is that it reveals that politics in Athens was not dominated by a privileged elite who had large incomes and illustrious ancestors and stood at a distance from the mass of citizens. When Pericles boasted that it was talent that counted when the Athenians selected men for positions of honor, not membership in a restricted group, he may have been exaggerating a bit. But he was not too far from the truth.[64]

3

Getting to Know Philip

Athens and Macedon to 348

When Aeschines first addressed the Assembly in 348, Athens was not enjoying a golden age. The Athenians still possessed the largest fleet in the Aegean, but it had not won them the hegemony that they had once held in the fifth century B.C. and had been eager to regain ever since. For a short time after the founding of the Second Athenian Confederacy in 378, it looked as if the goal of uniting all the Greeks of the Aegean under Athenian leadership might again be attained. But the goal proved to be elusive. The inhabitants of the islands and the cities that ringed the Aegean joined the Athenian Confederacy primarily out of fear of Sparta. Once the threat of Sparta was removed by the defeat of her hoplites at Leuctra in 371 and the subsequent invasion of the Peloponnese by the victorious Thebans, the members of the confederacy began to see little advantage in remaining under Athenian leadership. And when the Athenians took the step of concluding an alliance with Sparta, they undermined the main rationale for the confederacy, making it just a matter of time before the stronger, more independently minded members went their own way. To aggravate the situation further, the Athenians, who had posed as liberators, revived their imperialistic ambitions in northern Greece by seeking to retake their former colony Amphipolis, a move which must have increased the suspicions of their already skeptical allies.[1]

All these factors made Byzantium, Chios, and Rhodes ripe for rebellion by the time Mausolus, the ruler of Caria, encouraged them to break away from Athens in 358/57. The revolt, which came to be known as the Social War, caught the Athenians unprepared and without adequate funds to prosecute the war with full vigor. Their lack of money was so acute that the general Chares was forced to hire out Athenian troops to the rebellious satrap Artabazus in order to replenish their depleted coffers. Chares' strategem put a temporary end to their financial troubles, but it created a serious diplomatic problem: the Great King of Persia was furious and threatened to side with Athens' rebellious allies if they did not withdraw their support from his enemy Artabazus. Short of funds and unwilling to provoke further the wrath of the Great King, the Athenians had no choice but to come to terms with the rebels and grant them independence. Such a defeat at the hands of a few second-

41

rate powers was especially galling for a city like Athens with her glorious past and her perennial ambition to leadership in Greece.[2]

The years following the end of the Social War in 355 and preceding Aeschines' entry into politics in 348 were a period of agonizing reappraisal. The Athenians were now compelled to reassess their role in the Greek world: should they continue to pursue their dream of hegemony in Greece or should they renounce forever the goal of winning back the power they had held in the fifth century? Many joined in the debate. Isocrates, the self-appointed conscience of the city, lectured his fellow citizens about the evils of seeking a naval empire, which in the past had earned them nothing but hatred and danger. Aeschines himself would later echo these sentiments during the debate about peace with Philip in 346 when he spoke out against those who were encouraging the Athenians to imitate the exploits of their ancestors who built the magnificent Propylaea on the Acropolis. Their former eagerness to build an empire led to the disaster at Syracuse and the humiliating surrender to Sparta in 404. Daring should give way to caution, Aeschines counseled. The Athenians would do better to emulate those who fought against the Persians on behalf of Greece, not those who recklessly sought to gain more power.[3]

Others, like Aeschines' friend Eubulus, concentrated on improving public finances so that Athens would never again be forced to make peace for lack of money. It was probably during these years that Xenophon composed his *On Revenues,* a work which contained several practical suggestions for increasing public revenues. Demosthenes, too, was not without ideas. In his earliest preserved speech to the Assembly, he put forward a proposal to ensure faster mobilization of the fleet in times of emergency. Measures were also taken to collect overdue contributions to the *eisphora* and to reduce the number of exemptions from liturgies. Under the general direction of Eubulus, the Athenians made considerable progress in getting their house in order, and public revenues rose as a result.[4]

The defeat in the Social War was not the only major setback the Athenians suffered in the years that preceded Aeschines' entry into politics. Between the accession of Philip II to the Macedonian throne in 360/59 and his capture of Olynthus in 348, the Athenians saw their power in northern Greece decline to the point where even their position in the Thracian Chersonese was endangered. The goal of their ambitions in the region was the city of Amphipolis, which the Athenians had founded as their colony in 437/36 during the heyday of the Athenian Empire. The city lay on both sides of the river Strymon and commanded an area rich in timber and precious metals, valuable resources for the Athenians, who had to maintain a large fleet and mint coinage to pay the rowers who manned it. The colony had been captured by the Spartan commander Brasidas in 424 and was never retaken despite numerous efforts. During the early years of the fourth century the Athenians were too weak to continue these efforts, but the founding of the confederacy inspired them to revive their ambitions in the area. Around 370 they officially renewed their claim to Amphipolis. The following decade witnessed a series of unsuccessful campaigns, led first by Iphicrates, then by Timotheus, to regain the city. Timotheus brought many cities in the neighboring region under Athenian control, but when Philip II ascended the throne in 360/59, the former Athenian colony, now protected by a Macedonian garrison, was still not in Athenian hands.[5]

The continuing struggle to recapture Amphipolis became something of an obsession, dominating all Athenian strategy in northern Greece right down to the Peace of Philocrates in 346 when it was one of the central issues discussed by Aeschines during the First Embassy to Philip. To place Athenian aims in 346 in their proper perspective, therefore, we need to survey the gradual erosion of Athenian power in northern Greece and the growth of Philip's dominance. A short study of the period will also reveal a certain pattern in Philip's diplomacy, one which recurred in 348 and 346. Once we have sketched in this background we will be in a better position to understand Aeschines' account of Philip's overtures to Athens in these years as well as Aeschines' own actions during the First Embassy.

Philip's reign began amid defeat and chaos. His predecessor, King Perdiccas, had been killed in a battle with the neighboring Illyrians, leaving the Macedonians without a king and their army demoralized. As brother of the dead king, Philip quickly asserted his right to the throne and set about the task of acquiring the loyalty of the army with gifts, restoring its morale, and improving its organization. Philip had to work rapidly to meet the threats of hostile neighbors and ambitious pretenders who confronted him on all sides. From the north the Paeonians were making raids on his territory. In the west the Illyrians were preparing to follow up their victory over Perdiccas with an invasion of Macedonia. One of the Thracian kings to the east was supporting the pretender Pausanias. And to Methone, just south of the Macedonian capital at Pella, the Athenians were sending their general Mantias with three thousand hoplites to assist another pretender, Argaeus, in his bid to gain the throne.[6]

Philip dealt with these threats one by one. Instead of meeting Pausanias in a pitched battle, Philip sought to weaken him by winning over the Thracian king who was backing him. The Thracian king accepted the gifts Philip offered him and in return withdrew his support from Pausanias, whose campaign for the throne soon collapsed. Philip then tried the same tactic with the Athenians. Knowing their desire to retake Amphipolis, he removed the Macedonian garrison stationed there in hopes of inducing them to abandon Argaeus. The gesture failed, and Philip was forced to meet his rival in battle. Although he routed Argaeus' soldiers, Philip realized that one victory would not cause the Athenians to renounce their ambition to regain Amphipolis. Nor could he afford to have the Athenians as his enemies when his own borders remained vulnerable. To gain their friendship, Macedonian ambassadors were sent to Athens with the message that Philip was willing to withdraw his claim to Amphipolis if the Athenians would make peace with him. The Athenians welcomed the proposal, and peace was concluded, leaving Philip free to deal with the Paeonians and the Illyrians. It may have been at this time that the Athenian ambassadors Antiphon and Charidemus suggested to Philip that he help the Athenians retake Amphipolis in exchange for Pydna. We do not know how Philip responded to this suggestion, but it is clear that no formal agreement was reached, and the idea, if actually put forward during these negotiations, was soon dropped from consideration. Nevertheless, the proposal does illustrate the lengths to which the Athenians were ready to go in their efforts to regain Amphipolis.[7]

The alliance with Athens enabled Philip to devote all his resources to defeating the Illyrians and Paeonians. He first attacked the Paeonians and after defeating them compelled them to become his allies. Next he drove the Illyrians out of Macedonia and concluded a peace with them. With his kingdom safe from immediate threats, Philip turned his attention to the east and in 357 marched his troops against Amphipolis. Philip's siege of Amphipolis caused considerable alarm for the Olynthians who headed the league of cities in the Chalcidice. Apprehensive at the increasing power of their Macedonian neighbor, the Olynthians opened negotiations with Athens with the aim of forming a common front against Philip. To thwart this move, Philip once again employed his tactic of winning over the allies of his opponents. He countered the Olynthian request with an offer to turn over Amphipolis to the Athenians after its capture. The promise had obvious attractions for the Athenians, who at the time were busy fighting their rebellious allies. Unable to spare any troops for a campaign in northern Greece, the Athenians were seduced by Philip's offer and turned away the Olynthians. The failure of the Olynthian initiative left Amphipolis completely isolated, and the city soon fell to Philip. Contrary to Athenian expectations, however, Philip reneged on his promise to hand over the city and then marched his army against Pydna, an Athenian possession on the Aegean coast just south of Macedon. With their forces tied down elsewhere, the Athenians were powerless to retaliate against Philip for his deceit and could only stand by and watch as Philip captured Pydna.[8]

Philip's victories at Amphipolis and Pydna greatly strengthened his position, but they did nothing to allay the fears of the Olynthians. Despite their earlier failure to conclude an alliance, the Athenians and the Olynthians were now united in their distrust of Macedon and might in the future join forces. To preclude that eventuality, Philip turned to the Olynthians and requested that they allow him to march through their territory so that he could lay siege to Potidaea, an Athenian possession just south of their city. He declared that if they consented, he would surrender Potidaea to them after its fall. The offer was a generous one and not without advantages for Philip. Besides gaining for him the friendship of Olynthus and the cities of the Chalcidice, it would also prevent any rapprochement between Athens and Olynthus for the time being. The Olynthians, perhaps embittered by the Athenian rejection of their friendship, granted Philip their permission, and the Macedonian army began its assault on Potidaea, which succumbed to Philip in the summer of 356. On this occasion Philip was as good as his word and turned over the captured city to his new friends. Although he could easily defy the Athenians, who were distant and helpless, he could not risk offending the Olynthians and Chalcidians, who lived close to his own kingdom. Once again Philip's diplomacy worked wonders: by the pledge of a generous gift he deprived Athens of its only potential ally in northern Greece strong enough to defend Potidaea. After the loss of Potidaea and the alliance between Philip and the Olynthians, the Athenians no longer had a base from which to launch a campaign to retake Amphipolis. Their only remaining possession in the area was Methone, but in 354 that city too fell to Philip after a siege.[9]

Shortly after the capture of Potidaea in 356 Philip was drawn into Thracian affairs. His involvement there originated from an appeal for help made by the citizens of Crenides. Crenides was a colony of Thasos situated on the western edge of the kingdom of Thrace, an area rich in minerals. The territory had originally belonged to the Thracian king Cotys, but after his death in around 360/59 the Thasians appear to have taken advantage of the ensuing chaos in his kingdom to found Crenides with the obvious intention of gaining access to the region's valuable resources. Once the sons of Cotys settled their differences and divided their father's kingdom among themselves, Berisades, the king of the western portion, attacked Crenides, the foundation of which he no doubt considered an encroachment on his territory. The Thasians for some reason did not come to the aid of their colonists, who called on Philip to defend them. Philip provided much more than protection: he installed Macedonian settlers on their land, renamed the city Philippi, and proceeded to exploit the mineral resources of the adjoining countryside. Although Berisades did not live long enough to attempt retaliation, his son and heir Cetriporus was able to cobble together an alliance which included the Illyrians under King Grabus and the Paeonians under King Lyppeius. The Athenians also joined the league against Philip, motivated probably by their desire to regain a foothold in the area. Athenians hopes were soon dashed: Philip defeated each of the kings in turn and may have reduced them to subordinate allies.[10]

Several years later, in 352, Philip was once more embroiled in Thracian affairs. This time a request came from King Amadocus, who ruled the central part of Thrace, and the cities of Byzantium and Perinthos for help in a dispute with King Cersebleptes, who held sway over the eastern section of Thrace. Philip responded quickly and surrounded Cersebleptes at Heraion Teichos, but was later forced to break off the siege when he fell ill. Although this campaign led to one of the few setbacks Philip suffered during his reign, his invasion of eastern Thrace had serious implications for Athens. Up to this point in their war with the Macedonians the Athenians had struggled to win Amphipolis. Now Philip had advanced so far into Thrace as to threaten their possessions in the Chersonese. And a threat to the Chersonese was a threat to the grain supply that Athens drew from the regions around the Black Sea. If Philip could seize the Chersonese, he could cut off this supply of imports and force the Athenians into submission. It was no imaginary danger. After the Spartans won their victory at Aigospotamoi in 405 and gained control of the Hellespont, the Athenians were compelled to surrender and accept harsh terms. In 386 the Spartans again cut off their grain supply by taking the Hellespont and forced them to submit to the Peace of Antalcidas and to recognize Spartan hegemony in Greece. What had been a war to retake Amphipolis had now become a fight for survival.[11]

Philip's attack on Cersebleptes brought one significant benefit for Athens. Previously Cersebleptes, like his father Cotys before him, had fought against Athens for control of the Chersonese. In 357 the Athenian general Chares had forced Cersebleptes to conclude a treaty with Athens that required the three sons of Cotys to respect the freedom of the cities that were allies of Athens. As soon as the Social War erupted, however, Cersebleptes flouted the treaty and renewed his attempt to seize the Chersonese. Philip's attack in 352 caused Cersebleptes to change his attitude toward Athens. Completely surrounded by hostile neighbors, Cersebleptes knew that the Athenians were the only ones willing to help him against Philip. While besieged by the Macedonian army, Cersebleptes sent an appeal to Athens with an offer to surrender the cities he held in the Chersonese in return for military aid. The Athenians were slow to react, perhaps because of weak finances, but finally sent a fleet under Charidemus, who had formerly served Cersebleptes as a condottiere before gaining Athenian citizenship and being elected general. It was probably during the years after Philip's first attack on Cersebleptes that Charidemus supervised the construction of forts along the Thracian coastline. In the event of any future Macedonian attack, Cersebleptes could retreat to one of these strongholds and rely on the support of the Athenian navy. Protection of their new ally was not the only purpose of the forts: they also safeguarded the vital grain supply through the Hellespont.[12]

The Athenians were not alone in their concern about the growth of Philip's power in these years. Even though he was ostensibly their ally, the Olynthians too were becoming worried by Philip's conquests. Probably about the time Philip was making his assault on Cersebleptes, the Olynthians sent an embassy to Athens. For the moment they did not go so far as to propose an alliance, but limited themselves to a treaty of friendship. They clearly did not wish to provoke Philip and hoped to remain on good terms with him while simultaneously providing themselves with a friend to fall back on should Philip turn against them. Philip soon learned of these developments and on his return from Thrace made a demonstration against the Olynthians. We do not know what form this demonstration took, but it appears to have been no more than a warning of some sort. Nevertheless, it was now clear that a confrontation was in the offing.[13]

In late 349 Philip decided to test the loyalty of the Olynthians by asking them to surrender his step-brothers Arrhidaeus and Menelaus, who had been granted asylum in their city. The Olynthians, who must have regarded Philip's demand as an unreasonable infringement on their autonomy, refused to comply. This was too much for Philip. After all, he had made them a gift of Potidaea, and the surrender of two potential pretenders to his throne was the least they could do to repay the favor. Nor should we interpret his demand as merely an attempt to furnish a pretext for invading the Chalcidice: Philip's fear of pretenders was well founded in past experience. Philip at first refrained from attacking Olynthus itself, choosing instead to pick off the city's Chalcidian allies one by one. Their worst fears having materialized, the Olynthians appealed to Athens and asked for an alliance as well as troops to repel the Macedonian invasion. The Athenians did not hesitate this time and sent 200 lightly armed troops called peltasts and thirty triremes under Chares. These troops were not enough to check Philip's relentless advance: by the spring of 348 he had most of the Chalcidice under his control. In early 348 the Olynthians made another request for troops and were given 4,000 more peltasts, an additional 19 triremes, and 150 cavalry. Charidemus was summoned from the Hellespont to command the force and was able to make raids into Pallene and Bottiaia, but he is unlikely to have accomplished much aside from causing a temporary nuisance. Yet his raids were not without symbolic value for they displayed to Philip Athenian readiness to commit military forces to the defense of Olynthus.[14]

If that was the intention of Charidemus' offensive, the message did not go unheeded. When preparing for his final attack on Olynthus itself in early 348, Philip must have realized his task would be greatly simplified if he could deprive the city of the one ally that had come to its aid. In what had become a characteristic maneuver, Philip began to seek peace with Athens. The first offer to open negotiations was carried by the Euboean ambassadors that came to Athens in the spring of 348, probably in the Attic month of Munichion. Aeschines is our only source for this report of Philip's willingness to enter into talks and provides neither witnesses nor documents to corroborate his account. Yet his failure to do so need not be taken as an indication he invented the incident. When he told the story in 343, it was a relatively recent event, which must have been fresh in the minds of the court. Besides, Aeschines had nothing to gain from fabricating the event, which does nothing to enhance his own reputation nor to blacken Demosthenes' character. The offer to make peace certainly makes sense both in terms of Philip's strategic needs at the time and of his past behavior. In short, there is no reason to discard Aeschines' testimony on this point.[15]

Although this first offer met with no response, Philip did not give up trying. He quickly found another opportunity to convert the Athenians to his side. Not long after his first offer, a certain Phrynon from the Attic deme of Rhamnous was captured by pirates during the truce for the Olympic games of 348. After paying his ransom, Phrynon returned to Athens where he asked the Assembly to send an ambassador to Philip to demand back the money that had been extorted from him. The Assembly voted to entrust the mission to Ctesiphon, who journeyed to Macedon and obtained repayment of the ransom from Philip. His task accomplished, Ctesiphon brought the money back to Athens and reported to the Assembly in the manner he was required to. In addition to his report, Ctesiphon carried an important message from the king: Philip wished to inform the Assembly that it was against his will to wage war on Athens and that he desired to end hostilities.[16]

Ctesiphon's report was welcomed and his actions praised by the Assembly. Encouraged no doubt by Philip's words and the Assembly's reaction to them, Philocrates submitted a motion that Philip be permitted to send a herald and ambassadors to Athens for peace negotiations. The proposal was passed, but immediately attacked as illegal by an obscure politician called Lycinus, who then prosecuted its author Philocrates. With the aid of Demosthenes' eloquence, Philocrates was acquitted by a wide margin: Lycinus did not carry even one fifth of the votes cast by the court.[17]

All these events—Phrynon's capture and release, Ctesiphon's embassy, and Philocrates' decree and trial—are recounted by Aeschines in his speech of 343. He does not provide any evidence for his narrative, relying, as he himself says, on the memory of the court. His decision was quite reasonable since the events were not far removed in time and were familiar to everyone. Thirteen years later in his speech against Ctesiphon he gave an abbreviated version of the same events, which agrees closely with the earlier version of 343. Not only are the two accounts consistent with each other; they are also not contradicted by Demosthenes, who, in fact, is in agreement with his opponent about Ctesiphon's role. Aeschines did have a reason for exaggerating Demosthenes' part in securing the acquittal of Philocrates and may well have done so to stress his hypocrisy in first siding with Philocrates, then later denouncing him. Beyond that, Aeschines had no motive for tampering with the facts presented in his narrative, which we ought therefore to accept as essentially reliable. Yet although his account of these events is trustworthy, Aeschines leaves some important questions, especially about the motivations of the main actors, unanswered. For the most part, he did this because he was not interested in explaining the events in detail; his main intent was to paint Demosthenes as a hypocrite, not to give a thorough analysis of Philip's diplomacy in early 348. While Aeschines could ignore that task, we cannot.[18]

To make sense of Philip's offer and the Athenian response, it is necessary to recall the context of these events. The Athenians had sent two expeditions to Olynthus, a city Philip was at war with. As we have seen above, Philip had already tried to draw Athens away from Olynthus with an offer to make peace. It was probably this expression of good will, which encouraged Phrynon to petition the Assembly to send an ambassador to Philip with a demand to repay his ransom. Phrynon had, of course, ample justification for his request. After all, he had been captured during the truce for the Olympic games, a serious breach of religious custom. But he would not have made it unless he had some expectation that an ambassador might meet with success, and that expectation must have been nourished by Philip's previous offer to make peace. From the Assembly's point of view, there was nothing to lose by sending the ambassador. Even if Ctesiphon failed, Philip's refusal could be exploited as effective propaganda. The Athenians could point to the violation of the holy truce by the Macedonian pirates and Philip's tacit approval of their sacrilege by spurning Phrynon's request. What better proof that Philip was a sacrilegious barbarian, whom no pious Greek should trust? One should bear in mind that charges of impiety were potent weapons in the diplomatic struggles of the period. Philip was certainly not unaware of the value of maintaining a reputation for piety: he was at the very moment championing the cause of Delphic Apollo in his campaign against the Phocians, who had usurped control of his shrine. Were Philip to dismiss Phrynon's request, he would lay himself open to the charge of impiety while trying to pose as the avenger of Apollo. However much the Athenians pitied Phrynon in his distress, they may have secretly hoped that Philip would not honor his entreaty.[19]

All this cannot have escaped Philip's notice, but his main motive for repaying Phrynon was obviously to gain the goodwill of the Athenian people and thereby pave the way for peace negotiations. The gesture succeeded, and the Athenians voted to allow Philip to send a herald and ambassadors. We must not exaggerate the degree of Athenian enthusiasm for peace at this stage. The decree of Philocrates was only a proposal to begin negotiations; there was no guarantee given that the Athenians would accept whatever terms Philip might submit. The vote to allow him to send ambassadors was not a signal that the Athenians were intent on making peace at any cost. If the terms were not generous enough, they could always reject them. As eager as the Athenians may have been to learn about Philip's proposal, they had to wait for a while. Lycinus' prosecution must have temporarily delayed the sending of an ambassador with the Athenian reply.

All Aeschines tells us is that Philocrates was acquitted. He ends this section of the narrative without revealing what happened to Philocrates' decree after his acquittal. His reason for breaking off here is not hard to discern: he wanted to remind his audience of Demosthenes' early support for Philocrates in the first stages of the negotiations with Philip. Having established this point, he jumps ahead to another topic. But in doing so he leaves an important question unanswered: why did negotiations not go forward after the acquittal of Philocrates? Before the trial Philocrates' decree could not be implemented since it lay under a *hypomosia,* but after his acquittal that obstacle would have been removed, and the negotiations with Philip could have proceeded. Why did they not? In fact, Aeschines offers a hint when he slips in the chronological reference to the fall of Olynthus. Here is the key to the answer: Philocrates' decree was never carried out because the news of Philip's final attack on Olynthus must have arrived shortly after the trial. This news must have caused an immediate shift of opinion away from the aggressor Philip in favor of the Olynthians. As a result, plans for negotiations were dropped and another expedition, this one made up of hoplites, was sent to Olynthus. Luckily for Philip, bad weather held up the fleet carrying the Athenian reinforcements.[20]

We can now understand why the Athenians acted as they did, but another puzzle remains: why did Philip decide to launch his final assault on Olynthus before receiving the Athenian reply to his offer? It is conceivable that his offers to make peace were not really sincere, aimed only at arousing false hopes and putting the Athenians off their guard. It would not have been the first example of Philip's deceit: he had employed a similar strategem during the siege of Amphipolis. Or Philip may have genuinely wanted to make peace with the Athenians, but had grown impatient with the delay caused by Lycinus' prosecution and had chosen not to wait any longer before starting his campaign. Nor should we rule out the possibility that Philip misinterpreted the delay and wrongly took it as a rejection of his offer. Such a conclusion would have been mistaken, but understandable. After all, had not his earlier offer to make peace been ignored? Philip could easily have assumed that the failure of the Athenians to respond quickly was an indication of their lack of interest. In the absence of other evidence it is impossible to choose among these alternative explanations, but that does not matter a great deal. What is important is that one can make sense out of Aeschines' account of Philip's diplomacy in 348. Although we cannot pin down Philip's precise motivation in making the offer, his actions conform to the pattern we have seen at work again and again in his diplomacy: when confronted by an adversary, his first move is to deprive him of his allies, often by a promise of future gifts. This is not the last time we will see the pattern in operation.

When the storm that was holding up the fleet carrying the Athenian troops finally abated, they discovered that it was too late to help the Olynthians. The city had already been betrayed by some of its own citizens and had fallen to Philip before help could arrive. The treatment meted out to the Olynthians was unusually harsh: the city was looted, and its inhabitants enslaved. The consequences for Athens were devastating: all hopes of recovering Amphipolis by force of arms were now lost. The Athenians did not possess a single base in the region, and there were no friendly tribes or cities that would cooperate with them. They still maintained their hold on the Thracian Chersonese, where their position was bolstered by their new-found ally Cersebleptes. But Cersebleptes was isolated and surrounded by his enemies King Amadocus and the cities of Byzantium and Perinthos, which just a few years ago had summoned Philip to fight on their behalf. Even with Cersebleptes' cooperation, the Athenian position in the Chersonese was precarious.

After celebrating his victory at Olynthus in lavish style and with conspicuous generosity, Philip began to contemplate his next move. By the spring of 346 he had clearly resolved on a campaign against Cersebleptes. He could not let his previous failure in Thrace go unavenged. If he did not wipe out the memory of his defeat with a victory, his reputation and influence in the area would be seriously impaired. Such an expedition had an excellent chance of success for he could count on the friendship of Cersebleptes' neighbors. Furthermore, Cersebleptes' Thracian troops were no match for the seasoned veterans of the Macedonian army. Philip's only obstacle was Athens. As long as Cersebleptes could retreat to a stronghold on the coast, he could rely on Athenian assistance to cheat Philip of victory. To assure a favorable outcome for his campaign, therefore, Philip had to deprive Cersebleptes of his one remaining ally. With this purpose in mind, Philip would send another message to Athens communicating his desire to conclude peace.

The Decision to Begin Negotiations with Philip

The fall of Olynthus brought about a major shift in Athenian strategy in the war against Philip. Until 348 the Athenians had not tried to devise a comprehensive response to Philip's advance nor to coordinate the efforts of their various allies. So far their strategy had been confined to lending support to those who had been attacked by Philip. For example, they had sent ships under Charidemus to Cersebleptes only after Philip had broken off his unsuccessful assault on Heraion Teichos. The same was true in the case of Olynthus, to which troops had been sent only after Philip commenced his attack on the Chalcidian cities. And in each case the Athenians had trusted in their own resources and had not made any move to solicit the help of other powers. The fall of Olynthus made it obvious to Aeschines and Eubulus that Athenian arms alone were not sufficient to roll back Philip's progress. If the Athenians were to stop him, they would have to enlist the cities of southern and central Greece in their cause. Where the Athenians acting by themselves had failed, a coalition of Greeks might prevail.[21]

Aeschines made his debut in the Assembly speaking in favor of this initiative. All our information about his role in promoting and furthering the new policy comes from Demosthenes, who, it goes without saying, is far from impartial. Yet although Aeschines avoids any discussion of these activities, he does admit to his participation in them and does not contest his opponent's account, two good indications Demosthenes is telling the truth. Demosthenes may have embellished his account of Aeschines' speeches by making them sound more dramatic than they were in reality. But then again, Aeschines had been an actor, so the histrionics described by Demosthenes could easily be authentic.[22]

Demosthenes' account of Aeschines' actions after the fall of Olynthus is somewhat sketchy, but the little he does say gives us a valuable glimpse of the aims pursued by him and his friend Eubulus in late 348. According to Demosthenes, Aeschines addressed both the Council and Assembly, making speeches filled with dire warnings about the threat Philip posed to Athens and to Greece. To demonstrate that his fears were not unfounded, he invited Ischander, a native of Arcadia, to tell the Assembly how Philip had corrupted some of the leaders of his native city. What was needed in his opinion was to send embassies to all the Greeks with an invitation to come to Athens where they could discuss ways of opposing Philip. His oratory evidently hit the mark for when Eubulus submitted a proposal to send embassies, the

Assembly approved it and elected Aeschines as one of the ambassadors. He was sent to the Peloponnese and addressed the Arcadian Assembly at Megalopolis. Ischander's fears were justified: Aeschines' appeals to the Arcadians were countered by a man named Hieronymus, who spoke up for Philip.

On his return to Athens, Aeschines reported to the Assembly that the Arcadians were overjoyed that Athens was finally waking up and paying attention to the Macedonian threat. Despite these encouraging signs, there was still cause for concern. To illustrate the nature of the threat they faced, Aeschines recounted a troubling incident. During his travels in the Peloponnese, he encountered an Arcadian called Atrestidas returning home with a crowd of women and children following along behind him. Upon asking a passerby who these people were, Aeschines was told they were Olynthian captives whom Philip had given to Atrestidas as a gift. The incident deeply moved Aeschines: Greece is certainly in a lamentable state, he exclaimed, when such a tragedy as this passes unnoticed and without protest. He ended his report with a plea to send another embassy to Arcadia to denounce those who were doing Philip's bidding there. If the Athenians were to cast off their former passivity and follow his advice, his Arcadian friends assured him that Philip's cronies would be punished.[23]

Despite the exertions of Aeschines and the other ambassadors, the Greek states were unwilling to join in a coalition against Philip. At the time Greece was far too divided, and there was little chance of uniting all the cities, or even the major ones, in a common cause. In the Peloponnese the Spartans were attempting to reassert their leadership over their neighbors, while the Arcadians, Messenians, and Argives resisted their efforts. The Athenians maintained an alliance with Sparta while simultaneously trying to cultivate good relations with their opponents. But their friendship with the Spartans made them suspect in the eyes of the Arcadians and others. This suspicion probably accounts for the fact that, in spite of the optimism expressed in his reports to the Assembly, Aeschines met with no success in his endeavor to convince the Arcadians to side with Athens against Philip. In the Aegean Athens had lost her most powerful allies, Chios, Rhodes, and Byzantium, during the Social War. Chios and Rhodes were now under the influence of Mausolus of Caria, and Byzantium had demonstrated her eagerness to cooperate with Philip. The two most prominent states of central Greece, Phocis and Thebes, had been locked in a conflict over control of Delphi for over a decade. Although the Thebans enjoyed the backing of Thessaly, Locris, and Macedon, and had inflicted several defeats on the Phocians, a decisive victory remained out of reach, and the war dragged on inconclusively. The Athenians and the Spartans took the side of the Phocians early in the war and had delivered enough help to allow the Phocians to fend off defeat, but never a sufficient amount to tip the scale in their favor. As a result of this disunity, Athenian appeals for unity fell on deaf ears, and the ambassadors sent out under the Decree of Eubulus came home empty-handed.[24]

In the wake of the failure to form a united front against Macedon came a new offer to make peace from Philip. Our sole source for the new offer and the embassy of Aristodemus, who reported it to the Assembly, is once again Aeschines, who provides a detailed narrative and several pieces of evidence in his speech of 343. According to Aeschines, two Athenians, Iatrocles, the brother of Ergochares, and

Everatus, the son of Strombichus, were caught in Olynthus in 348 and taken prisoner by Philip's troops when the city fell. Some time later, their relatives petitioned the Assembly for an ambassador to be sent to ask Philip for their release. The Assembly approved the request and elected the actor Aristodemus, whose talents Philip was known to admire, to carry out the mission. Aeschines alleges that Philocrates and Demosthenes were instrumental in securing the Assembly's approval of the request made by the relatives.

Aristodemus was able to persuade Philip to free Iatrocles and Everatus, but owing to some pressing business, he was prevented from reporting about his embassy to the Council immediately after his return to Athens. The Council consequently heard his news from Iatrocles, and there was much indignation about Aristodemus' delay in making his report. Democrates of Aphidna then convinced the Council to summon Aristodemus, who dutifully obeyed. In his report Aristodemus announced that Philip was very well disposed toward Athens and in fact wished to become her ally. When he repeated this news to the Assembly, Demosthenes proposed that he be awarded a crown. Philocrates followed him by moving another decree calling for the election of ten ambassadors to travel to Macedon and negotiate with Philip about peace and alliance. Aeschines was nominated by his former fellow ephebe Nausicles, and Demosthenes by Philocrates. They and eight others including the actor Aristodemus were elected. After his earlier success with Philip, the Assembly was obviously eager to have Aristodemus join the new embassy, but the actor had already promised to perform in various festivals throughout Greece. To free him from his obligations, Demosthenes moved that ambassadors be directed to those cities where Aristodemus was scheduled to perform with a request that they not impose any fines on him for failing to honor his contracts. Once this hurdle was overcome, the First Embassy was ready to make its journey to Macedon. Aeschines gives no indication in his narrative of the dates when Aristodemus was first sent to Macedon, and when he delivered his report to the Assembly, but another passage in his speech of 343 reveals that the decision to send the First Embassy was made during the winter of 346, early in the Attic month of Anthesterion.[25]

How reliable is Aeschines' account of these events? To answer this question we must examine the evidence he furnishes and then determine whether or not it could have corroborated his assertions. At the end of his narrative, Aeschines has a number of decrees read out as well as a deposition of Aristodemus, who could not be present in court that day. There is nothing suspicious about Aristodemus' absence—as a popular actor, he was quite in demand throughout Greece and was probably performing abroad at the time. Aeschines does not specify which decrees the secretary actually read out, but does mention three in this section of his narrative:

1. A decree proposed by Demosthenes to award a crown to Aristodemus (2.17);
2. A decree proposed by Philocrates to elect ten ambassadors to negotiate with Philip (2.18);
3. A decree proposed by Demosthenes to send ambassadors to the cities in which Aristodemus was scheduled to perform (2.19).

It seems clear from what Aeschines says that the decrees of Demosthenes concerning Aristodemus were read out since he declares that the evidence he is submitting will show that it was Demosthenes who proposed the rewards for Aristodemus. The decree that granted a crown to Aristodemus must have stated the reasons why Aristodemus had merited the honor and therefore must have recorded something about his embassy to Philip, his role in gaining the release of Iatrocles, and the news he brought back from Macedon. The deposition of Aristodemus probably contained a fuller account of his embassy to Philip and the reports he gave to the Council and Assembly about Philip's willingness to seek peace. It is doubtful that it covered anything beyond his own actions on the embassy and his own statements in the report, and thus it is very unlikely it would have touched upon Demosthenes' alleged cooperation with Philocrates.[26]

The decree of Philocrates calling for the election of ten ambassadors to discuss peace with Philip was also probably read out by the clerk. This decree would have verified Aeschines' statement that Philocrates made the proposal and might also have stated that the proposal was inspired by Aristodemus' report of Philip's intentions. What it would not have proven is that Demosthenes was nominated by Philocrates to serve as ambassador. Inscriptions reveal that when a decree was passed to elect ambassadors, it was customary to record the name of the man who made the proposal, the reason for the proposal, and at the bottom, the names of the men who were elected. But no extant Attic inscription carries the names of the men who nominated them. While the evidence adduced by Aeschines probably proved that Demosthenes considered Aristodemus' actions praiseworthy, it is doubtful that either the deposition of Aristodemus or the decrees read out by Aeschines contained any information about his association with Philocrates. There can be no question that both men actively promoted negotiations with Philip, but we need not believe Aeschines' claim that they were working closely together.[27]

Having completed the preliminary task of separating good evidence from slander, we can now address a more important question: why did the Athenians decide to send the First Embassy to Philip in early 346? After the fall of Olynthus, Aeschines and Eubulus convinced the Assembly of the need for a more aggressive policy toward Philip and tried to form a coalition of Greek states to oppose him. Yet in early 346 the Athenians were enthusiastically responding to Philip's new invitation to make peace. What had caused them to change their minds?

The traditional view has been that the actions of the Phocians in early 346 were responsible for the volte-face in Athenian policy toward Philip. Supporters of this view point to another passage in Aeschines' speech of 343 where we learn that shortly before the Athenian decision to send the First Embassy, the Phocians requested military assistance from Athens and offered to turn over the fortresses of Alponon, Thronion, and Nikaia, which protected the pass of Thermopylai. The Assembly granted the request and instructed the general Proxenus, who was stationed at Oreos on the northern tip of Euboea, to proceed to Thermopylai and take control of the forts there. A resolution was also passed to equip fifty triremes and to mobilize all those under forty years of age. When Proxenus arrived at Thermopylai, however, the Phocians refused to allow him to occupy the forts. The news of their refusal reached Athens on the same day as the *spondophoroi* reported that the Phocians had also declined to accept the truce for the Eleusinian Mysteries. The reliability of Aeschines' account is unimpeachable for it is verified by the testimony of the *spondophoroi* and of the messengers sent by Proxenus as well as by a letter of Proxenus himself. According to the traditional view, it was this abrupt shift in Phocian policy which compelled the Athenians to seek peace with Philip in early 346. The refusal of the Phocians to hand over the forts to Proxenus and their severing of relations with Athens meant that Athens no longer had control of the Pass of Thermopylai. This left central Greece open to Philip, who could now descend upon the rest of Greece at will. With the last barrier to Philip's aggression removed, the Athenians had little choice other than to make peace with him.[28]

The traditional view has serious flaws. First of all, there is nothing in the text of Aeschines' speech of 343 that suggests such a conclusion. Nowhere in the passage in which he describes the Phocian change of mind does Aeschines state, or even imply, that the actions of the Phocians had any effect on the Athenian decision to send the First Embassy to Philip. Nor for that matter does Demosthenes in any of his writings ever suggest such a causal relationship. It is also crucial to note that Aeschines does not place his account of the Phocian refusal in his narrative of events that culminated in the decision to send the First Embassy; this information comes much later, in a section treating the reasons why Phocis surrendered to Philip in 346. The mention of the deliberations about peace is added here simply for chronological reasons. No causal link between the two events is even hinted at. Another weakness of the traditional view is that it clashes with what both Aeschines and Demosthenes tell us about the background to the Athenian decision. Each orator stresses the importance of two factors: first, the messages brought by Ctesiphon and Aristodemus, and second, the division within Greece, which made it impossible for Athens to convince other cities to unite in a common effort against Philip.[29]

A similar view is found in a speech delivered by Philocrates and reported to us in a fragment from Theopompus' *Philippika*. Theopompus obviously did not insert a verbatim transcript of the speech into his history, but like his predecessor Thucydides reproduced in his own words the general drift of Philocrates' argument. Even if the phrasing of the points made in the speech is not that of Philocrates, the basic points themselves must be his. The fragment does not indicate the occasion on which the speech was given, but the most likely is the meeting of the Assembly at which the Athenians voted to send the First Embassy. In the speech Philocrates describes the division among the Greeks and urges the Athenians to abandon all hopes of victory over Philip and make peace with him. Once more the connection is made between the disunity in Greece and the need to conclude peace with Philip. Like Aeschines and Demosthenes, Philocrates does not single out one state in particular as making a decisive difference and being primarily responsible for the change in Athenian policy. All three men stress the general situation in Greece, which made the offer from Philip so attractive.[30]

Not only does the traditional view clash with the evidence found in the ancient sources; it is also inconsistent with what we know about the events leading up to the decision to send the First Embassy. Even before the news of the Phocian volte-face reached Athens, there was already a general willingness to begin negotiations with Philip. Many were enthusiastic about Iatrocles' reports of Philip's desire for good relations with Athens. The Council did not let the matter drop, but voted on the motion of Demosthenes to summon Aristodemus to find out more about the possibility of making peace with Philip. The Council did not express the opinion of a small minority; its five hundred members, fifty selected from each of the ten tribes, were broadly representative of the entire citizen body of Athens. It is, therefore, strictly speaking incorrect to talk of a sudden change of opinion in Athens prompted by the abrupt refusal of the Phocians to accept Athenian aid. Even before the news of their refusal arrived, there was already widespread support for beginning peace negotiations with Philip.

The view that the Phocian refusal to hand over the forts at Thermopylai to Proxenus seriously threatened Athenian strategic interest is flawed. The Phocian refusal to entrust the forts at Thermopylai does not mean they were ready to hand them over to Philip instead. Nor was Philip in a position to seize them. True, Phalaecus, the leader of the Phocians, who was responsible for the shift in relations with Athens, appears to have made overtures to Philip in the next few months, but this should not be taken to imply that he was willing at this juncture to surrender Thermopylai to the Macedonians. Had Phalaecus invited the Macedonian army into Phocis in return for an alliance, Philip would still not have been able to gain undisputed supremacy in central Greece. In fact, by siding openly with the Phocians, Philip would have forfeited the loyalty of his Thessalian allies, who were implacably set on the defeat of Phocis. Not only would he offend the Thessalians, but the Thebans as well, who had been at war with Phocis for over ten years. The only way Philip could gain control of Thermopylai was by means of an alliance with the Phocians, but such an alliance would have alienated his most important allies in central Greece and thus canceled out any advantages he might have gained by possession of the Gates.

The decision of the Phocians did not make the situation in central Greece more clear-cut and force the Athenians to come to terms with Philip before the Macedonian army swept down from the north and marched through Thermopylai. Instead, it made the situation more complex and presented Philip with an intricate problem, about which, as we will see, he did not make any final decision until he was compelled to several months later. As far as the Athenians were concerned, the changed position of the Phocians made no difference to their relationship with Philip. And it is misleading to say they lost the Gates at Thermopylai since they never had them in the first place. What compelled the Athenians to send the First Embassy was their anxiety over the situation in northern Greece, not that in central Greece, and their failure to forge a coalition of Greeks against Philip. It should therefore come as no surprise that Phocian affairs were not even alluded to during the negotiations that Aeschines and his colleagues held with Philip during the First Embassy.[31]

The First Embassy was a large one by Athenian standards. The greater size of the embassy was probably due to two factors, the importance of the mission and the need to accommodate differing points of view. The Athenians must have realized that the future of their position in northern Greece rested primarily on the ability of these ambassadors to persuade Philip. Such a weighty responsibility could not be placed on the shoulders of two or three. Nor could it be entrusted to men who had no previous experience in dealing with Philip. For this reason Ctesiphon and Aristodemus were included among those sent to negotiate with Philip. The size of the embassy also allowed various points of view to be represented. Demosthenes and Philocrates, who had been the main proponents of peace with Philip, were the obvious choices for those in favor of a treaty with Macedon. They were probably joined by Ctesiphon, Aristodemus, Iatrocles, and Phrynon, who had also played a part in the move toward peace. Aeschines, on the other hand, was known for his attempt to rally the Greeks against Philip and was clearly selected to provide a more skeptical point of view. Dercylus and Nausicles, who appear to have been close associates of Aeschines, may have been chosen for the same reason. Aglaocreon of Tenedos was elected to represent the allies of Athens, that is, the members of the *synedrion* of the Athenian Confederacy. He, too, seems to have been allied with Aeschines during the negotiations and later testified for him at his trial in 343. More evidence for their close ties can be adduced from their views following the return of the embassy, when both Aeschines and the allies whom Aglaocreon represented were in favor of a more comprehensive peace treaty that would have been open to all the Greeks. Bringing up the rear in the embassy was a certain Cimon, about whom we know nothing.[32]

Aeschines' participation in the embassy should not be interpreted as an indication he had abandoned all hope of uniting the Greeks in a common cause. About the time the First Embassy set out for Macedon, the Assembly sent another set of embassies to the Greeks with a new invitation to come to Athens. The intent of the new appeal was slightly different than the earlier one made by Aeschines and Eubulus. While the ambassadors sent out in late 348 under the decree of Eubulus carried an invitation to join in alliance against Philip, these ambassadors were dispatched to summon the Greeks to join with the Athenians in making peace with Philip. Aeschines says very little about the ambassadors sent to the Greeks in early 346 apart from his charge that Demosthenes prevented them from participating in the negotiations with Philip's ambassadors by rushing through the ratification of the treaty before they could arrive in Athens. Nevertheless, it is clear that Aeschines wished to have these ambassadors take part in the discussion about the peace that took place after the return of the First Embassy, and equally evident that the new initiative represented a continuation of his previous efforts to form a coalition of all the Greeks. Aeschines knew that Philip owed his victories in large measure to the dissension among the Greeks and that a peace treaty between the Athenians and the Macedonians alone would not by itself put an end to the disunity that Philip had exploited for his own benefit. Only a comprehensive settlement could remove all the causes of division among the Greeks and assure harmony and concord. Aeschines may have also calculated that with all the Greeks behind them the Athenians could negotiate with Philip from a position of strength and force him to make concessions he might not otherwise agree to. Having observed that the Greeks were not interested in joining with Athens in making war against Philip, Aeschines appears to have now hoped they might be drawn together by the prospect of making a common peace with him. This was the situation as Aeschines made his preparations for this first journey to Macedon in the spring of 346.[33]

The First Embassy

The account of the First Embassy given by Aeschines in his speech of 343 is one of the most valuable pieces of evidence we have for the Peace of Philocrates. By furnishing a detailed narrative of the negotiations conducted in Macedon, Aeschines provides us with important information about Athenian aims and Philip's response. His narrative is all the more precious because Demosthenes has virtually nothing to say about the embassy in either of his speeches against Aeschines. His neglect of the topic is not surprising: in 343 he was prosecuting his opponent for his activities on the Second Embassy, not the First, and in 330 it was not relevant to his defense of Ctesiphon. Furthermore, Demosthenes did not wish after 346 to draw attention to his participation in the embassy that helped to negotiate the Peace of Philocrates, a treaty he later denounced as the product of treason and deceit. Aeschines' aim was just the reverse, which is the reason he deals with the First Embassy so thoroughly. Yet, despite its wealth of detail and anecdote, Aeschines' account has met with skepticism. Since it was presented by a defendant on trial for treason, the account has been suspected to be unreliable, replete with exculpatory fictions and misleading omissions. Our first task is therefore to examine Aeschines' statements closely, to answer the objections to them, and study the evidence adduced to corroborate his narrative.[34]

The only statement Demosthenes makes about the First Embassy is that during their journey Aeschines asked him to join in keeping an eye on Philocrates. Aeschines begins his account by refuting this charge. He argues that it made no sense for him to try to set Demosthenes against Philocrates since he knew of their close association prior to the embassy. He then proceeds to recount the discussions among the ambassadors while on their way to Macedon. Cimon expressed his fear that Philip would get the better of them. Demosthenes was not worried in the least. He assured the others he had much to say and was confident he would reduce Philip to stunned silence. His confidence was so great he predicted he would persuade Philip to return Amphipolis and the Athenians to recall their exiled general Leosthenes.[35]

As soon as the Athenian ambassadors arrived in Macedon, it was agreed that they would speak in order of age, the youngest, Demosthenes, speaking last. When they met with Philip, the Athenian ambassadors spoke first. Aeschines spoke in roughly the middle, after several older men and before Demosthenes and the other younger men. Aeschines' speech dealt primarily with Athenian claims to Amphipolis. After he finished, some of the other ambassadors delivered their speeches. Then came Demosthenes' turn to address the king. He began with a murky prologue, then halted and lapsed into complete silence, unable to continue. With consummate tact Philip invited him to take some time to recover and encouraged him to begin again. Demosthenes tried once more, but without success, and soon fell back into silence. Now that all the ambassadors had spoken, they retired to await Philip's reply.[36]

Aeschines' account of this part of the First Embassy is effectively told and has many features of a good anecdote. It begins with Demosthenes' vain boasts about his skill as an orator and his promise to overwhelm Philip with a flood of invincible arguments. During their first interview with Philip, Demosthenes is scheduled to speak last. We are told that it was agreed beforehand that the ambassadors would speak in order of age, but the arrangement also works well in dramatic terms: Demosthenes, who we are led to expect will outdo all the others, is kept until the end where his speech forms a climax. Ten other ambassadors speak, then after much waiting and anticipation Demosthenes rises to speak. Everyone sits up; Philip himself is excited at the prospect of hearing a dazzling display of Attic eloquence. But Demosthenes is able to get out only a few sentences before he is struck dumb by his own nervousness.

The tale is effectively told. The audience is led to expect an impressive conclusion, but is surprised *para prosdokian* with a comic twist, and Demosthenes is revealed to be a braggart and a buffoon. The portrait of Demosthenes is so unflattering that it has drawn the suspicions of several scholars who have put forward reasons for rejecting it. First, it is pointed out that it is unlikely that Demosthenes would have had trouble speaking before Philip during the First Embassy since he clearly had none when he spoke before the Macedonian king on the Second Embassy, only a few months later, as Aeschines himself says. Second, there is Demosthenes' claim that Aeschines never mentioned Amphipolis during the entire time they were in Macedon. Demosthenes further asserts that on his return to Athens Aeschines told the Assembly that although he had much to say about Amphipolis, he passed over the topic and allowed Demosthenes to discuss it. This assertion stands in direct contradiction to Aeschines' account of his own speech in which Amphipolis is a central concern. To be noted also is Aeschines' admission that Demosthenes intended to speak about Amphipolis. We should therefore not believe Aeschines' statement that he reported to the Assembly that Demosthenes was to speak about Amphipolis "if we had left anything out." As for Aeschines' later claim that Philip in his response to the Athenians ambassadors replied to Aeschines' arguments in detail, while neglecting to mention Demosthenes at all, that is flatly contradicted by Plutarch, who recounts that Philip replied to Demosthenes' speech with great care on that occasion.[37]

None of these arguments for disbelieving Aeschines has much force. The strongest argument in favor of trusting Aeschines here is that his statements are supported by the testimony of his fellow ambassadors, who appeared as witnesses on his behalf. He does not call them to testify until he has finished his account of the reports they made to the Assembly after completing the embassy, but he plainly states that these witnesses are testifying to all that he has said about what occurred on the journey to Macedon and in the court of Philip. Demosthenes, on the other hand, calls no witnesses to verify his assertions, but only has the clerk read out some verses of Solon. The poetry may have pleased the audience, but need not convince us that he was telling the truth.[38]

Second, there is no reason to think both Aeschines and Demosthenes could not have spoken about Amphipolis. We have only one account of an embassy that purports to give a version of three speeches delivered by different ambassadors from one state before a foreign assembly, but it is very instructive. This is Xenophon's account of the Athenian embassy to Sparta in 371. Of course, Xenophon's version of these three speeches is not a verbatim transcription of what was actually said at the time. Nevertheless, the historian would not have portrayed the speakers acting in a fashion contrary to normal diplomatic practice. In all likelihood, his account is a reasonably accurate summary of what the Athenian ambassadors said on the occasion. Xenophon was resident in the Peloponnese in that year, and if not actually present at the meeting in Sparta, could have heard about it from eyewitnesses. In the different speeches delivered by the Athenian ambassadors, Callias, Autocles, and Callistratus, several topics are treated, but each speaker is allowed to talk about a topic that a previous speaker has already touched upon. Thus Aeschines and Demosthenes could well have each planned to speak about Amphipolis. There were many arguments to be made on the subject, and one ambassador could not have been expected to cover all of them. Besides, it would be surprising if either Aeschines or Demosthenes did not plan to talk about Amphipolis. After all, the city had been the cause of the war between Philip and Athens.[39]

The passage from Plutarch cited by those skeptical of Aeschines' account of the embassy raises more questions than it answers. Plutarch was writing over four hundred years after the Peace of Philocrates; what source did he use for his version of these events? It cannot have been Demosthenes' speeches since nowhere in his works does the orator claim that Philip replied with great care to the speech he made on the First Embassy. Nor could Plutarch have confused the reply made by Philip to the speech Demosthenes delivered on the First Embassy with a reply made to another speech. The only other time Demosthenes delivered a speech in Philip's presence was during the Second Embassy, but neither Aeschines nor Demosthenes records anything about Philip's response to it. What is odd is that immediately after this detail about Philip's reply Plutarch repeats the sarcastic comments made by Demosthenes during his speech to the Assembly following the First Embassy, information he must have drawn from Aeschines' speech. Thus in the very same section Plutarch saw fit to take from Aeschines one piece of information about the First Embassy, yet in the previous sentence write something that directly contradicted that same source. If Plutarch did not find this item in Aeschines or Demosthenes, where did he find it? Theopompus is a possible source since Plutarch mentions him elsewhere as a source for his biography of Demosthenes. Theopompus treated the Peace of Philocrates in some detail in his *Philippika,* but none of the fragments of that work appears to treat the First Embassy. Given his hostile remarks about Demosthenes, however, Theopompus is unlikely to have recounted the First Embassy in a way that would have been more flattering to Demosthenes, especially when he could have used Aeschines rather damaging version. Plutarch may have simply contradicted Aeschines' version for the same reason as several modern scholars do: full of admiration for Demosthenes as an orator and a statesman and suspicious of Aeschines' malice, Plutarch, like his modern counterparts, may have found it incredible that Demosthenes had difficulty addressing Philip and therefore chose to alter the story to fit his own preconceptions.[40]

Essentially we are left to choose between an account given by a contemporary, which, although hostile, is nonetheless supported by the testimony of several witnesses, and another presented by a writer who was separated from the event in question by several centuries and probably had no other source for the First Embassy than the speeches of Aeschines and Demosthenes. Granting that Aeschines may have exaggerated certain details for the sake of dramatic effect, it would be wrong to question the essentials of his account. Demosthenes' general silence about the First Embassy may therefore be due in part to his reluctance to recall events that had been the cause of great embarrassment to him.

The most important conclusion to be drawn from Aeschines' account of the speeches delivered by the Athenian ambassadors is that Amphipolis was the main topic during the negotiations. Although the city had been under Philip's control for a decade and had not been in their possession for over three quarters of a century, the Athenians were still insisting on their rights to the former colony. After spending so many lives and so much money on their efforts to recover the city, they were not about to relinquish their claims meekly. That is why much of Aeschines' speech is devoted to a lecture about the basis for Athenian claims to Amphipolis, ranging from the mythical to the contemporary, from the historical to the legalistic. The only other topic that appears to have been raised during the First Embassy was the security of Athenian possessions in the Chersonese. This reveals that the negotiations dwelt on the situation in northern Greece, a conclusion that confirms the view that the First Embassy was sent because of Athenian concern about this area, not central Greece.[41]

In addition, there is no evidence that the Athenian ambassadors ever broached the topic of Phocis with Philip during the First Embassy. To be sure, the topic figured prominently during the Second Embassy, but neither Aeschines nor Demosthenes says it came up during the earlier negotiations. At first glance, a remark of Demosthenes reported by Aeschines might seem to indicate that the question of Phocis was dealt with during the First Embassy, but closer inspection of the remark shows such a conclusion is unwarranted. Aeschines reports that after the Athenian ambassadors withdrew and were by themselves, Demosthenes asked him why he had acted so arrogantly in Philip's presence. Was it because of the fifty ships that had been voted, but would never be equipped? He then accused Aeschines of having destroyed all chances for peace with Macedon. The fifty ships alluded to by Demosthenes must be the same ones that Aeschines later in his speech of 343 says were voted when the Phocians made their request for help and asked the Athenians to occupy the forts at Thermopylai. The significant point here is that nothing in Aeschines' narrative suggests he ever mentioned these fifty ships in his speech to Philip. Demosthenes attacked Aeschines for delivering what he considered to be an aggressive speech and voiced his fear that his hard-line approach might have endangered the success of their talks. He does not say Aeschines referred to the ships in his speech. He merely suggests to Aeschines that it was these fifty ships that gave him the confidence to take a harder line when speaking to Philip. The reason why Demosthenes adds that the fifty ships would never be equipped should be readily apparent: after the Phocians changed their minds and refused the help offered by the Athenians, there was no longer any need for them. In short, there are no grounds to believe that the question of Phocis was raised at this point.[42]

After this heated exchange between Aeschines and Demosthenes, the Athenian ambassadors were summoned to meet again with Philip. Neither Aeschines nor Demosthenes gives a detailed account of his reply. Aeschines says Philip responded at length to the points made in his speech, but does not disclose the substance of his remarks. Although impressed by Aeschines' oratory (so Aeschines says), Philip, as we discover from other sources, was not convinced by his arguments. He insisted that each side retain those territories already in its possession, or in other words, that Athens renounce its claim to Amphipolis in return for peace. Philip may have been eager to cease hostilities with Athens, but he was not desperate. Besides, he was not about to yield possession of an important area so close to Macedon. And he could not allow another power to control an area that lay across the route linking his own kingdom and his possessions in western Thrace, most notably Philippi with its rich gold mines.[43]

No source tells us whether the position of Cersebleptes was discussed by Philip in his reply to the ambassadors. All we learn from Aeschines is that the king promised not to lay his hands on the Chersonese before the treaty was concluded. His promise is very significant. It demonstrates that he was aware of Athenian concern about his upcoming campaign against Cersebleptes and their fear that he would not halt after defeating the Thracian king, but press on to the Hellespont. On the other hand, Philip may not have needed to say anything about Cersebleptes. It must have been obvious to the Athenians that any move to protect Cersebleptes and interfere with Philip's conquest of Thrace would have jeopardized their chances for peace with Macedon. If no peace treaty were concluded, nothing would restrain Philip from attacking the Chersonese after finishing off Cersebleptes. That is how Demosthenes interpreted the choice confronting Athens. At a meeting of the Assembly on Elaphebolion 25, after the treaty with Philip was ratified, Demosthenes strongly argued against admitting Cersebleptes' representative to the *synedrion* of the Athenian Confederacy, making him thereby eligible to swear the oaths to the treaty with Philip. If that were to happen, Demosthenes declared, it would destroy the peace with Philip. As we will see, his interpretation of the choice was shared by the Assembly, which voted to reject Cersebleptes' request to be included in the treaty.[44]

After finishing his reply to the ambassadors, Philip gave them a letter containing his proposals to be read out in the Assembly. The only information we have about the contents of the letter is Demosthenes' statement that it was studiously vague. To illustrate its general tone, he quotes a sentence: "I would have written more explicitly about the benefits I intend to confer on you if I were certain that the alliance will be made." However vague his words were, the excerpt unambiguously shows that Philip was not demanding an alliance at this point: he did not require Athenian troops to overcome Cersebleptes, only their promise not to intervene. Just the same, Philip must have realized that many Athenians would be reluctant to abandon Cersebleptes. To sweeten this bitter pill, he added a promise of future benefits in return for an alliance, but stopped short of specifying what these benefits might be. The strategy employed in the latter conforms to the pattern we have observed in Philip's diplomacy often before: when about to attack an enemy, he attempts to buy off their allies with a pledge of gifts.[45]

Philip gave his letter to all the ambassadors who had come to negotiate with him. This included Aglaocreon of Tenedos, who was representing the members of the *synedrion*. This means that Philip's offer of peace and alliance was extended to members of the confederacy as well as to the Athenians. Yet there is no indication that it applied to other allies of Athens that were not members of the *synedrion*. Since this set of allies had not sent their own ambassadors, they had no part in the negotiations in Macedon and were thus not included in Philip's offer.[46]

The proposals the First Embassy brought back from Macedon presented the Athenians with a clear-cut choice. If they were to accept peace with Philip, they would have to renounce their claim to Amphipolis and acquiesce in Philip's defeat of Cersebleptes. To balance these disadvantages were certain benefits. The treaty with Philip would put an end to the protracted war between the two powers. Peace after a long period of fighting was always a welcome prospect for the Athenians and should not be underestimated as a factor of great influence in the Assembly. The treaty would also guarantee the security of the Chersonese and thereby liberate the Athenians from their fear about the security of their grain supply. The alternative was to reject the treaty and to run the risks of continuing the war with Philip. Rejection would confer no immediate benefits and would compel Athens to increase the support sent to the beleaguered Cersebleptes. And if Cersebleptes were to fall, nothing would stand in the way of Philip's advance deep into the Chersonese. Whatever its drawbacks, the terms proposed by Philip were certainly better than the dangers that would result from continuing the war. Aeschines cannot have been very enthusiastic about the proposals. Indeed, when he advocated ratification on Elaphebolion 18, it was with a deep sense of regret. But Aeschines was hoping that the guarantees afforded by the treaty might be strengthened if the other Greek states could be persuaded to join in the agreement. Although the Athenians had not been able to roll back Philip's conquests or to win back Amphipolis by diplomacy, they could still forge a peace that would check further Macedonian advances.

4

Peace at Last

The Attic orators paint a dismal picture of Athenian politics. Their speeches over-
flow with stories of bribery, deceit, perjury, treason, and murder. Speakers in the
Assembly hire themselves out to foreign powers, magistracies are bought and sold
like merchandise in the agora, innocent men are condemned to death on flimsy
charges, and ambassadors conspire with the enemy to destroy Athens' allies. Indeed, if one were to believe everything one reads in their speeches, one might well
come to the conclusion there was not one honest politician in all of Athens. Among
the masterpieces of this sordid genre are the accounts of the Peace of Philocrates
given respectively by Aeschines and Demosthenes. Aeschines denounces Demosthenes for passing an illegal decree that prevented the Greeks from joining in the
peace with Philip. Demosthenes accuses Aeschines of plotting the destruction of the
Phocians with his partner-in-crime Philocrates. Aeschines charges Demosthenes
with browbeating the Assembly into accepting a dishonorable peace. Demosthenes
accuses Aeschines of delaying the swearing of the oaths for the treaty so that Philip
could have the time to crush Cersebleptes.

But accusations are only accusations. To win acceptance as trustworthy evidence, they must be accompained by strong credentials, in this case, documents and
the testimony of witnesses. If, on the other hand, we dismiss the unsubstantiated
slanders exchanged by Aeschines and Demosthenes and construct our account of the
Peace of Philocrates only from reliable information, a very different picture of the
treaty emerges.

The First Embassy Returns to Athens

Aeschines is the only one to give a detailed account of the events that occurred
between the return of the First Embassy and the debate in the Assembly about the
treaty with Philip on Elaphebolion 18 and 19. His account is found in his speech of
343 and is designed mainly to rebut Demosthenes' charge that he spoke in front of
the representatives from all of Greece during the debate about the treaty with Philip.
He also accuses his opponent of robbing the Greeks of the chance to participate in
the debate. Our first task will be to place Aeschines' account in context and to
examine its contents, paying close attention both to what he says and to what he

neglects to say. Next we will analyze his charge against Demosthenes. Finally we will discuss the nature of the debate that took place in the Assembly on about Anthesterion 30.[1]

Aeschines returned to Athens with the First Embassy late in the attic month of Anthesterion. The news they had to report was not as good as they had hoped it might be, but there was still some cause for optimism. Although Philip had refused to yield on the issue of Amphipolis, he had treated the ambassadors with respect and gave them the impression he was genuinely desirous of peace. He had assured them he would refrain from attacking Athenian possessions in the Chersonese, and his letter to the Assembly promised future benefits in return for an alliance. To judge from his choice of ambassadors he sent to represent him in Athens—Antipater and Parmenion, two men to whom he would later entrust positions of high responsibility—Philip was taking these negotiations very seriously.[2]

Despite Philip's refusal to accede to Athenian claims to Amphipolis, Aeschines and Eubulus were still hoping that the presence of the Greek ambassadors might strengthen their hand in the upcoming negotiations with Antipater and Parmenion. Before the departure of the First Embassy, they had persuaded the Assembly to send ambassadors to the Greeks with an invitation to come to Athens and discuss policy toward Macedon. By the time the First Embassy returned, they must have been expecting some response to their diplomatic initiative. But time was running out. Philip was marching on the Chersonese. Aeschines was later to describe how in early 346 the war with Philip was no longer for Amphipolis, but for Lemnos, Imbros, Skyros, the islands that formed the last line of defence for the Athenian grain route to the Black Sea. The general Chares was supposed to be guarding Athenian interests in the Chersonese, but no one knew where he was. The Assembly was growing so worried about the situation that it voted to dispatch the general Antiochus to discover his whereabouts.[3]

Amid such fears and expectations, Aeschines and his colleagues made their reports to the Council about their embassy to Philip. Aeschines informs us that at this meeting Demosthenes praised his fellow ambassadors and went so far as to propose that they all receive olive crowns and an invitation to dine in the *prytaneion* as a reward for their services to Athens. He also proposed that a truce be concluded with the Macedonian herald so that Philip's ambassadors could enter Attica. The truce was necessary since Athens was technically still at war with Philip, and thus his ambassadors could not set foot on Attic soil without a special dispensation. Aeschines' narrative is supported by the testimony of the other ambassadors and the texts of Demosthenes' decrees so we are entitled to regard it as trustworthy. What is striking about his account of the meeting is that there appears to have been no discord between him and Demosthenes at the time. Everyone agreed the embassy had achieved its goals, and therefore its members deserved the commendation of the Council. Despite their disagreements during the embassy, Aeschines and Demosthenes appear to have been on good terms when they reported to the Council.[4]

Although Aeschines does not mention it, the Council must at this meeting have instructed the *synedrion* of the Allies, that is, the members of the Confederacy, to consider the proposals brought back from Philip and invited that body to submit a resolution about the matter to the Assembly. Further in his narrative Aeschines cites this resolution and quotes its main provision. In their resolution the Allies noted that the ambassadors whom the Assembly had sent out to the Greeks were still abroad and accordingly proposed that the *prytanes* wait until after their return to convoke two meetings of the Assembly for the purpose of discussing peace with Philip. Aeschines also asserts he supported this resolution. Although he does not provide evidence to prove his assertion, we should probably accept his word here. After all, it was Aeschines who, along with Eubulus, urged the Athenians to send these embassies. His support for the Resolution of the Allies was probably motivated by his unwillingness to admit that his policy of rallying the Greeks behind Athens was a failure. He continued to hope that the Athenian ambassadors might bring back some encouraging news about the prospects for a coalition against Philip and therefore favored the Resolution of the Allies, which would have delayed the debate about the treaty until after their return. The resolution may in fact have heen drawn up at the suggestion of Aeschines, because Aglaocreon of Tenedos, the man whom the Assembly had appointed to represent the Allies on the First Embassy, was closely associated with Aeschines. The two men shared lodgings on both the First and Second Embassies, and in 343 Aglaocreon testified on Aeschines' behalf at his trial. After the Allies passed their resolution, it was either submitted to the Council, which would have then passed it on to the Assembly, or submitted directly to the Assembly.[5]

After reporting to the Council, the ambassadors gave an account of their negotiations with Philip to the Assembly at a meeting that probably occurred on or shortly before Anthesterion 30. In his speech of 343 Aeschines gives a rather amusing account of the reports made at this meeting. According to Aeschines, Ctesiphon spoke first and praised Philip's handsome appearance and polished manners. Philocrates and Dercylus followed and said only a few words. Then came Aeschines' turn. He commended Philip's eloquence and keen memory. As a favor to Demosthenes, he gave his younger colleague credit for covering any points about Amphipolis that the other ambassadors had passed over. Up to this point, all the ambassadors reported in the manner they had all agreed upon in advance. But Demosthenes, who spoke last, did not maintain this cordial tone. He began by scratching his head, then expressed his astonishment at his colleagues' speeches: how could they waste time reporting about their chitchat with Philip when they should be discussing weightier matters? It was very easy to report about an embassy, Demosthenes said and immediately proceeded to demonstrate how he thought it ought to be done. He first read out the decree containing the instructions given to the embassy, then abruptly declared that the ambassadors had fullfilled their mission. There was nothing more to it than that. Next he read Philip's letter and bluntly told the Assembly all that remained for them to do was to make up their minds.

Aeschines says that Demosthenes' report met with mixed reactions. While some admired its power and brevity, the majority found it uncouth and mean-spirited. But Demosthenes was not finished yet. He continued by belittling the praises showered on Philip by the other ambassadors. Ctesiphon was struck by his beauty; in his eyes Aristodemus was just as handsome. Someone said that the king had a good memory, but so do many people. When it came to conviviality, Philip was in no way superior to Philocrates. As for the claim that he was allowed to speak about Amphipolis, that was nonsense: Aeschines was incapable of sharing a topic with anyone. At the end of this rather unusual speech, Demosthenes made three proposals: first, that a truce be concluded with the Macedonian herald who had already arrived in Athens so that Philip's ambassadors could enter Attica; second, that after the arrival of the Macedonian ambassadors, the *prytanes* convoke two meetings of the Assembly to discuss not only peace, but also an alliance with Philip; and third, that the members of the First Embassy receive a vote of praise and an invitation to dine in the *prytaneion* on the following day. To attest to the truth of this account, Aeschines has the decrees of Demosthenes and the testimony of the other ambassadors read out. He also points out that the members of the court were witnesses to Demosthenes' speech in the Assembly.[6]

Such is Aeschines' account of the reports made by the First Embassy to the Assembly. While Aeschines may have taken some liberties with the precise wording of Demosthenes' report in order to make it sound more arrogant than it actually was, we have no grounds for questioning its essential veracity since it is confirmed by good evidence and nowhere contradicted by Demosthenes. But if we are to accept Aeschines' description of Demosthenes' speech, a question immediately arises: why was Demosthenes' attitude at this meeting so different from that he expressed shortly before in the Council? In front of the Council he was full of praise for his colleagues; in the Assembly he covered them with ridicule. Aeschines attributes the change to his opponent's jealousy for the applause he himself received, but that is the interpretation of a political rival. To understand why Demosthenes changed his attitude so dramatically between the two meetings, we need to consider what Aeschines leaves out of his account of the meeting of the Assembly that was held around Anthesterion 30.

Aeschines says Demosthenes made three proposals at this meeting. Two of these, the proposal to conclude a truce with the Macedonian herald and the recommendation that the ambassadors receive a vote of praise, are identical with the motions he passed in the Council and thus must have formed part of the *probouleuma* submitted to the Assembly around Anthesterion 30. The middle proposal, however, the one calling for the *prytanes* to convoke two meetings of the Assembly to discuss not only peace, but also an alliance with Philip, was new. The fact that Demosthenes introduced such a proposal at this meeting reveals that it was at this meeting that the Assembly discussed whether or not to hold a debate about Philip's proposals. This in turn means that the Resolution of the Allies, which dealt with this matter, must also have been submitted to the Assembly around Anthesterion 30.

Demosthenes' new proposal was very different from the Resolution of the Allies. Their resolution stipulated that discussion of the treaty with Philip not take place until after the return of the ambassadors whom the Assembly had sent out to the Greeks and be limited to a discussion of peace alone. Demosthenes' proposal did not contain these restrictions, thereby enabling the *prytanes* to schedule a meeting of the Assembly to debate both peace and alliance before the return of the Athenian ambassadors. What Aeschines fails to mention is that there was a debate at the meeting of the Assembly in late Anthesterion about postponing the scheduling of the debate about the treaty until after the return of these ambassadors. Demosthenes was clearly opposed to delaying the debate and moved a proposal that would allow the debate to take place as soon as possible. The Allies, probably supported by Aeschines and Eubulus, took a different position. They wanted the debate put off until after the Athenian ambassadors could report about the chances for having the rest of the Greeks participate in the negotiations with Macedon. Finally, it is clear that Demosthenes won this debate because it was his proposal that the Assembly endorsed. If it had not been passed, no copy of it would have been kept for Aeschines to cite in 343. The Resolution of the Allies, on the other hand, remained just that. It was not approved by the Athenian people and thus never became a decree of the Assembly. Demosthenes' sarcasm toward Aeschines at the meeting of the Assembly in late Anthesterion was therefore more likely to have been occasioned not by jealousy, but by a disagreement about what decision the Assembly should take in regard to the ambassadors sent to the Greeks.[7]

The reason for Aeschines' failure to mention these facts becomes apparent once we study the rest of his account of the events leading up to the debate about the treaty. After describing the ambassadors' reports to the Assembly, Aeschines refers to another decree of Demosthenes, this one reserving seats of honor at the Dionysia for Philip's ambassadors. He then sums up this part of his narrative by asserting that he has now proven that it was not he, but Demosthenes, who conspired with Philocrates to convince the Athenians to accept the treaty with Philip. He next turns to the charge that he had spoken in front of the embassies from the Greeks during the debate about the treaty. Aeschines begins his refutation of the charge by pointing out that if any foreign delegates had arrived in Athens at the time, they must have first appeared before the Council, which would then have granted them entry to the Assembly. The same would have applied for any ambassadors sent by the Athenians to the Greeks. Aeschines accordingly challenged Demosthenes to prove that any ambassador from the Greeks or any Athenian ambassador sent to the Greeks presented himself to the Council before Elaphebolion 18 and requested entry to the Assembly. Since Aeschines would not have made the challenge unless he was certain Demosthenes could not respond to it, we can conclude that no ambassadors arrived in Athens in this period. To lend further support to his argument, Aeschines brings forward the Resolution of the Allies passed prior to the debate about the treaty with Philip. In that document it is clearly stated that the ambassadors whom the Assembly had sent out to the Greeks were still abroad. This evidence firmly refutes Demosthenes' claim that there were ambassadors from all the Greeks present when the Assembly debated the treaty with Philip.[8]

After defending himself against this charge, Aeschines counterattacks by making an accusation of his own. He produces another decree of Demosthenes in which the *prytanes* were ordered to convoke two meetings of the Assembly on Elaphebolion 18 and 19 for a discussion of peace and alliance with Philip. Aeschines charges that Demosthenes by means of this decree surreptitiously deprived the ambassadors of the chance to participate in the debate about the treaty. Aeschines contrasts this decree with the Resolution of the Allies, which called for the Athenians to wait until the Greek embassies arrived before discussing the treaty with Philip. Aeschines slightly misrepresents here the intent of the resolution when he claims that the Allies expressed in it their desire that the debate be delayed until after the arrival of the ambassadors sent by the Greeks. In the passage he quotes from the resolution, however, there is no mention of embassies sent by the Greeks; the Allies only refer to the ambassadors sent out by the Athenian Assembly. Thus Demosthenes' decree setting the dates for the debate about the treaty prevented only the ambassadors sent by the Athenians from returning to Athens in time to report before that debate. Aeschines implicitly assumes that if the debate were held before the Athenian ambassadors could return, it must also have been held before the ambassadors sent by the Greeks could arrive in Athens. His assumption is not unreasonable. We can therefore accept Aeschines' basic point that Demosthenes' decree deprived the Greeks of the opportunity of participating in the debate in the Assembly about the treaty with Philip.[9]

Before we can evaluate Aeschines' charge, we need to determine where Demosthenes passed this decree, in the Council or in the Assembly. To begin with, it is important to distinguish this decree from the one he proposed and passed at the meeting of the Assembly during which the First Embassy made its report. At that meeting in late Anthesterion, Demosthenes only proposed that the *prytanes* call two meetings of the Assembly after the arrival of the Macedonian ambassadors, but did not specify the dates for those meetings. This decree, on the other hand, was passed after the arrival of the Macedonian ambassadors and set specific dates for the debate about the treaty. Evidence drawn from inscriptions indicates that the latter decree must have been passed in the Council. Inscriptions reveal that the normal procedure in such negotiations was for the foreign embassy to report first to the Council and to state its business. The Council then usually passed a decree to introduce the embassy to the Assembly at its next meeting and to place its business on the agenda. Since it was the Council that drew up the agenda and set the dates for meetings of the Assembly, Demosthenes' decree fixing the exact dates of the meetings must have been passed in the Council.

This conclusion is confirmed by evidence from Demosthenes' speech for Ctesiphon. In 330 Aeschines repeated his charge that Demothenes had cheated the Greeks of the opportunity to participate in the debate about the treaty and again cited his decree setting the dates for the debate. This time Demosthenes was speaking for the defense and was able to reply. We will discuss his reply later; all we should note here is that in it he acknowledges the fact that "as a member of the Council" (*bouleuon*) he proposed that the Macedonian ambassadors be introduced to the Assembly. This proposal must have been contained in the same motion fixing the dates for the debate about the treaty with Philip on Elaphebolion 18 and 19, since as we have just observed, the Council normally voted to introduce a foreign embassy to the Assembly at the same time as it voted to include its business on the agenda.[10]

We can now return to Aeschines' charge. Aeschines claims that Demosthenes' decree annulled the provisions of the Resolution of the Allies, which stipulated that the debate in the Assembly be limited to a discussion of peace alone and that it not take place until after the return of the ambassadors sent by the Athenians to the Greeks. But Aeschines omits one rather important fact: the Assembly never passed the Resolution of the Allies. There was thus nothing underhanded or illegal about the decree Demosthenes passed in the Council setting the dates for the debate. He was simply acting in accordance with the decree that the Assembly passed on his motion instructing the *prytanes* to convoke two meetings of the Assembly to discuss peace and alliance with Philip after the arrival of the Macedonian ambassadors. Demosthenes can certainly not be faulted for following the orders of the Assembly.

It is nevertheless true that Demosthenes did by means of these two decrees prevent the Assembly from hearing the reports of the Greek ambassadors before the debate on the treaty with Philip. Aeschines furthermore claims that Demosthenes also cheated the rest of the Greeks of the chance to share in the peace with Philip, thereby forcing the Athenians to make a separate peace with Philip. His argument rests, of course, on the assumption that the other Greeks would have sent ambassadors to Athens if they had had the chance to. Here again Aeschines omits a crucial fact, namely, that the Athenians had already invited the Greeks to join a coalition against Philip just over a year before, and at that time none of the Greeks appeared to have shown any interest in such a plan. One could therefore have argued in late Anthesterion that since the Greeks, when previously summoned by the Athenians, had not responded, they were unlikely to change their attitude now and heed the call of the Athenians. Indeed, Demosthenes probably used this line of argument when he spoke in the Assembly in late Anthesterion. As prosecutor in 343, Demosthenes was not able to reply to Aeschines' charge, but when his opponent repeated it in 330, he was speaking for the defense and had an opportunity to rebut it. At the later trial he did actually point out that long before early 346 the Greeks had already been "tested." If he found this argument powerful enough to make in 330, he may well have taken advantage of it in Anthesterion 346.[11]

One might object to this argument by drawing attention to the fact that the embassies sent out in late 348 had as their goal the formation of a coalition to wage war against Philip, whereas in early 346 the Athenians were negotiating with Philip about peace and wanted the Greeks to join them in concluding a comprehensive settlement with the king. Although they had not been interested in uniting to fight Philip, the Greeks might still be willing to participate in negotiations for peace. As we will soon see, the Greeks were in fact interested in negotiations with Philip in 346, but they saw no need to unite behind Athens in their dealings with the king, preferring instead to talk to him directly. That should come as no surprise. In 346 Philip was not seen as a common danger to the freedom of the Greeks. He had confined Macedonian expansion to northern Greece. In Thessaly he had come as liberator and as a champion of the Delphic Amphictyony, not as conqueror. The Athenians became alarmed at the growth of his power only because his victories in northern Greece had threatened their own traditional interests in the area. In seeing Philip as a threat in 346 the Athenians were almost alone among the states of central and southern Greece. Far from considering Philip a menace to their common freedom, many Greeks saw him as a potential ally who could lend them much needed assistance in their struggles against their rivals. Frustrated by the stalemate produced by the Third Sacred War, each of these states now hoped to win Philip over to its side and use his power to better its own position. None of the Greeks perceived the need to unite behind Athens in 346 either to wage war or to negotiate for peace. Each one wanted to convince Philip to take its side, and that was best done by appealing to him directly, not by participating in joint negotiations under Athenian leadership. That is in fact what the Greeks did in the next few months.[12]

The differences that separated Aeschines and Demosthenes in late Anthesterion and early Elaphebolion of 346 related not so much to ultimate aims as to how each man perceived the situation. Aeschines thought there still was a possibility that the Greeks might respond to an appeal for unity. Demosthenes did not and urged the Athenians not to wait for the return of their ambassadors before discussing the treaty with Philip. The situation in Thrace must also have contributed to Demosthenes' sense of urgency. Philip was probably besieging Cersebleptes at the time, and Athenian settlers were fleeing the Chersonese in panic. If the treaty was not approved quickly, Philip might change his mind and no longer feel bound by his pledge to keep his hands off the Chersonese. Aeschines clung to the hope that the Greeks might finally recognize the need to unite behind Athens, but the failure of his policy to produce any results caused the Assembly to abandon it and to come over to Demosthenes' point of view. Worn out by a war that had dragged on without success for ten years and worried about the security of the grain route through the Hellespont, the Assembly sided with Demosthenes and voted to have the *prytanes* hold two meetings of the Assembly to discuss both peace and alliance after the Macedonian ambassadors arrived. The truce concluded with the Macedonian herald, Philip's ambassadors entered Attica and proceeded to Athens, where they reported to the Council. After hearing their request for entry to the Assembly, the Council voted on the motion of Demosthenes to have the *prytanes* convene two meetings of the Assembly on Elaphebolion 18 and 19 to discuss peace and alliance with Philip. In the meantime, they were told, they could watch the plays about to be performed at the Dionysia in the seats of honor reserved for them by Demosthenes.

The Meetings of the Assembly on Elaphebolion 18, 19, and 25

The decree Demosthenes passed in the Council instructed the *prytanes* to hold one meeting on Elaphebolion 18 to discuss the treaty with Philip and another on Elaphebolion 19 to vote on the treaty. Aeschines and Demosthenes generously provide us with numerous statements about these meetings. Demosthenes refers to them several times in his speech of 343, and Aeschines gives a detailed account of them in his speeches of 343 and 330. But it is difficult to feel much gratitude for this generous supply of information: each man contradicts the other, and to make matters worse, Aeschines contradicts himself. The surest path through this maze of conflicting statements is to study each account in the order it was given and to examine carefully the evidence adduced to corroborate it. We must also keep in mind that after 346 the treaty became the object of harsh criticism. As a result, Aeschines and Demosthenes each tried to dissociate himself from it and to blame its faults on his opponent.[13]

    Demosthenes in his speech of 343 makes several serious charges about Aeschines' conduct at the two meetings. His first charge is that on the first day Aeschines reluctantly endorsed Philocrates' proposal to conclude peace and alliance with Philip, but on the second day he was more fervent in his support and urged the Assembly to pass a motion denying assistance to any Greek states that had failed to help Athens. This arrogant speech was allegedly made in the presence of ambassadors from all of Greece. His second charge is that Aeschines on the second day of the debate convinced the Athenians to accept Philocrates' version of the peace.

Demosthenes claims his own conduct was far different: on the first day he supported the Resolution of the Allies and tried to have the Assembly summon the Macedonian ambassadors. His third charge is that Aeschines, together with Philocrates and the other members of the First Embassy, attempted to fulfill Philip's request to exclude the Halians and the Phocians from the treaty by inserting a clause to that effect, but was forced to remove the clause by the shouts of the Assembly.[14]

Let us begin with the third charge. Demosthenes calls no witnesses nor brings forward any evidence to prove the charge. Could Phocis and Halus have been included in the terms of the decree of Philocrates about peace and alliance with Philip? The only allies known to have been included in the treaty were the members of the Confederacy, those who had representatives in the *synedrion,* but it does not appear that either Halus or Phocis were members of this group in early 346. And there is no evidence that Athens ever concluded any alliance with Halus before 346. The Phocians became allies of Athens in 356, but no source tells us whether they became members of the *synedrion* at the time or were just independent allies. Yet even if the Phocians were members of the *synedrion,* it is very doubtful they would have retained their *synedros* in Athens after Phalaecus broke off relations with them after his return to power in early 346. Demosthenes' third charge is thus a sham. Aeschines could never have conspired with Philocrates to exclude Phocis and Halus from the treaty since they were never included in its terms in the first place. Even if the Phocians had been members of the *synedrion,* it is hard to believe that Aeschines could have inserted this kind of clause. Such an exclusionary clause is unparalleled in all known Athenian treaties. All in all, it is best to explain Demosthenes' failure to call witnessess for this charge by his inability to find anyone who was willing to commit perjury.[15]

We cannot evaluate Demosthenes' first and second charges until we look at Aeschines' reply to them, but one detail in the second charge does not ring true. Demosthenes claims that on the first day he proposed to summon the Macedonian ambassadors. That is odd when we consider that the agenda for that meeting called for a discussion of the treaty with Philip. As we have noted, it was normal procedure in such debates to introduce the ambassadors who had come to negotiate the treaty and to allow them to speak to the Assembly. After they spoke, debate from the floor ensued. If there were any questions about the issues presented by the ambassadors, they could be raised during the course of the debate. Besides, there was no need for Demosthenes to propose in the Assembly on Elaphebolion 18 that Philip's ambassadors be summoned. The decree he passed in the Council shortly before had already granted them entry to the Assembly.[16]

Aeschines in his speech of 343 deals with each of Demosthenes' charges separately. We have already looked at his decisive refutation of the charge that he insulted the Greek embassies that were present during the debate about the treaty. Aeschines does not reply directly to the third charge about the Phocians, preferring instead to show how their defeat was caused by their own mistakes, not by any schemes concocted by Philocrates and himself. As for the charge that he spoke in favor of Philocrates' proposal on the second day, Aeschines simply reads out the text of Demosthenes' own decree setting the dates and procedure for the meetings. There it is explicitly stated that no speeches were to be given during the meeting on

Elaphebolion 19 when the vote about the treaty was taken. Surprisingly enough, Aeschines does not deny he spoke in favor of peace with Philip on Elaphebolion 18. In fact, he gives a short summary of the speech he delivered on that day. In it he warned the Athenians not to reject Philip's offer of peace while they could still obtain a good settlement. He predicted that a refusal to ratify the treaty would land them in the same position as the Athenians found themselves in 404 when the Spartans dictated harsh and humiliating terms of surrender. To confound Demosthenes' claim to have spoken on behalf of the Resolution of the Allies, Aeschines brings forward Amyntor of Erchia to testify. According to Amyntor, Demosthenes showed him a proposal that he himself had drawn up and was considering submitting to the *proedroi* who ran the meetings of the Assembly. The proposal contained terms that were exactly identical to those of Philocrates' decree.[17]

Our analysis of the information found in the speeches of 343 yields interesting results. Although their accounts of the meetings of Elaphebolion 18 and 19 differ in many regards, they agree on one key matter: on Elaphebolion 18 Aeschines reluctantly backed the proposal of Philocrates that the Athenians conclude peace and alliance with Philip. Aeschines does not admit in his speech of 343 that it was the proposal of Philocrates he favored, but that is obviously due to his reluctance to mention the name of Philocrates, who had shortly before been convicted of treason in absentia. But earlier, at the trial of Timarchus in late 346, Aeschines was not ashamed of his connection with Philocrates and boasted that he worked with him to bring about peace with Philip. Significant too is the fact that neither orator says Aeschines supported the Resolution of the Allies during the debate about the treaty. On the other hand, Demosthenes' charges that Aeschines spoke on behalf of Philocrates' proposal with greater conviction on Elaphebolion 19 and that he attempted to exclude the Halians and the Phocians from the treaty are obviously no more than baseless slanders. Aeschines refutes the first charge by reading from the decree Demosthenes passed in the Council, the second is highly improbable, and neither is supported by any evidence. Demosthenes' claim that he championed the Resolution of the Allies also lacks any foundation of evidence. Indeed, the testimony of Amyntor shows that he too was in favor of peace and alliance with Philip. Ironically enough, Aeschines and Demosthenes, despite their bitter hostility toward each other in 343, had on Elaphebolion 18 of 346 shared precisely the same position in regard to the treaty with Philip.[18]

In 330 Aeschines presented a very different account of the meetings of Elaphebolion 18 and 19. In his speech against Ctesiphon he states that at the first meeting the Resolution of the Allies was read out. The resolution proposed that the Assembly only discuss peace and that all Greek states that wished could join in the treaty provided they did so within three months' time. Aeschines claims he argued for this resolution on the first day of the debate and after the meeting went away convinced that on the next day the Assembly would ratify it. On the following day, however, Demosthenes seized the rostrum and declared that it was senseless to vote for a resolution Philip would never accept. He then called on Antipater, who announced that Philip would not accept the provisions contained in the Resolution of the Allies. Intimidated by Demosthenes' maneuver, the Assembly passed Philocrates' proposal, which included both peace and alliance with Philip and excluded the other Greeks.[19]

Aeschines' account given in 330 bears a curious resemblance to Demosthenes' account of 343. In 343 Demosthenes claimed to have championed the Resolution of the Allies; in 330 Aeschines asserts that he was the one who backed the Resolution of the Allies. In 343 Demosthenes accused Aeschines of urging the Athenians to pass Philocrates' proposal at the second meeting of the Assembly; in 330 Aeschines charges Demosthenes with having pressed the Assembly to accept Philocrates' version of the treaty. Aeschines' later account is vulnerable to the same objections brought against Demosthenes' charges: no witnesses are summoned to verify them, and they are inconsistent with the decree regulating the procedure for the meetings of Elaphebolion 18 and 19. And if Demosthenes did actually go to the rostrum and speak on Elaphebolion 19 in defiance of the provisions of his own decree, it is remarkable that Aeschines did not draw attention to the incident in 343. If true, the charge would have done much to strengthen his case and to expose the hypocrisy of Demosthenes. Why then did he not bring it up in 343? Furthermore, Aeschines' later account is implausible. As we observed above, Philip's ambassadors should have been present in the Assembly during the debate on Elaphebolion 18. Why did it not occur to someone then to ask them what they thought of the Resolution of the Allies? And if Aeschines in fact urged the Athenians to ratify the Resolution of the Allies in 346 instead of Philocrates' version of the treaty, why did he not say so in 343 when he was doing his best to dissociate himself from Philocrates? All these arguments point to the inescapable conclusion that Aeschines' later account of the ratification of the treaty is worthless as historical evidence. In 343 Aeschines knew that the court could still recall the events of Elaphebolion 346 and kept closer to the facts. In 330 he was confident that most people had forgotten about the events of sixteen years ago and felt free to invent these fictions.

Aeschines' later account, though in general unreliable, contains one valuable piece of evidence: it gives the contents of the Resolution of the Allies that Demosthenes only alluded to in 343. The resolution reveals that even after the defeat of their previous resolution, the Allies in the *synedrion* continued to place their hopes in a comprehensive peace settlement. Aeschines may have helped to draft this resolution, whose aim was similar to that of the other Resolution of the Allies he may have sponsored. If he really did favor at one time this form of the treaty, his support for it was short-lived since on Elaphebolion 18 he endorsed Philocrates' proposal for peace and alliance. His decision not to speak for the Resolution of the Allies may have been prompted by the defeat of their earlier resolution and by the apparent unwillingness of the Greeks to rally behind Athens. Alternatively, he may have walked into the Assembly on Elaphebolion 18 with the intention of leading the fight for the resolution with its plan for a comprehensive peace, but soon have changed his mind after hearing the Macedonian ambassadors declare that Philip would never consent to its terms.[20]

Whatever the reason for his change of mind, Aeschines' support for Philocrates' proposal was less than wholehearted, and motivated by fear for the consequences of its rejection rather than any conviction about its intrinsic merits. Aeschines knew that turning down Philip's offer of peace and alliance would mean the continuation of the war with Macedon, a war which the Athenians had little chance of winning. Just to hold their position in the Chersonese, they would have to mobilize all their resources. If they did not, Macedonian troops would overrun their possession in the Chersonese. No Athenian wanted to repeat the aftermath of Aigospotamoi. Eubulus put the choice confronting the Assembly quite bluntly: either the Athenians accept the proposal of Philocrates or go down to the Piraeus at once, pay the *eisphora,* and divert the money in the Theoric Fund toward the prosecution of the war. Aeschines says that there were many who opposed acceptance of the treaty and urged the Athenians to continue fighting. Aristophon was one of the most outspoken of this group. He upbraided the Assembly, calling it an act of cowardice to give up Amphipolis in return for such a treaty. The Athenians had plenty of allies, a fleet of three hundred triremes, and annual revenues of four hundred talents. With resources like these it would be shameful to make peace with Macedon. But few were evidently convinced by his speech. On Elaphebolion 19 the Assembly voted to pass Philocrates' proposal to conclude peace and alliance with Philip, thus ending their ten-year war for Amphipolis.[21]

The Athenian decision to accept Philip's offer of peace and alliance was fatal to Cersebleptes' position. The Thracian king was counting on Athenian soldiers and triremes to strengthen his defenses against Philip. Now that the Athenians had become allies of his enemy, he had little hope of withstanding Philip's invasion. Cersebleptes must have been aware of the negotiations between Philip and the Athenians, because sometime around early Elaphebolion he sent Critobulus of Lampsakos to act as his representative in Athens. Critobulus may in fact have been sent in response to the request carried by the Athenian ambassadors sent out at the suggestion of Aeschines to invite the Greeks to participate in their negotiations with Philip. Knowing that Philip was trying to win the Athenians over to his side, Cersebleptes possibly hoped that the conclusion of a comprehensive peace settlement might save him from Philip's onslaught. If those were his hopes, the Assembly put a quick end to them. Seeing the indifference of the other Greeks and the opposition of the Macedonian ambassadors to a kind of Common Peace, the Assembly abandoned that alternative and chose to accept Philip's package of peace, alliance, and future unspecified benefits.

In their rush to embrace Philip, the Athenians preferred not to remember their previous commitment to their Thracian ally. Indeed, Aeschines tells us that his name never came up during the debate about the treaty, and Demosthenes, who accuses his opponent of bringing about the destruction of Cersebleptes, nowhere states that the Assembly deliberated about his fate on Elaphebolion 18 and 19. But Critobulus was determined to bring Cersebleptes to the attention of the Athenians. On Elaphebolion 25 Critobulus was introduced to the Assembly and asked the Athenians to include Cersebleptes among their allies so that he could swear the oaths to the treaty on the king's behalf.[22]

Aeschines gives an account of Critobulus' request in his speech of 343. After the Assembly voted to conclude peace and alliance with Philip, the treaty was sent to the *synedrion* to be ratified by the Allies. Since the Allies' version of the treaty was rejected by the Assembly, their approval was needed for the version the Assembly had finally endorsed. The Allies proved to be compliant and reported their decision to accept peace and alliance with Philip to the Assembly at a meeting on Elaphebolion 25. After their report, Philocrates passed a motion instructing the members of the *synedrion* to swear the oaths to Philip's ambassadors at the *Strategeion*, the headquarters of the Athenian generals located in the agora. It was at this meeting that Critobulus made his request. According to Aeschines, Critobulus stated that Cersebleptes had sent him as his representative. Since only the Allies of Athens, that is, the members of the *synedrion*, were eligible to swear the oaths to the treaty, Critobulus asked that Cersebleptes be enrolled among the Allies. After Critobulus finished speaking, Aleximachus of Pelekes submitted to the *proedroi*, who presided over meetings of the Assembly, a proposal to allow Cersebleptes' representative to swear the oaths to the treaty. At this point, Demosthenes, who was serving as one of the *proedroi* at the meeting, rose and declared that he would not submit Aleximachus' proposal to a vote and break the peace with Philip. He compared Cersebleptes to a person who showed up late at a sacrificial meal and tried to take part in the ritual and to enjoy its benefits without having made any offerings of his own. If the king wanted to become one of the Allies, it was too late now; he should have submitted his request at the earlier meeting that was designated for that purpose. But the crowd in the Assembly shouted him down and demanded that the other *proedroi* put the motion to a vote. The other *proedroi* obeyed, and Aleximachus' proposal was voted on despite the impassioned protest of Demosthenes. After the meeting was adjourned, the Macedonian ambassadors received the oaths from the members of the *synedrion*.[23]

Aeschines marshaled an impressive phalanx of witnesses to corroborate his account. To attest to his narrative of the meeting in the Assembly, Aeschines called on Aleximachus and the other *proedroi* who presided at the meeting. To disprove Demosthenes' charge that he prevented Critobulus from taking the oaths, he summoned as witnesses the Athenian generals who administered the oaths and the representatives of the Allies in the *synedrion* who swore the oaths. With eight *proedroi*, several generals, and dozens of representatives, there must have been quite a crowd in the court that day. Yet although Aeschines gives a detailed account of the incident and a horde of witnesses to support it, his narrative contains one puzzling omission: he never tells us whether Aleximachus' proposal passed or not. All he says is that the *proedroi* submitted it to a vote. One also wonders why Aeschines, who spared no effort to furnish supporting evidence for his account, neglected to have Aleximachus' proposal read out. If the proposal passed, Aeschines would certainly have said it did, since its passage would have revealed that Demosthenes had attempted to thwart the will of the Athenian people. On the other hand, if the proposal did not pass, Aeschines' failure to mention its rejection would not be surprising since the Assembly's decision to turn down Critobulus' request would have shown that Demosthenes was acting in accord with the wishes of the Athenian people in trying to exclude Cersebleptes from the treaty. Such considerations strongly suggest that the Assembly did not pass Aleximachus' proposal, thereby rejecting Critobulus' request.

Other evidence confirms this inference. In his speech of 330, Aeschines charges that Demosthenes plotted with Philocrates to exclude Cersebleptes from the treaty. The charge is without foundation, but Aeschines reveals that Cersebleptes was not included in the treaty because he had no *synedros* in Athens, clearly implying that Critobulus' attempt to have him enrolled among the Allies was unsuccessful. The letter sent by Philip to the Athenians in 340 when the Peace of Philocrates was slowly unraveling lends further confirmation. Although scholars are divided about the authenticity of the letter, some pronouncing it genuine, others seeing in it the work of the historian Anaximenes, the information contained in it is for the most part reliable. In the letter Philip scolds the Athenians for their inconsistent attitude toward Cersebleptes. When the king wanted to swear the oaths to his ambassadors, the Athenian generals prevented him and denounced him as an enemy of Athens. Now that they want to pick a quarrel with Philip, however, the Athenians have started to call him a fellow citizen. Philip is clearly alluding to the attempt of Critobulus to have Cersebleptes included in the treaty between himself and the Athenians. The evidence of the letter thus reveals that our inference about Aleximachus' motion is correct: the Athenians must have rejected his proposal to make Cersebleptes a member of the *synedrion* and to allow Critobulus to swear the oaths on his behalf. Otherwise the generals would not have barred Cersebleptes' representative from the ceremony. One can now understand why Aeschines asked the generals to testify that he did not prevent Critobulus from swearing the oaths: it was they who had driven Critobulus away, not Aeschines.[24]

As it turned out, the Assembly's rejection of Critobulus' request had no effect on Cersebleptes' fate. Aeschines, when refuting Demosthenes' charge that his actions brought about the king's downfall, presents a letter from Chares reporting the Cersebleptes capitulated to Philip on the day before the Assembly met to hear Critobulus' request. The vote of the Assembly, though it did not alter the situation in Thrace, indicates nevertheless that the Assembly shared Demosthenes' analysis of the situation. The Athenian knew that the price of peace and alliance with Philip was the sacrifice of their Thracian ally. Although it is never easy to turn one's back on a former ally, the Athenians could have had few regrets about the decision. The Thracian kings had never been the most faithful of friends. Cersebleptes, like his father Cotys before him, had attempted to wrest control of the Chersonese from the Athenians and had come to terms with them only out of fear of his co-heirs and Philip. In 343 Demosthenes tried to pin the blame for Cersebleptes' surrender on Aeschines, but the real causes of his defeat were Philip's astute diplomacy, the overwhelming superiority of the Macedonian army, and Athenian self-interest.

Elaphebolion 346 was a month of disappointment for Aeschines. His efforts to have the Greeks send embassies to Athens and to form a united front under Athenian leadership in the negotiations with Philip failed to stir any enthusiasm abroad. Aeschines tried to keep his initiative alive by asking that the negotiations with Philip be postponed until after the arrival of the Athenian ambassadors sent out to rally the Greeks, but the Assembly had lost patience with a policy that had been so fruitless. The Athenians were also well aware of the situation facing them. Philip was besieging Cersebleptes in eastern Thrace, and Chares did not have enough troops to rescue him. To save Cersebleptes they would have had to mobilize their entire fleet and risk several thousand hoplites on a campaign that held little promise of victory. Instead, they chose to succumb to Philip's offer: renounce all claims to Amphipolis and abandon Cersebleptes in return for peace, alliance, and the security of the Chersonese. The Athenians did not have to be hoodwinked into accepting the treaty with Philip. They were fully cognizant of the unpleasant alternatives between which they had to choose. Aeschines also understood the situation and reluctantly urged the Assembly to vote for Philocrates' proposal to conclude peace and alliance with Philip.

And not to be forgotten were the benefits promised by Philip in his letter. What sort of benefits might the Athenians now request in return for ratifying the treaty and turning their backs on Cersebleptes? That was a question Aeschines would soon begin to ponder.

5

The End of the Third Sacred War

The Second Embassy

After ratifying the treaty with Philip, the Athenians could put to rest their fears about the Chersonese. The only task remaining was for the Athenian ambassadors to travel to Macedon and receive the oaths from Philip and his allies. At this point the Peace of Philocrates, as the treaty would come to be known, appeared to be a success: Philip gained his victory over Cersebleptes, and the Athenians gained security for their interests in the Chersonese. In the meantime, however, a new issue had arisen. In central Greece, the Third Sacred War had dragged on for a decade. All the major powers of Greece—Phocis, Thebes, Thessaly, Sparta, and Athens—were caught up in the conflict. Philip, too, had entered the fighting on the side of Thessaly and had won a major victory over the Phocians in 352, but had chosen to remain aloof since then. By the spring of 346, all of the contestants had grown weary of the conflict and wanted to see it resolved.

This kind of military stalemate was nothing new for the major Greek powers. In the years after the Peloponnesian War, the Greeks had several times tried to put an end to their interminable conflicts by concluding a Common Peace. These comprehensive peace treaties were usually negotiated under the supervision of the Great King of Persia, who took advantage of them to maintain his power and influence in the Aegean. But the year 346 marked a turning point in Greek history. Instead of appealing to Persia, the Greeks sought the leadership of another monarch, Philip of Macedon. The negotiations in Macedon that brought an end to the sacred war were of paramount importance since they signaled the entry of Macedon as the arbiter of affairs in central and southern Greece.[1]

The new situation presented the Athenians with a difficult question: what kind of relationship should they have with Philip? The First Embassy had dealt with Athenian relations with Philip in northern Greece and had resolved their disputes about that area for the moment. But the Athenians had never before had to confront the possibility of Philip establishing his power south of Thessaly. Was the development to be welcomed or feared? Should the Athenians cooperate with Philip to advance their mutual interests in the region? Or were their interests in central Greece incompatible? Might it then be a good idea to preserve the status quo and shut out Macedonian influence from any territory south of Delphi? Unfortunately, there had

been no discussion of central Greece during the meetings of the Assembly in Elaphebolion. Demosthenes later claimed that the fate of the Phocians and the Halians
was brought up in the debate about the treaty with Philip, but those charges we have
found to be baseless. As far as we can tell, the negotiations that culminated in the
Peace of Philocrates concentrated exclusively on Amphipolis and the Chersonese.
Thus when Aeschines and the other Athenian ambassadors sent to receive the oaths
from Philip arrived in Pella in Macedon and found embassies from all over Greece
each trying to sell Philip their own proposal for ending the sacred war, they were
without instructions about how to proceed.

After the representatives of the Allies had sworn the oaths to Philip's ambassadors, the Athenian ambassadors who had been elected to receive the oaths from
Philip made ready for the journey to Macedon. It appears that everyone who went on
the First Embassy was reelected to serve on the Second Embassy. The Assembly,
evidently satisfied with the previous round of negotiations in Macedon, saw no
reason to deny the ambassadors the honor of bringing to a conclusion what they had
so ably begun. In addition to receiving the oaths from Philip and his allies, the
Assembly instructed the ambassadors to try to obtain the release of all Athenian
prisoners held in Macedon and to do anything else that might bring benefit to
Athens. This final instruction was a general clause often tacked on to orders given to
ambassadors to empower them to deal with matters that might arise in the course of
negotiations but lay outside the scope of their actual instructions. The most significant omission from the orders is the absence of any instructions relating to the sacred
war. In fact, Demosthenes was later to argue that the Athenian ambassadors should
pay no attention to the negotiations conducted with Philip by the other Greeks about
the sacred war since nothing in their instructions compelled them to. And Aeschines
was able to justify his participation in these talks only by citing the clause that
allowed the ambassadors to deal with matters not covered explicitly in their instructions. As the members of the First Embassy left Athens, all they expected to do in
Macedon was to receive the oaths from Philip and to negotiate the release of the
Athenian prisoners.[2]

After giving the Second Embassy its instructions, the Assembly ordered the
Council to supervise the departure of the embassy. In accordance with this decree,
Demosthenes, who was a member of the Council, passed on Munichion 3, the Attic
month after Elaphebolion, a decree ordering the ambassadors to depart immediately
and instructing the general Proxenus to convey them to their destination. Three years
later, Demosthenes claimed that he moved this decree so that the ambassadors would
sail to the Hellespont as soon as possible and compel Philip to swear the oaths to the
treaty. According to Demosthenes, this would have forced Philip to restore the
places he had taken from Athens and to keep his hands off the rest. But that is not
what happened. Once the ambassadors reached Oreos on the northern end of Euboea, where they met Proxenus, the ambassadors did not proceed by sea, but instead
took a roundabout route to Pella, which consumed twenty-three days. During this
time, Philip was helping himself to a generous portion of Thracian territory, including Doriskos, the Sacred Mount, and a collection of fortresses. Demosthenes says he
tried to prevent this, but was thwarted by Aeschines. As a result of Aeschines'
alleged treachery, all of Thrace fell into Philip's hands. To prove these charges,

Demosthenes has several documents read out, including a letter of Philip, the decrees of Philocrates, and another decree containing instructions about the swearing of the oaths. Then several witnesses are called to testify that the embassy could have caught Philip at the Hellespont.[3]

Demosthenes gathers an impressive array of evidence, but his entire point rests on the assumption that the territory in Thrace was covered by the terms of the Peace of Philocrates. We know that this was not the case. As we noted before, Cersebleptes' kingdom was not included in the terms of the treaty, since Cersebleptes was not a member of the *synedrion* of Allies. Although the fortresses in Thrace were probably established under the supervision of the Athenian general Charidemus, they could not be described as Athenian possessions and thus did not fall under the terms of the treaty. On the contrary, the forts lay in Thracian territory and were held by Thracian troops. Even if the Athenian ambassadors had sailed posthaste to the Hellespont and received the oaths from Philip before his army captured the fortresses, it would not have stopped him from overrunning all of Thrace. It therefore made no difference where the ambassadors met Philip.[4] Whatever Demosthenes might have said in 343, Philip clearly kept his word in 346. The king confined his conquests to Thrace and left Athenian possessions in the Chersonese untouched. His good faith in regard to the treaty may have made an impression on Aeschines. If Philip had proved to be as good as his word in regard to the Chersonese, could he not also be trusted to keep his promise about benefiting Athens in other regards?

When the Athenian ambassadors arrived in Pella at the end of Munichion, they found that they were not the only ambassadors who had arrived in Macedon. Embassies had also come from Thebes, Thessaly, Sparta, Phocis, and a host of other Greek states. These embassies had converged on Pella for the same reason, namely, to see how Philip intended to resolve the Third Sacred War. To understand what these embassies hoped to achieve, it is necessary to cast a glance backward over the history of this war and to analyze the general situation in Greece in early 346. It will then be possible to place the proposals Aeschines made to Philip in their proper context.[5]

The dispute that led to the outbreak of the sacred war went back to 371. After their victory at Leuctra in that year, the Thebans went on a diplomatic offensive and brought a charge of sacrilege against the Spartans before the Amphictyonic Council in Delphi. Another charge was lodged against the Phocians, who were allies of Sparta. The council declared both the Spartans and the Phocians guilty and condemned them to pay a large fine to the god at Delphi. Neither the Spartans nor the Phocians complied, and the fine remained unpaid. Finally in 356 the council threatened to place a curse on any state that failed to pay its debts to the god. Rather than submit to this threat, Philomelus, a prominent Phocian, persuaded his fellow citizens to seize the temple at Delphi. The Thebans and the Locrians marched out to defend the temple, but their forces were driven back by a Phocian army led by Philomelus. Philomelus strengthened his position by concluding alliances with Athens and Sparta. The Thessalians, traditional enemies of the Phocians, sided with the Locrians and the Thebans. Thus, what began as an accusation of sacrilege expanded into the Third Sacred War for Delphi, which locked all the major powers in Greece in conflict.[6]

Philip did not enter the war until 353. After a serious defeat at the hands of the Phocians under Onomarchus (Philomelus lost his life in a battle with the Thebans), the Thessalians appealed to Philip for help. Philip marched his army into Thessaly, but suffered two defeats and was forced to withdraw from the area. Undaunted by these reverses, Philip returned to Thessaly in the next year and trounced the Phocian army at Crocus Field. Onomarchus, the Phocian commander, lost his life, and Phocis itself was only saved from invasion by the quick reaction of the Athenians. An Athenian fleet under Nausicles promptly landed troops at Thermopylai and occupied the pass to cut off Philip's progress. Philip used the opportunity afforded by his victory to advertise his piety to the god of Delphi and to prove to the Greeks he came as an avenger of sacrilege, not as a conqueror. He had over three thousand Phocian prisoners drowned for looting Apollo's temple.[7]

Despite his overwhelming victory, Philip chose not to finish off the sacred war in the five years that followed. At first glance, this appears puzzling. One cannot explain his long absence from the region as the result of pressing business elsewhere. True, Philip made two invasions of Thrace and subdued all of the Chalcidice in the next few years. But these campaigns took up only two years, leaving Philip ample time to return to central Greece. Part of the reason may have been his lack of confidence in the ability of the Macedonian army to bring the war to a close. After all, he had only defeated the Phocian army, and his victory owed a great deal to the cavalry of his Thessalian allies. His own troops had suffered defeat twice before finally pulling off a victory. But if Philip were to invade Phocis and strike at Delphi, he would have to confront not only the Phocians, but also their allies, the Athenians and the Spartans, who would not allow their ally to be crushed. On the other hand, the continuation of the sacred war was very much to Philip's advantage. As long as Sparta, Thebes, Phocis, Thessaly, and Athens remained locked in stalemate, Philip had a free hand to extend his power and influence in northern Greece. Were any one of these powers to emerge as undisputed leader of the Greeks, Philip might find his ambitions thwarted. The prolongation of the conflict had the further advantage of keeping Thessaly dependent on Philip for protection against the aggressive Phocians. Once that threat was removed, Philip might have a hard time justifying Macedonian interventions in Thessaly and would have to compete with the Thebans for influence in the area. Philip thus had no incentive to end the sacred war for the time being. He could afford to wait until circumstances improved his chances for an easy victory over the Phocians.

After Philip's withdrawal, the war dragged on much as it had before. Phayllus succeeded to Onomarchus' position as leader and rebuilt the Phocian army. Phayllus succumbed to a fatal disease sometime around 351 and was replaced by Phalaecus. Phalaecus' policy departed from that of his predecessors, who had maintained close ties with Athens. When Callias of Chalcis led the Euboeans in their struggle to drive out Athenian influence from the island, Phalaecus supplied him with mercenaries. Our information about Phalaecus' move is so scanty that it is difficult to discern his motive, but his willingness to pursue a policy that threatened to jeopardize Phocian relations with Athens is clear. Luckily for the Athenians, popular sentiment in Phocis turned against Phalaecus. His use of temple funds to finance the war effort against Thebes evidently disturbed many Phocians, who began to accuse him of appropriating sacred property. In 347 Phalaecus was deposed by a triumvirate com-posed of the generals Deinocrates, Callias, and Sophanes, who lost no time in launching an investigation into the charges against him. The investigation resulted in the conviction and punishment of Philon, one of Phalaecus' generals.[8]

In the same period, the Thebans, who had lost several cities to the Phocians and were worn out by the protracted conflict, turned to Philip and asked him to send troops. The request was a splendid opportunity for Philip since it gained him the friendship of Thebes and enabled him to enhance his reputation as the champion of the Amphictyonic cause. Philip sent a small contingent of troops to the Thebans, which enabled them to win a victory over the Phocians at Abai, thus placing them in Philip's debt. But Philip made sure that the force was not large enough to tip the scales decisively in favor of the Thebans. For the moment Philip had no wish to see the war brought to an end.[9]

It may have been this Theban victory that caused the new Phocian leaders in early 346 to appeal to their old allies Athens and Sparta. In return for their military support, the Phocians offered to entrust to the Athenians the forts controlling the pass at Thermopylai. The Athenians voted to accept the offer and commanded their general Proxenus, who was stationed at Oreos on the northern end of Euboea, to take over the forts. Before Proxenus could act, Phalaecus threw out the triumvirate and seized power again for himself. Phalaecus told Proxenus he was in no need of Athenian assistance and refused to grant him control of the forts around Thermo-pylai. The Spartans received the same rebuff. Phalaecus then added insult to rebuff. When the Athenian *spondophoroi* arrived in Phocis in early 346 to announce the truce for the Eleusinian Mysteries, they were rudely informed that the Phocians would not receive the truce. Having broken off ties with Athens, Phalaecus placed his hopes in Philip and sent an embassy to Macedon. He was not the only one to do so. In the same period, the Thessalians, Thebans, Spartans, and several other com-munities also sent embassies to Philip.[10]

When Aeschines and the other Athenian ambassadors arrived in Pella, the diplomatic situation was tense and confused. The Phocians were seeking Philip's support, or at least his neutrality, so they could continue their war against Thebes. The Thessalians were there to demand that Philip put an end to Phocian control of Delphi and to restore to them their traditional position of honor in the Amphictyonic Council. The Thebans wanted Philip to help them end the sacred war so they could recover the cities conquered by the Phocians. The Spartans hoped that Philip would weaken their Theban enemies by dissolving the unification of Boeotia under their leadership.[11]

After Philip returned in triumph to Pella in the Attic month of Thargelion, following his victory over Cersebleptes two months before, Aeschines and the other ambassadors met to discuss what they would say to the king. Aeschines is the only one to recount the events of the meeting, but there is no reason to question his account, which is supported by the testimony of the other ambassadors. The meeting was confined to a discussion of the instructions they had received from the Assembly until Aeschines spoke up and urged his colleagues not to ignore what was going on around them. After drawing attention to the other Greek embassies present, he reminded them that their instructions included an order ''to do whatever good they might.'' He admitted that their instructions did not command them to ask Philip to put down the arrogance of the Thebans and to rebuild the walls of the Boeotian cities. His explanation for the omission was that the Assembly wished to provide itself with an excuse in case the ambassadors failed to persuade Philip. They should therefore not be afraid of stirring up the anger of the Thebans. Instead they should remember the boast of Epaminondas, who said that he would drag the Propylaia down from the Acropolis and set it up on the Cadmeia in Thebes. In the middle of Aeschines' speech, Demosthenes interrupted and protested that they should not stick their noses into other people's business. Moreover, they should certainly not set the Greek cities against one another. Demosthenes said that he was going to pay no attention to the fact that Philip was setting out for Thermopylai. No one was going to accuse him of saying what he ought not say nor of failing to say what he should. The ambassadors then agreed that everyone should say what he wanted to in his speech to Philip.[12]

This discussion, which took place at a seemingly routine meeting of the Athenian embassy, was of crucial importance and marked a turning point in Athenian foreign policy. During Elaphebolion 346 Aeschines and Demosthenes disagreed only about the terms of the treaty with Philip, whether it should include an alliance or not, and whether the other Greeks should be allowed to share in the peace with Philip. Demosthenes won this battle, and the Assembly voted to accept Philocrates' version of the treaty, which included both peace and alliance and limited eligibility to the allies of Athens who were members of the *synedrion*. Aeschines, though initially opposed to this version of the treaty, finally yielded and voiced his support for it. After their arrival in Pella, however, an entirely new dispute broke out between the two men. While their disagreement over the treaty with Philip was short-lived, their quarrel over Athens' new relationship with Philip was to last far longer.

It was clear to Aeschines that Philip had to put an end to the sacred war and return the temple at Delphi to the Amphictyons. Philip had acquired his influence in Thessaly by promising the Thessalians that he would champion their cause in the sacred war. To maintain his position in Thessaly Philip had to make good on his promise. If Philip were to march against the Phocians, there was little the Athenians could do except to stand by and watch. The Athenians had been eager and willing to defend Thermopylai earlier in 346, but Phalaecus had spurned their help and placed his trust in Philip. For these reasons the fate of Phocis was out of Athenian hands. Both Aeschines and Demosthenes must have known this at the time. Demosthenes said that he would pay no attention to Philip's movement toward Phocis. Aeschines took a different approach. There was no sense in opposing Philip's intention to end the sacred war, but Aeschines could at least urge Philip to impose a lenient settlement on the Phocians.[13]

The defeat of Phocis worried Aeschines less than the victory of Thebes. Thebes had been seriously weakened by the sacred war and had lost several important cities in Boeotia to the Phocians. The defeat of Phocis would free Thebes from a crippling war and restore her lost territory. To inhibit the resurgence of Thebes, Aeschines planned to urge Philip to humble Thebes by liberating the Boeotian cities from Theban control. Aeschines' proposal was not an original one. The Spartans had employed the same strategy in their attempts to weaken Theban power earlier in the century. Aeschines' motive for the proposal appears to have been nothing more than a desire for vengeance against a traditional enemy. His approach was utterly dissimilar to the policy advocated by Isocrates at the time. In his *Philippus,* Isocrates encouraged the king to work toward *homonoia,* unity, among all the major powers of Greece. Where Aeschines took a rather narrow view of the situation and looked only at Athenian interests, Isocrates took a Panhellenic view, counseling a comprehensive solution to the problems besetting Greece. Besides bringing peace and freedom to the Greeks, Isocrates advised Philip to invade the Persian Empire in order to liberate the Greeks of Asia and conquer the Persians. Neither of these proposals figures in Aeschines' speeches. Aeschines had obviously fastened on Philip's promise of benefits and wanted him to humble the arrogant Thebans as a favor to Athens. His goals went no further than this.[14]

Why did Demosthenes oppose Aeschines' proposal? Some have maintained that Demosthenes disagreed with Aeschines at this point because he wished to keep Theban strength intact in the hope that Thebes might later join with Athens in an alliance to halt Philip's advance into Greece. Were this Demosthenes' true aim, however, we would expect to find some trace of it in his speeches delivered in the following years. But far from appearing pro-Theban in this period, Demosthenes in his addresses to the Assembly showed no reluctance to appeal to anti-Theban sentiments in Athens. Besides lacking support in our sources, this view of Demosthenes' aims suffers from implausibility. No one in 346 could have foreseen the circumstances that gave rise to the alliance between Athens and Thebes in 339. Even then it was a close thing: Demosthenes was able to persuade the Thebans to accept the alliance against Philip only by offering enormous concessions.[15]

The only evidence we have about Demosthenes' motives at this meeting of the ambassadors in Pella is Aeschines' statement that Demosthenes objected to his plans on the grounds they would stir up dissension among the Greeks. In the statements he made in subsequent years, Demosthenes reveals that he was not pro-Theban at the time, but simply suspicious of Philip's designs. While the weakening of Thebes might be advantageous to Athens, the surrender of Phocis and the liberation of the Boeotian cities would have allowed Philip to extend his influence perilously close to Attica. The capitulation of Phocis would place Philip in control of Thermopylai and give him unimpeded access to central Greece. If Philip were to go farther and liberate the Boeotian cities, he would establish a cordon of Macedonian client states that would henceforth look to him for security in much the same way as the Arcadians and Messenians had looked to Thebes for protection of their freedom after Epaminondas shattered Sparta's hold on the Peloponnese. A set of Macedonian client states on the border of Attica would have been a very disturbing development indeed. Even though the situation as it existed in early 346 was not without its drawbacks, it still had the virtue of preserving a certain balance of power with Phocis pitted against Thebes and both these states blocking Philip's access to central Greece and Attica. By stirring up anti-Theban sentiments in Greece and increasing tensions among cities, Aeschines was playing right into Philip's hands. In Demosthenes' eyes the proposal put forward by Aeschines would have allowed Philip to exploit the disunity of the Greeks to extend Macedonian power. Thebes might be an enemy of

Athens, but although hostile, Theban strength was worth preserving as a buffer between Athens and Macedon.

The differences between Aeschines and Demosthenes that surfaced at this meeting were to form the basis for the debate between the two men during the next several years. Aeschines hoped to convince Philip to liberate the cities of Boeotia; Demosthenes opposed the plan for the reason it would have dangerously increased Philip's power in central Greece. Aeschines saw no risk in the plan; Demosthenes' suspicions led him to distrust Philip's intentions. Yet while Aeschines and Demosthenes differed about policy toward Thebes, there is no indication they differed about the question of Phocis. That is not surprising. Both men must have realized that the Athenians were in no position to alter the outcome of the sacred war after Phalaecus' rejection of their help. They could only approve or disapprove of Philip's actions, but there was little sense in disapproving. The best they could do was to praise Philip's aim of ending the war and hope that the settlement imposed on the Phocians would not be too severe.

Not long after Philip returned to Pella in Thargelion, the king met with the Athenian ambassadors. Demosthenes later claimed that it was at this point that Philip bribed Aeschines, Philocrates, and the other Athenian ambassadors. According to Demosthenes, Philip first sent messages to each of the ambassadors and gave them gold. Demosthenes himself refused the gift. Philip became worried that if some of the ambassadors declined to take his gifts, they would later denounce those who had accepted them. Philip thus decided to make a collective gift to all the ambassadors and offer it as a gift of hospitality, although it was really meant as a bribe. Demosthenes put a stop to this gambit by asking Philip to use the money to pay the ransom of the Athenian prisoners held in Macedonia. Philip found it impossible to deny Demosthenes' request. He could not say he was unable to spend the money on the captives since he had already given it to the other ambassadors. Were he to say that, he would give away the fact that they had already received gifts from him. In this predicament Philip had no choice but to release the prisoners. Nevertheless, he held off carrying out his promise and said he would send them home in time for the Panathenaia.[16]

It is crucial to analyze how much of this story is supported by evidence and how much is unsubstantiated. After recounting the incident at Aeschines' trial in 343, Demosthenes called on Apollophanes and others "who were present" to testify. These witnesses must be those who were present when Philip offered the guest-gift to all the Athenian ambassadors and declared he would send the prisoners home in time for the Panathenaia. But Demosthenes does not provide any evidence to back up his charge that Philip communicated privately with the ambassadors and offered them gold, which most of them accepted. Despite Demosthenes' effort to place Philip's actions in a bad light, there was nothing suspicious about a Macedonian king offering a guest-gift to all the ambassadors. It was a Macedonian custom to bestow such presents on those who came to visit the king. Philip was acting no differently than Menelaus and Helen in the *Odyssey* when they give Telemachus gifts as the young man makes ready to leave Sparta and return to Ithaca.

Demosthenes' charge of bribery is without foundation, but the incident he describes is worth studying more closely since it illustrates the cultural divide that separated the Macedonian court from the democracy of Athens. During the reign of Philip II, the Macedonians had still not progressed much beyond the Homeric way of life in many respects. In the absence of any formal legal or political institutions such as those found in Athens and Sparta, Philip maintained his power inside and outside of Macedonia by cultivating personal friendships, distributing gifts, and dispensing favors to put others in his debt. Since he was ruler of the Macedonians, the advantages gained by his friendships would benefit all Macedonians. His offer of gifts to the ambassadors was thus a normal part of the diplomatic etiquette of the Macedonian court, and Demosthenes' interpretation of his traditional generosity is unwarranted.

But the custom of giving gifts to ambassadors was viewed with deep suspicion by the Greeks who lived in the poleis of central and southern Greece. The Athenians regarded the custom with such distrust that they made it illegal for an ambassador to receive gifts. In their eyes such gifts were dangerous because they created a personal bond between the foreign king and the ambassador, a bond that might prevent the ambassador from fulfilling his duty to the city to which he owed his complete loyalty. Thus when Demosthenes refused the gift proffered by Philip, he was acting quite correctly by Athenian standards. But his suggestion to spend the money on the Athenian prisoners was unlikely to have been aimed at foiling Philip's plot because that plot was a figment of a prosecutor's overzealous imagination. Demosthenes' suggestion is better interpreted as a tactful attempt to decline Philip's hospitality without causing offense. If the ambassadors were to refuse the gift outright, they would have insulted Philip; if they had accepted it, they might have faced prosecution on their return to Athens. As a way out of this dilemma, Demosthenes proposed that Philip use the gift to free the Athenian prisoners. This avoided the appearance both of ingratitude and of venality. When prosecuting Aeschines three years later, however, Demosthenes tried to exploit the incident to arouse the suspicions of the members of the court, who, as good Athenian citizens, found the custom contrary to their notion of proper diplomatic conduct.[17]

Either on the same day or shortly after Philip offered his gift, the Athenian ambassadors delivered their speeches to the king. Demosthenes gives no account of these speeches, but Aeschines devotes a considerable section of his speech of 343 to them. Aeschines first recounts the speeches Demosthenes gave and describes how his opponent listed in tedious and sycophantic detail all the kindnesses he had shown the Macedonian ambassadors during their stay in Athens. Aeschines then passes on to a summary of his own speech. He provides no witnesses to corroborate his account, and his failure to do so is surprising when we consider that he had his colleagues testify about all the events on the First Embassy and about the private conference they held before meeting with Philip on the Second Embassy. Nonetheless, Aeschines' account of his own speech to Philip is consistent with what he declared at the private conference he would say in his speech to Philip, and his description of that meeting is supported by his colleagues' testimony. On the other hand, his description of Demosthenes' speech to the king deserves a measure of skepticism. The caricature of his enemy is clearly the product of malice, an attempt on Aeschines' part to portray Demosthenes as a hypocrite who once flattered Philip as fervently as he later denounced him.[18]

By his own account, Aeschines praised Philip's aims as righteous and just. He qualified his endorsement only by insisting that when the Amphictyons met at Delphi, they should punish just those who were guilty and not the communities from which they came. There was good precedent for Aeschines' approach. The Greeks had made a similar proposal to the Thebans in 479. Despite Theban collaboration with the Persians, the Greeks promised to lift their siege of the city and not to harm its citizens if the leaders of the pro-Persian faction were surrendered to them. Once the Thebans agreed to this solution and handed over the designated leaders, they were spared any further punishment. On the surface Aeschines' proposal seemed just and humane, but the motive behind it was far from idealistic. In another passage from his speech of 343, Aeschines discloses his opinion that Phalaecus and his associates were the only ones guilty of sacrilege. It is no coincidence that this was also the view of the pro-Athenian generals in Phocis, who had previously tried to fasten all the blame for the theft of the sacred funds on one of Phalaecus' companions. Despite the humane appearance of his proposal, Aeschines was in reality asking Philip to carry out a purge of the anti-Athenian elements in Phocis. Aeschines may have been sincerely interested in saving the rest of the Phocians from destruction. But the solution he proposed to achieve that end was also a means of pursuing a vendetta against the man who aided the enemies of Athens in Euboea and had rebuffed the Athenian attempt to assist Phocis by occupying Thermopylai.[19]

With regard to Thebes, Aeschines advocated a harsher policy. He pointed out to Philip how the Thebans had violated the oaths they had sworn to the Amphictyony by destroying several cities in Boeotia. Thebes should be part of Boeotia, not Boeotia subject to Thebes. In conclusion, Aeschines warned Philip that any favors granted to the Thebans would gain the king no gratitude.[20]

Neither Aeschines nor Demosthenes tells us how Philip responded to the speeches of the Athenian ambassadors. All we know is that Philip later gave the ambassadors a letter to be read to the Assembly. According to Demosthenes, who had the letter read out and discussed its contents at Aeschines' trial in 343, the letter contained no mention of Thebes and no promise to liberate Boeotia. Not even Aeschines claims Philip made any specific promise to liberate Boeotia. Aeschines does say that Philip's companions avowed that Philip would rebuild the walls of the Boeotian cities, but provides no evidence for his statement. Even if the statement were true, the rumors circulated by these companions cannot be taken as sure proof of Philip's intentions. It is impossible to determine whether the companions were privy to Philip's actual plans or just hazarding a guess about his intentions. Or they may have been trying to impress Aeschines by boasting about their free access to the king and invented this bit of "insider" information to make the gullible Athenians think they were on closer terms with Philip than they actually were. In short, there is no reason to believe that Philip endorsed Aeschines' proposals for Phocis and Thebes.[21]

In fact, Philip had good reasons for rejecting Aeschines' advice. It was certainly not in Philip's interests to liberate the cities of Boeotia at that time. He had no need to weaken Thebes in 346; ten years of war had already seen to that. Thebes was simply not a threat to Philip. Far otherwise; the Thebans were dependent on Philip and in no position to stand in his way. They had received a contingent of Macedo-

nian troops in 347 and needed his help to end the sacred war and to regain the
Boeotian cities lost to Phocis. The Thebans had nothing to gain from challenging
Philip, had gained from cooperating in the past, and stood to gain even more if Philip
marched against the Phocians. The Thebans had no reason to defy Philip, and Philip
had no reason to regard them as enemies. On the other hand, the liberation of the
Boeotian cities would have brought few benefits and created many problems for
Philip. To begin with, it would have cost him the friendship of Thebes, which it was
not in his interests to forfeit. Second, it would have forced him to act as the guarantor
of Boeotian freedom. If the cities in Boeotia were to be liberated, they would have to
be protected against Thebes, and that was a commitment Philip cannot have been
eager to make. He had seen how the Thebans were obligated to defend the freedom
of the Messenians and others in the Peloponnese repeatedly between 368 and 362.
These campaigns were a serious drain on Theban resources and prevented her
leaders from pursuing initiatives in other regions. The balance of power in central
Greece had worked to Philip's advantage from 356 to 346. It had kept Phocis,
Thebes, and Athens locked in conflict and had given Philip carte blanche to subdue
much of northern Greece. The liberation of Boeotia would have disturbed this
balance of power by weakening Thebes and putting Athens in a stronger position.

Despite these obvious drawbacks for Philip, some scholars have claimed that
Philip planned to turn against the Thebans after gaining control of Thermopylai,
provided the Athenians attacked them from the rear. But if that was Philip's plan,
Philip should have asked the Athenian ambassadors to send an army into Boeotia.
None of our sources, however, indicates that he made such a request, nor does our
evidence record any attempt by Aeschines and Philocrates to convince the Assembly
to send troops against the Thebans. In the next month, at a meeting of the Assembly
on Skirophorion 16, Philocrates passed a measure calling for the dispatch of Athenian troops in the event that some power tried to prevent the Amphictyons from
meeting in Delphi. But this measure was unambiguously directed at the Phocians,
who held the temple at the time and were reluctant to surrender it to the Amphictyons. The measure could not have been aimed at the Thebans, who were in no
position to prevent anyone from entering Delphi.[22]

What Philip's actual plans were remains unknown to us in the absence of any
trustworthy evidence. All we can do is to examine what he said and did. It appears
that Philip assured the Thessalians he would restore them to their position of honor
on the Amphictyonic Council. That assurance, however, did not stop him from
telling the Phocians he was their friend and ally. To the Athenian ambassadors he
gave a letter and a pledge to allow their prisoners to return home in time for the
Panathenaia. Aeschines hoped that Philip would adopt his proposal to liberate the
cities of Boeotia, and Philip's promise in his letter to do anything for Athens as long
as it was consistent with his honor and reputation must have encouraged him to think
Philip would follow his advice. Yet it is equally clear that Philip made no specific
promises at the time. While Philip may have given Aeschines the impression he
would heed his advice, he was too shrewd to bind himself to anything definite.
Indeed, Philip may not have had any plans at all. He was in no hurry to reach a
solution to the conflict and certainly not eager to resort to arms unless he had to.[23]

Once the conference between Philip and the Athenian ambassadors was over,

Philip swore the oaths for the Peace of Philocrates. In the next few days Philip gathered his army and marched south into Thessaly. There the Athenian ambassadors received the oaths from Philip's Thessalian allies in a hostelry near the temple of the Dioscuri in Pherai. This business concluded, Philip asked the Athenian ambassadors to help him resolve a dispute between Pherai and Halus. Our sources reveal nothing about the nature of the dispute nor the form of settlement. Demosthenes later painted a heart-rending picture of the sufferings the settlement inflicted on the people of Halus, but his account lacks supporting evidence and should not be taken seriously.[24]

The Athenian ambassadors probably parted company with Philip at Pherai and then crossed to Oreos on Euboea. They took with them the letter Philip had given to be read out to the Assembly. The letter contained his promise to do anything for the Athenian people that did not damage his honor and reputation and a statement about the Athenian prisoners. He assured the Assembly he never intended to demand payment of ransom and pledged their swift return. Of course, he did not mention the money he had already received for the release of several prisoners. That would have diminished the intended effect of his magnanimous gesture.[25]

After the Athenian ambassadors left for Oreos, Philip collected troops from his Thessalian allies and continued his march toward Thermopylai. By the time the Athenian ambassadors reached Athens, the Macedonian army was drawing near to Phalaecus and his troops, who had taken up a position at Nikaia.[26]

The Meeting of the Council after the Return of the Second Embassy and the Meeting of the Assembly on Skirophorion 16

Aeschines returned to Athens with the Second Embassy in early Skirophorion with hopes that Philip would fashion a settlement to the sacred war that favored Athens. He had received no specific promise, yet had made his case forcefully in Pella, and Philip's letter, though vague, appeared to encourage optimism. In his speech of 343, however, Demosthenes drew a very different picture of Aeschines' aims at the time. According to Demosthenes, Aeschines came back from Macedon with treason in his heart. Aeschines deceived the Assembly about the king's intentions and lulled them into a false sense of assurance, which Philip exploited to crush the Phocians. Aeschines was thus a willing accomplice in the destruction of Phocis, an instrument of Philip's ambition, and a traitor to the city. The ever vigilant Demosthenes boasts that he denounced the nefarious scheme of Aeschines and Philocrates before the Council, but to no avail. In the Assembly he was shouted down by these two scoundrels, and his warnings shunned. The charges are serious and form the centerpiece of the accusations Demosthenes brought against Aeschines in 343. Demosthenes builds his case with consummate oratorical skill and supports it with some evidence. But rhetoric is not proof.

Demosthenes' charges require close investigation. Demosthenes begins by describing the meeting of the Council at which the Second Embassy reported after its return to Athens. The Council was packed with spectators. Before this multitude

Demosthenes arose and denounced the other ambassadors, demonstrating how their negotiations with Philip had reduced the city to a deplorable state. He exhorted the Council not to abandon Phocis and Thermopylai. The Council, now alerted to the danger by Demosthenes, drew up a *probouleuma* containing all his proposals. But the Assembly never heard the *probouleuma* at its meeting on Skirophorion 16 for Aeschines and Philocrates made sure it was never read out.[27]

Demosthenes cites no evidence for his sensational account of his report to the Council until after finishing his account of the subsequent meeting of the Assembly. Only at this point does he have the clerk read out the *probouleuma* of the Council. For good measure he throws in the testimony of the man who drew up the motion. What the *probouleuma* actually stated is something of a mystery. Demosthenes quotes no phrases from it nor paraphrases its contents, only drawing attention to what was missing from it, namely, the customary vote of thanks and invitation to dine in the *prytaneion,* honors, which he claims, had hitherto never been denied to any ambassador. He then challenges Aeschines to produce a decree of the Council praising the Second Embassy and offers to yield up part of his time if the defendant can find such a decree.[28]

The *probouleuma* is the sole evidence Demosthenes submits to support his charge that he denounced the other ambassadors to the Council. He provides no evidence at all to show that the Council endorsed his proposal not to abandon Phocis and Thermopylai. In the absence of any confirming evidence, we are entitled to doubt his claim to have persuaded the Council to pass such a measure. In fact, it is hard to believe he could have made this proposal at the time. True, the Athenians had been able to land a force at Thermopylai after the defeat of the Phocians at Crocus Field and prevented the victorious Philip from seizing the pass in 352, an argument that serves as a constant refrain in Demosthenes' speech of 343. But the situation in 346 was radically different, and we should not be seduced by a specious analogy. Phalaecus had cut Phocian ties with Athens in 346, and there was no large Athenian force in the immediate vicinity. Besides, there is no hint that the Phocians had requested Athenian help in Skirophorion or were willing to accept it. There was simply no question of the Athenians going to the defence of Phocis at the time. Even if they had wanted to, it would have taken far too long to mount an expedition large enough to make a difference. Finally, it is necessary to recall that during the Second Embassy Aeschines and Demosthenes had differed only about policy toward Thebes, not about Phocis, whose fate the Athenians were powerless to influence since Phalaecus' rejection of their assistance several months earlier. Demosthenes' claim that he persuaded the Council to pass a motion about Phocis is not only unsubstantiated, but also implausible.[29]

Did Demosthenes really denounce the other ambassadors at this meeting of the Council? The only evidence Demosthenes brings forward is the *probouleuma* that the Council passed on that day. Demosthenes says the *probouleuma* granted no honors for the ambassadors and interprets this omission as a condemnation of their actions. Is his interpretation justified? Even if one accepts his interpretation of the *probouleuma,* one would also have to admit that the absence of honors was a condemnation of all the members of the embassy, Demosthenes included, for he did not receive honors either.[30]

There is a more plausible explanation for the Council's failure to vote honors for the Second Embassy. In point of fact, it was technically illegal for the Council to award honors to a magistrate for his service during a term of office before he laid down that office and submitted his accounts to the *logistai*. Nonetheless, it was possible for the Council or Assembly to vote that honors be awarded to a magistrate as long as a clause was added to the effect that the honors would not be conferred until after the candidate passed his *euthynai*, or audit, of his activities. This is apparently what happened in the case of the First Embassy. When the ambassadors returned in late Anthesterion and reported to the Council, Demosthenes passed a vote of honors for the embassy, honors which were presumably not awarded until after they had passed their *euthynai*.

But why did these same men not receive a vote of honors from the Council after their return from the Second Embassy? The answer to this question is to be found in the changed circumstances of Skirophorion. When the ambassadors reported to the Council in Elaphebolion, there was no disagreement among them about the negotiations with Philip. Even the querulous Demosthenes had nothing but praise for his colleagues. The Council, seeing harmony and goodwill reigning among the ambassadors, was confident that all the ambassadors would pass their *euthynai* and decided to go ahead and pass a vote of honors subject, of course, to the standard proviso. The situation in Skirophorion was different. During the Second Embassy Aeschines and Demosthenes had quarreled bitterly about what to say to Philip. Their disagreement must have been obvious to the Council when the ambassadors made their report. Demosthenes may indeed have attacked Aeschines and the others just as he claims to have.

The Council, knowing that Demosthenes did not approve of Aeschines' conduct, must have felt less than certain that no trouble would arise during the *euthynai* for these ambassadors. Instead of passing a provisional vote of honors at this time, the Council understandably decided to play it safe and wait until after all the ambassadors had passed their *euthynai*. If they did, the Council could always confer honors later. The Council neither endorsed nor rejected Demosthenes' charges; it merely suspended judgment for the time being. Although Demosthenes soon afterward laid an accusation against Aeschines at his *euthynai*, he did not bring the suit to court until 343. Thus, at the time of Aeschines' trial, the Council, if it had not completely forgotten about the matter, was still waiting to see if Aeschines would pass his *euthynai*. So by the time of the trial the embassy had still not received a vote of praise from the Council. We can now understand Demosthenes' confidence in challenging Aeschines to produce a decree of praise. Yet while he was no doubt correct that such a decree did not exist, Demosthenes' interpretation of the Council's failure to vote honors at this stage ought to be rejected. The Council refrained from voting honors out of prudence, not as a condemnation of the ambassadors' conduct.[31]

Skepticism about Demosthenes' account should not end here. Questionable too is his allegation that the *probouleuma* passed by the Council was not read out in the Assembly on Skirophorion 16 because of chicanery on the part of Aeschines and Philocrates. Demosthenes says that never before had a *probouleuma* of the Council not been read out in the Assembly, and this should incline us to suspect that it never happened on Skirophorion 16 either. Certainly Demosthenes brings forward no evidence to support this incredible charge when he could have done so. It is far more likely that the *probouleuma* passed by the Council was noncommittal, calling for an open discussion of the points raised by the ambassadors' reports without endorsing the position of either Aeschines or Demosthenes.[32]

Following the meeting of the Council, the Assembly met on Skirophorion 16 to hear and discuss the reports of the ambassadors. At this crucial meeting in 343, Demosthenes claimed that Aeschines deceived the Athenian people by assuring them that Philip was about to save the Phocians and liberate the cities of Boeotia. Despite its importance to the prosecution's case, Aeschines has relatively little to say about the meeting, and neither man provides much evidence. As a result, we must scrutinize Demosthenes' account very closely and pay careful attention to his summary of the main points in Aeschines' speech.

To begin with, Demosthenes charges that Aeschines did not report about the negotiations with Philip, as he was supposed to. Aeschines instead boasted that he had persuaded Philip to follow a policy that suited Athenian interests in regard to the Amphictyony and other issues. Next he launched into a tirade against the Thebans, going over the main points he had made in his speech to Philip. Thanks to his efforts, the Athenians would soon hear that Thebes was under siege and cut off from the rest of Boeotia, that Plataia and Thespiai had been rebuilt, and that the money stolen from Apollo had been recovered, not from the Phocians, but from the Thebans, who were the real culprits. Aeschines then reported the remarks of a Euboean, who said he had heard Philip had agreed to hand over Euboea in return for Amphipolis. To round out this list of benefits, Aeschines alluded to the restoration of Oropos.[33]

There is much in Demosthenes' account that is similar to the information found in Aeschines. Demosthenes says that Aeschines repeated the main points of his anti-Theban speech to Philip; Aeschines admits to having delivered such a speech and to having informed the Assembly that he had urged Philip to liberate the Boeotian cities. What Aeschines does not say, but Demosthenes lays great emphasis on, is that Aeschines believed he had convinced Philip to follow his advice. There is good reason to believe Demosthenes here since his charge is supported by other evidence, namely, a remark Demosthenes himself makes in his speech *On the Peace,* which was delivered in the summer of 346, not long after the meeting of the Assembly on Skirophorion 16. In this speech Demosthenes says that certain men (presumably Aeschines is being alluded to) assured the Athenians that Philip would rebuild Thespiai and Plataia, save the Phocians, divide Thebes into villages, and return Euboea to Athens. Yet nowhere in this speech does Demosthenes say that Aeschines or anyone else reported that Philip had actually promised to perform these actions. Aeschines appears to have thought Philip would follow his advice despite the absence of any explicit commitment. Even after Philip failed to act as Aeschines predicted, Aeschines tried to explain it away by claiming that despite his intention to liberate the Boeotian cities, Philip was prevented from achieving his goal by the joint opposition of the Thebans and the Thessalians. Aeschines was not deceived by Philip, for Philip never made any concrete promises. Nor did Aeschines deceive the Assembly, for he only reported what he had said to Philip and what he actually believed would happen.[34]

Next there are Aeschines' statements about Euboea. Demosthenes never says that his opponent reported to the Assembly that Philip had promised to hand over Euboea to the Athenians in return for their renunciation of claims to Amphipolis. All Demosthenes states is that Aeschines reported a rumor he had heard from a Euboean about such an exchange. There were obviously many rumors flying about Pella when the Greek embassies met Philip, and this piece of gossip was certainly among the wilder ones. Euboea could have been considered to be in Philip's sphere of influence in 346, but it was not one of his possessions to trade. Philip simply did not have the power to ''hand over'' Euboea to the Athenians. Aeschines himself recounts that he repeated to the Assembly the worried remarks of Cleochares of Chalcis, who, as a citizen of one of the smaller cities, expressed his fears about the secret plans being made by the major powers of Greece.

The two versions of the story are not incompatible. Cleochares could well have heard a rumor in Pella that Philip intended to swap Euboea for Amphipolis with the Athenians. Despite the inherent implausibility of the rumor, Cleochares did have some grounds for concern; had not the Athenians years before proposed to Philip that they hand over Pydna in exchange for Amphipolis? And had not Philip made a gift of Potidaia to the Olynthians? After hearing this rumor, Cleochares might well have expressed his justifiable anxiety about the clandestine negotiations of the larger powers, either to Aeschines or to someone else, who then related it to Aeschines. If this explanation is true, it would provide additional support for the view that Aeschines' statements in the Assembly on Skirophorion 16 about Philip's plans were based on little more than his own hopes, nourished in part by rumors such as this one. What Aeschines told the Assembly was irresponsible to the extent that he was basing his prediction about Philip's actions on little more than rumors, but it was not dishonest for he never claimed to have received from Philip assurances that Philip had not given.[35]

As for Demosthenes' actions in the Assembly on that day, we have little to go on. Aeschines alleges Demosthenes voiced approval for his actions during the Second Embassy and even proposed honors for the ambassadors, but provides no evidence to prove his statement. His failure to cite evidence is all the more striking when we recall that he had the clerk of the court read out the decree of praise proposed by Demosthenes for the First Embassy. One thing is certain: Aeschines and Demosthenes were clearly at odds by this point. They had quarreled in Pella and probably revealed their differences to the Council after their return to Athens. And shortly after this meeting of the Assembly, Demosthenes laid a charge against Aeschines before the *euthynoi*, the magistrates who received accusations arising from a magistrate's *euthynai*. From what we know of their relationship both before and after Skirophorion 16, it is highly improbable that they were on good terms that day.

What Demosthenes really said at the meeting is another question. By his own account, Demosthenes says he told the Assembly he did not believe Philip would act as Aeschines predicted, but was prevented from speaking and delivering his report to the Assembly by Aeschines and Philocrates, who made fun of him and got the Assembly so convulsed in laughter that it refused to listen to him any longer. How much of this is reliable is hard to tell. Yet Demosthenes' opposition to Aeschines and Philocrates at this meeting should not be questioned. The best evidence for his actions on Skirophorion is again his speech *On the Peace* delivered shortly afterward. There Demosthenes says he expressed strong reservations about his opponents' view of Philip's intentions. What is striking is that he does not accuse Aeschines and Philocrates of treason, only of being naive and misguided.[36]

After the reports of the ambassadors and the ensuing debate, Philocrates proposed a motion, which the Assembly passed. Demosthenes blames this decree for the destruction of the Phocians, but a study of its provisions casts doubt on his charge. One part of the decree extended the alliance between Philip and the Athenians to the descendants of Philip. Another dealt with the Phocians. The decree merely demanded that the Phocians surrender control of the temple at Delphi to the Amphictyons. This was hardly equivalent to an unconditional surrender, nor were the Phocians compelled to yield any territory. They were not even told to withdraw from the cities they held in Boeotia. If anything, the decree of Philocrates was mild and restricted in its demands. It left the Phocians in command of their army, all their territory, and the land they had conquered in Boeotia. The decree in no way amounted to an abandonment of the Phocians. It was the Phocians who had abandoned the Athenians several months before. Demosthenes thus completely misrepresents the effect of this decree, and his interpretation of its consequences should not be accepted.[37]

The decree of Philocrates is better understood in the light of the solution Aeschines proposed to Philip for ending the sacred war. Aeschines had admitted Philip's goal of ending the war was just. To end the war all that was necessary was for the Phocians to return the temple at Delphi to the control of the Amphictyons. The seizure of the temple had been the *causa belli;* the return of the temple had to be the first step in any solution to the conflict. Aeschines also realized that to satisfy the Thebans' and Thessalians' thirst for vengeance, some punishment had to be inflicted upon the Phocians. As we saw above, Aeschines' proposal was to punish only those who were responsible for the theft of the temple treasures, that is, Phalaecus and his associates. Aeschines must have reported his proposal to the Assembly and have assured the Athenians that this was the way Philip intended to save the Phocians. If the Phocians consented to surrender Delphi to the Amphictyons, he told them, the rest of the nation would go unharmed. Confident that this was Philip's intention, the Assembly urged the Phocians to surrender the temple to the Amphictyons. Knowing that Phalaecus might not go along with this plan willingly, the Assembly backed up its demand with the threat of force. Philocrates' decree was thus directed more against Phalaecus than against the Phocians.

Before the meeting of the Assembly adjourned, most of those who had served on the First Embassy, including Aeschines and Dercylus, were reelected to serve on another embassy to Philip. Obviously pleased with the results of their diplomacy so far, the Assembly asked the ambassadors to continue their good work. Demosthenes, however, would not be a member of this embassy. No longer in agreement with his colleagues, he chose to resign from the embassy and dissociate himself from any future negotiations with Philip.[38]

The Surrender of Phocis

As the Third Embassy made ready to bring Philip news of the Assembly's decision, Phalaecus was finding his own position more and more isolated. Philip had marched his Macedonian troops and Thessalian allies to the pass at Thermopylai. To the east, the Thebans were preparing to invade Phocis once Philip attacked. And now the Athenians had declared they too would march against Phocis if the temple at Delphi were not handed over to the Amphictyons. Philip's diplomacy had worked wonders. His promise to end the sacred war had enabled him to maintain the loyalty of the Thessalians. The Thebans had enjoyed his support in the past and were now counting on his aid to regain the Boeotian cities they had lost to Phocis. The Athenians were also hoping for benefits from the king. Aeschines and Philocrates had led them to believe Philip would have Phalaecus prosecuted, protect the Phocians from a harsh punishment, and break the Theban hold on Boeotia. Having isolated Phalaecus by winning over all the major powers in the region, Philip was in a strong position and could afford to bide his time. The next move was up to Phalaecus.

While Aeschines was optimistic, Demosthenes' suspicions had increased. He had strong doubts about Philip's promises and was skeptical of Aeschines' motives. After his defeat in the Assembly, he decided to take his battle into court. Since he had finished his duties as ambassador after making his report to the Assembly, Aeschines now had to submit a statement of his accounts to the *logistai*. Even though the ambassadors had received no money from the public aside from traveling expenses, they still had to submit an account of their finances as part of normal procedure. After the *logistai* examined and approved these accounts, anyone who wished could bring a charge against the ambassadors before the *euthynoi*. It was during this part of the *euthynai* procedure that Demosthenes planned to initiate his prosecution of Aeschines.[39]

Aeschines must have known about Demosthenes' intention to accuse him before the *euthynoi* and did his best to thwart him. When Demosthenes appeared before the *logistai* to give his accounts, Aeschines came forward with a large crowd of witnesses and tried to prevent the board from summoning his opponent. Aeschines argued that the *logistai* could not summon Demosthenes since he had already passed his audit sometime before. Presumably Aeschines was referring to the fact that Demosthenes had passed his audit for the First Embassy in Elaphebolion or Munichion. Aeschines' motive behind this maneuver is transparent: he wanted to provide himself with an excuse for refusing to submit his own accounts to the *logistai* since after he did so, Demosthenes would lay his charge against him before the *euthynoi*. Demosthenes is our only source for this curious incident, but his story ought to be trustworthy since it is supported by the testimony of several witnesses. The argument Aeschines presented was patently specious. If an ambassador had passed his audit for one embassy, that did not exempt him from having to sumbit his accounts for a subsequent embassy. The *logistai* wcrc not taken in by Aeschines' sophistry for soon afterward Demosthenes was able to charge him with treason before the *euthynoi*.[40]

Demosthenes was not the only one to accuse Aeschines. A man named Timarchus also came forward to lodge a formal charge. We do not know whether Timarchus was acting in concert with Demosthenes or had taken this step on his own initiative. Timarchus is not known to have had any previous connection with Demosthenes, and their brief association may have begun at this point. Timarchus and Demosthenes were both members of the Council in 347/46, but there is no trace of cooperation between them while serving in that body. The only thing known about Timarchus' activity in the Council that year is that he authored a proposal making it a capital offense to transport weapons or ship's tackle to Philip. Timarchus had several prominent friends, the most influential of which was Hegesander, the brother of Hegesippus, who convinced the Athenians to take the side of Phocis at the beginning of the sacred war. Given his past hostility to Philip and his association with the pro-Phocian politician Hegesippus, Timarchus had a strong motive for prosecuting Aeschines, who was singing Philip's praises and encouraging the Athenians to march against Phocis if they refused to surrender the temple at Delphi. However brief their association may have been, Timarchus might have been the one who brought Demosthenes into contact with Hegesippus with whom he had had no previous connection. Hegesippus became a valuable ally of Demosthenes in the years ahead, accompanying him on his mission to the Peloponnese in 344/43 and joining him in opposition to Philip's proposals for the revision of the Peace of Philocrates in the next year.[41]

About this time Aeschines became ill. He sent his brother to the Council to say he was unable to join the Third Embassy for the moment. Aeschines' doctor went along with his brother to support his statement. Demosthenes alleges Aeschines was feigning illness so he could stay behind and keep an eye on him. According to Demosthenes, Aeschines was afraid that in his absence his opponent would pass a decree in favor of the Phocians that might have saved them. Even a small display of support would have foiled Philip's plan. Demosthenes' charge that Aeschines was shamming sickness is probably false, and his claim that the Athenians could have prevented the defeat of the Phocians is implausible. The Phocians were surrounded on all sides by states that were hostile to Athens and friendly to Philip. The Athenians had been able to stem the rout of the Phocian army six years before because their fleet was off the coast of Thermopylai. In 346, however, they could not have sent an army to join Phalaecus by land, and it would have taken too long before they could have mobilized the fleet with transports and sailed to the pass.

Yet even if Phalaecus had requested Athenian aid in Skirophorion 346 (there is no indication that he did), Athenians would not necessarily have been willing to entrust their forces to a leader who had been so unreliable in the past. Demosthenes gives the impression that the Athenians turned against the Phocians only because Philip and Aeschines had tricked them. He neglects to mention that Phalaecus had given them ample cause for distrust. Demosthenes' motive for inventing this tale about Aeschines' anxiety about his intentions and feigned illness should be obvious: he wanted the court to believe that the Phocians could have been saved by Athenian action in 346 and that Aeschines blocked his efforts to rescue them. In 343 his story may have fooled some members of the court, but in 346 both Aeschines and Demosthenes must have known that the Athenians were powerless to alter the outcome of events in Phocis. That was now to a large extent, but not completely, in Philip's hands.[42]

Before the Third Embassy set out without Aeschines around Skirophorion 21, the word of the Assembly's decision on Skirophorion 16 had already reached Phalaecus. In Demosthenes' opinion, this news deprived the Phocians of their last hope for Athenian support and forced them to capitulate to Philip. This misrepresents the strategic situation at the time. As we have seen, Athens could do nothing to prevent the defeat of Phocis, and Phalaecus was already isolated before he received this news. With the Macedonian and Thessalian armies in front of him and the Thebans ready to march from the east, Phalaecus had a considerable incentive to begin negotiations with Philip. Nor should we believe that Phalaecus began to negotiate at this juncture because the Athenians had failed to march out to attack the Thebans as part of a master plan worked out by Philip, who would then invade Boeotia with the Phocians joining in. There is no evidence that Philip ever formulated such a plan, and it made no sense for Philip to invade Boeotia. And if Philip were really set on the destruction of the Theban army in 346, it is hard to understand how the refusal of the Athenians to play along would have made any difference. He could still have appealed to Phalaecus to join him in a campaign against Thebes, and Phalaecus, if presented with such an invitation, would have eagerly accepted. With the Phocian army added to his own, Philip would have found the Thebans no match. If Philip did ever have such a plan, the main obstacle to it would not have been the Athenians but the Thessalians, who were implacably set on punishing Phocis.[43]

Why then did Phalaecus start negotiations with Philip? All the Athenians wanted was for the Phocians to surrender the temple at Delphi. What risk was there in this for Phalaecus? Here it is important to recall the proposal Aeschines made to Philip at Pella to spare the people of Phocis and to punish only the guilty, by whom he meant Phalaecus and his associates. Aeschines probably reported this to the Assembly, and word of the proposal must have reached Phalaecus. Phalaecus naturally did not wish to be sacrificed on the altar of a general settlement in central Greece so he offered to bargain with Philip. A deal was quickly struck: Philip agreed to allow Phalaecus and his troops safe passage out of Phocis. The deal contained several attractive features for Philip. He now gained control of Thermopylai, which sealed off access to Thessaly and Macedon from central Greece. He obtained the surrender of Phocis and won credit for ending the sacred war without fighting a pitched battle. And he furthered his reputation as the champion of the god at Delphi by returning his temple to the Amphictyons. It apparently did not matter to Philip that Phalaecus and his mercenaries, who were thought to have profited the most from plundering the temple, were allowed to escape unpunished. This was certainly not the solution that Aeschines had envisaged and had led the Athenian people to expect. And it may not have been the solution that Philip himself had anticipated. But the settlement suited Philip, and that was all that counted for the moment.[44]

Dercylus and the rest of the Third Embassy were in Chalcis on Skirophorion 24 when they heard the news of the settlement between Philip and Phalaecus. Stripped of troops by the departure of Phalaecus and his mercenaries, the Phocians had no choice but to surrender. The news of these events threw the ambassadors into confusion. Instead of continuing on their journey to Philip, they turned around and headed back to Athens to announce the surrender of Phocis and to receive new instructions. They arrived home on Skirophorion 27 and reported these unexpected developments to a shocked Assembly meeting in the Piraeus. The Athenians had been led to believe Philip would end the sacred war by punishing only Phalaecus while leaving the rest of Phocis unharmed. Now they heard that Phalaecus had been allowed to depart with his mercenaries, leaving Phocis at the mercy of Philip and his allies. What was worse was that Philip was in control of Thermopylai. Only the territory of their Theban enemies lay between the Macedonian army and the border of Attica. Philip had failed to act as they had been led to expect; what would he do next? One man, Callisthenes, decided that the Athenians could take no chances. He passed a decree ordering that all women and children be brought from the countryside and placed behind the walls of the city, that the fortresses be made ready to resist an invasion, and that the Piraeus be secured. Despite these emergency measures, the Assembly nevertheless ordered the Third Embassy to proceed to Delphi. Although the Phocians had surrendered, the Amphictyons had not yet decided on their punishment. There was still a possibility that a harsh sentence might be avoided. Aeschines had by this time recovered from his bout of illness and joined the rest of the ambassadors on their journey to Delphi.[45]

Sometime after the meeting on Skirophorion 16, two letters came to Athens from Philip. Demosthenes had these letters read out at the trial of Aeschines in 343. He does not quote from them, but says they contained a request for troops and arrived in Athens after Skirophorion 16. Nothing in his description of these letters suggests that Philip was asking the Athenians to march north into Boeotia and attack Thebes from the rear. Aeschines also referred to Philip's request, which he places in roughly the same period. His references to these letters show that Philip wanted the Athenians to send troops to Phocis, not against Thebes. Aeschines furthermore states that Demosthenes and others warned that Philip would make hostages of these soldiers if they were sent. This warning would only have made sense if Philip was asking the Athenians to send troops to join him in Phocis. If they were requested to attack Thebes, Demosthenes could never have made this prediction about Philip's intentions.[46]

Why did Philip want these troops? We can rule out the explanation Demosthenes is alleged to have given in 346. If he had really believed this, he would have repeated it at Aeschines' trial in 343 and would have claimed credit for persuading the Athenians not to entrust their hoplites to the perfidious Philip. Instead, Demosthenes says that Aeschines and Philocrates should have urged the Athenians to march out and defend the Phocians. Aeschines' view of the situation at the time is similar. In his account, the Athenian refusal to send troops at this critical juncture was responsible for the ruin of Phocis. But Aeschines excuses Philip for their fate, blaming instead the Thessalians and the Thebans, who were united in their hatred for Phocis and forced Philip to accept the harsh sentence meted out by the Amphictyons. Aeschines faults Demosthenes for opposing the dispatch of troops to the Phocians and causing their misfortune. Each orator attributes a different motive to Philip for the request, but neither presents any evidence beyond the letters. Of course, the only person who could have explained to the court what Philip's motives were was the king himself, and neither orator could have summoned him to testify.[47]

The only context for Philip's request is the period before his arrangement with Phalaecus. After Phalaecus and his troops departed and the Phocians were forced to capitulate, Philip was in complete control of Thermopylai and Delphi and no longer in need of Athenian troops. Before this, Philip obviously wanted Athenian help to strengthen his hand against Phalaecus in the hope that an overwhelming show of force would encourage him to surrender or the Phocians to overthrow him. The Athenians would not have been able to march through Boeotia to help Phalaecus, but the Thebans might have permitted them to cross their territory to aid Philip against Phalaecus. The Assembly had in fact voted on Skirophorion 16 to send troops if the Phocians refused to surrender the temple at Delphi, and the Third Embassy was carrying this message to Philip when they heard at Chalcis the news of the Phocian surrender. Aeschines' claim that the Athenian failure to send troops caused the destruction of the Phocians misrepresents the situation in the early summer of 346. The Athenians had promised to send troops, and they would certainly have done so if Phalaecus had remained intransigent. When Phalaecus saw the handwriting on the wall and came to an agreement with Philip, Athenian troops were no longer necessary.

Nor did this alleged failure to send troops have an effect on the fate of the Phocians after their surrender. What left Phocis vulnerable to the wrath of the Thebans and Thessalians was the departure of Phalaecus' troops. Phalaecus' exit also deprived Philip of a scapegoat on whom he could have directed all the anger of the vindictive Amphictyons. Both Aeschines and Demosthenes exaggerate the role of Athenian actions in the events of 346. The absence of Athenian troops did not bring about the fall of Phocis, and their presence would not have saved that much lamented state. Each politician naturally wanted to fix the blame for the tragedy on the other and accordingly declared that his opponent's influence on Athenian actions was the decisive factor in 346. Not only are the charges on both sides groundless; they are also misleading in a larger sense insofar as they create the false impression that Athenian actions were more important than they actually were. Like all politicians, both Aeschines and Demosthenes inflated the importance of their state's role on the stage of international events. In reality, Athens was only one player among many. The main part in the drama belonged to Philip, but even he did not have complete mastery over the plot.

After the surrender of the Phocians, Philip convened a meeting of the Amphictyons in the sanctuary of Apollo at Delphi. Aeschines and the rest of the Third Embassy attended the meeting and represented Athens. The situation had not turned out as Aeschines had hoped it would, and the Phocians were now at the mercy of their enemies, who held a majority of seats on the Amphictyonic Council. The Oetaeans were the most vengeful of all: they proposed that all the adult males of Phocis be thrown off a cliff. In spite of the failure of his plan to punish only Phalaecus, Aeschines did not give up. He did his best to convince the Amphictyons that the Oetaeans' proposal was too draconian and succeeded in persuading the Council to permit representatives from Phocis, who had not been admitted to the meeting, to speak in their own defense. With Aeschines' help, the Phocians were able to dissuade the Amphictyons from imposing the punishment urged by the Oetaeans. The punishment they received was still severe, but it was a distinct improvement over the one they barely escaped. The Amphictyons ordered the Phocians to surrender the three cities they held in Boeotia to the Thebans and to make a payment of sixty talents a year to the temple at Delphi until all the money Phalaecus and his predecessors had absconded with was repaid. The Amphictyons did not stop there. Their aim was not just to punish Phocis but to destroy it as a military power. They ordered the destruction of all the cities in Phocis. The Phocians were henceforth to live in villages of no more than fifty houses each and were not permitted to acquire horses or weapons. The Thebans and Thessalians had suffered from the Phocian invasions for over a decade. They intended to make sure Phocis would never be able to make war on them again.[48]

Demosthenes' opinion was that Philip had plotted the destruction of Phocis all along, but there are grounds for thinking that the harsh conditions imposed by the Amphictyons were not Philip's idea. Above all, it is necessary to recall that Philip did not yet have a seat on the Amphictyonic Council and that the Thebans and the Thessalians held the majority of votes. After ten years of fighting, they did not require Philip's urging to inflict a vindictive sentence. In fact, the evisceration of Phocis was not in Philip's interest. The balance of power in central Greece had been favorable to the Macedonians, allowing them a free hand in northern Greece. For that reason Philip showed no inclination prior to 346 to end the sacred war and disrupt this balance. But by 346 he found that he had to return Delphi to the Amphictyony for otherwise he would lose the confidence of the Thessalians. And to retain the friendship of the Thebans he had to help them recover the Boeotian cities lost to Phocis. With these goals accomplished, his position as the leading power in central Greece was secure.

The destruction of Phocis, however, upset the balance of power that favored Philip before 346. Without a strong Phocis to check them, the Thebans might, once they had recovered from the ravages of the sacred war, attempt to reassert their influence in central Greece and even to push northward into Thessaly as they had done twenty years before. Indeed, after Philip was defeated at Byzantium in 340 and led his troops against the Scyths, the Thebans took advantage of his absence to seize Nikaia. Second, without the threat of a strong Phocis to the south, the Thessalians would feel less dependent on Philip's protection against their inveterate enemy and be free to expand their power southward. This is not speculation: it is what actually happened in 339 when the Amphictyons declared war on the Locrians of Amphissa and elected the Thessalian Cottyphus to lead an army against them. The Thessalians, who held the largest block of votes on the Amphictyonic Council, were unquestionably behind the decision.

Far from stabilizing the situation in central Greece in a way friendly to Macedonian interests, the destruction of Phocis removed the barrier between Thebes and Thessaly and created a power vacuum in central Greece, which in turn led to the clash of these two powers and set off the crisis of 339. The resulting split in Philip's allies made it possible for Demosthenes to draw Thebes away from Philip in that year and to form a united front of Greeks against Macedon. Had Phocis not been shattered in 346, the Thebans might not have dared to seize Nikaia, and the Thessalians would have found their path to Amphissa blocked. In a sense, therefore, the settlement of 346 settled nothing; it only sowed the seeds for the next round of conflict. This crisis was to confront Philip with the greatest challenge he had faced since the early days of his reign. We do not know whether Philip understood then the implications of the settlement of 346. The surrender of the Phocians without a battle was certainly a welcome victory for Philip, and the gratitude he gained from the Thebans and the Thessalians cemented his position in central Greece. He also enhanced his reputation for piety by avenging the god of Delphi and punishing the impious Phocians. But it was not the complete triumph for Philip that Demosthenes says it was. Perhaps the greatest irony of 346 is that the person who may have benefited most from the punishment of the Phocians was not Philip, who celebrated a victory in Delphi that year, but Demosthenes, who decried the settlement. For the destruction of Phocis was the ultimate cause of the crisis of 339, which gave Demosthenes his opportunity to form the alliance with Thebes, the keystone of his league of Greek states against Macedon.[49]

After the meeting of the Amphictyony, Aeschines and the other members of the Third Embassy returned to Athens, where they reported the punishment imposed on the Phocians. The panic of Skirophorion 27 now gave way to anger. It was now evident that Philip was not about to attack Athens, as Demosthenes, Hegesippus, and Callisthenes had led the Assembly to fear. But the knowledge that they were out of danger was not cause for rejoicing. The harsh punishment inflicted by the Amphictyons outraged the Assembly, which had been led by Aeschines to expect something far less severe. As a result, the Athenians decided to protest the settlement by refusing to send a delegation to the Pythian games, which were that year celebrated under Philip's presidency. Indignation still ran high a little later when the Amphictyons sent ambassadors to Athens asking for approval of their decision to award to Philip the two seats on the Council formerly held by the Phocians. Many in the Assembly voiced their objections to the request, but cooler heads prevailed. Demosthenes criticizes Aeschines for being the only one to speak up in favor of the request, but his own speech *On the Peace* delivered on the same occasion reveals that Aeschines was not alone in giving this advice to the Assembly. Demosthenes, too, counseled the Assembly not to oppose the Council's decision. Refusal to condone the measure might afford the Amphictyons a pretext for declaring a sacred war on Athens. The Thebans and the Thessalians would never follow Philip against Athens simply to further Macedonian ambitions, Demosthenes argued, but furnished with a common cause to unite them, they might conceivably join forces and march on Attica. Demosthenes' fears were probably exaggerated. Philip had accomplished his goals and showed no intention of attacking Athens either in 346 or in the next several years. We do not know what arguments Aeschines used to dissuade the Assembly from rebuffing the Amphictyons, but he, too, must have realized that witholding their approval of Philip's honors would have been a futile gesture of protest that would have only set Athens against the rest of the Amphictyons and have played into Philip's hands.[50]

The Prosecution of Timarchus

His duties as ambassador finally completed, Aeschines still had one piece of unfinished business to attend to. He knew that Demosthenes and Timarchus were preparing to bring their case against him to court. Their strategy was obvious: they planned

to take advantage of the angry mood prevailing in Athens and to persuade the court
to vent its wrath on Aeschines, the man who had encouraged the Assembly to trust in
Philip's promises. Aeschines had to act quickly and strike a blow against one of his
accusers before they could attack him. Demosthenes, who was the younger of the
two prosecutors, would have appeared to be the more vulnerable target, but his
reputation so far was impeccable, and his ability as a speaker was formidable.
Aeschines chose instead to move against Timarchus, hoping that by convicting him
he could discourage Demosthenes from going through with his prosecution. Timarchus had been active in politics for several years, long enough to acquire an
unsavory reputation, which offered Aeschines a promising opportunity for an easy
victory in court. In addition to the usual suspicions of bribery and extortion that have
a way of dogging the reputations of many politicians, there were rumors circulating
that Timarchus had leased his favors to several lubricious customers. There appears
to have been nothing illegal about such transactions so long as the man who sold his
body did not address the Council or Assembly, hold public office, or bring a public
charge. The reasoning behind this prohibition appears to have been that the person
who was willing to sell himself for shameful acts could not be trusted to put the
public interest ahead of private gain. After all, if a man agreed to sell himself to
satisfy another's lust, might he not also sell himself to a foreign leader to satisfy his
ambition? The law also denied the privileges of public office to a man who squandered his patrimony, failed to perform military service, threw his shield away in
battle, or treated his parents dishonorably. The citizen who defied this prohibition
could be prosecuted under a procedure for the scrutiny of *rhetores*.[51]

Aeschines brought his case against Timarchus to court sometime in late 346,
before his enemies had a chance to proceed with their own case against him. As
Aeschines himself tells us, it was his first prosecution. In the beginning of his
speech, he turns his inexperience to good advantage, citing it as proof of his modest
way of life. After thus demonstrating that he is not a habitual prosecutor who brings
suits only to vex other law-abiding citizens, he asserts that Timarchus is an enemy
both to Athens and to himself. Aeschines could not deny his personal motive in
prosecuting Timarchus for a public offense, but by identifying his own interest with
that of Athens, he protects himself from the charge of prosecuting Timarchus solely
out of personal enmity. In our system of criminal justice, where a public prosecutor
brings the case, such statements are unnecessary. Since the public prosecutor is an
employee of the state, one assumes that he or she is acting in the interest of his or her
employer. In Classical Athens, however, a private citizen who brought a public
charge had first to establish his credentials as a public-spirited Athenian before
launching into his case. It was necessary for him to show that his prosecution was in
the public interest, not just for his own advantage, and that his own blameless life
and service to the community gave him the right to bring others to justice for their
misconduct. If Aeschines were to be the first to cast judicial stones, he had to prove
that his own life was without public or private sin.[52]

To show what a good citizen he is, Aeschines gives the court a rather puritanical
civics lesson. He expatiates upon the rule of law in democracies and lectures on the
importance of a good upbringing as preparation for the duties of Athenian citizenship. He notes the regulations laid down to supervise the conduct of those who train

the youth, the penalties for relatives who hire out children as prostitutes, and the law which disqualifies those who sell their bodies from holding public office. Next he moves on to the law about proper conduct in the Assembly and stresses personal rectitude as a prerequisite for advising the people. The aim of this lengthy disquisition on public and private morality is to set the standards against which Timarchus' conduct should be judged.[53]

The narrative portion of Aeschines' speech is a masterpiece of sophistic pleading. Without a shred of relevant evidence, Aeschines ruthlessly attacks Timarchus as a consummate debauchee. Aeschines alludes briefly to Timarchus' unsavory reputation during his youth and early manhood, then describes his liaison with the notorious voluptuary Misgolas. To prove his allegations, Aeschines challenges Misgolas to swear to the statement he has prepared for him and submits the testimony of Phaedrus and several others. Yet all Aeschines says about these men is that they knew Timarchus resided with Misgolas for a time and that Phaedrus had once gone with Misgolas to search for Timarchus after the latter had failed to show up for the procession at the Dionysia. Aeschines describes how the two men found Timarchus dining with some foreigners at a lodging house and frightened them off with a threat of prosecution for attempting to corrupt a youth, but that does not prove Misgolas succeeded in corrupting Timarchus. As for the summons to testify, we do not know if Misgolas in fact swore to the statement or not, and Aeschines' words strongly indicate he did not expect his witness to comply.[54]

Aeschines skips over Timarchus' alleged dealings with another customer named Anticles and proceeds to recount his dissolute stay with Pittalacus. Aeschines says that Pittalacus was a public slave when he kept Timarchus, who had now fallen so low that he was willing to sell himself to someone who was not even freeborn. The following part of the narrative, however, undercuts this statement because Aeschines represents him as enjoying the full rights of a free man. While living with Pittalacus, Timarchus fell in with Hegesander, who had recently returned from the Hellespont, where he had served as a treasurer to the general Timomachus. Hegesander was the brother of Hegesippus, who was to become one of Aeschines most dedicated opponents in the coming years. Aeschines accuses Hegesander of embezzling funds entrusted to him and of luring Timarchus away from Pittalacus. By his account, Timarchus and Hegesander broke into Pittalacus' house, ransacked his possessions, then tied him to a post, and whipped him. When Pittalacus attempted to bring a suit against them, Hegesander retaliated by claiming him as his slave. A man named Glaucon came to Pittalacus' rescue and asserted he was a free man. The case was submitted to Diopeithes of Sunion for arbitration, yet appears to have been dropped in exchange for Pittalacus' dropping his suit against Timarchus and Hegesander. Although Aeschines adduces the testimony of Glaucon to support his account of Timarchus' dealings with Pittalacus and Hegesander, there is no reason to believe Glaucon had knowledge of anything beyond Hegesander's dispute with him about Pittalacus' status. Aeschines also summoned Hegesander, who to no one's surprise refused to swear to the statement prepared for him.[55]

To strengthen his rather feeble case, Aeschines draws on rumors about Timarchus' activities. In particular, he tells a story that allegedly reveals how the entire Assembly was aware of Timarchus' sordid reputation. Timarchus had sometime earlier passed a decree in the Assembly instructing the Areopagus to review his proposal about certain dwellings on the Pnyx. After completing its report, the Areopagus sent one of its members, Autolycus, to deliver its recommendation to the Assembly. At one point in his report, Autolycus, whose sober habits made him unacquainted with the unsavory reputation of this district of the Pnyx, said that Timarchus was more familiar with the buildings in question than he was. The Assembly took this as an unwitting allusion to Timarchus' debauchery and burst out laughing. Despite reprimands from Autolycus and the political leader Pyrrander, the Assembly would not quiet down and kept on laughing.[56]

After establishing (to his own satisfaction at least) that Timarchus had misused his body for shameful purposes, Aeschines sets out to prove that the defendant had treated his inheritance in a similar fashion. According to Aeschines, Timarchus had squandered the large fortune he received from his father Arizelus, but the testimony he cites proves only that Timarchus had collected a loan from Metagenes and had sold a house to Nausicrates. There is no way of testing Aeschines' charge that Timarchus wasted all his money from these transactions on decadent pleasures. He further alleges that Timarchus cheated his uncle Arignotus out of property he was supposed to oversee for his benefit and calls Arignotus to testify that the council turned down his request to continue receiving public assistance on account of his disabilities. But this testimony merely shows that Arignotus claimed that he was needy enough to require public assistance. It does not prove that Timarchus was the cause of his indigence.[57]

Aeschines links Timarchus' profligacy in his own affairs with his misconduct in public office. These charges recall an important theme brought up at the beginning of the speech, namely the connection between private morality and trustworthiness in public office. Aeschines provides Timarchus with a *cursus scelerum,* describing his venality in a post on Andros, as a member of the Council, and as an inspector of troops in Eretria. His sole piece of evidence in support of this scandalous resume is an anecdote about a charge made by Pamphilus of Acherdous. At a meeting of the Assembly, Pamphilus allegedly shouted that a man and a woman were robbing the Athenian people. When asked to identify the man and the woman, Pamphilus pointed his finger at Hegesander and Timarchus. Yet, as Aeschines himself admits, the accusation was never investigated nor led to a prosecution for stolen funds. Aeschines did not even bother to call on Pamphilus to confirm his version of the story.[58]

Aeschines was well aware of the weaknesses of his case and knew exactly how his enemies would attack it. In reply to the anticipated objections about his lack of evidence, Aeschines defends his use of hearsay and rumor as proof of Timarchus' misdeeds. He cites the recent cases arising from the revision of the citizen lists by the demes. In these cases, the courts often made up their minds on the basis of their own knowledge of the lives of those who were appealing against the decisions of their demes. The Areopagus, too, looks not only at the evidence and arguments presented by the litigants, but also draws on its own knowledge of the defendant's actions and reputation. Aeschines predicts that the defense will insist that he produce documents and witnesses to demonstrate that Timarchus entered into contracts with his lecherous customers. He ridicules this demand for evidence by reminding the court how neither party in such a transaction would commit its terms to writing nor bring the other party to court for failure to fulfill its obscene terms.[59]

Aeschines was also aware that out of all those who intended to speak for Timarchus, Demosthenes would be the most dangerous to his case. In his speech, therefore, he does his best to undermine in advance the arguments Demosthenes might use. For instance, he derides the argument Demosthenes would make that Timarchus was not a prostitute because he did not ply his trade in a registered house of prostitution. Nonsense, Aeschines retorts; any house that Timarchus walked into became ipso facto a house of prostitution. If Demosthenes tries to argue that "common knowledge" can be inaccurate, Aeschines advises the court to remember the words of Hesiod, who called rumor divine and immortal, and the verse in the *Iliad* where Homer mentions rumor. The court may have had a hard time recalling the latter since the verse is absent from all extant manuscripts of Homer's poem.[60]

One of Aeschines' main concerns was that Demosthenes would bring up the punishment of the Phocians and try to fasten the blame for the recent debacle on himself. Aeschines' reply to the threatened accusation is revealing. Rather than denying his role in recent events, Aeschines boasts that he and Philocrates were responsible for the treaty with Philip. He cautions the court not to be overhasty in its judgment of Philip. The Athenians should wait and see if Philip will provide the benefits he had promised in his letters to the Assembly.[61]

Another of Timarchus' supporters was rumored to be a general who would take Aeschines to task for sullying the reputation of handsome young men like Timarchus. Aeschines reports hearing that the general will accuse him of hypocrisy since Aeschines himself has enjoyed passionate friendships with youths, pursuing them in the gymnasia and writing poems full of longing and affection. Evidently sensitive to the charge that he was lacking in refinement, Aeschines launches into a learned disquisition on the proper type of friendship between men and youths. He draws a distinction between the kind of love celebrated by the poets and the sort of lust indulged in by Timarchus and his associates. The digression serves several functions. In part, it provides the court with some poetic relief after the depressing catalogue of Timarchus' vices. At the same time, it enables Aeschines to avoid appearing too puritanical in his denunciation of Timarchus' misdeeds. Finally, it gives Aeschines the opportunity to portray himself as a cultured gentleman, well versed in the canon of respected works of literature and not insensitive to the charms of young men.[62]

By our standards, Aeschines' case against Timarchus is incredibly weak. Whatever the truth of his allegations, however, Aeschines succeeded in blackening his reputation to the point where the court was willing to convict Timarchus and punish him with loss of citizen rights. Before condemning Aeschines for his unscrupulous tactics, one ought to bear in mind that he brought his prosecution in self-defense and that the case Demosthenes brought against him in 343 was not stronger. Sordid as it may have been, this was the way one played the game of politics in Classical Athens. Without firm rules of evidence and magistrates trained and empowered to enforce them, Aeschines could expect his opponents to resort to the lowest forms of character assassination. Better to strike first than to await the inevitable onslaught of slander and abuse.[63]

The court's verdict indicates that Demosthenes' attempt to divert its attention by bemoaning the fate of the wretched Phocians did not succeed. The Athenians were certainly angry about the punishment of the Phocians, but they apparently did not hold Aeschines responsible for it. Indeed, there was no reason for them to do so. The Athenians had been in no position to help the Phocians. Aeschines had done his best to convince Philip to spare the Phocians, when he spoke to the king in Pella. After his plan to make scapegoats of Phalaecus and his followers was not adopted, it was Aeschines who was able to persuade the Amphictyons to impose a punishment that was much milder than what the vindictive Oetaeans proposed. If anything, the Athenians had reason to feel grateful to Aeschines, and Demosthenes was not yet able to convince them otherwise. Demosthenes would have to wait several years before Athenian memories of 346 faded to the point where they might believe a different version of the Phocian tragedy.

The conviction of Timarchus provided Aeschines with some consolation after the disappointments of the summer of 346. His hopes for a satisfactory conclusion to the sacred war and for benefits from Philip had not materialized. But that did not stop him from continuing to place his trust in Philip's promises. If the Athenians would be patient, Philip might find a way to prove himself true to his word.

6

Entre Deux Guerres

In the years following 346, Aeschines' position in Athenian politics suffered a decline from which it never fully recovered. In 346 he served on three important embassies, played a major role in bringing about peace with Philip, and eliminated his political enemy Timarchus. A mere three years later, Aeschines was fighting for his political life, barely escaping conviction on a charge of treason brought by Demosthenes. Not long after, his election as ambassador to Delphi was canceled, and his opponent Hyperides appointed in his place. And in 340, the Peace of Philocrates, the treaty which had been a source of pride to Aeschines only six years earlier, came to an ignominious end when the Athenians declared war on Philip. As Aeschines' influence waned, Demosthenes' position steadily rose. By the end of the decade, it was Demosthenes' voice that dominated the Assembly, rousing the Athenians to take a more aggressive stance toward Philip and drowning out the objections of critics like Aeschines.

The decline of Aeschines' fortune was not entirely caused by Demosthenes' attacks on his policy. The policy Aeschines first adopted during the Second Embassy and then pursued for the next few years was based on his faith in Philip's promises. In his letters to the Athenians Philip had pledged to bring benefits to Athens, and Aeschines, impressed by the king's generosity and gracious behavior, decided to take him at his word. The fate of Aeschines' policy thus depended not so much on his own ability to sway the Assembly as on Philip's ability to make good on his promises. Without some benefits to show for Athenian loyalty, Aeschines' policy had little chance of long-term popularity in the Assembly. Aeschines received his first disappointment after the fall of Phocis, but this did not stop him from continuing to place his trust in Philip's generosity. To understand the course of Aeschines' political career after the Peace of Philocrates, therefore, we must look not only at events in Athens, but also at Philip's aims, resources, and needs in these years.

The period of Aeschines' career after the trial of Timarchus is less well documented than the events surrounding the Peace of Philocrates. In the speech he delivered against Ctesiphon in 330, Aeschines devotes some space to a discussion of Demosthenes' activities in the years 345–40, but has next to nothing to say about his own. In his reply to that speech, Demosthenes makes a few scattered remarks about his opponent's action in the period, and these provide most of the very small amount of information we have about Aeschines during these years. The speech Aeschines delivered in his own defense in 343 is a valuable source for his views and policy toward Philip in that year, but tells us nothing about what he was actually doing to implement that policy. The main source of information about events in Athens in this period are the speeches Demosthenes delivered in the Assembly and the speech Hegesippus gave in response to Philip's proposals to revise the Peace of Philocrates. Although these speeches contain several attacks on policies pursued by certain unnamed opponents, it is uncertain who their opponents are and whether or not their views are being reported accurately. Confronted with such a dearth of evidence, one is always faced with the temptation to overinterpret the few known facts or to interpret the actions of leaders in the light of later events, thereby ignoring the immediate context in which they occurred. In the case of Philip it is tempting to interpret all his campaigns and diplomacy in the years 345–340 as parts of a grand strategy that had as its goal the invasion of Asia. Since Aeschines constantly voiced his support for Philip at the time, one might assume that he was in sympathy with this alleged plan for a Panhellenic crusade against Persia and consistently opposed Demosthenes' earlier attempt to enlist Persian backing out of his desire to further Philip's plans. Although these assumptions have provided convenient perspectives from which to analyze the events of the period, none of them finds any corroboration in our sources.[1]

Such assumptions have led to a mistaken view of the Athenian response made to the appeal of the Persian king in 344/43. In that year, the Persian king sent an embassy to the Athenians to ask them if they still intended to maintain their friendship with him and to request that they send troops to help him suppress the revolt of Egyptian subjects. The Athenians replied that they would not send troops, but promised to abide by their friendship with the Great King provided that he did not attack any Greek cities. In his commentary on Demosthenes' speeches, the Alexandrian scholar Didymus identified this Persian embassy with one which Demosthenes alluded to in a speech delivered in 341/40. Since Demosthenes says that the Athenians rejected the terms brought by that embassy, Didymus concluded that the reply the Athenians gave to the Great King in 344/43 was "more haughty than was necessary." Didymus added that an embassy from Philip was also present in Athens at the same time as the Persian embassy. Some have identified the Macedonian embassy with that led by Pytho of Byzantium, who was sent by Philip to appeal to the Athenians during this period. Pytho delivered a message to the Assembly that Philip was willing to amend any clause in the Peace of Philocrates that the Athenians did not find to their liking. The presence of these two embassies has been seen as an important moment of decision for the Athenians. The alleged rebuff given to the Persian embassy and the warm reception granted to Philip's ambassador Pytho have been viewed as a victory for a pro-Macedonian party led by Aeschines and Eubulus, who supported Philip's plan to unite all of Greece in a Panhellenic crusade against Persia. In similar fashion, the different responses given to the two embassies have also been interpreted as a defeat for the anti-Macedonian party headed by Demosthenes and Hegesippus, who hoped to employ the resources of the Great King in their struggle against Philip.[2]

This view has serious flaws and is propped up by nothing more than unwarranted inferences. To begin with, we cannot be certain that the Macedonian embassy that Didymus says arrived in Athens at the same time as the Persian embassy was identical with the one led by Pytho. The identification of the two embassies is a guess; although we cannot rule out the possibility, there is no evidence that compels us to accept the identification. Furthermore, it is clear that Didymus, who was notorious in antiquity for his carelessness, was mistaken in his identification of the Persian embassy of 344/43 with the one mentioned by Demosthenes in 341/40. Each of these embassies arrived at a different time and carried different messages to the Assembly. They cannot be identical. This mistake on Didymus' part undermines his view that the Athenian response to the Persian embassy of 344/43 was a haughty rejection. True, the Athenians declined to send troops to the Great King for his expedition against Egypt, but that was only half of their response. The Persian king also asked them if they would maintain their friendship with him. This was no idle question, and the Athenian answer was of some importance to the Great King. The Great King was then about to invade Egypt in order to suppress a revolt that had lasted two decades. If he could not get military assistance, he could at least gain an assurance from them that they would not interfere in his efforts to subdue his rebellious subjects. The Athenians had aided the rebels before, and their promise not to do so again would have been a gain for the Great King. He therefore asked the Athenians if they still considered themselves his friends. The Athenian response was conditional, but essentially favorable to the Great King. Their promise to maintain their friendship clearly implied that they would not seek to thwart his plan to reconquer Egypt. Nor was the Athenian response expressed in language that the Great King would have found offensive. The Athenians were merely repeating the terms on which their friendship with Persia had been based. All they were saying in effect was "you keep to your part of the bargain, and we will keep to ours." Indeed, the Great King appears to have been grateful for the Athenian declaration since a few years later he offered them his assistance against Philip.[3]

The Athenian response can in no way be interpreted as an endorsement of a Panhellenic crusade against Persia, such as the one proposed by Isocrates in 346. Far from declaring their hostility toward the Great King of Persia, the Athenians in their response declared themselves his friends, provided, of course, he met certain conditions. Nor are there any grounds for believing that Philip at this juncture envisaged any such campaign against the king of Persia. Philip, though clearly on the point of leading an invasion of Persia when he died in 336, does not appear to have considered such a move as early as 343. If he did, it was certainly one of the best kept secrets of antiquity. Nor do we ever hear of Aeschines urging the Athenians to join in this kind of an expedition under Macedonian leadership. There is no trace of this policy in his speeches, and Demosthenes, who is quick to point to any support voiced by Aeschines for Macedonian aims, never credits him with such a policy. Aeschines' support for Philip was based on his hope that the king would deliver the benefits he had promised in 346. None of these promises had anything to do with an invasion of Asia.[4]

After the Peace of Philocrates, Philip turned his attention not to Asia, but to his neighbors in northern Greece. Unlike Attica, which shared borders with only one major power, Thebes, and a geopolitical nonentity, Megara, Macedon was surrounded by many tribes and cities, none of which Philip could ignore for long. In the

years leading up to 346, Philip had eliminated the most serious threats to his kingdom from the east. Olynthus and the cities of the Chalcidice had been subdued, and
the Thracian kings had either been won over or defeated. In the years after 346,
Philip therefore moved to increase his power and influence in the areas to the west of
Macedon. Soon after his victory in the sacred war, Philip led his army against tribes
in Illyria. In 343/42, if not earlier, the king marched into Epirus, deposed King
Arrybas, and placed his compliant nephew Alexander on the throne. After strength-
ening his western flank, Philip shifted his attention to Thrace to secure and extend
his power in that region. Philip did not ignore events in central and southern Greece,
but his interventions there were directed solely at maintaining the status quo and
lending help to his friends in the Greek cities. In the Peloponnese, Philip inherited
the role Thebes had played in the 360s. He supported Argos and Messene with
money and mercenaries, keeping them strong enough to resist Sparta and prevent her
from reasserting her traditional hegemony in the area. At the same time Philip helped
to keep friends in Elis and Euboea in power. Yet with the exception of some short
expeditions to Euboea, Philip never ventured south of Thermopylai during the six
years after the Peace of Philocrates. The only time Philip himself led troops south in
this period was to put an end to discord that had arisen in Thessaly. His business
there finished, he returned to continue his campaigns in northern Greece.[5]

Demosthenes, whose speeches of the 340s raised paranoia to an art form, saw
Philip's actions in a different light. He repeatedly denounced Philip's meddling in
Greek affairs as evidence of a grand strategy aimed at overcoming Athens, the
champion of Greek liberty. Demosthenes oratory is stirring and rightly admired, but
his interpretation of Philip's actions deserves a large measure of skepticism. Philip's
moves were hardly aggressive, and it was not in the king's interest to disrupt the
balance of power, which continued to keep the Greeks divided and unable to hinder
his progress in northern Greece. Philip's aims after 346 remained basically the same
as they had been before 346. His abiding interest was to prevent the emergence of a
Greek community that could challenge his supremacy in Thessaly and Thrace.

While Philip sought to maintain the status quo, Demosthenes was doing everything in his power to disrupt it. In late 344 Demosthenes convinced the Assembly to
send him to the Peloponnese to warn the Greeks about Philip's plot to conquer them.
Politics in Athens had changed a great deal since 348. Just four years ago, Demosthenes had been urging the Athenians to make peace with Philip, and Aeschines
telling the people of Megalopolis about the dangers Macedon posed to Greek freedom. But Demosthenes was no more successful in 344 than Aeschines had been in
348. The only fruit of Demosthenes' mission to the Peloponnese was that the
Argives and Messenians sent embassies to Athens to protest his allegations. They
even went so far as to accuse the Athenians of hypocrisy, posing as the defenders of
Greek freedom while simultaneously supporting the Spartans, who were bent on
enslaving the entire Peloponnese. They were joined in their protest by Philip, who
sent ambassadors to reply to Demosthenes' slanders that he had failed to keep his
promises to the Athenians. Such a charge was absurd, they said; the king had never
made any specific promises to the Athenians.[6]

Demosthenes defended his policy to the Assembly in his *Second Philippic*. In
his speech, he unambiguously alludes to certain opponents, who are obviously

Aeschines and Philocrates. He summarizes some of their arguments and thus gives us some indication of what their own policy was at the time. From what Demosthenes says, Aeschines' policy appears not to have altered since 346. He continued to claim that Philip was friendly to Athens; Philip's real enemies were the Thebans. Philip was merely waiting for an opportunity to attack the Thebans. There were rumors circulating that he was about to fortify Elateia on the border of Boeotia. Philip would have rebuilt the Boeotian cities and given them their independence in 346, Aeschines explained, had he not been hemmed in by the Theban infantry and the Thessalian cavalry.[7]

Demosthenes replied to these criticisms by calling it foolish to think that Philip considered the Thebans his enemies when the king was doing all he could to oppose their enemies, the Spartans. If Philip was a friend of Athens, he had shown no indication of it. Despite his promises in 346, the Athenians had still received no solid benefits as a result of the Peace of Philocrates whereas Philip had gained control of Thermopylai and the Thebans had regained the portion of Boeotia that had been wrested from them by the Phocians.[8]

Demosthenes' speech reveals that opinion in Athens was now divided between those who were in favor of maintaining peace with Philip and those who suspected his designs. Aeschines remained one of the main proponents of the Peace of Philocrates, holding on to the hope that Philip would eventually deliver the benefits he had written about in his letters of 346. But two years had passed since the conclusion of the treaty, and the Athenians had yet to receive any tangible gains from their relationship with Philip. This played into the hands of men like Demosthenes and Hegesippus, who had been opposed to cooperate with Macedon all along. They were now able to point to Philip's failure to make good on his promises. They used this failure as evidence to prove their argument that Philip's promises had never been sincere, but were held out only as bait to keep the Athenians in his camp while he seized Thermopylai and crushed the Phocians. Aeschines had been able to defeat these opponents of the peace in 346 with his conviction of Timarchus, but by 344 the tide was beginning to turn. Demosthenes had grown powerful enough in the Assembly to convince the Athenians to send him on a mission to warn the Greeks of Philip's sinister plans. But the failure of his mission did nothing to enchance his prestige, and circumstances did not yet favor his aggressive policy.

Philip realized that the Athenians were growing impatient with his delay in providing them with the benefits he had promised in 346. Not too long after Demosthenes' embassy to the Peloponnese, probably in early 343, Philip attempted to improve his relations with Athens by responding to the criticisms leveled at the peace by Demosthenes and others. He sent Pytho of Byzantium and several other ambassadors from his allies to announce to the Athenians that he was willing to revise the terms of the Peace of Philocrates. Pytho urged the Athenians not to condemn the peace, but to amend any clause they found unsatisfactory. Naturally Pytho could not promise that Philip would accept any proposal the Athenians might put forward. Pytho had not been sent to negotiate with the Athenians with plenipotentiary authority, but to relay a message from Philip. The message contained an invitation to begin negotiations about revising the peace and nothing more. Hegesippus, our main source for Pytho's embassy, however, later interpreted

Philip's message as a pledge to accede to any Athenian demands. Hegesippus' motive in doing this is readily apparent: after Philip had rejected the demands Hegesippus made, the orator wished to demonstrate that the king had not been bargaining in good faith. To establish that, he had to claim Pytho had implied Philip would consent to any revision the Athenians wished to make. But Pytho is unlikely to have implied this, and Philip would certainly not have committed himself so unreservedly.[9]

After Pytho delivered his message from Philip to the Assembly, Hegesippus then proposed that the clause in the treaty providing that both powers retain only those territories that they already possessed be amended to read that each power should hold those territories that belonged to them. This revision was clearly aimed at the recovery of Amphipolis, which the Athenians stubbornly persisted in regarding as their own. According to Hegesippus, Pytho and the other ambassadors did not object to this proposal. Hegesippus read into their silence an expression of approval, but his interpretation is implausible. Pytho and the other ambassadors had no authority to accept or reject a proposal submitted by the Athenians. Philip kept the power of decision to himself. If they remained silent, it was because they knew that whatever they said would not be binding and so did not wish to mislead the Athenians.[10]

Hegesippus and several others were then elected as ambassadors and instructed to travel to Macedon and present the Athenian proposals to Philip. In addition to asking for a revision of the clause pertaining to territory, the Athenians made two more demands: first, that Philip return to them the island of Halonnesos, and second, that Philip pledge to defend the freedom of the Greeks who had not sworn the oaths to the Peace of Philocrates. Halonnesos was an island in the north Aegean, which had been seized by pirates whom Philip later expelled. The Athenians still regarded it as their possession and insisted that Philip return the island to its rightful owner.[11]

After hearing the Athenian proposals, Philip gave his reply. He rejected Hegesippus' new version of the clause about territory. The king had no intention of yielding Amphipolis, which gave him control of valuable resources and lay between Macedon and his colony of Philippi. He did, however, propose that all disputes between the Athenians and himself be submitted to arbitration. As for Halonnesos, he denied that the Athenians had a right to demand it back since it was not in their possession when he took it. On the other hand, he was willing to promise to defend the freedom of the Greeks. Beside responding to the Athenian proposals, Philip made several of his own. He invited the Athenians to join with him in a campaign to suppress piracy in the Aegean. To foster closer ties between Athens and Macedon, he suggested that they conclude agreements about legal procedure designed to encourage trade. He also urged the Athenians to submit their dispute about Cardia to arbitration. Cardia was a city in the Chersonese that was allied with Philip. When the general Chares tried to install Athenian settlers in their territory, the Cardians objected and appealed to Philip. If the Cardians refused to honor the terms of the arbitrator's decision, Philip declared he would compel them to. Finally, he repeated his promise to confer benefits on Athens and claimed that he valued the friendship of the Athenians more than that of the other Greeks. Philip incorporated these proposals in a letter to the Athenians, which he gave to Hegesippus and the other ambassadors to read to the Assembly. At the same time, he sent his own ambassadors to Athens to urge the Assembly to accept his proposals.[12]

The negotiations followed the same pattern as they had in 346. The Athenian ambassadors returned to Athens where they would have reported about their embassy and delivered the letter to the Council and the Assembly. They were followed by the Macedonian ambassadors, who attempted to persuade the Assembly it was in their interest to endorse Philip's proposed revision of the treaty. After their speech, Hegesippus rose and violently attacked all of Philip's proposals. He argued that Philip's refusal to recognize the validity of the Athenian claim to Halonnesos represented a dangerous precedent. Was all property seized by pirates now to be regarded as the property of the person who happened to recover it without regard for the rights of its original owner? The gift of Halonnesos was no great benefit to Athens—all Philip really wanted to do was to make a display of Macedonian power and Athenian weakness. And for the Athenians to submit their claims to arbitration would only be a further sign of weakness. Philip's offer to coerce the Cardians into accepting the result of arbitration carried the same message: it implied that the Athenians were powerless to compel the Cardians to recognize their rights.[13]

The motives behind Philip's other proposals were also suspect. Philip said he wanted to suppress piracy, but his real aim was in Hegesippus' opinion to make Macedon into a naval power that could rival Athens. The agreements about legal procedure were not necessary to promote commercial relations between Athens and Macedon. Trade had flourished under Philip's predecessors without any such treaty. The true object of Philip's proposal was to force Athens to recognize Macedonian claims to Potidaia. Hegesippus then defended his own version of the territorial clause and accused Philip of hypocrisy for inviting the Athenians to suggest revisions for the Peace of Philocrates, then rejecting the revisions they had submitted to him. Amphipolis belonged to Athens and all the Greeks. The king of Persia and even Philip himself had declared the city Athenian territory. Philip could not hide behind the terms of the Peace of Philocrates. Hegesippus denounced that treaty as illegal since it did not conform to earlier Athenian decrees about Amphipolis. And Philip's pledge to defend the freedom of the Greeks was contradicted by his recent actions. Had not the king robbed Pherai of its freedom, marched against Ambracia, and conquered the Elean colonies in Epirus so that he could make a gift of them to Alexander? In sum, Philip's promise of benefits was empty. Philip had had plenty of opportunities to fulfill his promise, and several years had passed without Philip surrendering the territories in Thrace he had unjustly seized from the Athenians. Where were his much vaunted benefits?[14]

Despite the distortions of Hegesippus' rhetoric, it is still possible to discern the strategy underlying Philip's proposals. Philip clearly understood that the Athenians were angry about the events of 346. He had won the Athenians over with a promise of benefits, just as he had gained allies throughout his career, but had not yet delivered on his promise. He now tried to allay their sense of disappointment by offering the gift of Halonnesos and by promising to help them in their dispute with Cardia. Philip could obviously not yield to territorial demands, but he could consent to submitting his differences with Athens to arbitration. To promote closer ties, he put forward the possibility of an agreement to encourage trade and a joint campaign against pirates. He could not offer more than this for fear of offending his other Greek allies. Philip appears to have been genuinely interested in avoiding a break with Athens, but higher on his list of priorities was maintaining the settlement of 346. He could not restore Phocis or liberate Boeotia from the Theban yoke without shattering that settlement. Hegesippus demanded some substantial benefits in return for Athenian friendship, but Philip could not satisfy those demands without alienating the rest of the Greeks. What he could offer was not enough to convince the Assembly to turn a deaf ear to Hegesippus' slanders. As a result, the Assembly appears to have turned down Philip's proposals. Though Athens and Philip remained at peace for the time being, the ties that bound them together were slowly unraveling.

What was Aeschines' attitude to all of this? Demosthenes tells us that when Philip sent Pytho of Byzantium and ambassadors from his other allies to present his charges of Athenian injustice, Aeschines spoke out in agreement. What Demosthenes neglects to say is that Pytho also invited the Athenians to submit proposals for the revision of the peace. Aeschines would naturally have welcomed the invitation, for it demonstrated what he had maintained all along, namely that Philip was indeed friendly to Athens and eager to give proof of his goodwill. Unfortunately, we are otherwise in complete ignorance as to what Aeschines did at the time. In 330, Aeschines criticized Demosthenes for advising the Athenians not to accept Halonnesos from Philip, unless the king were to admit that he was returning the island to its rightful owner, not granting it as a gift. The evidence is not as substantial as we might like it to be, but what testimony there is indicates that Aeschines supported Philip's proposals to revise the treaty. It is also clear that Hegesippus, one of Aeschines' opponents, was the one who was elected as ambassador to conduct the negotiations with Philip, not Aeschines and his associates. No source informs us about the reasons for the choice of Hegesippus. Perhaps the Assembly thought that Aeschines and those in favor of peace had given away too much in 346. Unhappy with the results of the Peace of Philocrates, the Assembly may have decided that a more aggressive spokesman was needed to express Athenian dissatisfaction with the treaty.[15]

The paucity of evidence about Aeschines' activity in this period is possibly the most regrettable gap in our information about his career. Aeschines had risked his reputation on the hope that Philip would finally grant Athens the benefits he had alluded to in 346. Pytho's message must have given him cause for optimism since it revealed that Philip was interested in fostering good relations with Athens. But the proposals that Hegesippus brought back from Macedon must have been a disappointment. Aeschines had asserted that Philip intended to liberate Boeotia from Theban rule and confer other benefits, but his letter and his ambassadors had nothing to say about Boeotia. And the gift of Halonnesos was a rather niggardly display of generosity. Yet the main problem was that too much damage had been done in 346, and Philip was unable to repair it. Those opposed to observing the peace could always point to the draconian treatment of the Phocians and the recovery of Theban power in Boeotia. These were the main causes of discontent in Athens, which Philip's proposals did nothing to address. The major shortcoming of Philip's revisions was that they did not compensate for these perceived losses. If Aeschines failed to convince the Assembly to accept Philip's offers, it was not entirely his fault. Philip's package of benefits was not all that attractive, and Aeschines would have had an uphill struggle convincing the Athenians to see otherwise. Aeschines had trusted in Philip to provide him with proof of Macedonian goodwill. Philip let him down.

The next blow to the Peace of Philocrates was the prosecution of the author of the treaty. Sometime after the debate about the revision of the treaty, Hyperides, a man who had not played a prominent role in politics up to this point, accused Philocrates of having received bribes from Philip in return for proposing decrees that were contrary to the best interests of the Athenians. Hyperides initiated his prosecution by using the procedure of *eisangelia,* by which he made his accusation in the Assembly. After Hyperides presented his charge, Demosthenes by his own account jumped up and shouted that Philocrates was not the only guilty ambassador. He then invited the other men who had served on the embassies to Philip in 346 to denounce the king, but they remained silent. Philocrates did not stay in Athens to stand trial, but fled before his case came to court. Aided by the conspicuous absence of the defendant, Hyperides found it easy to secure a conviction. Philocrates was condemned to death in absentia, and all his property was confiscated.[16]

Although both Aeschines and Demosthenes interpreted Philocrates' flight as a confession of guilt, it may not have been a guilty conscience that drove him into exile. With the opponents of his treaty growing more and more confident after ambushing Philip's attempt to revise it, Philocrates may have lost his nerve and fled out of fear that he might not receive a fair trial. His flight may thus say less about his culpability than it does about the political atmosphere in Athens at the time. The repeated attacks on Philip had begun to sway public opinion. All those who spoke kindly about Philip were now regarded with suspicion; those responsible for the Peace of Philocrates, which had done so much to damage Athenian interests, were suspected of treason.[17]

Events outside Attica played into the hands of those opposed to peace with Philip. Sometime in late 343, Philip sent mercenaries to Megara in an attempt to help his friends Perillus and Ptoiodorus, two leading men in the city. Perillus had enjoyed Philip's hospitality in Macedon and had apparently attracted the suspicions of some of his compatriots, who hauled him into court not long after his return. Thanks to the efforts of his friend, the wealthy Ptoiodorus, Perillus escaped conviction. As it turned out, his rivals' suspicions were justified. After his acquittal Perillus went back to Macedon where he collected mercenaries for a coup d'état, which Ptoiodorus was plotting. We do not know the outcome of the plot; it may have been thwarted by an expedition of Athenian troops summoned by the Megarians, which Plutarch appears to place in this period. Whatever the fruit of Ptoiodorus' machinations, the incident was soon cited by Demosthenes as further evidence of Philip's designs against Athens.[18]

Philip also appears to have had a hand in the troubles that occurred in Elis about this time. The details are sketchy, but Philip seems to have supplied his friends in Elis with money and enabled them to seize power. Philip's intervention in Euboea, separated from Attica by only a narrow strip of water, was even more alarming. Civil war had broken out in Eretria after the expulsion of Plutarchus, and one faction was driven out and fled to Porthmos, a nearby town. The winning faction realized that they would not be completely safe as long as their enemies remained in the neighborhood so they appealed to Philip for troops. Philip saw another opportunity to gain friends by bestowing favors and sent Hipponicus with a thousand mercenaries to take Porthmos. Demosthenes claims that Philip installed Hipparchus, Automedon, and Cleitarchus as tyrants in Eretria after Hipponicus stormed Porthmos, but his use of the word "tyrant" is more likely to be an expression of his dislike for their connection with Philip than an accurate description of their constitutional position. Philip's supporters had also established themselves in control of Oreos in Euboea.[19]

A common pattern can be seen in all these incidents. In each case, a local political struggle led one side to appeal to Philip, who then distributed gifts to his friends in the form of money or mercenaries. In none of these incidents does Philip appear to have taken the initiative nor to have committed Macedonian troops. Philip merely responded to requests made by Greeks who asked for his assistance in their own struggles for power. The events in Megara, Elis, and Euboea were all isolated incidents, conflicts arising from domestic rivalries. But these facts did not prevent Demosthenes from seeing in them the coordinated parts of a grand strategy aimed at isolating Athens and destroying Greek liberty. Armed with this evidence of Philip's hostile intent, Demosthenes now judged the time ripe to bring his battle against Aeschines into court.

Demosthenes made a total of five charges in the speech he delivered against Aeschines at the trial. First, he accused Aeschines of giving false reports and preventing him from reporting the truth. His second charge is that Aeschines had given advice that was contrary to the interests of the Athenian people. For his third charge, Demosthenes says that Aeschines had disobeyed the instructions of the Assembly while serving as ambassador. Aeschines' fourth crime was to have deprived the city of valuable opportunities by reason of his delays. For all of these misdeeds, Demosthenes' indictment concludes, Aeschines received gifts from Philip. Demosthenes' main charge is that of bribery, which is also the weakest of all five. As we have already seen, the charge is not supported by any evidence. The other charges are not especially strong either. For this reason, Demosthenes concentrates most of his oratorical fire on circumstantial evidence, in particular, the disadvantages brought by the peace and Philip's failure to act as Aeschines and Philocrates had predicted in 346 that he would. The entire first third of his speech is devoted to demonstrating how the reports Aeschines and Philocrates made after the Second Embassy led directly to the downfall of Phocis. Demosthenes draws an unfavorable contrast between the successful Athenian effort to defend Thermopylai against Philip in 352 and the surrender of Phocis to Philip in 346. He argues that the security of the Athenian possessions in the Chersonese was no compensation for the defeat of Phocis because the Chersonese was already held by the Athenians when the treaty was sworn. Not only does Demosthenes emphasize the losses suffered by the Athenians; he constantly reminds the court of the gains won by Philip and the Thebans.[20]

Demosthenes devotes less attention to the events of the Second Embassy itself. He blames the loss of the Thracian fortresses on Aeschines because of his refusal to sail directly to Philip and receive the oaths from him before the Macedonian army could overrun them. Of course, he claims that Aeschines and his fellow ambassadors received large gifts from Philip once they arrived in Pella and that Aeschines helped the king to write his letter to the Assembly. This was the letter that deceived the Athenians into thinking that they had nothing to worry about.[21]

Demosthenes' speech is not only an attack on Aeschines; it is also a defense of his own actions in 346. Demosthenes denies that he ever spoke in favor of Philocrates' version of the treaty with Philip, and claims instead to have backed the Resolution of the Allies. Not surprisingly, he has a hard time explaining the honors he proposed for the Macedonian ambassadors when they came to Athens. At several points he contrasts his own patriotism with the treason of Aeschines and Philocrates. For instance, he asserts that he tried to speed the Second Embassy on its way by setting an early date for its departure. Had the embassy followed the instructions set down in his decree, Philip would not have had a chance to overwhelm Cersebleptes and to seize the Thracian fortresses. Demosthenes also recalls how he attacked Aeschines and Philocrates after the return of the Second Embassy.[22]

Most of the speech Aeschines delivered in his defense consists of a point-by-point refutation of Demosthenes' accusations and slanders. Aeschines' style of presentation differs significantly from that of his accuser. Demosthenes tends to fling out an accusation without much evidence or argument, then refer back to it later in his speech as if it had already been incontrovertibly proven. Aeschines' exposition is more careful and methodical. He patiently moves through the events of 346 in chronological order, pausing only to summon witnesses, to cite a decree, or to remind the court of the circumstances surrounding his actions in 346. Aeschines' aim in giving a detailed narrative is not only to defend his own actions and place them in the proper context, but also to expose the hypocrisy of Demosthenes, who once promoted the Peace of Philocrates as vigorously as he later excoriated it. Aeschines accordingly begins at the very outset of the negotiations with Philip, describing how Demosthenes urged the Athenians to make peace with the king as early as 348. Aeschines takes up Demosthenes' charge of collaboration with Philocrates and tosses it right back at him. It was not I who worked closely with Philocrates, Aeschines retorts; Demosthenes was the one who advocated Philocrates' version of the treaty with Philip. To provide further embarrassment for his opponent, Aeschines has the clerk read out Demosthenes' decree of honors for the Macedonian ambassadors. Nor does Aeschines allow the court to forget the decree of Demosthenes that robbed the other Greeks of the chance to join in the peace with Philip. Aeschines then recounts how Demosthenes opposed the attempt to have Cersebleptes included among the allies eligible to swear the oaths to Philip. As a member of the Second Embassy, Demosthenes delivered a sycophantic speech to Philip and was considered so untrustworthy by his colleagues on the embassy that none of them would consent to dine with him.[23]

Aeschines' refutation of Demosthenes' charges is generally thorough and convincing. His narrative of the events culminating in the ratification of the Peace of Philocrates is corroborated at important points by the evidence of decrees and witnesses. In reply to the charge that on Elaphebolion 19 he browbeat the Assembly into accepting the alliance with Philip, Aeschines simply produces the decree that limited the debate on the treaty to the previous day, thereby showing that he could not have addressed the Assembly on the nineteenth. Aeschines admits that he reluc-

tantly supported the Peace of Philocrates, but reminds the court of the desperate
situation at the time, which left the Athenians with no choice but to come to terms
with Philip. He attributes the defeat of Phocis to the reckless policies of Phalaecus
and Philip's failure to fulfill his promises to the Athenian refusal to send troops.[24]

Aeschines' defense of his own action and of the treaty mark an important shift in
his attitude toward Philip. In his speech against Timarchus in 346, Aeschines
claimed credit for the Peace of Philocrates. In 344 he was still speaking positively
about the treaty and predicting that Philip would soon grant the benefits he had
promised in his letters of 346. But when Philip finally offered some ''benefits'' in
343, the Assembly took the advice of Demosthenes and Hegesippus and rejected
them as inadequate compensation for the losses the Athenians suffered in 346. By
the time of his trial later in the year Aeschines found it impossible to defend the
treaty on the basis of Philip's promised benefits. The only course left to him was to
defend the treaty for the benefits that peace had brought. In his speech Aeschines
makes no attempt to defend the alliance with Philip, which, as he points out, he was
never in favor of in the first place. On the contrary, it was Demosthenes who was
primarily responsible for the conclusion of the alliance. Aeschines himself had
advised the Assembly to limit the debate to the question of peace alone. But after the
alliance was concluded, Aeschines encouraged the Athenians to hope for benefits
from Philip. By 343 his attitude had changed. In his speech he no longer celebrates
the virtues of the treaty, but portrays it as the lesser of two evils. His defense of the
treaty toward the end of his speech is not based on his faith in Philip's promises but
on the lessons of history, which taught that Athens had always prospered more in
times of peace than during wars. The Athenians should continue to observe the peace
with Philip for the advantages that peace, not Philip, confers.[25]

Aeschines was acquitted of Demosthenes' charges by a very narrow margin.
The close vote is surprising given the patent weaknesses of Demosthenes' case and
the strength of Aeschines' defense. It is also astonishing that so many cast their
tokens against Aeschines when he had three of the most prominent Athenians of his
day, Eubulus, Phocion, and Nausicles, testify on his behalf. Demosthenes' ability to
come so near to a conviction was in part due to the power of his stunning oratory, but
a more influential factor may have been the political atmosphere. Shortly before the
trial, the Assembly had rejected Philip's proposals, and Philocrates, who had moved
the treaty with Philip, had fled Athens to avoid prosecution. Philip's meddling in
Elis, Megara, and Euboea no doubt also had an effect on the court.[26]

Aeschines' speech is valuable for revealing how the rejection of Philip's proposals for the revision of the treaty affected his position. It was not impossible for
Aeschines to defend the alliance with Philip on the grounds that Philip would sooner
or later make good on his promises of 346. And after the conviction of Philocrates,
one could not call for improved ties with Macedon without being accused of treason.
The best Aeschines could now do was to prevent the tension between Athens and
Philip from escalating into an outbreak of war. But Aeschines' position was ham-
pered by the lack of a clear-cut alternative to Demosthenes' policy. He could attack
the policies of his opponents and accuse them of stirring up war, but was unable to
propose any measures that might place peace on a firmer foundation by advocating
closer relations between Athens and Macedon. This made it difficult for him to

mount an effective opposition to Demosthenes, Hegesippus, and the others who were bent on forcing a showdown with Philip.

A reflection of Aeschines' shift in policy can be seen in the debate about Diopeithes' command, which took place in the year following Aeschines' trial. Around the time of Pytho's embassy, the Assembly had sent Diopeithes with a group of settlers to the Chersonese to protect Athenian interests there. Several cities in the area cooperated with Diopeithes and provided the settlers with land, expecting defense against their enemies in return. The people of Cardia, however, refused to go along; they defiantly told the Athenians to settle in their own territory. Their refusal angered Diopeithes, who tried to compel Cardian compliance by force of arms. The Cardians appealed to Philip, who was about then negotiating with the Athenians about the revision of the Peace of Philocrates. Philip included in his package of revisions a proposal to submit the dispute to arbitration, but the Assembly, egged on by Hegesippus and Demosthenes, rejected Philip's idea. Unable to convince the Athenians to accept a peaceful means of resolving the conflict, Philip sent some troops to strengthen the Cardians' defenses. Diopeithes waited until Philip departed into northern Thrace and then made a series of raids on Philip's Thracian allies along the Aegean coastline. This violation of the treaty prompted Philip to write yet another letter to the Assembly (he had by now become a regular correspondent), protesting Diopeithes' incursions.[27]

In the speech he delivered during the debate occasioned by Philip's letter, Demosthenes reports the remarks of several of his opponents. The thrust of these remarks bears a close resemblance to the policy Aeschines advocated at his trial during the previous year. In fact, Demosthenes groups those who criticize Diopeithes with the same cabal that blamed Chares for the defeats Athens suffered in 346. Of this group Aeschines was a proud member. According to Demosthenes, the speakers of this persuasion demanded that the Assembly recall Diopeithes and put him on trial. In their opinion, it was Diopeithes who was the greatest threat to the peace and freedom of the Greeks. Far from stirring up war, Philip had no hostile designs on Athens. What the Athenians should do is to observe the terms of the treaty with Philip and enjoy the benefits of peace. Since Philip has observed the peace, Demosthenes' opponents held that the Athenians are obligated to do likewise. There is no longer any talk of benefits to be reaped from friendship with Philip. The choice is peace or war.[28]

Demosthenes in his reply to these arguments hammered home the need for Athenian preparedness in the face of Macedonian aggression. He takes Philip's hostile aims for granted and even has the temerity to argue that Philip's campaigns in northern Thrace were aimed at subduing Athens. In Demosthenes' eyes, Philip had already broken the peace and was at war with Athens. To claim that the Athenians have a choice between peace and war is false: Philip has already made the decision to wage war. Since Philip is de facto at war with them, it is imperative to look for allies.[29]

Demosthenes had already made some progress in this direction during early 342. Not long after Aeschines' trial, Demosthenes, Hegesippus, and Polyeuctus went on another embassy to the Peloponnese and succeeded in winning over Megalopolis, the Achaeans, the Arcadians, the Argives, and the Messenians, whom

Aeschines in 348 and Demosthenes in 344 had courted without result. The shift in Peloponnesian opinion may have in part been caused by Archidamus' departure with a Spartan army for southern Italy. The main obstacle to previous Athenian efforts to form an alliance with the Peloponnesians had been Athenian ties with Sparta, but with Archidamus and a large number of Spartan soldiers away defending Tarentum, the fear of Sparta no longer stood in the way of Demosthenes' goal of forming a coalition against Philip. Philip's recent actions must have made Demosthenes' warnings more convincing. The Macedonian contribution to the bloodshed in Elis and Megara was a disturbing example of Philip's tactics, and his promise to the Aetolians to make a gift of Naupactos was a direct threat to the Peloponnese.[30]

Callias of Chalcis, the man who led the Euboeans to victory over the Athenians in 348, was also becoming worried about Philip's actions. Aeschines later claimed that Callias turned to Athens only after falling from grace with Philip and failing to secure help from Thebes, but his animus toward Callias, who worked closely with his rival Demosthenes, makes his interpretation suspect. Callias' fears were more likely to have been activated by the growing power of Philip's friends in Eretria and by the mercenaries sent by Philip to capture Porthmos for his friends in Oreos. Callias himself had enjoyed the friendship of Philip, but these developments represented a threat to Euboean independence. Finding the price of Macedonian friendship too high, Callias sent ambassadors to Athens to see if he could obtain a better bargain from the Assembly. Callias was probably aware that Demosthenes was casting about for allies and would be willing to make a generous bid for an alliance with Euboea. His demands were substantial: he offered the Athenians an alliance with Chalcis and in return asked for help against Philip's allies in Oreos and Eretria. Once liberated, these cities would not rejoin the Athenian Confederacy, to which they had belonged prior to 348, and pay contributions to its treasury, but instead would join with Chalcis and form a Euboean League under the leadership of Callias.

Many years later, Aeschines criticized the arrangement for depriving Athens of Euboean contributions to the treasury of the confederacy. Demosthenes responded by accusing Aeschines of collaborating with Philip's friends in Oreos and Eretria. Demosthenes' charge is yet another piece of unsubstantiated slander, but Aeschines' criticism is also off the mark. The Athenians lost the Euboean contributions as a result of their defeat on the island in 348, not from the alliance Demosthenes promoted in 342. Demosthenes may not have liked the terms of the alliance with Chalcis, but he knew that the only way Callias could rally the Euboeans behind the leadership of Chalcis was to summon them to defend the independence of the island from outside interference. If Callias were to promise to Athens to bring Euboea back into the confederacy, he could not very well pose as liberator. Aeschines later saw the concessions made by Demosthenes as proof of his venality and ridiculed his policy of providing help first, concluding alliances afterward. But Demosthenes' policy was a sensible one given the circumstances. Philip had won allies by providing benefits; if the Athenians were to compete with him at this game, they, too, would have to back their words up with friendly actions. The Assembly agreed with Demosthenes and in the following months sent Athenian hoplites to drive out Philistides from Oreos and Clitarchus from Eretria. Accustomed to suffering defeat, the Athenians suddenly had something to celebrate. Aeschines' policy of trusting Philip had brought Athens nothing; Demosthenes' policy of rallying the Greeks was beginning to produce tangible results. In recognition of his achievements in Euboea, the Assembly voted to grant Demosthenes a crown and to have this honor announced in the theater of Dionysus.[31]

As Demosthenes' influence rose, Aeschines' position became weaker. The decline in his fortunes is well illustrated by two incidents that occurred between his trial and the outbreak of war with Philip in 340. Sometime during this period, Demosthenes seized Antiphon, an Athenian who had lost his citizenship during the review of the citizen lists in 346, and brought him before the Assembly, where he accused him of having promised to Philip to burn down the dockyards of the Athenian fleet. Aeschines immediately objected to the manner in which Demosthenes made the arrest. Demosthenes claimed to have found Antiphon hiding in a house, but Aeschines pointed out that he had acted illegally by entering a house without a decree authorizing him to do so. Despite its increasing suspicion of Philip, the Assembly recognized the correctness of Aeschines' argument and decided to have Antiphon released. But the matter did not end there. Demosthenes' allegations aroused the suspicions of the Areopagus, which launched an investigation of its own. The Areopagus evidently concluded that there was something to Demosthenes' accusation and had Antiphon arrested a second time. Urged on by the Areopagus, the Assembly decided to get to the bottom of the matter and had Antiphon tortured. Antiphon must have confessed for he was subsequently executed.[32]

Antiphon may have been guilty or may simply have been the victim of anti-Macedonian hysteria whipped up by Demosthenes. Demosthenes, the main source for the incident, provides no details and takes Antiphon's guilt for granted. That Antiphon confessed does not confirm Demosthenes' accusation since confessions obtained by torture are notoriously unreliable as evidence. The most one can infer is that the Athenians thought there was enough evidence against Antiphon to justify his execution. Nor is there any reason to see Aeschines' defense of Antiphon as a sign of his complicity in his alleged plot. Aeschines' objection to the first arrest was based on a sound legal argument and was clearly aimed at preventing Demosthenes from fomenting a witch-hunt against Philip's supporters. But the confession of Antiphon did much harm to his credibility and aroused the doubts of the Areopagus, which led to one of the worst humiliations Aeschines was to endure.

Not long after the execution of Antiphon, the Athenians elected Aeschines to represent them in a dispute over the temple on Delos, which the inhabitants of the island had claimed as their own property. The case had come before the Amphictyons in Delphi, and Aeschines may have been elected because of his success in persuading that body to accept a milder punishment for the Phocians. In an unusual move, the Assembly invited the Areopagus to review the election of Aeschines and granted them the power to appoint a replacement if they saw fit. The unusual procedure was probably employed because the dispute involved a religious matter and thus came within the sphere of business overseen by the Areopagus. The Areopagus decided to strip Aeschines of his post and entrusted the task of defending Athenian interests to Hyperides, who ably presented the Athenian brief and obtained a favorable judgment from the Amphictyons.[33]

Demosthenes says that the Areopagus based its decision to deprive Aeschines of his post on its suspicions about his loyalty. His interpretation of their move gains support from their selection of Hyperides, a man who had recently demonstrated his patriotism by convicting the traitor Philocrates, as his replacement. Yet whatever doubts the Areopagus may have had about Aeschines' loyalty, neither they nor anyone else went as far as to indict him for treason during these years. His acquittal in 343 appears to have deterred his opponents from further judicial attacks. Nevertheless, the slanders of Demosthenes had made an impression on the Areopagus, which apparently held politicians to a higher standard than the Assembly did.

It is tempting to blame the decline of Aeschines in the later 340s on the unrelenting demagoguery of Demosthenes and Hegesippus. One could argue that Philip was genuinely interested in forging better ties with the Athenians and adduce his offer to revise the terms of the treaty of 346 as proof of his sincerity. On the other hand, the hostile interpretation of Philip's motives put forward by Demosthenes and Hegesippus is certainly farfetched. By his actions after 346, Philip showed he had little interest in undermining Athenian power. The Macedonian army remained far north of Thermopylai for the entire period, with the sole exception of short expeditions into Thessaly. Demosthenes' idea that Philip's campaign in Thrace was actually directed at Attica is ludicrous. The king's assistance to Cardia was nothing more than the protection of an ally whose freedom had been threatened. Demosthenes repeatedly asserted that Philip was obsessed with the defeat of Athens, but Philip's words and actions tell a different story. Philip's invitation to discuss the revision of the Peace of Philocrates was certainly made in good faith, and Hegesippus' allegations about the sinister motives behind the proposals of 343 exceed the limits of credibility.[34]

There can be no question that Demosthenes and Hegesippus present a distorted picture of Philip's action to justify their own policy of opposition to Macedon. But twisting the truth is part of the stock in trade of many politicians. Furthermore, it does not explain why the Athenians preferred to listen to their slanders about Philip and to follow their proposals. Whatever Philip's motives may have been, two things were indisputable. First, the position of Athens was worse after 346 than it had been before. Second, Philip had greatly increased his power and influence after the Peace of Philocrates. Aeschines argued at his trial that the Athenians would have been in a far worse position if the treaty had not been ratified, but this argument was too hypothetical to carry much weight in the Assembly. Aeschines could not deny that Philip, Thessaly, and Thebes had gained in 346 and that Athens had lost, and these two facts provided Demosthenes and Hegesippus with their most potent argument. Events after 346 only helped to strengthen their case. Philip's aid to his friends in Euboea, Megara, and Elis, and Philocrates' flight from Athens to avoid prosecution appeared to confirm their worst predictions.

In 346 Aeschines had placed his trust in Philip's promises and assured the Assembly they would reap large benefits from their Macedonian alliance. When events did not turn out as predicted, Aeschines argued that Philip's failure to deliver on his promises was caused by the Athenian refusal to send troops at the critical moment. In the next years, Aeschines clung to the hope that Philip was only waiting for an opportunity to deliver the gifts he had promised. But the benefits Philip finally came up with were too little, too late. The Athenians had been led to expect the liberation of Boeotia from Theban control. In 343 they were presented with the puny gift of Halonnesus, an offer to have their dispute with Cardia submitted to arbitration, a treaty regulating judicial procedure, and an invitation to rid the Aegean of pirates. None of these proposals brought the Athenians gains large enough to offset their losses of 346. In comparison with the lavish promises Aeschines made after the Second Embassy, these benefits were mere crumbs. After the failure of Philip's attempt to revise the treaty, Aeschines was forced back to the uninspiring alternative of defending peace for the sake of peace.

Philip's inability to come up with more attractive proposals was not a sign of hostility to Athens. Contrary to Demosthenes' hyperbolic claims, Philip's overriding interest was in maintaining a status quo that was advantageous to Macedon. The settlement approved by the Amphictyons in 346 guaranteed a delicate stability in central Greece, and Philip had no desire to disturb it. And he could not yield to Athenian demands to free Boeotia without disrupting this settlement. In northern Greece, Philip could not reasonably be expected to return Amphipolis nor to abandon his allies in Cardia to the depredation of a freebooting general. Philip valued the friendship of the Athenians and tried to place the alliance on a stronger basis. But Athens was not his only ally, and his obligations to his other friends prevented him from finding some strategic or territorial advantage to bestow on Athens. In the final analysis, the two sides clashed because one side found the balance of power to its liking, while the other did not.

If Aeschines failed to convince the Athenians to follow his policy of cooperation with Philip, it was not entirely his fault. Aeschines may have oversold the advantages of the Macedonian alliance, but Philip also did not provide him with the benefits for Athens that he needed to make the case for his policy compelling. When given a choice between Aeschines, whose predictions of Macedonian largesse never materialized, and Demosthenes, whose embassies had gained allies for Athens in Euboea and the Peloponnese, the Assembly naturally chose the latter.

7

Decline and Exit

From the Siege of Byzantium to the Defeat at Chaeronea

In the last phase of his career, Aeschines made a series of attempts to play a major role once again on the Athenian political scene, only to find himself repeatedly upstaged by Demosthenes. But Demosthenes' triumphant performance in the Assembly did not bring Athens victory over Philip in the battlefield. In 338 the Athenians and their Greek allies suffered a crushing defeat at Chaeronea, which put an end to Demosthenes' hopes of pushing Philip back to his homeland behind Mount Olympus. Looking back in 330 on the events leading up to Chaeronea, Demosthenes charged Aeschines with standing in the way of his plans and working hand in hand with Philip to promote Macedonian aims. Aeschines retorted that he always had Athenian interests at heart. Had the Athenians followed his advice, he countered, they would never have suffered the ignominious defeat at Chaeronea. Were Aeschines' criticisms of Demosthenes' policies justified? Did his own proposals represent a patriotic alternative, or were they merely obstructionist measures, aimed at furthering Philip's ambitions?

In 340 Aeschines witnessed the final collapse of his attempts to preserve peace with Philip. The outbreak of hostilities occurred in the Hellespont, where tensions between Philip and Athens had been building up ever since the defeat of Cersebleptes in 346. The immediate cause of the war lay in the suspicions Philip's conquests aroused in his allies Perinthos and Byzantium. Both of these cities had enjoyed Philip's protection against the Thracian kings in previous years, but by 340 had started to worry that their erstwhile liberator might turn oppressor. The people of Perinthos decided to appeal to Athens. We do not know what form the negotiations took nor what the outcome was, but the shift in allegiance was naturally regarded by Philip as an act of disloyalty and ingratitude for past favors. Philip moved quickly to punish Perinthos for its treachery, launching a siege in early 340. Reinforced by soldiers and catapults from Byzantium and supplied with money from local Persian satraps, the people of Perinthos put up a stiff resistance. After several fruitless months, Philip left a token force to continue the siege and took the rest of his troops to attack Selymbria and his other disloyal ally, Byzantium. At about the same time, he launched a sort of preemptive strike against Athens by seizing the fleet bringing grain from the Black Sea. In another of his letters to the Assembly, Philip defended his action on the grounds that the fleet was carrying supplies to his enemy Selymbria. The provocation was more than the testy Assembly could tolerate. The stele on which the terms of the Peace of Philocrates were written was smashed to pieces, and preparations were immediately made to help Byzantium.[1]

Once the war began, Aeschines did not give in to anger and frustration and withdraw from politics. During the debate about the reform of naval organization in 340, Aeschines doggedly attacked Demosthenes' proposals to alter the old system and forced him to amend them. Demosthenes' proposals were formulated to remove the inefficiencies and inequities of the old system whereby the wealthiest twelve hundred Athenians were divided into twenty symmories of sixty members each. These symmories paid contributions to purchase equipment for the fleet and provided the men who served as captains of the triremes. In 346 Demosthenes had already noted how rich men like Meidias could manipulate the system to minimize their contributions and to avoid serving as captains. The cumulative effect of these abuses was to place a disproportionate share of the burden on the less wealthy members of the symmories, who found it difficult to pay their assigned sums. Demosthenes proposed to remedy these problems by placing the entire responsibility for the fleet in the hands of the Three Hundred, the richest stratum of Athenian society, who had served as the "Leaders," "Second Men," and "Third Men" of the symmories.

Demosthenes says that his reform met with fierce opposition from the Three Hundred and alleges that Aeschines "damaged" his proposal in return for a "friendly loan" from the Three Hundred. Aeschines, on the other hand, accuses Demosthenes of surreptitiously removing captains from sixty-five fully manned ships. It is unclear what Aeschines means by this. Demosthenes may have initially proposed not only that the Three Hundred furnish all the funds for the fleet, but that they also provide all the captains for the triremes. If so, Aeschines may have pointed out that three hundred was too small a number to create a pool of trierarchs large enough to staff the fleet over a long period of time, given that many would plead various excuses or claim occasional exemptions. Whatever the thrust of his criticisms, Aeschines appears to have compelled Demosthenes to alter his reform in some significant way, for his opponent implies that it was changed as a result of his objections. Demosthenes in his characteristic way later took all the credit for the reform and boasted that the naval reorganization brought Athens power and glory, presumably an allusion to the defeat of Philip at Byzantium in 340. To judge by the results of the reform, Aeschines' criticisms in no way damaged Demosthenes' proposal. Far from obstructing efforts to fight Philip, Aeschines may in fact deserve some of the credit for the success of the naval reform that helped to save Byzantium from the Macedonian army.[2]

Aeschines' support for the war was matched by his friends Phocion and Eubulus. Despite their previous advocacy of peace, both men were just as patriotic as Demosthenes when it came to defending Athenian interests against Philip. In early 340 Phocion led the Athenian troops that drove out the pro-Macedonian tyrant from Eretria and later in the same year commanded the fleet sent to rescue Byzantium. Eubulus' activities are less well attested, but Demosthenes attributes to his authorship a decree that was somehow responsible for the outbreak of the war. Despite the differences Aeschines, Phocion, and Eubulus had with Demosthenes in the past, once war loomed on the horizon, they all closed ranks and devoted their collective energies to defeating Philip.[3]

With the help of the Athenian fleet, the Byzantines were able to withstand the Macedonian siege. Sometime before the spring of 339, Philip was forced to break off the siege and marched his troops north to deal with King Atheas. Atheas ruled a tribe of Scythians near the Danube in Upper Thrace and had earlier requested Philip's protection against a neighboring tribe. In return, he had offered to adopt Philip as his son and make him his successor. But after the king of the neighboring tribe died, Atheas informed Philip that he no longer stood in need of his protection and that his own son would succeed to his throne. Philip replied by asking Atheas for a contribution for his siege of Byzantium. Atheas declined, citing the harsh climate and poor soil of his native land. Philip's request for a contribution indicates that his supplies were running low, forcing him to terminate his siege without a victory. To test Atheas' loyalty, Philip marched his troops north and asked for permission to cross his territory so he could set up a statue of Heracles at the mouth of the Danube. The stubborn Atheas refused again, provoking Philip to attack. The Scythians were defeated, and Atheas paid for his intransigence with his life. The Macedonian soldiers, denied victories at Perinthos and Byzantium, finally won a chance to help themselves to booty and made the most of the opportunity, seizing women, children, and cattle, but discovering no gold. The victory must have done much to restore the morale of the Macedonian soldiers and to repair the damage done by successive defeats to Philip's reputation as commander among his own men, but the campaign kept the king far away from Greece for several crucial months. During this time, the settlement of 346 began to fall apart. No longer under the watchful eye of Philip, several of the Greek states took advantage of his absence to settle old scores.[4]

In early 339, the Amphictyons held their regular spring meeting at Delphi. Aeschines, who attended the meeting as a *pylagore,* and Demosthenes, who was not there, give different accounts of what happened, but both agree that at the meeting the Amphictyons, acting on the advice of Aeschines, declared war on the Locrians of Amphissa for cultivating the sacred Plain of Crisa. Aeschines claims to have saved Athens from a serious charge of sacrilege and to have turned the tables on the Thebans and the Locrians. Demosthenes derides his claim and substitutes his own interpretation of the events in Delphi: Aeschines was acting on the orders of Philip, who was seeking a pretext to enter central Greece so he could strike at Attica. The incident was the most controversial event in Aeschines' career and set in motion a chain of events that culminated in the Battle of Chaeronea. Aeschines and Demosthenes, though discussing the meeting at length, give very little in the way of evidence. Two facts, however, are indisputable: first, Philip was hundreds of miles away at the time, and second, there were differences among the Amphictyons that had not been resolved by the settlement of 346.[5]

Aeschines gives a detailed narrative of the meeting, casting himself in the role of the righteous avenger of Locrian impiety. According to his own account, Aeschines was elected *pylagore* that spring along with his friend Meidias and a certain Thrasycles. Together with the *hieromnemon* Diognetus, they made their way to Delphi. After their arrival in Delphi, they learned from a friendly source that the

Locrians of Amphissa, who were allies of the Thebans, would bring a charge of sacrilege against Athens during the meeting of the Amphictyons. The formal charge would be that the Athenians had placed a dedication of golden shields in front of the new temple of Apollo before it had been consecrated and had written over the dedication an inscription saying that the shields were spoils taken from the Persians and Thebans when they fought against the Greeks. The real cause was probably Theban and Locrian resentments over Athenian support for Phocis during the Third Sacred War, a topic which the Locrian *hieromnemon* actually brought up at the meeting. The Athenian *hieromnemon* Diognetus had fallen ill on his arrival in Delphi so he asked Aeschines to take his place at the meeting of the Amphictyons. Aeschines entered the meeting and was rising to speak when he was interrupted by a member from Amphissa, whom he describes in rather unflattering terms. This rude fellow began to shout that the Athenians should be banished from the temple for their impiety and went on to recite a long list of complaints against the city. Aeschines relates that he listened to this tirade with mounting anger and indignation. When he finally got a chance to speak, he drew the attention of the Amphictyons to the Plain of Crisa below the shrine and pointed out the buildings set up there by the people of Amphissa in the sacred area dedicated to Apollo. Summoning up all his histrionic skills, Aeschines vowed to come to the aid of the god and punish the impious. Next he turned to the Amphictyons and asked them how they could perform the sacrifices standing ready at the altars while men were under the curse for cultivating sacred land. He ended by reminding them that the curse on the land also applied to those who failed to punish men who transgressed the god's orders.[6]

Aeschines describes with great pride how his words caused the meeting to forget about the Athenian dedication and to demand the punishment of the Amphissans. The heralds summoned all men of Delphi, both free and slave, as well as the *pylagores* and *hieromnemons* to report next day to the Thyteion. On the following morning, all these men marched down to the plain and set about burning down houses and buildings, when suddenly the Locrians of Amphissa appeared en masse ready for battle. Righteous indignation soon gave way to panic, and the crowd, which had left Delphi that morning filled with holy conviction, fled in undignified disorder back to the temple.

The next day, Cottyphus, a Thessalian *hieromnemon* who was presiding over the meeting, called an assembly of all those present in Delphi. Charges flew thick and fast against the people of Amphissa. It was finally decided to hold an emergency meeting of the Amphictyony at Thermopylai at which they would deliberate about measures to be taken against the Amphissans. Aeschines returned to Athens with his companions and reported about the events of the meeting to the Council. But the Council did not recommend to the Assembly that the Athenians send a representative to the emergency meeting. According to Aeschines, Demosthenes prevented the Athenians from joining in the campaign against the Amphissans by convincing an inexperienced member of the Council to draw up a *probouleuma* proposing that the *hieromnemon* and the *pylagores* attend only the regular meetings of the Amphictyony and not take part in the emergency meeting. By another ruse, Demosthenes managed to get an unwary Assembly to ratify the measure with the upshot that the Athenians did not participate at the meeting in Thermopylai at which the Amphictyons voted to march against Amphissa and chose Cottyphus to lead the army. The Thebans also abstained from the meeting. Cottyphus marched into Amphissan territory and, in Aeschines' estimation, dealt with them rather leniently, imposing a trifling fine for their enormous crimes. Philip was still far away fighting the Scyths during these events and did not return until much later. By then the Amphissans had not paid the fine, so the Amphictyons invited Philip to lead his army against the god's enemies.[7]

Demosthenes criticizes Aeschines' account as implausible. His main objection is that the Locrians could not have initiated proceedings against the Athenians without first delivering a summons. Aeschines did not defend the Athenians against a Locrian charge, but instead was bribed by Philip to create confusion and to have the Amphictyons declare a sacred war so that Philip could enter central Greece. Demosthenes brings forward no evidence to corroborate his version of what transpired at the meeting. His criticism of Aeschines' account is based entirely on procedural grounds, but the criticism is not relevant. Aeschines says that the Locrians were about to introduce a resolution, or *dogma,* for the Amphictyonic Council to vote on. Demosthenes' criticism is based on the assumption that the Locrians were initiating a form of judicial proceeding against the Athenians. Indeed, we can go one step further and say that Demosthenes falsely assimilates the procedure for moving a *dogma* in the Amphictyonic Council with the procedure for initiating a lawsuit in Athens in a deliberate attempt to mislead the court, which would probably have known nothing about the details of Amphictyonic procedure. This is made clear when Demosthenes asks "who served as witness to the summons?" He is referring to a well-known aspect of Athenian legal procedure whereby the plaintiff was required to have witnesses present when he delivered his summons to the defendant. Thus, Demosthenes' only argument to discredit Aeschines' account is worthless.[8]

There is still the larger question raised by Demosthenes' allegation that Aeschines was bribed by Philip. Demosthenes furnishes no witnesses to prove the charge, which rests solely on circumstantial evidence. To evaluate the charge, we need to examine Demosthenes' explanation of Philip's motives at the time. According to Demosthenes, Philip needed a pretext to convince the Thessalians to allow him free passage through Boeotia to reach Attica. His description of Philip's motives is implausible. Philip did not need a sacred war to enter Greece. He already wielded considerable influence among the Thessalians, who were in his debt for defeating the Phocians and restoring them to their position of honor in the Amphictyony. As for the Thebans, Philip had an alliance with them and knew that there was a great deal of anti-Athenian sentiment in their ranks. As Aeschines' narrative reveals, the Thebans were still angry about Athenian support for the Phocians during the Third Sacred War and had not forgotten Aeschines' plea to Philip for the liberation of Boeotia from Theban control. And if the alleged plot between Philip and Aeschines was aimed at convincing the Thebans to allow the Macedonian army to march through Boeotia, it was a dismal failure for the immediate result of the "plot" that allowed Philip to seize Elateia was to alienate the Thebans to the point where they were willing to listen to Demosthenes and to conclude an alliance with Athens. It is also difficult to comprehend why, if Philip wished to gain the consent of Thebes, he concocted a plot in which the Locrians, the traditional allies of Thebes, were to be accused of sacrilege, attacked by an Amphictyonic army, and punished with a fine.

Furthermore, if there really had been a plot, it was timed extremely poorly, for the sacred war broke out when Philip was far removed from the scene, fighting the Scyths in the north. It certainly would have made more sense for the conspirators to have delayed the Amphictyonic declaration of war until Philip could return to Greece where he could fully exploit the situation created by the plot. Finally, if Philip wanted to stir up this sacred war to persuade the Thebans to side with him against Athens, it is strange that we never hear of Philip using the sacred war in his negotiations with the Thebans. Demosthenes' account of the speeches given by Philip's ambassadors in Thebes later that year contains not a word about the sacred war. Diodorus' account of Philip's appeal to Thebes does not report the content of these speeches, but does state that the Athenians were worried that the Thebans would join Philip because they were his allies. The only evidence of Philip using the sacred war to further his aims that Demosthenes can cite comes from a letter addressed to his Peloponnesian allies. But Demosthenes never asserts that Philip engineered his plot to win them over to his side.[9]

Demosthenes' charges of bribery and conspiracy are implausible, lack evidence, and should therefore be rejected. Aeschines' account of the outbreak of the sacred war is backed up only by the decree passed by the Amphictyons condemning the Amphissan sacrilege and calling for an emergency meeting. He furnishes no evidence for his narrative of the meeting at which he accused the Amphissans of impiety; but Demosthenes agrees that he delivered such a speech. Furthermore, Demosthenes' attempt to discredit the rest of his opponent's narrative is specious. What we know for certain is that Aeschines denounced the Amphissans, that the Amphissans attacked the Delphians and Amphictyons in the sacred plain below the temple, that Cottyphus called a meeting at which the Amphictyons voted to hold an emergency session at Thermopylai to discuss measures against Amphissa, and that the Athenians did not send representatives to the emergency session. We can probably go further and trust in its essentials Aeschines' claim that the Locrians of Amphissa started the quarrel by accusing the Athenians.[10]

It is not necessary to invent a plot hatched by Aeschines and Philip to explain these events. All of the principals in the dispute—the Athenians, the Thessalians, and the Thebans—had enough grievances among them to ignite a conflict without Philip's lighting the flame. The Thebans had several complaints. They and their allies the Locrians were still angry over Athenian support for the Phocians during the last sacred war. The Thebans no doubt also resented Aeschines' proposal to have Philip liberate Boeotia from their control. In addition, they felt cheated when Philip handed over Nikaia to the Thessalians after the defeat of Phocis. During Philip's absence from Greece, they took matters into their own hands and grabbed the coveted territory from the Thessalians. This naturally infuriated the Thessalians, who then seized on Aeschines' accusation against the Amphissans to hit back at the Thebans by punishing their ally. We should bear in mind that it was the Thessalian Cottyphus who presided over the meeting that condemned the Amphissans and who later led the Amphictyonic army against them. The Thessalians controlled a large bloc of votes on the Amphictyonic Council and no decision against the Amphissans could have been taken without their consent. Aeschines, of course, would have welcomed the opportunity to lash out at an ally of Thebes and to restore Athenian prestige in the Amphictyony. Indeed, it was not Philip's involvement that sparked the conflict, but his absence. While Philip was close by and able to intervene quickly, the Athenians, Thebans, and Thessalians did not dare disturb the settlement arranged by Philip in 346. Once Philip was far away and his prestige at a low ebb after his setbacks at Perinthos and Byzantium, each of these powers felt free to pursue vendettas that the settlement of 346 had restrained, but not eliminated.[11]

Aeschines' actions at the meeting were clearly directed against Amphissa and Thebes. He felt that he was defending the honor of Athens and seeking to promote Athenian interests. His hostility to Thebes is a familiar theme. He had encouraged Philip to humble the arrogance of Thebes in 346 and for several years afterward had clung to the hope that the king might still follow his advice. In the spring of 339 he finally found his chance to humiliate Thebes. Nothing in his speech of 330 shows that he had any higher aim than defending Athens and attacking Thebes and her ally when he made his charge against the Locrians.

Though we can discard Demosthenes' charges of bribery and collusion, Aeschines is still open to the accusation that he inadvertently helped Philip by creating a situation favorable to his designs. The best way to find out whether Aeschines' actions in Delphi helped Philip or not is to look at the situation that confronted the king upon his return to Greece in late 339. The situation Philip encountered at the time was fraught with difficulties. During his absence, the Thessalians had led the Amphictyons into a sacred war without his consent and had defeated the Locrians without his help. Such an assertion of leadership in the Amphictyony was a challenge to his own influence in the body. It also demonstrated that the Thessalians were capable of going their own way and were no longer under Philip's control. Worse still was the dangerous split between the Thebans and the Thessalians, two of his most important allies. The Thebans had angered the Thessalians by taking Nikaia, and the Thessalians had retaliated by punishing the Locrians. With Athens openly challenging his position in Greece, Philip could not afford any disunity in his own ranks.

Philip's first task was to reassert his hegemony in Thessaly and in the Amphictyony. Luckily for him, the Amphissans had not paid the fine imposed on them by the Amphictyony after Cottyphus' campaign. This gave Philip a pretext for renewing the sacred war against Amphissa. Once elected general by the Amphictyons to prosecute the war, he was able to summon troops from Thessaly and gain control of the situation there. The Thessalian troops, after joining up with the Macedonian army, would have to march to Philip's orders. With Thessaly back in his grip, Philip now conveniently forgot about his duty to conduct the Amphictyonic expedition against Amphissa. Philip marched his army south on the road to Amphissa, but on reaching Cytinion, he did not continue south, but suddenly veered east and led his troops to Elateia in Phocis, right next to the Boeotian border. From there he tried to win over the Thebans. Of course, Philip could not appeal to them as Amphictyons and expect them to join in a campaign against their Locrian allies. Although the sacred war had proven useful in his effort to reassert his position in Thessaly and in the Amphictyony, it had not become a distinct liability in dealing with the Thebans.

Instead, Philip's ambassadors reminded them of all the benefits the king had bestowed upon them in the past, especially his assistance during the Third Sacred War. Philip never conferred favors without strings attached. He now expected his Theban friends to reciprocate. His other means of appealing to the Thebans was to invite them to join in an assault on Athens, or at least, to allow him to march his army through Boeotia so as to strike at Attica. At the same time, he realized that the Thebans would not fall in next to the Thessalians unless he resolved the dispute about Nikaia. As a result, he offered a compromise solution, proposing to give the territory to the Locrians.[12]

In one of the most renowned passages in Greek literature, Demosthenes describes the panic that overtook the Athenians when they heard about Philip's presence in Elateia. The *prytanes* immediately called a meeting of the Council and summoned the Assembly. When the Athenians gathered on the Pnyx and the herald called for speakers to address the Assembly, no one rose except for Demosthenes. He moved that the infantry and the cavalry proceed immediately to Eleusis to make a show of force. He also proposed that an embassy of ten men travel to Thebes and offer to come to their assistance against Philip. The Assembly passed his proposals and elected him to head the embassy to Thebes. Demosthenes, more interested in celebrating his own achievement than in revealing the details of the treaty, tells us only that the Thebans accepted his proposed alliances and passes over in silence its provisions. By informing us about these provisions, Aeschines shows that the Thebans may have been won over less by Demosthenes' eloquence than by the enormous concessions he was willing to make to the Thebans. The terms of the treaty called for Athens to pay two thirds of the expenses of the war and to yield the command of the allied army entirely to the Thebans. Despite Aeschines' criticisms, this was probably a necessary concession since the campaign against Philip took place in territory under Theban control. It was customary in Greek alliances for the allied army, when in the territory of one of the allies, to obey the generals from that state. The burden of paying two thirds of the expenses was heavy, but it was Boeotian territory that would be devastated by the campaign, not Attic. At sea the Athenians were forced to share the command with the Thebans in spite of the fact that the Theban fleet was almost nonexistent. The next provision must have been especially galling to Aeschines: the Athenians were required to recognize Theban control of Boeotia. Demosthenes probably recognized that Aeschines' proposal to Philip to liberate Boeotia was one of the major causes for Theban hostility to Athens and that the Athenians would have to reject in explicit terms this aim if they wanted to gain their friendship. From the events that followed in the next months, the Athenians appear to have also agreed to assist the Thebans in defending Amphissa. Philip, of course, had nothing to offer in response to this. He could postpone his expedition against Amphissa indefinitely, but he could not renounce it without appearing hypocritical and offending the Thessalians. Ironically enough, it was Aeschines, who, by helping to stir up the sacred war, had placed this trump card in Demosthenes' hand. This had not been Aeschines' intention, and he never claimed any credit for it later. Had he had his way, the Athenians would have helped the Thessalians to punish Amphissa.[13]

One cannot argue that the declaration of the sacred war was to Philip's advantage. As subsequent events themselves show, the conflict created an intractable problem for Philip, one which he was unable to solve by diplomacy. His only way out of the impasse was to try to exploit anti-Athenian sentiment in Thebes, but his attempt foundered, and Philip found himself facing the combined armies of Athens, Thebes, and several other Greek communities that had joined Demosthenes' Hellenic League. This was by far the largest Greek army Philip had so far been up against. His victory over the Phocians in 352 had only been gained after two defeats, and his final triumph over them in 346 had been won without a spear being cast. Up to this point, Philip had been able to isolate his enemies and defeat them one by one. He now was confronted by the coalition Demosthenes had striven to build since 344. Aeschines thus did not inadvertently help to create a situation favorable to Philip. If Aeschines erred in his judgment, it was in trying to convince the Athenians to take part in the Amphictyonic campaign against Amphissa. Had the Athenians followed his advice, it might have destroyed any chance for a rapprochement between Athens and Thebes. In this regard, Demosthenes was far more prescient than Aeschines.

Having been turned down by the Thebans, Philip decided to return to his role as leader of the Amphictyony and to appeal to the Peloponnesians for support in his campagin against Amphissa. His appeal was fruitless insofar as none of the Peloponnesians came over to his side, but it may have had the beneficial effect of providing several of them with an excuse not to enter the war on the other side for few of them fought with the Athenians and Thebans. As leader of the Amphictyony, Philip turned against Amphissa, which had in the meantime been reinforced by the Thebans and mercenaries under Chares. By pretending to retreat from Amphissa, Philip lured these troops away from the city, then doubled back to capture it before the Greeks could rush back to defend it. After the capture of Amphissa, a stalemate ensued. The only other military actions attested between the capture of Elateia and the Battle of Chaeronea are two skirmishes in western Boeotia.[14]

After briefly regaining center stage at Delphi, Aeschines was again thrust back into the shadows by Demosthenes. Just as he had not deserted the Assembly after the outbreak of war in 340, Aeschines did not abandon politics after the conclusion of the alliance with Thebes. Aeschines recounts that he criticized the sending of ten thousand mercenaries under Chares and Proxenus to protect Amphissa. His criticism was probably based on the argument that these troops were needed to strengthen the army in Boeotia or that it was poor strategy to divide the Greek forces in the face of the Macedonian army. Once more his criticism was shortsighted. The agreement to send troops to Amphissa is likely to have been one of the conditions demanded by the Thebans in exchange for their alliance. To refuse to send these troops would have strained relations with Thebes, and that would have been to the advantage of no one other than Philip. Aeschines, however, never saw the need for cultivating good relations with Thebes.[15]

Demosthenes' prestige in the Assembly was so great in this period that he had no trouble thwarting an attempt by Philip to conclude peace. The evidence for his offer is rather vague, consisting of some statements by Aeschines and a pair of brief references by Plutarch. Aeschines speaks of negotiations initiated by Philip with the magistrates of the Boeotian League and halted by Demosthenes, while Plutarch twice mentions a proposal made to the Athenians. Neither Aeschines not Plutarch provides us with any details about the proposals. All that can be inferred is that Philip advanced them sometime before the Battle of Chaeronea. Plutarch says that Phocion recommended accepting Philip's offer, and Aeschines may have shared his opinion, since he later criticized Demosthenes for rejecting them. But it was Demosthenes who held sway in the Assembly. Demosthenes had no intention of listening to Philip and probably interpreted his offer as a sign of weakness. Demosthenes was determined to force a showdown with Philip and confident that the combined forces of the Athenians, Boeotians, and other Greek allies were assured a victory over the Macedonian army.[16]

In hindsight it was easy for Aeschines to criticize Demosthenes for his overconfidence before Chaeronea. Yet one must recall that before 338 Philip had won most of his victories against tribes in the north, whose armies were of a far lower caliber than those fielded by the Athenians and Thebans. Philip's record against the Phocians was hardly impressive. His victory at Crocus Field had been preceded by two defeats, and his victory in 346 was achieved without bloodshed after Phalaecus found himself surrounded by Macedonians, Thessalians, and Thebans. In 338, however, the Thebans were opposing him and had been joined by Athens and troops from Euboea, Achaea, Corinth, Megara, Leucas, Corcyra, and probably Acarnania. These combined forces probably outnumbered the Macedonians and Thessalians under Philip, giving Demosthenes good reason for optimism. In Demosthenes' view it made no sense to compromise with Philip. Since Philip was bent on destroying Greek freedom (so Demosthenes argued), a treaty would only have delayed the inevitable confrontation. The moment had come for the Greeks to crush Philip once and for all. Demosthenes was not about to throw away the chance he had sought for six years.

Having exhausted all his options, Philip had no choice but to fight. On Metageitnion 9, 338, which fell in August, the two armies clashed at Chaeronea. The outcome was exactly the opposite of what Demosthenes expected: Philip routed the Greek army and inflicted devastating losses. A thousand Athenians fell in battle; two thousand more were taken prisoner. The Boeotian losses were equally severe. Demosthenes is reported to have thrown away his shield and fled the battlefield in disgrace.[17]

Demosthenes' oratory had convinced the Athenians to expect the worst from Philip, and after the disaster at Chaeronea they set about preparing for the worst. The Assembly decreed that women and children be evacuated from the countryside and placed inside the walls. On the motion of Hyperides, the Council was instructed to go in arms to the Piraeus and secure the harbor against attack. To make up for the losses at Chaeronea, the Assembly summoned men older than fifty to military duty. Demosthenes moved proposals to strengthen the city's defenses and was appointed to the task of overseeing the import of food supplies. Requests were sent to Andros, Ceos, Troizen, and Epidauros for assistance. Another measure granted the Areopagus the power to execute all those who deserted the city during the crisis. Dozens of wealthy citizens voluntarily stepped forward to contribute money for the city's protection. In this atmosphere of panic, Hyperides went so far as to propose an unheard of measure: he moved that the slaves of Attica be freed and the disen-franchised and metics be given citizenship so they could serve in the army and repel Philip's anticipated invasion.[18]

Philip did not fulfill Demosthenes' dire predictions. Instead of marching on Attica, Philip released all the Athenian prisoners without ransom and sent his son Alexander and his general Antipater to Athens with an offer to conclude a treaty of peace and alliance. Philip had no desire to annihilate Athens; his aim remained the same as it always had been, that is, to maintain Athenian friendship without allowing them to strengthen their position to the point where they could challenge Macedo-nian power. The settlement Philip imposed reflected this aim. The Athenians were to receive the gift of Oropos, a territory that the Thebans had seized from them in 366. Eight years earlier, when Philip achieved his settlement of the Third Sacred War, it made little sense for him to reward the Athenians at the expense of his loyal ally Thebes. With Thebes now a defeated foe, the situation was different. The restoration of Oropos could be used to punish Thebes and to give evidence of Philip's goodwill toward Athens. To balance this gift, however, Philip insisted that the Athenians renounce their confederacy. The only overseas possessions they were to retain were Lemnos, Scyros, Samos, and Delos. The loss of the confederacy was more a blow to Athenian pride than to her power, since in 338 it was only a shadow of the vigorous organization founded in 378. In other regards Philip's terms were lenient. There was no demand for a Macedonian garrison stationed on the Acropolis, a change of constitution, or a purge of political opponents.[19]

The Thebans received much harsher treatment. Unlike the Athenians, they were compelled to pay ranson for the release of their prisoners and the recovery of their dead. Philip then placed a garrison in Thebes and forced the city to accept the recall of three hundred political exiles. Besides detaching Oropos from their control Philip restored the cities of Plataia, Orchomenos, and Thespiai. The king may also have curtailed the powers of Thebes within the Boeotian League. Even if no actual changes were made in the constitution of the league, the restoration of the three cities that had traditionally resisted Theban hegemony would have done much to limit Theban influence in the organization.[20]

Aeschines was elected along with his old associate Phocion and a political newcomer named Demades to serve as members of the embassy that negotiated the treaty with Philip. There was probably very little negotiating for them to do since the terms were clearly dictated by Philip. Some of the treaty's terms bear a curious resemblance to the proposals Aeschines made to Philip in 346. During the Second Embassy Aeschines had urged Philip to deliver his promised benefits to Athens and to end Theban domination in Boeotia. Aeschines finally received his wish in 338, but he could not have been ecstatic about the package it came in. Though Thebes was humbled and Athens gained Oropos, Aeschines never appears to have boasted about the results of his embassy to Philip, which had occurred in such humiliating circumstances. It is also doubtful that Philip had Aeschines' earlier suggestions in mind when he decided upon the form of the settlement of 338. The idea of weaken-ing Thebes was a punishment for recent disloyalty, not the delayed fulfillment of a long-range strategy adopted at the instigation of Aeschines in 346.[21]

After arranging settlements with Athens and Thebes, Philip led his army to the

Isthmus, where he received the capitulation of Corinth. Thence he marched to the Peloponnese where he demanded that Sparta give up certain areas claimed by its neighbors. When the Spartans remained intransigent, Philip invaded their territory and made gifts out of the disputed territories to the cities that claimed them. Argos received a large portion of the Argolid south of Thyrea, Messene the Denthalitis, Tegea the Skiritis area, and Megalopolis Belemina. Besides placing all these cities in his debt, Philip also created a cordon sanitaire around Sparta to keep its army from disturbing his settlement both within and beyond the Peloponnese.[22]

Philip's next move was to place his settlement on a firmer basis. In the winter of 338/37 he summoned the Greeks to send representatives to Corinth. There he invited them to participate in a Common Peace modeled on the previous arrangements known by the same name. By the terms of the treaty, all the Greeks were guaranteed their freedom and autonomy in return for a pledge to defend the security of the Macedonian throne. To preserve stability and peace, all the Greeks swore that they would not pass any revolutionary measures such as unlawful executions, confiscations of property, redistribution of land, cancellation of debts, or the liberation of slaves for the purpose of insurrection. They also pledged to refrain from interfering in the affairs of other states by overthrowing their established governments or providing exiles with a base from which to launch assaults. If any community were to violate the oath, all the rest were obligated to punish the offender by expulsion from the settlement and by military action. To enforce these provisions and to resolve disputes among members, a *synedrion* or council was established. Each community sent a delegation of representatives to the *synedrion*, the number of representatives probably proportional to the size of the military contribution made to the army of the alliance. Either at this meeting or a subsequent one, Philip had the *synedrion* vote for war against Persia and elect himself leader of the Greek forces.[23]

The Common Peace of 338 and the League of Corinth were the fruit of the lessons Philip had learned from the failure of the settlement of 346 and of his previous relations with the Greeks. Prior to 338 Philip had won over the cities of central and southern Greece one by one, offering each some reward to gain its friendship. To the Thessalians he had restored their position of honor in the Amphictyony. For the Thebans he had forced the surrender of the Phocians and freed their lost territory in western Boeotia. In Euboea he had given succor to men like Hipparchus and Clitarchus, who were vying for power against local rivals. In Megara he had supplied Ptoiodorus and Perillus with mercenaries. In the Hellespont he had gained allies by subduing Cersebleptes and had defended Cardia against Athenian encroachments. But the policy had its drawbacks. To help one community, Philip had to take its side against its enemies, who thus became his enemies. Second, the policy was directed mainly at short-term advantages by exploiting conflicts, but was not conducive to long-term stability. Third, Philip's intervention in the internal affairs of the Greeks was anathema to their hallowed traditions of constitutional government and local autonomy. While help for conspirators like Ptoiodorus and Perillus may have won him friends, it also alienated Greek opinion. Philip may in 346 have expected the Amphictyony to maintain peace and order among its members. If he did cherish this belief, the recent sacred war certainly demolished it.[24]

The new arrangement was admirably designed to provide the stability that the settlement of 346 was unable to achieve. In exchange for the promise to respect their freedom, the Greeks promised to uphold the new status quo Philip had installed. As long as the arrangement lasted, Demosthenes could no longer accuse the king of attempting to enslave the Greeks. One might interpret Philip's willingness to entrust the resolution of disputes to the *synedrion* as a sign of implicit trust in his allies. Another explanation is more plausible. By turning over the responsibility to the *synedrion,* he could maintain his own position of leadership without being forced to take sides in any quarrel among his allies. If one city went away disappointed with a decision rendered by the *synedrion,* it would have only its fellow Greeks to blame. And by committing the members of the league to punishing infractions of the Common Peace, Philip made the Greeks share the responsibility for disciplining disobedient members. With such an arrangement in place, Philip could avoid some of the unpleasant duties of policing the status quo. When the settlement was put to the test during the war stirred up by King Agis of Sparta in 331, it worked fairly well: few of the Greeks rallied to Agis' cause, and the *synedrion* cooperated with Philip's successor Alexander in bringing its leaders to justice. Long experience with the quarrelsome Greeks had taught Philip that the job of arbitrating their disputes was a thankless task. It was better to devote his energy and resources to the campaign in Asia, which would bring him glory and booty that he could distribute to the Greeks without fear of offense.[25]

Philip's settlement put a temporary end to the kind of diplomacy Aeschines had practiced. Aeschines had served his community on embassies whose mission was to conclude alliances and peace treaties. Since almost all the Greeks had now agreed to a Common Peace and were joined in one grand alliance, Aeschines' skills were no longer in demand. Aeschines was not the only one who found himself out of a job. Demosthenes, too, received little employment as an ambassador during the next fifteen years. Since power rested in the hands of the Macedonian kings and their lieutenants, the main way to advance the position of Athens was to do favors for these men in the expectation that they would reciprocate. The most skilled practitioner of the new style of diplomacy was Demades, who had been one of the prisoners released by Philip after Chaeronea and had accompanied Aeschines and Phocion on the embassy to conclude peace. Demades quickly adjusted to the new realities of power, urging the Athenians to accept the terms offered by Philip, to confer honors on the king, and to join the Common Peace and the League of Corinth. Diplomacy was replaced by flattery. In the following years, Demades secured honors for Euthycrates, an Olynthian who had helped Philip during his assault on his native city. Similar honors were awarded at his suggestion to someone, probably a Macedonian, who had helped Athenian ambassadors during negotiations with Philip. Demades may also have been responsible for the honors granted to Alcimachus, a Macedonian from Pella, and to Philip's general Antipater.[26]

The goodwill Demades earned by these gestures proved to be helpful after Philip's death in 336. After Alexander succeeded to the throne and departed to fight the Illyrians and Triballians far to the north, the Thebans with the encouragement of Demosthenes and other Athenians rose in revolt. On his return Alexander moved quickly to surround Thebes and to prevent the spread of the revolt, then took the city by assault. Angry with the Athenians for fomenting the revolt, Alexander demanded that they surrender his most dedicated enemies including Lycurgus and Demosthenes. Demades, however, drew on the goodwill he had accumulated by past favors and persuaded the king to accept a milder alternative whereby the Assembly passed a decree calling for the trial at Athens of all the men demanded by Alexander. Demades was then elected to go as ambassador to the king, who also granted his request to allow the Athenians to grant refuge to the Theban refugees. Demades' willingness to flatter the Macedonians in return for favors such as these made him indispensable for the Assembly. The money he received through his connections with the Macedonian court and the extravagant liturgies financed by this money helped him to earn prestige and gain election to the important post of Treasurer of the Military Fund.[27]

Though Aeschines had acquired much experience in negotiating with Philip, this new form of diplomacy apparently did not appeal to him. Phocion is reported to have found Demades' style of negotiating distasteful, and Aeschines seems to have held a similar attitude. Significant also is the fact that Aeschines did not capitalize on his previous relations with Philip the way Demades did. Demosthenes made no distinction between Aeschines and men like Demades, but significant differences did exist between their respective approaches to Athenian policy toward Macedon. Aeschines had supported peace and alliance with Philip in 346 out of the hope that by cooperating with Philip on an equal basis Athens would gain benefits from the relationship. Demades was willing to adjust to the new realities after Chaeronea and to recognize Macedonian hegemony in return for small favors.[28]

Aeschines ran into many of the same difficulties in the period 340–338 as he had encountered in the years leading up to 340. His major problem was his inability to hit upon an attractive alternative to Demosthenes' policy. Before 340 Aeschines tried to convince the Athenians that peace was preferable to war, but Demosthenes' success in gaining Greek allies and in expelling Philip's supporters from Euboea were achievements he could not compete with. Demosthenes' influence continued to rise after the outbreak of the war with Philip in the Hellespont, and Aeschines had no choice but to do his patriotic duty and serve the city in the struggle. During the meeting of the Amphictyony in 339 he defended Athens against the charges of the Locrians and backed the declaration of war against Amphissa. These actions were done to meet an immediate threat and did not form part of some wider strategy for advancing Athenian interests. After his return to Athens, Demosthenes again seized the initiative and dissuaded the Athenians from participating in the war against Amphissa. And when Philip surprised the Athenians by marching to Elateia, Aeschines had no ideas to offer the Assembly. Demosthenes had a clear vision of his goals and presented a decisive plan of action. Once again, his plan met with success by concluding an alliance with the Thebans. Aeschines may have advised the Athenians to accept peace with Philip before Chaeronea, but by then it was too late to counter Demosthenes' prestige in the Assembly. After the defeat at Chaeronea, there was no longer any possibility of forming an alliance on equal terms with Philip. Philip was the victor, and Athens the defeated city obliged to accept his terms. The new realities gave rise to a new form of cooperation and a new type of politician exemplified by Demades. Aeschines' approach to Athenian relations with Macedon was now outmoded. As a result, his active career in the Assembly and as an ambassador came to an end.

Waiting for the Final Performance

The last period of Aeschines' political activity forms more of an epilogue to his career than a climax. Following the defeat of Athens, Aeschines' only appearance on the public scene was his prosecution of Ctesiphon for proposing an illegal measure to praise Demosthenes. Although the charge was formally brought against Ctesiphon, the accusation focused primarily on Demosthenes' political career and was clearly an act of revenge for past slights. Aeschines had repeatedly tried to dissuade the Assembly from following Demosthenes' advice, and the crushing defeat at Chaeronea seemed to bring him a certain measure of vindication. Aeschines' criticisms of his rival finally appeared to receive confirmation: Demosthenes' policy had led directly to the worst defeat Athens had suffered since Aigospotamoi. Yet despite the verdict that the course of events seemed to have rendered on Demosthenes' leadership, Aeschines hesitated for almost two years before launching his attack, then waited another six years before bringing his case to court. To understand the reasons for the delay, we need to examine events in Athens and in Greece after Chaeronea and consider how they may have affected Aeschines' tactics during the final phase of his political duel with Demosthenes.

Immediately after Chaeronea, the Athenians took out their anger not on Demosthenes, but on the general Lysicles, who was one of the commanders at the battle. The indictment against Lysicles was brought by a newcomer called Lycurgus, who made his mark by convincing the court to put the unlucky general to death. The verdict would appear to indicate that the Athenians blamed their defeat primarily on military errors committed on the battlefield rather than on the policies made in the Assembly. Indeed, Demosthenes' reputation remained so high that the Athenians elected him to deliver the oration at the public funeral given for those who had fallen at Chaeronea. This rare distinction did not deter some politicians from trying to make Demosthenes into a scapegoat for the defeat, but none was able to repeat Lycurgus' triumph over Lysicles. Aeschines was surprisingly not among the men who attacked Demosthenes in the aftermath of Chaeronea. He may have been content to let others take the risk of prosecution or may have judged the time inopportune.[29]

Aeschines later charged that Demosthenes fell into disfavor in the months after Philip's victory. In 330 he claimed that the Assembly refused to approve proposals that bore his authorship and declined to elect him Athenian representative to the *synedrion* of the League of Corinth when he put himself forward as a candidate. Aeschines' fellow ephebe Nausicles received the post instead. Aeschines is our only source for Demosthenes' failure to gain election to this position so we cannot determine whether the charge is baseless or not. Even if Aeschines' statement is correct about Demosthenes' losing out to Nausicles, the Assembly may have preferred the latter to the former so as not to offend Philip, not as a sign of disfavor to Demosthenes. To send Demosthenes as Athenian representative to sit in the *synedrion* would not have been a wise move from a diplomatic perspective. Philip would not have enjoyed seeing Demosthenes in Corinth seated among his allies. Nausicles, who never appears to have been an outspoken enemy of Philip and was associated earlier with Aeschines, was no doubt viewed as a more appropriate candidate.[30]

Aeschines' other charge that the Assembly would not ratify Demosthenes' proposals is certainly exaggerated. We know from Aeschines himself that on Thargelion 29 in the spring of 337 Demosthenes passed a decree in the Assembly calling on the tribes to meet during the next month on Skirophorion 2 and 3 to elect superintendents and treasurers for work on the city's fortifications. At the meeting of his tribe Demosthenes was elected superintendent for the repair of the walls and received ten talents to fund the project. So much for Demosthenes' alleged unpopularity. Demosthenes also held the powerful position of Superintendent of the Theoric Fund, another fact reported to us by Aeschines.[31]

The project proposed and supervised by Demosthenes was an early example of the many internal improvements the Athenians devoted their energies to in the years after Chaeronea. Now that military campaigns were no longer draining their resources, the Athenians, both as a community and as individuals, began to spend their money on public building projects. Lycurgus, who assumed the position of Superintendent of the Theoric Fund around 336, appears to have initiated many of the projects. He is credited with constructing a palaestra at the Lyceum and a stadium near Ardettos. He may also have been responsible for the reconstruction of the theater of Dionysus. Other measures were taken to ensure the transport of grain from abroad, and in 325/24 a colony was sent to the Adriatic to secure a supply of grain from that region. The motive behind the founding of the colony was probably the desire to find an alternative to supplies from the Black Sea, which could be intercepted by the Macedonian fleet in time of conflict. Aeschines appears to have taken no active interest in these projects. He later explained his intermittent involvement in public life as the result of his modest means. His lack of funds would have been an even greater disadvantage in this period when his diplomatic skills were no longer in demand and when private generosity to public projects was one of the only means left to win renown in the Assembly. Demosthenes, in contrast, commanded substantial resources and made a generous contribution of one hundred *minai* to the project of repairing the walls of Athens, which he helped to supervise.[32]

Demosthenes' generosity inspired a little-known politician named Ctesiphon to propose honors for him sometime shortly before the end of his term of office in the summer of 336. Ctesiphon was so enthusiastic that he praised Demosthenes not only for donating money, but also for his outstanding record of achievement in public life. This was apparently more than Aeschines could take. Aeschines attacked the decree as illegal, thus blocking temporarily the award of honors. Aeschines had three reasons for his charge. First, the law of Athens made it illegal to confer honors on a magistrate for his performance in office before he laid down that office, submitted his accounts, and had his conduct approved by the boards of the *logistai* and the *euthynoi*. Second, Ctesiphon's proposal to have Demosthenes' honor announced in the theater of Dionysus appeared to contravene the law that restricted such announcements to the Council and Assembly. Third, Aeschines maintained that the Ctesiphon's proposal contained false statements, namely the assertion that Demosthenes had provided the Athenians with excellent advice throughout his career. On these legal grounds, Aeschines accused Ctesiphon of moving an illegal decree and attempted to deny Demosthenes the honor of a crown.[33]

Aeschines must have made his charge against Ctesiphon before Demosthenes completed his term of office in Skirophorion 336. Yet the statements in the speech he delivered at the trial of Ctesiphon reveal that the case did not come to court until the summer of 330. Since the decision to follow through on a prosecution appears to have lain in the hands of the prosecutor, we need to examine why Aeschines chose to delay bringing the case to court and why he finally did so in 330 and not earlier. Aeschines, himself, does not say why he chose this moment, but he must have had a good reason. In politics, as in acting, one's success is often dependent on good timing. Demosthenes understood this when prosecuting Aeschines for his conduct on the Second Embassy. The conviction of Timarchus showed him that the time was not ripe in 346 so he waited until 343 when Athenian attitudes toward Philip had changed and circumstances were more propitious. Although Aeschines is silent about the reasons that inspired him to stage his prosecution in the summer of 330, we can study the events of the period and consider how they may have affected Aeschines' decision.[34]

The assassination of Philip in the summer of 336 and the resulting uncertainty in Greece was probably the reason why Aeschines did not proceed immediately with his case against Ctesiphon. The violent death of Philip encouraged Demosthenes to believe that Macedonian power in Greece had ended. According to Aeschines, Demosthenes was jubilant at the news of the king's murder. He quickly recovered from his grief over the death of his daughter and confidently predicted that Alexander would stay in Pella and study the entrails of sacrificial beasts, not daring to leave Macedonian. On his motion, the Council voted to make an offering of thanksgiving for the welcome news.[35]

Demosthenes' rejoicing was premature. Philip's son and successor Alexander quickly mastered the situation in Macedonia, then promptly moved south to gain the support of the Thessalians for his election to the position of leader of the League of Corinth. From Thessaly he marched to Corinth where the members of the *synedrion* voted to make him their leader. With Greece again under Macedonian hegemony, Alexander departed to subdue rebellious tribes in the north. During his absence, the Thebans rose in revolt, but once more Alexander astonished his opponents. After his victory in the north, he hurried to surround Thebes with his army before they could rally support from the other Greeks and demanded their surrender. When the Thebans refused to capitulate, Alexander's army launched an assault and took the city. The Thebans who were not fortunate enough to be killed in the battle were sold into slavery, their city destroyed, and their territory divided up among their Boeotian neighbors.[36]

These sudden reversals are likely to have made an impression on Aeschines. He saw how swiftly events could change from one month to the next and how risky it was to count on favorable circumstances for more than a few weeks. This uncertainty did not end after the destruction of Thebes. In the spring of 334 Alexander led his army into Asia and began his campaign of conquest against the Great King. No Greek army had ever attempted such an expedition before, and final victory was by no means a foregone conclusion. This meant the uncertainty that had caused Aeschines to delay his prosecution in 336 continued as long as Alexander faced the possibility of defeat in Asia. According to Aeschines, Demosthenes was still confident in 333 that Alexander was about to be crushed. Just before the Battle of Issos, Demosthenes is alleged by Aeschines to have prophesied the victory of the Persian king. In his confidence, Demosthenes compared Aeschines to a bull whose horns had been gilded in preparation for sacrifice. When the news reached Athens that Alexander had routed the Persian army, Aeschines was still not free from worry since the Great King remained alive and in command of vast numbers of troops.[37]

It is tempting to believe that Aeschines' decision to bring his case against Ctesiphon to court in 330 was prompted by the defeat of the forces led by King Agis III of Sparta in the autumn of 331 or the spring of 330. Despite Philip's careful arrangements in the Peloponnese in 338, Agis was able to rally many of the states in the region behind him and defeated the Macedonian commander Corrhagus. Agis then laid siege to Megalopolis, one of the cities that did not take his side against the Macedonians. The Spartans appealed to Athens to fight alongside them, but the Assembly at the urging of Demades decided it was more prudent not to intervene. Their refusal was probably a good decision since the Macedonian general Antipater soon raised an army of forty thousand troops and confronted Agis near Megalopolis. The Peloponnesians were severely outnumbered, and Antipater won a decisive victory over Agis, who lost his life in battle.[38]

Aeschines alluded in his speech of 330 to Agis' war and Demosthenes' actions at the time, but does not place much emphasis on the topic. The most significant point to notice about Aeschines' criticism of Demosthenes' conduct during the war in the Peloponnese is that he never suggests that Athens should have joined Agis and was mistaken to have remained loyal to the Common Peace. His aim in this section is rather to demonstrate Demosthenes' hypocrisy and cowardice. He recalls Demosthenes' jingoistic words about war with Alexander, then observes how everytime an opportunity to start hostilities presents itself, Demosthenes does nothing. To illustrate his point, he adduces three opportunities that Demosthenes failed to exploit. The first was just after Alexander crossed to Asia, the second prior to the Battle of Issos, when Alexander seemed to be trapped, and the third during Agis' uprising. According to Aeschines, Demosthenes' initial reaction was to utter a few cryptic phrases about the city's impotence. Aeschines goes on to say that Demosthenes later took credit for bringing about the revolt of Thessaly and Perrhaibia, a claim that Aeschines derides as ludicrous. Nowhere does Aeschines even suggest that Agis' uprising presented Athens with a splendid opportunity, which Demosthenes foolishly threw away. Aeschines' criticism is directed not at Demosthenes' policy but at his character. He attempts to show how despite all his bluster about fighting Alexander, Demosthenes always runs from battle whenever there is a chance to rise up in arms.[39]

The reason why Aeschines brought his case against Ctesiphon to court in 330 is to be found not in Greece but in Asia. Before Alexander's final triumph over the Great King at Gaugamela in the autumn of 331, all the enemies of Macedon held on to the hope that Alexander would be defeated. The aftermath of Gaugamela put an end to that hope. After Alexander's victory, it gradually became evident that the Great King no longer had the power to overwhelm the Macedonian army. Aeschines was fully aware of the consequences of Gaugamela in the summer of 330 when he described the Great King as fleeing for his life. For Aeschines this meant that the threat of a Macedonian defeat bringing Demosthenes into power again had vanished. In contrast to Demosthenes' actions during Agis' war, which are alluded to just once, Aeschines refers to Demosthenes' taking Persian gold on four different occasions in his speech against Ctesiphon. By linking Demosthenes with the losing side in Asia, Aeschines appears to have calculated that the Athenians would take the Persian defeat at Gaugamela as a final verdict on Demosthenes misguided policies. Indeed, Aeschines' very last charge in his speech is that Demosthenes, by accepting Persian gold, has brought shame on those Athenians who died fighting at Marathon and Plataia.[40]

Aeschines had some reason to feel confident when he finally brought his case against Ctesiphon in the summer of 330. There was not only the recent triumph of Alexander, but also his victories in two previous encounters with Demosthenes, who stepped forward at the trial to defend Ctesiphon. Although Demosthenes had often prevailed in the Assembly, Aeschines had bested him twice in court, first by convicting Timarchus, second by winning his own acquittal in 343. In the intervening period, however, Aeschines appears to have forgotten nothing and learned nothing. His speech against Ctesiphon is replete with bitterness over past defeats and goes over much of the ground already covered by his speech of 343. Aeschines dwells largely in the past, nourishing old grudges, but without a vision of Athens' future. In previous speeches he vigorously defended his policy toward Philip and had a clear sense of the direction Athens ought to take. By contrast, the speech against Ctesiphon appears to be more detached from contemporary events which Aeschines regards with a certain bewilderment.[41]

Aeschines' style of presentation, too, is much the same as that of his speech against Timarchus delivered sixteen years earlier. He begins with a brief introduction containing many of the standard platitudes about the role of law in a democracy, the evils of oligarchy, and the importance of private morality in public life, which are also found in the earlier speech. Both speeches contain extensive discussions of the statutes relevant to the respective cases with careful attention paid to the intent of each law. Like the speech against Timarchus, Aeschines' speech against Ctesiphon provides a lengthy narrative of his opponent's career divided into different periods and entertains the court with various selections of poetry. The organization of the material is slightly mechanical, and one gets the impression that Aeschines learned how to construct a speech from reading a rhetorical handbook, whose precepts he followed with unswerving fidelity.[42]

Though his primary aim is to attack Demosthenes' reputation and to deny him honors, Aeschines pays careful attention to the legal grounds for declaring Ctesiphon's decree illegal. His first charge is that the decree violates the law forbidding the award of crowns to magistrates who have not yet submitted their accounts to the *logistai* and received approval from the *euthynoi*. The reason for this law, Aeschines explains, is that in the past dishonest magistrates used to have their associates pass honorary decrees for them before their term of office expired. Thus when they submitted their accounts and were discovered to have embezzled public funds, the court would be reluctant to convict them out of fear that a guilty verdict would make a mockery of the Assembly's decision to grant honors. Aeschines observes that Ctesiphon could have avoided breaking the law by calling for the award to be granted only after Demosthenes had passed his *euthynai,* but failed to do so.[43]

Since Demosthenes held an office supervising work on the walls and had not yet passed his *euthynai* at the time of Ctesiphon's decree, Aeschines would appear to have the law squarely on his side. Yet it is necessary to look at the precise wording of the law on which Aeschines relies. Aeschines paraphrases the law twice before actually quoting it. In his first paraphrase he says the law explicitly forbids the award of a crown to those subject to audit (*hypeuthynous*). The second paraphrase is similar to the first: Aeschines states that if someone is subject to audit for one office, even a very small one, the lawgiver does not allow this man to be given a crown before he undergoes his *euthynai.* It is suspicious that Aeschines does not have the clerk read the text of the law until the end of the section in which he makes his charge. Here the version of the law is slightly different: the law forbids the crowning of an office (*arche*) subject to audit. This is a subtle variation, but it has crucial significance for the legality of Ctesiphon's decree. This version implies that it was only illegal to award a crown for a term of office, that is, for the performance of the duties attached to an office, before the magistrate to receive the award passed his audit for that office. This means that the law did not prohibit a person who held an office from receiving crowns before undergoing his audit, but only a crown for his performance in that office. In other words, a magistrate still subject to audit might be able to receive a crown for some remarkable achievement, for a generous donation of money, or for earlier public service.[44]

What kind of decree had Ctesiphon in fact proposed? Curiously enough, Aeschines never has Ctesiphon's decree read out during his discussion of the laws about crowns, but only quotes a few phrases from it in two later passages. In the first passage we read that Demosthenes was praised for his merit and virtue, in the second for having dug trenches around the walls of Athens. Aeschines says this work caused the public burial grounds to be torn up, an event that occurred right after the Battle of Chaeronea when the Athenians were expecting an imminent attack by Philip. This would place Demosthenes' supervision of work on the trenches in late 338, a year before his election to the post of supervising work on the walls. Aeschines says this was only one of several good deeds listed in the decree. In the second part of the decree Demosthenes was praised for constantly saying and doing what was best for the Athenian people and credited with concluding the Theban alliance of 339. Demosthenes also quotes this phrase in his speech and adds that he was commended for donating a sum of money toward the work on the walls. The contents of Ctesiphon's decree indicate that Demosthenes was not praised for his performance in the office of *teichopoios* but for his generosity and earlier public service.[45]

In his response to Aeschines' legal arguments, Demosthenes rightly draws attention to the fact that Ctesiphon did not praise him for any of the tasks that were subject to *euthynai,* but on the grounds that he had donated money. He highlights the very issue that Aeschines ignores, namely, the nature of the praise contained in the decree. Demosthenes stresses the fact that he was not praised for acquitting his duties as a magistrate and has Ctesiphon's decree read out to underline his point. He then sums up his argument briefly and forcefully: I made a contribution. I am praised for that reason. I am not subject to audit for what I gave. It is clear that Demosthenes adopted a narrower interpretation of the law about crowns. Whereas Aeschines construes its provisions as banning the award of crowns for any reason to a magistrate still subject to audit, Demosthenes holds that it only applies to crowns awarded for the performance of duties in office, not to other types of commendation.[46]

Several considerations favor Demosthenes' interpretation of the law. First, the text of the law is more likely to have read "an office subject to audit" rather than "magistrates subject to audit" since the former is the wording Aeschines gives right after the statute is read out to the court. Demosthenes' interpretation of the phrase is certainly the more natural one. Second, Demosthenes' interpretation is more in line with the intent of the law as explained by Aeschines, who says it was aimed at magistrates who embezzled money during their terms of office, then had friendly speakers pass decrees of praise for their performance in office. Third, there is an argument from common sense. If the law prohibited any magistrate who was subject to audit from receiving a crown, it would have been impossible for a general like Phocion, who must have been reelected often, to receive a crown for a victory won in his first year of office as long as he remained in office. Fourth, Demosthenes adduces the examples of Nausicles, Diotimus, Charidemus, and Neoptolemus, all of whom received the honor of a crown for acts of generosity during their terms of office. These decrees do not show that the Athenians regularly ignored the law about crowns, but instead that Demosthenes' interpretation of the law was the customary one and had been followed often before. This means that Ctesiphon's decree was not covered by the law cited by Aeschines and was therefore not legal.[47]

Aeschines' other legal argument against Ctesiphon is also weak. Aeschines charges that Ctesiphon illegally called for Demosthenes' award to be proclaimed in the theater of Dionysus. Aeschines reads out a law stating that a crown awarded by the Council can only be proclaimed in the Council, one awarded by the Assembly only in the Assembly "and nowhere else." He lays great emphasis on the words "and nowhere else," insisting that the prohibition allows for no exceptions. Aeschines then warns the court that Demosthenes will try to deceive them by citing a Dionysiac law, which is not relevant to the case. This law prohibits proclamations of an award in the theater of Dionysus, but permits exceptions if the Council and Assembly so approve.[48]

The argument Aeschines presents to refute Demosthenes on this point is a sophisticated example of Athenian casuistry. Aeschines starts by reminding the court there are procedures for resolving contradictions between existing laws. It is the duty of the *thesmothetai* to search out these contradictions and bring them to the attention of the *nomothetai*. If there existed a contradiction between the law on which he rests his case and the Dionysiac law, therefore, one of the laws should have been repealed. Since both laws are still in force, there must be no conflict between them. And if there is no conflict between them, then the Dionysiac law cannot permit awards made by the Assembly to be proclaimed in the theater. The exception permitted by the Dionysiac law must apply to another class of awards, namely crowns granted by foreign cities. In support of his interpretation of the law, Aeschines points to the regulation requiring that all gold crowns that are announced in the theater must be dedicated to Athena. Yet if the Assembly voted to have the award of a gold crown proclaimed in the theater of Dionysus, it would in effect be granting and taking away an honor at the same time. Aeschines argues that it is right that crowns granted by foreign cities and proclaimed in the theater not remain in the hands of their recipients lest they place more value on courting the popularity of foreigners than on securing the approval of the Athenian people.[49]

This elaborate argument rests on one crucial assumption, which is that the law about the proclamation of crowns placed an absolute ban on proclamations elsewhere than the Council and Assembly. One might easily argue that there was no such absolute ban implicit in the law and that the Dionysiac law created an exception to the general rule. Aeschines' way of removing the apparent contradiction between the two laws is not the only solution. Indeed Demosthenes is able to give the names of several Athenians who had received crowns from the Assembly that were proclaimed in the theater. Demosthenes gives no evidence for his assertion, but that is presumably because the court was familiar with the customary practice, which is attested in several inscriptions.[50]

From a casual reading of the two speeches, one might think that Aeschines lavishes so much verbiage on the legal aspects of the case and Demosthenes so little because the laws favored Aeschines. On closer inspection, however, Aeschines' legal objections to Ctesiphon's decree are revealed to be specious. The great amount of effort and ingenuity invested in his discussion of the laws were required to bolster what was actually a rather weak case from a legal perspective. But Aeschines' main interest was not in the legality of Ctesiphon's decree. His primary objective as to destroy Demosthenes' reputation.[51]

The main part of Aeschines' speech attacks Ctesiphon's praise of Demosthenes for "constantly speaking and doing what is best for the people." Aeschines claims it is illegal to place false statements in a public document, then proceeds to show that Ctesiphon's praise is a complete lie by reviewing Demosthenes' entire career. There is some question as to which law Aeschines is referring. Moreover, it is suspicious that after his thorough discussion of the laws relating to the award of crowns, he neglects to quote the law or to have it read to the court.[52]

Aeschines divides his rival's career into four periods and commences his assault by examining Demosthenes' actions during the war against Philip that ended with the Peace of Philocrates. The first section is for the most part an abbreviated version of the narrative of these events presented in his speech of 343, but with some new charges thrown in to freshen up the otherwise stale material. He repeats the charge that Demosthenes worked hand in hand with Philocrates and conspired with him to deprive the Greeks of the chance to join in the peace treaty. He adds the new charge that Demosthenes tried to have the Assembly meet as early as Elaphebolion 8 to speed up ratification of the treaty. In 343 Demosthenes blamed Aeschines' vigorous support for Philocrates' version of the treaty for the defeat of the allies' proposal to extend its terms to all the Greeks. Aeschines now flings the charge back at Demosthenes, claiming that the allies' version would have been accepted if it had not been for Demosthenes' intervention on Elaphebolion 19 and his threats about Macedonian displeasure. Aeschines' account is strikingly at odds with his own testimony of 343 and lacks supporting evidence.

Aeschines also dredges up the decree Demosthenes passed to give Philip's ambassadors seats of honor at the Dionysia as proof of his hypocrisy in claiming to champion opposition ot Macedon. This time, however, he tosses in a new detail, alleging that Demosthenes rented mule carts for Philip's ambassadors and accompanied them as far as Thebes on their return journey. This anecdote, too, is unsupported by evidence. Finally, he accuses Demosthenes and Philocrates of excluding Cersebleptes from the treaty by passing a decree requiring the representatives of the Athenian allies to swear the oaths to Philip's ambassadors. Since Cersebleptes had no representative in Athens at the time, Aeschines claims that the decree had the consequence of barring Cersebleptes from the peace with Philip and thereby sealing his doom. Our analysis of the charge shows that it misrepresents the situation and is contradicted by Aeschines' earlier and better-documented account of the incident.[53]

Aeschines next examines Demosthenes' actions during the peace with Philip. He takes Demosthenes to task for undermining the treaty with Philip and gives a distorted account of his ties with Callias of Chalcis. Aeschines faults Demosthenes for collaborating with this scoundrel, a consummate opportunist who was notorious for shifting allegiances more frequently than the treacherous Euripos, famous for its unstable currents. According to Aeschines, the alliance with the Euboean cities engineered by Demosthenes and Callias cheated the Athenians of the contributions they would have paid the city had they become members of the *synedrion*. Aeschines' account of the alliance is misleading and does not take contemporary circumstances into account. That does not prevent him from charging that Demosthenes snatched a bribe of three talents for his alleged deceit. His only evidence for this bribe is a decree voted by the people of Oreos, which records a loan of one talent made by Demosthenes to the city to pay its contribution to the Euboean League formed by Callias. Such a loan is hardly incriminating.[54]

Aeschines directs most of his fire at the third period of Demosthenes' career, which covers the war against Philip that ended with the Battle of Chaeronea. Aeschines retells with obvious pride the story of the outbreak of the sacred war during the meeting of the Amphictyons in the spring of 339. He stresses his own role in defending Athens against the Locrian charge of sacrilege and rallying the Amphictyons to take revenge on the people of Amphissa for cultivating the Plain of Crisa. His own piety and patriotism are placed in sharp contrast to the venality of Demosthenes, who is accused of taking bribes from the impious citizens of Amphissa. Aeschines continues by attempting to discredit Demosthenes' diplomacy with Thebes later in 339 by attributing the success of his negotiations to circumstances and minimizing Demosthenes' responsibility for the alliance. All Demosthenes is credited with is concluding the alliance on terms that were extremely disadvantageous for Athens and forcing a showdown with Philip that resulted in disaster. Aeschines has less to say about the fourth period that takes Demosthenes' career from the defeat at Chaeronea down to the time of the trial. In this section he singles out several occasions when Demosthenes could have started war with Philip and Alexander, but backed down out of sheer cowardice.[55]

The remainder of the speech treats various topics and attempts to anticipate Demosthenes' possible replies to his accusations. He urges the court to apply the letter of the law and to insist that Demosthenes reply to his charges in order without diverting their attention onto irrelevant topics. He compares Demosthenes indecent lust for praise with the modesty of earlier Athenians, who did not seek extravagant honors after defeating the Persians. In response to the charge that he should have attacked Demosthenes earlier, Aeschines offers the excuse that his modest lifestyle prevented him from constant meddling in politics.[56]

One of the more serious accusations Aeschines anticipates is that he brought his prosecution to please Philip. Demosthenes never makes this precise charge, but several times accuses Aeschines of being the hireling of Philip and Alexander. Aeschines' defense against the charge is rather feeble: he points out that he initiated his prosecution when Philip was king and before Alexander came to the throne. This, of course, does not refute the suspicion that he launched his prosecution to do a favor to Philip. Despite Aeschines' weak reply, there is no reason to take the charge seriously. Aeschines had plenty of reason to attack Ctesiphon's decree without Macedonian encouragement. Besides, if Alexander really wanted to remove Demosthenes as a threat to his power, he would have done what he attempted to do in 335, that is, to have demanded that the Athenians surrender him into his custody.[57]

As the tone of the speech makes clear, Aeschines was still bitter over the defeats Demosthenes had inflicted on him between 346 and 338. His aim was to restore his own prestige by damaging Demosthenes' reputation. One should not underestimate Aeschines' desire for revenge as a motive for bringing the suit. In his speech against Timarchus, Aeschines himself explains that private hatreds are often the driving force behind public charges and are thus responsible for promoting the common good. This attitude, which appears strange to us, was widely accepted in Classical Athens. We expect our prosecutors to act as professional employees of the state, who bring cases to protect the public safety and have no personal motive for convicting the defendant. Without a professional judiciary, however, the Athenians had to rely on the private enmities of individual citizens to guard the interest of the community. Viewed from this perspective, Aeschines had plenty of justification for attacking Demosthenes in court. After all, Demosthenes was the one who began the feud by linking up with Timarchus in 346 to bring a charge against Aeschines and came within inches of convicting him in 343. It was an axiom of Greek morality that one should always repay one's enemies in kind. There is no need to search any further to find a reason for Aeschines' prosecution. Aeschines was only striking back at the man who had tried to destroy him. He could not find a means of attacking him directly so he settled on a prosecution of Ctesiphon's decree as a way of tarnishing Demosthenes' reputation.[58]

By devoting the bulk of his speech to an assault on Demosthenes' policies, Aeschines virtually invited Demosthenes to defend his own career at length. It was an invitation Demosthenes clearly welcomed. In the opening of his speech, Demosthenes states his reluctance to boast about his own achievement, but in the rest of the speech this reluctance is nowhere evident. One must still admit that Demosthenes had an impressive list of achievements to celebrate. His basic strategy in the speech is quite simple: he alternates between describing his own services to Athens and denouncing Aeschines' lack of patriotism. The allegations of treason not only undermine Aeschines' credibility as a prosecutor, but also enhance by contrast the glory of his own deeds. His greatest sources of pride are his law on the trierarchy, his victory over Philip on Euboea, and his tireless diplomacy, which won Athens many allies.[59]

Perhaps the most brilliant part of the speech is his treatment of the Athenian defeat at Chaeronea. For Aeschines, Chaeronea was an unmitigated disaster for Athens. Demosthenes makes no attempt to avoid the topic or to minimize its impact on Athens, though he points out that his policy ensured that the campaign took place on Boeotian, not Attic soil. While Aeschines offers no consolation for the defeat, Demosthenes says that the Athenians fought for a noble cause, Greek freedom, and lost only because fortune turned against them. Whatever the truth about Demosthenes' responsibility for the defeat, one can understand why the Athenians would prefer Demosthenes' interpretation of history to that of Aeschines. In fact, their attitude after Chaeronea indicates that they blamed the defeat on the military incompetence of the general Lysicles, whom they condemned to death, rather than on the misguided policy of Demosthenes, whom they honored by selecting him to deliver the eulogy over the fallen soldiers.[60]

The verdict in the trial was devastating for Aeschines. Ctesiphon was acquitted by a wide margin, Demosthenes was vindicated, and Aeschines was humiliated by failing to gain even one fifth of the votes. This meant that he lost the right to prosecute on public charges. He may have retired to Rhodes, but our information for his life after the trial is all drawn from biographers, who contradict each other. The defeat did more damage to his reputation than anything else. As we have seen, his career was essentially over by 337 after being on the decline for some time. Though Demosthenes' accusations of treason were baseless, the trial nevertheless exposed Aeschines' weaknesses as a politician. Throughout his speech, Demosthenes repeatedly draws attention to critical moments when Aeschines had no advice to offer. When Demosthenes was vigorously courting allies, Aeschines had no alternative to provide. He had counseled cooperation with Philip, but he had nothing to show for his policy. When Philip seized Elateia, Aeschines did not stand up and tell the Assembly what to do. In contrast to Demosthenes' lavish generosity with his own money, Aeschines had never performed a liturgy. When Demosthenes constantly demanded what services he had done for Athens, Aeschines could not say that he had served as trierarch, paid for a chorus at the Dionysia, or contributed to some public building project. Of course, it was not his lack of patriotism, but his lack of funds. Yet whatever his shortcomings, Aeschines certainly did not deserve to be grouped with those who had betrayed the freedom of the Greeks.[61]

8

Conclusion

A study of Aeschines' career shows how mistaken it is to speak in terms of a single pro-Macedonian party either in Athens or throughout Greece. Aeschines' approach to relations with Philip and Alexander differed in crucial respects from the position of Isocrates, whose ideal of Panhellenic unity he never espoused, and of Demades, whose style of diplomacy he chose not to imitate. In fact, Aeschines' own position often differed, ranging from initial opposition to a policy of close alliance with Philip. Contrary to Demosthenes' claims, the Greeks who cooperated at one time or another with Philip and later with Alexander did not form a single band of traitors, who were united by a single approach. There were several shades of opinion, and any account of the period that does not take into account this diversity in approaches to Philip will present an oversimplified picture of the events that led to the establishment of Macedonian hegemony.

Aeschines' own attitude to Philip shifted several times in response to changing circumstances. There was no sudden conversion to Philip's cause, but a gradual adjustment to the new realities created by the king's growing power. Aeschines began his career in 348 by supporting Eubulus' attempt to rally the Greeks against Philip. Like many other Athenians, Aeschines was shocked by Philip's harsh treatment of the Olynthians. The correct response to these atrocities appeared to be a broad coalition to resist Philip's advances. Up to this point, Athens had relied on allies in northern Greece in the attempt to check Philip's progress, but these had fallen one by one to Philip's masterful combination of diplomacy and military prowess. The time had come for Athens to alert all the Greeks to the general threat Philip posed to their freedom.

Aeschines' mission to the Peloponnese to implement this strategy was an intense disappointment. There he found the Arcadians more concerned about the threat of Sparta and unalarmed by Philip's conquests. Instead of considering him a danger, many Greeks saw Philip as a potential benefactor in their local conflicts. Yet the lack of interest displayed by the Arcadians and others did not discourage Aeschines, who continued to urge the Athenians to pursue the goal of a coalition against Philip. Even after the Athenians decided to open negotiations with Philip in 346, Aeschines did not abandon the hope of rallying the Greeks, if not in opposition to Philip, at least in a comprehensive peace treaty, which could serve to arrest Philip's advance. But these repeated appeals fell on deaf ears. The embassies sent by Athens in early 346

149

to summon the Greeks received little or no response since each city was about to send its own embassy to Philip in the expectation of winning him over to its side.

The Athenians themselves were under pressure to reach a separate agreement with Philip. Macedonian conquests in Thrace threatened their possessions in the Hellespont and placed their grain supply at risk. Unwilling to pursue a policy that had so far failed to bear fruit, the Athenians preferred to accept the treaty of peace and alliance offered by Philip and endorsed by Demosthenes and Philocrates. Aeschines bowed to the inevitable and reluctantly advised the Assembly to ratify the treaty that would become known as the Peace of Philocrates. His disillusionment with the goal of uniting the Greeks under Athenian leadership appears to have been permanent. He never attempted to revive his failed policy and later scoffed at Demosthenes' efforts to build a grand alliance against Philip. It was not the gifts of Philip that brought about his shift of opinion. What caused Aeschines to change his mind was the frustration caused by hard experience.

The Second Embassy marked a further shift in Aeschines' views. Seeing embassies from other Greek cities that had come to Pella to ask Philip to take their side in the sacred war, Aeschines decided it was only right to propose a solution to the conflict consonant with Athenian interests. After all, Philip had promised to confer benefits on the Athenians if they consented to become his allies. Now that the alliance was concluded, Aeschines naturally expected Philip to make good on his promise. Aeschines knew that Philip was about to march south with the intention of restoring the temple at Delphi to the Amphictyons. There was no risk in this for Athens provided that Philip did not yield to the wishes of his allies Thebes and Thessaly to impose a harsh punishment on the Phocians, who had been allies to Athens and held the temple under their control. On the other hand, it was in Athenian interests to make Phalaecus and his associates into scapegoats to satisfy the desire for vengeance of the Thebans, Thessalians, and other members of the Amphictyony. Phalaecus and his friends had been responsible for severing the ties between Athens and Phocis that went back to the beginning of the sacred war, while their opponents within Phocis had remained loyal to the Athenian alliance. The punishment of Phalaecus would not only allay the wrath of the Amphictyons; it would also restore the friends of Athens to power in Phocis.

Given these circumstances, Aeschines urged Philip to confine the punishment for the sacrilege against the temple to Phalaecus and his friends and to spare the rest of the Phocians. At the same time, he proposed that Philip liberate the cities of Boeotia from the Theban yoke. If Philip wished to show that he was a true friend of Athens, there was no better way than to weaken one of her traditional enemies. Philip apparently listened to these proposals and did not discourage Aeschines from hoping that he would follow his advice, yet did not give him any definite assurances. Nevertheless, Aeschines returned to Athens convinced that Philip was about to act in Athenian interests and predicted in the Assembly that the Phocians would be spared, Phalaecus punished, and the cities of Boeotia liberated. His new policy toward Philip was prompted by his analysis of the general situation in Greece, his assessment of Athenian interests, and Philip's earlier promise to confer benefits. Unlike Isocrates, who advised Philip to reconcile the warring Greeks, Aeschines acted only to further Athenian goals. Aeschines did not require the incentive of Macedonian gold to arrive at this policy. His decision was based on his own conception of where Athenian interests lay.

Demosthenes did not share Aeschines' confidence about Philip's intentions. Nor did he hesitate to voice his suspicions about Philip before the Council and Assembly. He had objected to the proposals Aeschines announced he would put to Philip when the ambassadors met to discuss what they would say to the king. Once back in Athens, Demosthenes openly disagreed with his colleague and at the first possible opportunity accused him of treason before the *euthynoi*. Demosthenes' suspicions about Aeschines' proposals and Philip' motives appeared to receive confirmation by the events that followed: Philip allowed Phalaecus to leave and escape punishment, the Amphictyons imposed a draconian settlement on Phocis, and the Boeotian cities remained under Theban control. But Philip had not acted out of a desire to harm Athens as Demosthenes later claimed. Phalaecus had found himself surrounded and isolated and had understandably preferred to reach a separate agreement with Philip rather than act out the part written for him by Aeschines. Phalaecus' solution suited the interests of Philip, to whom it may have come as a surprise, but it left Phocis defenseless and prey to the vengeance of Thebes and Thessaly. Although Philip may have wished to preserve Phocis as a counterweight to the influence of Thessaly and Thebes, there was now no possibility of diverting their wrath onto the head of the absent Phalaecus.

Despite Philip's failure to act according to his predictions, Aeschines did not abandon his trust in the king's promises. He traveled to Delphi after the departure of Phalaecus and was able to dissuade the Amphictyons from imposing the drastic punishment of total destruction demanded by the Oetaeans for the defeated Phocians. The Phocians were very grateful for Aeschines' intervention and later showed their appreciation by sending a delegation to testify at his trial in 343. But the punishment was still much worse than what Aeschines had led the Athenians to expect. Demosthenes and Timarchus thought that they could fasten the blame for the suffering of Phocis on Aeschines at their planned prosecution, but Aeschines struck first by prosecuting Timarchus. Though without a shred of firm evidence for his charges, Aeschines was still able to exploit Timarchus' unsavory reputation to secure a conviction. Demosthenes may have tried to influence the verdict by linking Aeschines with the punishment of Phocis, but the court did not allow recent events to sway its judgment. In fact, Aeschines went so far as to boast of his role in negotiating the Peace of Philocrates and to predict that Philip would soon make good on his promises.

In the years after 346 Aeschines continued to place his trust in Philip's promises to confer benefits and urged the Athenians to do the same. Demosthenes and others claimed that these promises had been nothing more than a stratagem designed to fool the Athenians. Aeschines replied that circumstances alone prevented Philip from liberating Boeotia and saving Phocis. In 343 Philip finally responded to the criticisms of Demosthenes and others by offering to consider Athenian proposals for amending the Peace of Philocrates. Aeschines must have greeted the offer with enthusiasm for it appeared to bear out what he had maintained all along, namely, that Philip was a true friend of Athens. Whatever hopes Aeschines cherished were soon dashed. Demosthenes and Hegesippus convinced the Athenians to make demands that Philip could not accept. Philip tried to keep the negotiations alive by offering a few minor concessions, but they were not enough to compensate for the losses the Athenians thought they had suffered in 346. The benefits Aeschines had so warmly recommended to the Athenians turned out to be too little, too late.

The failure of these negotiations compelled Aeschines to change his stance once again. He was now on the defensive, unable to justify his previous support for Philip and the Peace of Philocrates by pointing to Philip's promised benefits. Philip's enemies quickly sensed that it was the time to go on the offensive. Hyperides accused Philocrates of treason. The author of the treaty with Philip realized that events had turned against him and fled from Athens before his trial. He was condemned to death in absentia and his property confiscated. Encouraged by Hyperides' example, Demosthenes brought his case against Aeschines to court in 343. Aeschines defended himself by reminding the court of the situation in 346 and how circumstances had forced the treaty on Athens. Unable to convince the Athenians it was worthwhile to remain faithful allies of Philip, he could only plead with them to refrain from becoming his enemies and to keep the peace, which was preferable to war. Thanks in part to the strong support of Eubulus, Phocion, and Nausicles, Aeschines won acquittal by a narrow margin. But the damage done to his reputation was severe, and his influence in the Assembly declined in the following years. His denunciation of Demosthenes' illegal treatment of Antiphon was at first successful, then became an embarrassment when Antiphon confessed under torture to plotting with Philip to burn down the dockyards of the Athenian fleet. Aeschines retained enough popularity to gain election as ambassador to Delphi, but the suspicions aroused in the Areopagus by his conduct in the Antiphon affair caused his removal from the post.

As Aeschines' fortunes declined, Demosthenes' influence rose. Demosthenes began to pursue the goal of uniting the Greeks in a coalition against Philip, the policy Aeschines had earlier espoused, then later abandoned. Demosthenes had more success with the policy than Aeschines primarily because times had changed. Before 346 Philip had confined his activities to northern Greece and was not perceived as a threat to the cities of central and southern Greece. After 346, however, Philip started to meddle in the affairs of this area, causing many to heed the warnings Aeschines had sounded in 348. Demosthenes brought many of the Peloponnesians over to the Athenian side and drove Philip's supporters out of Euboea. But Aeschines was skeptical of Demosthenes' aggressive policy and blamed it for disrupting the peace with Philip.

After war broke out with Philip, there was no longer any peace for Aeschines to defend so he was compelled to change his position yet again. Aeschines now worked to ensure that Athens had the military wherewithal to defeat Philip. When Demosthenes introduced his reform of the trierarchy, Aeschines criticized its weaknesses and helped to improve its provisions. According to Demosthenes, the reform was responsible for the Athenian victory over Philip at Byzantium in 340. Since the final version probably included changes made at the insistence of Aeschines, Aeschines is due some of the credit for its results. Aeschines' speeches at Delphi in the spring of 339 also demonstrated his devotion to Athens. In response to the Locrian charge of sacrilege, Aeschines vindicated Athenian innocence and turned the anger of the Amphictyons against Amphissa. Aeschines' righteous indignation, whether feigned or real, helped Athens out of a temporary crisis, but his advocacy of Athenian participation in the sacred war was probably shortsighted. Demosthenes realized that Athens might need Theban support once Philip returned to Greece and that joining in the war against Amphissa would only alienate a potential ally. The events of the next several months proved that Demosthenes' advice was sound.

Yet Aeschines cannot be charged with acting in Philip's interests either knowingly or by accident. There are no grounds for doubting that his primary motive was to shield Athens from attack. In the following months Aeschines was once more reduced to criticizing Demosthenes' policy without being able to change its course. He protested Demosthenes' conduct of the war and refusal to negotiate with Philip to no avail. After the crushing defeat at Chaeronea, the Athenians called on Aeschines, Phocion, and Demades to conclude a new treaty with Philip. This was no great honor because the terms they brought back to Athens were dictated by the victor and stripped Athens of the confederacy of Allies, the last vestige of her former imperial glory. The final phase of Aeschines' career was a period of waiting for a final attack on Demosthenes, which turned out to be a dismal failure. It was a humiliating end to a career that had been filled with frustrations.

The years of Aeschines' greatest influence were in the middle of the 340s. After this period he never recovered his popularity, though he remained intermittently active in politics. During this period Aeschines gambled in effect on the goodwill of Philip. He based his support for Philip on the belief that Philip had been sincere in his promise of 346 to help Athens. Aeschines was correct in arguing that Demosthenes' suspicions about Philip's motives were not justified: Philip had certainly never revealed any desire to destroy Athens, either in this period or later. When Demosthenes and others attacked him in their speeches, Philip did not use their hostility as an excuse to break off relations. Instead he offered to amend the terms of the Peace of Philocrates. When he had an opportunity to besiege Athens after Chaeronea and subject it to the treatment Olynthus suffered, he preferred to offer a peace treaty.

What Aeschines failed to understand was that Philip, although wishing to retain the friendship of Athens, did not desire to see the city become stronger. Philip's main goal was to maintain the balance of power among the Greeks and to prevent any individual city from becoming powerful enough to challenge his ascendancy. Philip could not do as he pleased; he had to remain on good terms with as many Greeks as he could while keeping his enemies, such as Sparta, few and isolated. Aeschines did not realize that it was not in Philip's interest in 346 to weaken Thebes by liberating the Boeotian cities. If Aeschines erred in overestimating Philip's commitment to Athenian interests, Demosthenes veered to the other extreme of exaggerating Philip's hostility. Despite Demosthenes' jeremiads against Macedonian perfidy, there is no evidence Philip was bent on the destruction of Athens. Philip demonstrated his willingness to cooperate with Athens on several occasions, but that cooperation had its limits. Aeschines and Demosthenes, though differing on most issues, did share one trait in common: they mistakenly thought that relations with Athens were Philip's main concern. Their misconception had tragic consequences for Athens.

Though his policy underwent several shifts, Aeschines always placed Athenian interests first. This set him apart from Isocrates, who saw Philip as an instrument for realizing the dream of unity and concord among the Greeks. In 346 Isocrates advised Philip to reconcile all the major powers of Greece and to direct their common hatred against Persia. Aeschines in that year looked no further than the goal of punishing Athens's enemy Thebes and restoring Athens' friends in Phocis. In his *Letter to Philip,* Isocrates expressed his satisfaction with Philip's settlement and his plan to invade Asia. In Aeschines' opinion Chaeronea was a disaster for Athens, and Philip's settlement was no cause for rejoicing.

Nor did Aeschines ever imitate the example of Demades, who was eager to play the politics of flattery and trade Athenian honors to Macedonian overlords in return for favors and influence. Demades' style was not compatible with the kind of diplomacy Aeschines had practiced. Aeschines wanted Athens to cooperate with Philip as an equal partner. When that was no longer possible, Aeschines appears to have withdrawn from political activity. Finally, Aeschines does not deserve to be placed in the company of men like Ptoiodorus of Megara and Clitarchus of Euboea. Aeschines never used Philip's money or soldiers to seize power for himself and suppress his enemies. Despite Demosthenes' charges of treason, Aeschines did not betray Athens or attempt to subvert the city's political institutions for personal gain. When he advocated cooperation with Philip, it was from a conviction that such a policy was advantageous to Athens. When Philip was at war with Athens, Aeschines worked to achieve Athenian victory.

A careful examination of Aeschines' career reveals that it is necessary to distinguish among varying degrees and types of support for Philip and Alexander. There was a spectrum of responses to the growth of Macedonian power, ranging from stubborn resistance to willing subordination. Even such a diehard enemy of the Macedonian kings as Demosthenes occasionally saw the need for cooperation. To divide the politicians of Greece into two monolithic parties of pro-Macedonians and anti-Macedonians does not do justice to the rich variety of opinion in Greece at the time.

Appendix 1

Was Aeschines Ever an Associate of Aristophon?

At the trial of Ctesiphon in 330, Demosthenes (18.162) said that Aeschines used to follow not only Eubulus, but also Aristophon. This is a rather odd statement since in the same passage Demosthenes relates that Aristophon and Eubulus found themselves opposed to each other on every issue save that of Athenian relations with Thebes. Earlier, in 343, Demosthenes (19.291) claimed that Aeschines joined Aristophon in accusing Philonicus and in so doing attacked the policy of Eubulus. These are the only two references to a close relationship between Aeschines and Aristophon. There is nothing in the speeches of Aeschines to suggest that such a relationship ever existed. Aeschines mentions Aristophon four times, twice in his speech against Timarchus in 346 (Aeschin. 1.64, 158) and twice in his speech against Ctesiphon (Aeschin. 3.139, 194). His references to Aristophon on the earlier occasion are neither complimentary nor derogatory. In the other speech, Aeschines compares Aristophon unfavorably with Cephalus. He recalls Aristophon's boast about his seventy-five acquittals in prosecutions for proposing illegal decrees, but contends that Cephalus, who had never once been indicted on this charge, was more admirable. Striking also is Aristophon's apparent lack of support for Aeschines at his trial in 343, at which his close friends Phocion and Eubulus testified. On the other hand, Aeschines' hostile remarks about Chares, an ally of Aristophon, suggest that the two men may have actually been opponents (Aeschin. 2.71).[1] Furthermore, we know that Aeschines and Aristophon took different sides during the debate about the Peace of Philocrates on Elaphebolion 18.[2] As for Demosthenes' claim that Aeschines joined in the prosecution of Philonicus, we should note that Aeschines in 346 stated he had never before prosecuted any Athenian (Aeschin. 1.1). After his prosecution on Timarchus, Aeschines could still boast in 343 that he had never prosecuted anyone at their scrutiny after leaving office (Aeschin. 2.182). It is always possible that Aeschines exaggerates his lack of experience as a prosecutor to please the court, but it is more likely that Demosthenes' invented Aeschines' friendship with Aristophon and dated it to the period of his association with Eubulus to portray Aeschines as a duplicitous hypocrite.

Appendix 2

The Chronology of the Olynthus Campaigns and Philip's Peace Offers

Both Diodorus (16.52.9, 53.2) and Dionysius of Halicarnassus (*Amm.* 1.9–10), drawing on Philochorus (*FGrHist* 328 F 56), place the beginning of Philip's war with Olynthus in the archonship of Callimachus (349/48) and put the capture of Olynthus in the following archonship, that of Theophilus (348/47). Diodorus (16.55.1) and Demosthenes (19.192) relate that after the fall of Olynthus, Philip celebrated the Macedonian Olympia, a festival held in the autumn, in the Attic month of Boedromion at the earliest.[1] Since neither author indicates the length of the interval between Philip's victory and his celebration of the Olympia, and since the precise date of the Olympia is unknown, this information yields nothing more than a *terminus ante quem* of the autumn of 348 for the fall of Olynthus.

From the passages of Philochorus quoted by Dionysius we learn that the Athenians sent three expeditions to Olynthus, but nothing about the month or the season in which each was sent. We have no means of giving a more precise date for the first expedition, but it probably fell in the autumn of 348.[2] Evidence from Demosthenes allows us to date the second expedition to late Elaphebolion or early Munichion. Philochorus (*FGrHist* 328 F 50) states that the second expedition was led by Charidemus and included 18 triremes, 4,000 peltasts, and 150 cavalry. The cavalry on this expedition appears to be identical with the cavalry which crossed to Olynthus and was criticized in its absence by Meidias (Dem. 21.197).[3] Since this cavalry squadron had previously gone to Euboea after the Dionysia (Dem. 21.162–64), which took place in the middle of Elaphebolion, its departure for Olynthus cannot be dated before the end of Elaphebolion at the earliest and probably belongs to early Munichion.[4] It is unlikely that the cavalry on this expedition is the same as that sent on the third expedition, for that expedition occurred much later. Furthermore, the third expedition never reached Olynthus, which fell before it could arrive, yet Demosthenes (21.197) says that the cavalry from Euboea actually crossed to Olynthus.[5] The fact that Charidemus appears to have been summoned from the Hellespont whereas the cavalry departed from Euboea cannot be used as evidence against the identification. All Philochorus states is that Charidemus arrived with the cavalry; he does not state where the unit originated.

The third and last expedition to Olynthus was also sent in the archonship of Callimachus (349/48) and must be the one which was delayed by bad weather and failed to reach Olynthus before it was betrayed (Suidas *s.v.* Karanos). The delay caused by the bad weather cannot have lasted more than a few weeks at the most, and that means less than a month separated the departure of the third expedition and the fall of Olynthus.[6] For the former to have occurred in 349/48 and the latter in 348/47, the expedition must be placed in late Skirophorion and the fall of Olynthus in early Hekatombaion.

156

Philip's first offer to make peace was communicated to the Assembly by the Euboeans who came to Athens to discuss peace (Aeschin. 2.12). The Euboean embassy was presumably sent right after the final defeat of the Athenian troops under Molossus, who succeeded Phocion as commander on Euboea (Pl. *Phoc.* 14.1). Phocion was still on Euboea after the Dionysia, but Molossus' defeat took place soon after his departure so the Euboean embassy should probably be placed in late Munichion.

Aeschines (2.12) informs us that Phrynon was captured "not much time later" than the Euboean embassy, sometime during the truce for the Olympic games of 348. The games may have begun on July 31 of that year, but we do not know when the truce for the games began.[7] We are told that the athletes had to report a month early, and it is reasonable to assume that the truce must have begun even earlier to assure them a safe journey to Olympia. Certainly nothing excludes the possibility that the truce began as early as Thargelion. If Phrynon returned to Athens later in that month, Ctesiphon could have made his trip to Macedon and back by the middle of Skirophorion. Immediately upon his return, Ctesiphon would have reported to the Assembly about Philip's renewed offer of peace, and Philocrates would have made his proposal at the same meeting of the Assembly. Lycinus' indictment of Philocrates must also belong to this meeting of the Assembly. Nothing prevents us from placing the trial, which would only have consumed one day, right after the meeting of the Assembly. It may have preceded the departure of the final expedition to Olynthus, but is unlikely to have occurred after the fall of the city.

Schaefer correctly saw that the news of Olynthus' capture must have reached Athens after the trial of Philocrates. Schaefer reasonably suggested that the news of Olynthus' capture and Philip's harsh treatment of its citizens was the reason why the decree of Philocrates was never put into effect.[8] Markle, on the other hand, claims that the fall of Olynthus was the reason the Athenians showed such willingness to negotiate with the king after Ctesiphon delivered his report to the Assembly.[9] Markle's reconstruction contains a serious flaw: it does not explain why the Athenians did not begin negotiations with Philip after they had already voted to do so. Lycinus' prosecution of Philocrates only blocked the implementation of the decree temporarily by placing it under a *hypomosia*. Once Philocrates was acquitted, the *hypomosia* would have been lifted, and negotiations could have gone forward.

Appendix 3

Athenian Embassies to the Greeks Between 348 and 346

Both Aeschines and Demosthenes agree to the extent of saying that the Athenians sent embassies to rally the Greeks against Philip after the fall of Olynthus, but it is unclear how many sets of embassies were sent and when they were sent. The best method of approach is to lay out all the evidence that Aeschines and Demosthenes provide about these embassies and then to examine how modern scholars have interpreted this evidence.

Demosthenes (19.10–12) in his speech as prosecutor in 343 reports how Aeschines with the support of Ischander addressed the Council and Assembly and convinced the Athenians to send ambassadors to all the Greek states with an invitation to come to Athens where they could discuss how best to oppose Philip. Aeschines was then sent as an ambassador to Arcadia and on his return reported to the Assembly that he spoke against Hieronymus before the Ten Thousand in Megalopolis. Later in the same speech Demosthenes (19.302–6) repeats the story and adds a few more details. He tells once more how Aeschines warned the Athenians about Philip and persuaded them to send embassies "almost as far as the Red Sea." He mentions Ischander again, but this time identifies him as an Arcadian who claimed to represent the pro-Athenian elements in the region. Eubulus then passed a decree to send out embassies, and Aeschines was elected as an ambassador to the Peloponnese. On his return to Athens, Aeschines told the Assembly that he had met Atrestidas returning from Macedon with thirty Olynthian captives whom Philip had given them as a gift. Aeschines advised the Athenians not to give up their efforts, but to send more embassies.

Aeschines (2.79) in his response to Demosthenes agrees that he had indeed spoken against Philip in Arcadia and denies none of the allegations made by Demosthenes about his activity in that period. No mention is made of the decree of Eubulus, nor of Aeschines' mission to the Peloponnese, by either orator in the speeches delivered at the trial of Ctesiphon in 330.

There is no reason to question the fact that the embassies were sent out to the Greeks sometime after the fall of Olynthus and that Aeschines served as an ambassador to the Peloponnese. The problem arises when we try to determine whether the embassies sent out under the decree of Eubulus were the same ones that were expected to return to Athens in Elaphebolion 346 (Aeschin. 2.58–60). To refute the claim of Demosthenes (19.16) that on Elaphebolion 18, 346, he had spoken in front of the ambassadors whom the Athenians had summoned from the Greek cities, Aeschines says that there were no ambassadors from the Greek cities in Athens at the time and adds that the ambassadors whom the Athenian had sent out to ask the Greek cities to send delegations had not yet returned to Athens when the date for this meeting of the Assembly was set. Aeschines (3.68) reiterates this charge in his speech of

158

330. On that occasion Demosthenes (18.22–24) simply denies that the Athenians had sent any embassies to the Greeks at that time. Long before, he states, the Greeks had already been tested.

We can now consider the views of modern scholars about these embassies. Schaefer thought that there was only one set of embassies, which were sent shortly after the fall of Olynthus in late 348 or early 347.[1] He pointed to the story told by Demosthenes about Aeschines meeting Atrestidas with the Olynthian captives. Assuming that Atrestidas must have received these captives shortly after the fall of Olynthus, Schaefer placed the time of Aeschines' meeting with Atrestidas not too long after the fall of Olynthus, or in other words, in late 348 or early 347. Schaefer went on to assert that Aeschines is not telling the truth when he states that the ambassadors sent to the Greeks were expected to return to Athens in Elaphebolion 346.

Cawkwell objected to this dating.[2] "Of course the meeting with Atrestidas coming from Philip with a gift of Olynthian prisoners proves nothing. Philip could have made the gift one or eighteen months after the fall of Olynthus." Cawkwell proposed instead to identify the ambassadors sent out under the decree of Eubulus with those mentioned by Aeschines in his defense of 343 and later in his attacks on Demosthenes in 330. Since these ambassadors did not return to Athens before the meetings of the Assembly on Elaphebolion 18 and 19 of 346, Cawkwell argued that the ambassadors sent out under the decree of Eubulus must have been sent out in early 346, not in late 348 or early 347. Cawkwell also observed that there is no reason to doubt Aeschines' claim that the Athenian ambassadors were expected to return to Athens in Elaphebolion 346 since he quotes a resolution of the Allies in which it is clearly stated that the ambassadors had not yet returned. This resolution was submitted at the same time as Demosthenes' proposal to hold the meetings of the Assembly on Elaphebolion 18 and 19 and thus must date from that same month in 346. Cawkwell further noted that Aeschines is consistent on this matter, asserting in both of his speeches that the ambassadors were expected in Athens at this time, whereas Demosthenes states in the earlier speech that Aeschines delivered his remarks on Elaphebolion 18 to an Assembly that included representatives from all of Greece, whereas in his later speech he changes his story and claims that the Greeks had already been approached long ago, as well as accusing Aeschines of lying about the Athenian ambassadors sent in early 346 to summon the Greeks.

Markle attacked Cawkwell's attempt to redate the decree of Eubulus.[3] He pointed out that Cawkwell's argument contained one serious flaw: we know that Aeschines, who had been sent out as an ambassador under the decree of Eubulus, returned to Athens after his mission in time to be elected to represent Athens on the First Embassy to Philip and also to journey to Macedon and back before the Dionysia of 346, which began on Elaphebolion 10. Thus, if Cawkwell were correct in assuming the ambassadors who were expected back in Athens in Elaphebolion 346 were the same as those who were sent out under the decree of Eubulus, Demosthenes, when challenged by Aeschines to give the name of any ambassador who had returned to Athens by Elaphebolion 18, could have named Aeschines.

Cawkwell replied to these objections.[4] He first drew attention to the fact that he had not overlooked this difficulty in his original article, where he argued that Aeschines' mission was of a different nature from that of the other ambassadors sent out under the decree of Eubulus. He further assumed that Aeschines had been sent out to the Arcadians immediately and returned home promptly, whereas the others were to make longer journeys to more cities. Second, Cawkwell objected that if Eubulus' decree belonged to late 348, Aeschines, when he wished to prove that Demosthenes was wrong, need not have asked if any of the ambassadors had returned, but had only to read out the date of the decree of Eubulus to show that the embassies were sent to the Greeks over a year before Elaphebolion 346. Third, Cawkwell claimed that if the embassies sent out under the decree of Eubulus belonged to 346, Aeschines could have explained his change of policy from rallying the Greeks for a war against Philip to supporting the negotiations for peace by saying that the situation had changed between the autumn of 348 and early 346, but this was not the case since Aeschines "sought to explain the change from his policy on the Arcadian embassy in terms of the situation in Elaphebolion 346." Cawkwell's final objection was that Demosthenes could not have stood up in court and given evidence, since the law forbade a man to give evidence in his own case.

Cawkwell's objections are easily answered. The assumption that Aeschines' mission was of a different nature from that of the other ambassadors sent out under the decree of Eubulus is very fragile, and Cawkwell does not attempt to prop up his case by adducing parallel examples.[5] The second objection, that if the decree of Eubulus belongs to late 348, Aeschines simply needed to read out the date of the decree to prove that Demosthenes was wrong in asserting there were ambassadors from the Greeks present in Athens in Elaphebolion 346, fails to grasp the situation in this period. As Cawkwell himself admits elsewhere,[6] there were two sets of embassies, those sent out under the decree of Eubulus and another group sent out under a later decree, which had not yet returned to Athens by Elaphebolion 18, 346. Thus, when Aeschines is attempting to prove that the embassies sent out under the later decree had not yet returned by Elaphebolion 18, it would have been irrelevant to cite the decree of Eubulus since the return of the ambassadors sent out under that decree was not at issue. The third objection of Cawkwell rests on the assumption that when Aeschines complained about the failure of the other Greeks to come to the aid of Athens and about corrupt politicians exploiting the war for private gain, he was referring only to the situation in the month of Elaphebolion 346. But the description of the circumstances described in the passage could just as well have applied to a much longer period, one that began several months before Elaphebolion.[7] Indeed, it is hard to believe that the Athenians would have given up the search for allies after a little more than a month. The sense of isolation described by Aeschines here was no doubt the product of a long period when no other Greeks came to their aid, not just a few weeks. Cawkwell's final objection shows a lack of understanding of Athenian judicial procedure. The law did prohibit a man from giving evidence in his own suit, but did not prevent him from answering questions posed by the other party during the trial.[8] Aeschines is not requesting Demosthenes to give evidence, but is merely asking him to respond to a question. This procedure is well attested in other speeches delivered in Athenian courts.

It is clear that there was a set of embassies expected back in Athens in Elaphebolion 346, since as Cawkwell had rightly stressed, their absence from Athens at the time is explicitly mentioned in a Resolution of the Allies cited by Aeschines. It is equally obvious that these embassies were not the same as those sent out under the decree of Eubulus. None of these ambassadors, who had been sent out not long before Elaphebolion 346, had returned to Athens by the eighteenth of that month, whereas Aeschines, who had been sent out under the decree of Eubulus, had already been back in Athens for some time before Elaphebolion 346 and in the meantime had served on an embassy to Philip. One question now remains: when was the decree of Eubulus passed?

As Schaefer observed, the only clue for the dating of Eubulus' decree is to be found in the story of Atrestidas and the Olynthian captives told by Aeschines.[9] Schaefer simply assumed that it must have occurred not too long after the Macedonian capture of Olynthus, in the spring of 347 at the latest. We can put this dating on a firmer basis by determining when Philip would have distributed the Olynthian prisoners as gifts to Atrestidas. Both Demosthenes (19.193–95) and Diodorus (16.55.1–4) relate that Philip gave to Satyrus the daughters of Apollophanes of Pydna, who had been sent to Olynthus after their father's death and were captured by Philip's soldiers when the city fell. Both authors identify the occasion as the Olympia, which Philip celebrated after he captured Olynthus. To distribute booty and prisoners from a campaign immediately afterward was indeed the traditional practice that

Philip was following at the festival.[10] Besides, why would he have waited over a year to distribute his spoils? Thus, Atrestidas must have received his gift of Olynthian prisoners from Philip at the Macedonian Olympia. If Aeschines, while an ambassador to the Peloponnese, met Atrestidas returning from the Macedonian Olympia, Aeschines must have been sent out during the time the festival was being celebrated or shortly before, in other words, right after the fall of Olynthus. The decree of Eubulus must therefore have been passed directly after that event. Finally, one of the greatest weaknesses in Cawkwell's arguments for dating the decree of Eubulus in early 346 is his apparent inability to explain why no effort was made to organize opposition to Philip until over a year after the capture of Olynthus. It makes far more sense to place the decree of Eubulus immediately after the fall of Olynthus, when indignation over the treatment of the unfortunate city was running high, than over a year later, when the memory of the debacle was already beginning to fade.

Appendix 4

When Did the *Spondophoroi* Report the Phocian Refusal?

The question of when the *spondophoroi* reported the news of the Phocian refusal to accept the truce for the Eleusinian Mysteries has been the object of controversy. Pickard-Cambridge maintained that the *spondophoroi* had been sent to announce the truce for the Greater Mysteries and placed the date of their return in Boedromion 347.[1] Most other scholars have argued that these *spondophoroi* were sent to announce the truce for the Lesser Mysteries, which began in the middle of Gamelion,[2] but have been unable to agree about whether they returned to Athens before or after the truce began. Schaefer, following Bohnecke, placed their return toward the end of Gamelion.[3] Cloché preferred the middle of Gamelion.[4] Cawkwell also placed their return after the beginning of the truce, but moved the date down to early Anthesterion.[5] In the most recent discussion of the problem, Markle had proposed that the *spondophoroi* must have returned in early Gamelion, before the truce began.[6]

There can be little doubt that the *spondophoroi* who announced the Phocian refusal to accept the truce must have been those sent to announce the truce for the Lesser Mysteries. Aeschines (2.132–33) states that the *spondophoroi* reported the news not long before the Athenians made peace with Philip. This must refer to the vote of the Assembly on Elaphebolion 19 to pass the decree of Philocrates. If the *spondophoroi* reported to the Assembly shortly before this, they must have been the *spondophoroi* sent for the Lesser Mysteries, which occurred in Anthesterion, not those for the Greater Mysteries, which took place in Boedromion, half a year before Elaphebolion.[7]

We can now turn to the question of whether the *spondophoroi* would have returned to Athens before or after the truce for the Lesser Mysteries began. Unfortunately, references to the activities of the *spondophoroi* are few: only two inscriptions provide us with any dates. The first of these is a decree passed by the Assembly in 367 instructing a herald to go to the Aetolian League and to demand their release.[8] The decree was passed during the prytany of the tribe Oineis, which we know was the third prytany of the year and probably ran from Boedromion 14 to Pyanopsion 20. However, this decree does not help us to determine when the *spondophoroi* normally returned to Athens. That year the *spondophoroi* had been illegally detained and thus had not been able to return to Athens at the regular time. There is no way of knowing how long it would have taken the Athenians to discover that they had been arrested and who had arrested them. All we can safely infer from the inscription is that the arrest of the *spondophoroi* was announced to the Assembly some time before Pyanopsion of that year. This does not get us very far.

At first glance another inscription appears more promising.[9] This one records three payments made to the *spondophoroi* in the archonship of Cephisophon (329/28). There may have been more payments made during the year since the entries for the seventh, eighth, and ninth prytanies have not been preserved. In the first prytany, which ran from Hekatombaion 1 to Metageitnion 6, 250 drachmas were paid out to the *spondophoroi* sent to the islands to announce the Greater Mysteries.[10] Another amount, this time not preserved, was paid to the *spondophoroi* in the fourth prytany, which ran either from Pyanopsion 20 to Maimakterion 25[11] or from Pyanopsion 19 to Maimakterion 24.[12] A third amount, again unpreserved, was paid to the *spondophoroi* in the tenth prytany, which lasted either from Thargelion 24 to Skirophorion 29[13] or from Thargelion 25 to Skirophorion 30.[14]

Markle argued from the information found in this inscription that the *spondophoroi* must have returned to Athens before the beginning of the truce.[15] He noticed that the payment made during the first prytany occurs first in the list of payments for that prytany and concluded that this payment must therefore have been made very early in the prytany. Since the prytany began on Hekatombaion 1 and the truce for the Greater Mysteries did not begin until Metageitnion 15, the *spondophoroi* would have had forty-four days to proclaim the truce before it began. He assumed that the payment made in the tenth prytany was made to the *spondophoroi* sent to announce the Greater Mysteries and that this payment was also made early in the prytany. He thereby concluded that the *spondophoroi* who received this money would have had seventy-nine days in which to make their journey. He argued against Cawkwell that the payment made during the fourth prytany must have been made to those *spondophoroi* sent out to announce the truce for the Lesser Mysteries.[16] Since this payment is one of the last entries for that prytany, Markle argued that it was made late in the prytany. Even if it was made on the last day of the prytany, the *spondophoroi* would still have had forty-eight days to complete their task before the truce began on Gamelion 15.

This is all guesswork. The inscription only indicates the periods during which the *spondophoroi* received their payments. It does not tell us when they left Athens and gives us no idea when they returned. The information found in the inscription cannot be used as evidence to show that all the *spondophoroi* must have returned to Athens before the truce began.

Since the inscriptions do not offer any indication of the date on which the *spondophoroi* returned to Athens, we must try another approach. We know that the *spondophoroi* not only announced the sacred truce, but also concluded the truce with each of the cities to which they came.[17] In addition, we know that Greek treaties sent into effect the instant both parties swore the oaths for them; there is no example of a Greek treaty that went into effect at some future date after the parties had sworn to it.[18] Thus the *spondophoroi* could not have concluded the sacred truce with any city until the period of the truce had begun. Otherwise, if the *spondophoroi* concluded the truce with any city before the period of the truce for the Lesser Mysteries began on Gamelion 15, we would have a situation where the truce with a city was in effect before the period of the truce had started. Of course, this meant that most cities must have concluded their truces with the *spondophoroi* after Gamelion 15 for the Lesser Mysteries since they could not have concluded the truce with all the cities on the same day. Thus, when the inscription regarding the sacred truce for the Mysteries states that the truce was to begin on Gamelion 15, what was actually meant was that this was the date on which the *spondophoroi* began to conclude the truce with the individual cities.

Comparative evidence lends support to this view. We know that the truce for the Olympic games was announced in Sparta, not before, but during the truce for the games.[19] If this explanation is the correct one, it would also account for the fact that the period of the truce before the Mysteries was longer than the period after the festival. If the *spondophoroi* had to announce and conclude the truce with many cities before the starting date of the festival, a fairly long time, at least three weeks, would have been required for them to complete their task.[20] The length of the truce after the festival, however, had only to be so great as to allow those who had come to the festival to return to their cities.

It is also more likely than not that the *spondophoroi* completed their task and returned to Athens before the Mysteries began. Since the truce was designed to afford protection for the Greeks who wished to attend the Mysteries when traveling to Eleusis, the *spondophoroi* must have concluded the truce with all the cities before the festival began. The Athenians themselves wished to know before the ceremonies commenced whether any city had refused the truce or had violated it so that their magistrates could take the appropriate measures and, if need be, to bar citizens from such cities from participation in the holy rites.[21] For these reasons, we can safely assume that the *spondophoroi* must have reported to Athens before the Lesser Mysteries took place, that is, sometime before Anthesterion 20–26.

On these grounds we can conclude that the *spondophoroi* who announced the news of the Phocian refusal to accept the truce must have returned to Athens sometime between the middle of Gamelion, when the truce began, and Anthesterion 20–26, the period during which the Lesser Mysteries appear to have been celebrated. Since we have no means of determining how long their journeys were, it is impossible to calculate the date on which they normally returned.[22] Nonetheless, it must have taken them a couple of weeks and possibly as long as a month. This would place their return in the middle of Anthesterion.

Appendix 5

The Thracian Fortresses

All these fortresses appear to have been located on the coast of the Propontis or on the northern Aegean. Ganos (Aeschin. 3.82; X. *An.* 7.5.8) lies on the shore of the Propontis opposite Proconnesos.[1] It has been suggested that Serreion Teichos (Aeschin. 3.82; [Dem.] 7.37; Dem. 9.15) is to be identified with Ganos, but this is doubtful.[2] Doriskos (Aeschin. 3.82; Dem. 8.64; 9.15; 10.8, 65; 18.70; 19.156, 334) lay on the shores of the Aegean at the mouth of the river Hebros (Hdt. 7.58–59). Serrion (Dem. 9.15 [where it is distinguished from Serreion Teichos]; 10.8, 65; 18.27, 70) was situated west of the Chersonese on the coast between Doriskos and Maroneia (Livy 31.16.4; Strabo 7, Fragment 47), and is possibly to be identified with Serreion Akte, which Herodotus (7.59) placed near Doriskos.[3] The location of Ergiske (Aeschin. 3.82; [Dem.] 7.37; Dem. 18.27) is unknown. So is that of Myrtenon (Dem. 18.27).[4] Harpocration (*s.v.* Myrtanon) merely calls it a fort in Thrace. It had been suggested that Ganias (Γανίαδα: Aeschin. 3.82) is actually Paniai, changed to alliterate with Ganos, which precedes it in Aeschines' list, and that Paniai is to be identified with Bisanthe, which lay on the shore of the Propontis northwest of Ganos, but this is fanciful.[5] The name may simply refer to the territory of Ganos.

It is clear that all these forts lay in Thracian, not Athenian, territory (cf. Dem. 18.27). The troops that held these forts were placed there by an Athenian general (Dem. 9.15). We are not told whether they were Athenian, Thracian, or mercenaries. This general should be Charidemus, who was in command of Athenian operations in the Hellespont at this time (Philochorus *FGrHist* 328 F 50). Markle claims on the basis of [Dem.] 7.36 that some of these forts were held by Athenian troops.[6] This is unlikely: in this passage Hegesippus only says that the Athenians had possession of these places (ἐχόντων) when Philip seized them, but fails to specify what he means by this vague expression, which could mean anything. They were probably held by mercenaries hired by Charidemus or by Thracians (Philochorus *FGrHist* 328 F 50).

Markle also claims that these forts were established on the motion of Eubulus in 347/46. His sole evidence for this is Dem. 18.70. In this passage Demosthenes is discussing the protests he made after the Peace of Philocrates about Philip's seizure of these forts, which Aeschines claims, destroyed the peace between Philip and Athens. To prove that he was not responsible for the conflict that broke out in 340, Demosthenes (18.73) had a number of decrees read out, including the one moved by Eubulus. This indicates that the decrees belong to the period after the peace was made in 346, not before. The decree of Eubulus mentioned in this passage therefore could not have been passed before the Peace of Philocrates and could not have dealt with the establishment of the Thracian fortresses.

165

Appendix 6

The Date of Philocrates' Speech in Favor of Peace with Philip

In Book 25 of his *Philippika,* Theopompus (*FGrHist* 115 F 164) gives a version of a speech delivered by Philocrates in favor of peace with Philip. This book of the *Philippika* appears to have covered events from 347 down to at least the arrival of the Macedonian ambassadors in Athens during Elaphebolion of 346.[1] Books 23 and 24 appear to have recounted the fighting in Euboea in 348 and the war between the Thebans and the Phocians.[2] These books may have also dealt with Philip's campaign against Olynthus in 348.[3] Book 26 included a speech of Aristophon against the proposals for peace brought back by the First Embassy (εἰ τὴν εἰρήνην δεξαίμεθα). It is highly unlikely that this speech was contained in a flashback to an event that took place long before the other events narrated in Book 26, since Greek historians did not insert speeches in direct discourse into such flashbacks. The speech of Aristophon must have been delivered on Elaphebolion 18, the day on which the Assembly debated the proposals brought back by the First Embassy.[4] At first glance the speech of Aristophon would appear to go with that of Philocrates, both speeches forming a pair, one for the peace, one against. One might object to this on the grounds that Theopompus would not have split the debate in the Assembly on Elaphebolion 18 between two books. Given our ignorance of Theopompus' method of arranging his material into books, however, we cannot rule out the possibility that he may have split the debate between two books. Another possible occasion for the speech of Philocrates is the meeting of the Assembly at which Philocrates made his proposal to send the First Embassy.[5] Unfortunately, we have no means of choosing between the two alternatives. All we can say with certainty is that the speech was delivered sometime between late 347 and early 346, not later than Elaphebolion of that year.

166

Appendix 7

Aeschines and the Third Embassy

In his speech of 343 Demosthenes charges that after being elected to the Third Embassy, Aeschines feigned illness in order to remain behind in Athens and keep an eye on him. After the embassy's premature return to Athens, however, Aeschines illegally rejoined the embassy and accompanied it to Delphi. In his reply to this charge, Aeschines asserts that he did nothing illegal at the time.

Demosthenes (19.121–30) alleges that before the Third Embassy left Athens, Aeschines met with his fellow ambassadors and expressed his fear that Demosthenes, who had resigned from the embassy (cf. Dem. 19.172), might succeed in calling an extra emergency meeting of the Assembly while they were away and have a decree passed in favor of the Phocians. They accordingly decided to leave Aeschines behind to keep watch on Demosthenes. Unable to resign legally from the embassy without a reason, Aeschines sent his brother and his doctor to the Council. There his brother made a sworn statement (ἐξώμοσεν) that Aeschines was ill.[1] The Council then elected Aeschines' brother to serve in his place. Important to note is the fact that despite his assertion that Aeschines could not resign from his post without a reason, Demosthenes never explicitly states in his account of his brother's report to the Council that Aeschines resigned from his position as ambassador. All he says is that his brother made a sworn statement about Aeschines' illness.

Demosthenes continues by asserting that Aeschines later joined the Third Embassy despite his resignation after the embassy returned to Athens prematurely. To prove that Aeschines resigned from his post, Demosthenes has an entry from the public records kept in the Metroon (there is no reason to delete γράμματα at Dem. 19.130) and a decree in which Aeschines is mentioned read out to the court. Demosthenes does not say that either of these documents contained Aeschines' statement of resignation. He simply implies that the two documents that the clerk is about to read out prove that Aeschines resigned from his post. Whether these documents actually proved this or not, we have no way of knowing, since Demosthenes does not quote from them. We are therefore entitled to regard his claim with skepticism. If these documents contained an unambiguous reference to Aeschines' resignation, we would have expected Demosthenes to quote the relevant passage. The possibility remains that these documents did not contain Aeschines' resignation but consisted only in a copy of the sworn statement made by his brother about Aeschines' illness. Demosthenes (19.129–30) also has the ambassadors who went to Delphi testify, but their testimony pertained only to events in Delphi (ὑπὲρ ὧν ἐκεῖ διεπράξατο).

Aeschines (2.94–96) prefaces his reply to the accusation with a charge that Demosthenes had one decree read out, but passed over another in silence. Unfortunately, he does not specify which decrees he is referring to.[2] He then gives his own version of what took place. At the meeting of the Assembly during which he was elected as ambassador to the Amphictyons, Aeschines claims he was already feeling under the weather. Despite the signs of incipient illness, Aeschines did not resign after his election, but promised to go on the embassy, his health permitting. But when the other ambassadors reported to the Council prior to their departure, Aeschines sent his brother and his doctor to report that he was not yet feeling up to another journey. They did not go to present his resignation, Aeschines says, since it was against the law for those elected by the Assembly to present their resignations to the Council. Despite his failure to have the statute containing this regulation read out, there is no reason to doubt its existence. The fact that Demosthenes presented his own resignation to the Assembly, not the Council, would appear to support his assertion.[3] Aeschines then relates that by the time the Third Embassy returned from Chalcis to announce Phalaecus' settlement with Philip, he had regained his strength. When the Assembly urged all the ambassadors who had originally been elected to proceed to Philip, Aeschines decided that he could not disappoint the Athenian people and made the journey with the other ambassadors.

Although Aeschines does not bring forward any evidence to prove his version of the story, we should still reject Demosthenes' charge. First of all, Demosthenes never proves that Aeschines was not ill when the Third Embassy left Athens for the first time. Both Aeschines and Demosthenes agree that Aeschines' brother made a sworn statement to the Council to the effect that he was ill, and this statement was entered into the public records and subsequently read out by the clerk at Aeschines' trial in 343. Thus one of the pieces of evidence Demosthenes adduces to prove his charge indicated that Aeschines was ill at the time, and Demosthenes never demonstrates that this was not true. Second, we should reject Demosthenes' charge that Aeschines joined the Third Embassy without official authorization. Demosthenes never proves that Aeschines actually resigned nor that his brother was elected to serve in his place. If he never resigned his position and his brother was never elected to replace him, he did not need to be formally reinstated in his position after the premature return of the Third Embassy. This argument receives support from the fact that Aeschines is known to have spoken at the meeting of the Amphictyony at Delphi.[4] All ambassadors in Classical Greece received credentials (*symbola*) to present to the officials of the states to which they were sent.[5] These credentials certified that the ambassadors were the legitimate representatives of the community that had sent them. If Aeschines had in fact resigned his post, he would not have received credentials and would have been unable to speak at the meeting of the Amphictyons. His participation at that meeting strongly suggests that Demosthenes' charge is false.

Appendix 8

The Chronology of Events from 344 to 340

The chronology of events in the period from 344 to 340 has been the subject of considerable dispute. Some events and speeches, however, are firmly dated. Demosthenes' *Second Philippic* and the Persian appeal to Athens are firmly dated to the archonship of Lyciscus (344/43). The trial of Aeschines and the reply of Hegesippus to Philip's proposals are securely placed in the next archonship, that of Pythodotus (343/42). In addition, we are told that the trial of Aeschines took place three years after Demosthenes made his accusation. This should not be taken to mean precisely three years, but indicates that the trial belongs to the latter half of 343 rather than the earlier half of 342. The main problems relate to the dates of the Antiphon affair and Aeschines' election as ambassador to represent Athens in the dispute about Delos, which are not precisely dated by our sources, and the relative chronology of Aeschines' trial and the speech of Hegesippus, which are both placed in the same year.[1]

Scholars have differed widely in their attempts to date the Antiphon affair and the dispute about the temple on Delos. Schaefer dated both incidents to 344. He argued that Aeschines would never have praised the Areopagus as he did in his speech against Timarchus in 345 (his date for the speech) after that body had deprived him of the post awarded to him by the Assembly. Schaefer also detected an allusion to Aeschines' removal from this post in a comment made by Demosthenes at Aeschines' trial in 343 (αὐτὸν οὐκ εἴᾱτε πρεσβεύειν). Wüst disagreed with Schaefer's assessment of the tone of Aeschines' remarks about the Areopagus in the speech against Timarchus. Wüst detected sarcasm in these remarks and claimed that the sarcasm was caused by his anger about the Areopagus' decision to rob him of his post as ambassador. Wüst therefore placed these two incidents before the trial of Timarchus in 345 and after the *diapsephisis* of early 346 by which Antiphon lost his citizenship. Ramming disagreed with Wüst's interpretation of Aeschines' comments about the Areopagus in the speech against Timarchus, showing that there was no reason to find them sarcastic. He placed both the arrest of Antiphon and Aeschines' removal from his post as ambassador in 345, but did not justify his selection of this year in preference to some later date. Ramming's dating was nevertheless endorsed by Wankel, who called it "wahrscheinlich." Sealey has been the only one to place the arrest of Antiphon at a much later date. Proceeding on the assumption that "extraordinary measures against individuals and Antiphon's promise to burn the dockyards are more appropriate to war-time than to peace," Sealey moved the arrest of Antiphon down to the period after the outbreak of the war with Philip in 340/39.[2]

A look at the evidence is called for. Demosthenes explicitly states that the arrest and trial of Antiphon occurred before the Areopagus disqualified Aeschines from serving as ambassador to Delphi. Thus both of these incidents must be placed after the *diapsephisis* of 346/45 deprived Antiphon of his citizenship. On the other hand, the fact that Demosthenes recounts both incidents before mentioning the embassy of Pytho need not indicate that both events occurred before that embassy. Demosthenes' order of presentation indicates only that both events occurred in roughly the same period. There is no reason to assume that Demosthenes was narrating events in strict chronological order, and nothing in the text of his speech implies that he was. We should also reject Schaefer's attempt to arrive at a *terminus ante quem* by detecting an allusion to the removal of Aeschines from his post as ambassador to Delphi in Demosthenes' speech against Aeschines in 343. The passage might allude to that incident, but it could easily allude to some other incident.[3]

This leaves us with a *terminus post quem* of the middle of 346 when Antiphon lost his citizenship in the *diapsephisis* of 346/45. Since Antiphon is alleged to have made his incendiary promise to Philip, his arrest must belong to the period before the king's death in 336. This *terminus ante quem* can be moved back a few years for at the end of the passage in which these incidents are recounted, Demosthenes declares that they reveal how Aeschines showed his pro-Macedonian sympathies before the war broke out (πρὸ τοῦ πολεμεῖν). Since Demosthenes identifies Philip's seizure of the fleet carrying grain to Athens as the outbreak of the war, the *terminus ante quem* must be 340/39.[4]

Can we narrow these rather wide limits of 346/45 and 340/39? Here an *argumentum e silentio* helps us to make some progress. When Demosthenes prosecuted Aeschines in 343, he spared no effort to prove that Aeschines had been acting in Philip's interests and did not confine himself to the events of the Second Embassy, the actual subject of his indictment. If Aeschines' defense of Antiphon and Antiphon's subsequent confession of guilt had occurred not long before the trial, it is unlikely that Demosthenes would have neglected to mention it in his speech against Aeschines in 343. The incident would have contributed a good piece of circumstantial evidence to a case that was otherwise rather weak. Demosthenes certainly found it worthwhile to recount the incident in 330; why not in 343? On the other hand, if we place the arrest of Antiphon after 343, these problems do not arise. For these reasons, the arrest of Antiphon and Aeschines' election as ambassador to Delphi ought to be placed in the period 342–341.

The next question concerns the order of events in 343/42. Ever since Schaefer, scholars have separated Pytho's embassy and the speech Hegesippus made in reply to Philip's proposals to amend the peace by an interval of up to a year. While noting that Demosthenes' speech against Aeschines contains an allusion to Hegesippus' embassy to Philip, Schaefer drew attention to the absence of any mention of Philip's campaigns in Epirus and Ambracia, events discussed by Hegesippus in his speech. From these observations, Schaefer concluded that the embassy of Hegesippus must have occurred before Aeschines' trial, which was then followed by Hegesippus' speech.[5]

Placing Hegesippus' speech after Demosthenes' speech at Aeschines' trial creates a serious problem: why does Hegesippus neglect in his speech to mention the Macedonian intervention in Euboea, Philip's lending aid to his friends in Elis and Megara, and the trial of Philocrates, incidents that are all referred to by Demosthenes in his speech? Various explanations have been advanced to account for these omissions, but none of them satisfactory. It is simply impossible to understand why Hegesippus, whose aim in his speech is to document Philip's assaults on Greek freedom and to discredit the king's supporters in Athens, would not have used these events to bolster his arguments. A much more likely order of events places the speech of Hegesippus several months before the trial of Aeschines, with the trial of Philocrates and the events in Elis, Megara, and Euboea occurring in the interval. On the other hand it is easy to understand why Demosthenes does not mention Philip's campaigns in Ambracia and Epirus at the trial of Aeschines. Furnished with several more convincing examples of Philip's aggression nearer to Attica, he chose to pass over Philip's activities in a more remote area. Since Aeschines' trial probably belongs to the last half of 343, we should accordingly place the speech of Hegesippus in the middle of the summer of 343 and the events in Elis, Megara, and Euboea in the late summer or early fall of 343. Aeschines' trial then follows in the late fall of 343.[6]

The course of negotiations with Philip in 343 followed the same pattern as the negotiations of 346. When Philip wished to make peace with Athens in 346, he sent a message with Iatrocles and Aristodemus, who reported it to the Assembly. As soon as this message was received, the Athenians voted to send ten ambassadors to Philip (Aeschin. 2.16–17). These ambassadors left in the middle of Anthesterion (see Appendix 4) and traveled to Macedon, where they presented the Athenian proposals for peace. On the same day Philip replied to these proposals and delivered his own counterproposals for peace and alliance (Aeschin. 2.18–39). These proposals were written down in a letter that Philip gave to the ambassadors to read out to the Assembly (Aeschin. 2.45). The Athenian ambassadors then returned to Athens in late Anthesterion and reported to the Council and Assembly, where the letter of Philip was read out (Aeschin. 2.45–54). The Macedonian ambassadors were introduced to the Assembly on Elaphebolion 18 to present Philip's version of the treaty, after which the Athenians discussed the issue of peace and alliance.[7] On the next day, the Athenians voted to accept the treaty (Aeschin. 2.61; Dem. 19.57).

The pattern in 343 was no different. Pytho was sent to Philip to announce the king's willingness to discuss revision of the peace ([Dem.] 7.18). Hegesippus was then elected with several others to journey to Macedon and present to Philip the Athenian proposals for the revision of the treaty ([Dem.] 7.2; Dem. 19.331). After hearing the Athenian proposals, Philip offered his response to them and submitted his own proposals. These proposals were written down in a letter, which the Athenian ambassadors carried back to Athens ([Dem.] 7.46). These proposals were discussed at a meeting of the Assembly during which Hegesippus delivered his speech. The only difference between the two sets of negotiations was that in 343 Philip's proposals appear to have been rejected by the Assembly. But the entire course of the negotiations in 343 should not have taken any longer than those of 346, which lasted less than two months from Iatrocles' message to the ratification of the Peace of Philocrates. Even if Hegesippus' embassy had to wait in Macedon for the arrival of Philip the way the Second Embassy had to in 346, the entire course of the negotiations in 343 from Pytho's embassy down to the rejection of Philip's proposals should not have lasted more than three months. There is certainly no reason to think that several months intervened between the completion of Hegesippus' embassy and the discussion and rejection of Philip's proposals by the Assembly, as Schaefer proposed. Pytho's embassy must threfore have come to Athens in the spring of 343 with Hegesippus' embassy to Macedon and the debate about Philip's proposals in the Assembly following soon afterward.

Appendix 9

The Legal Grounds for Aeschines' Objection to Antiphon's Arrest

Hansen believes that Aeschines' criticism of Demosthenes' arrest of Antiphon was based on the argument "that summary arrest of a citizen is unconstitutional."[1] This is clearly wrong. First of all, Antiphon was not a citizen. Demosthenes (18.132) states that Antiphon had lost his citizenship. His status is also evident from the fact that he was later tortured, a procedure from which all Athenian citizens were legally protected.[2] Second, Demosthenes gives Aeschines' reason for objecting to the arrest: he went into a house without the authorization of a decree (ἐπ' οἰκίας βαδίζων ἄνευ ψηφίσματος). Antiphon was clearly inside a house since Demosthenes describes him as "hiding." No one was allowed to enter into the house of another man in Attica without his permission unless one had prior authorization from the Council or Assembly. For instance, the trierarch who delivered the speech against Mnesibulus and Euergus relates that he only attempted to enter the house of Theopompus after receiving an order from the Council requiring all trierarchs to recover any missing gear from their predecessors "by any means they could" ([Dem.] 47.18–21). We should compare the reluctance of Hagnophilus to enter the house of the trierarch in his absence even after he had been summoned by the latter's slaves ([Dem.] 47.60). Note also the stipulation that a man could not enter into another man's house to deliver a summons, but had to shout the summons from the street if the defendant happened to be inside.[3] Demosthenes accused Antiphon of being a spy and thus considered him subject to summary arrest. His arrest was similar to that of Anaxinus, whom Demosthenes also accused of being a spy (Dem. 18.137; Aeschin. 3.223). Hansen lists Anaxinus' case as an instance of *eisangelia*, but this clashes with the evidence of Aeschines, who describes the procedure as an arrest (σύλληψιν).[4] Furthermore, Anaxinus was a foreigner from Oreos and in no other case do we know of a person who was not either an Athenian or a metic being prosecuted by *eisangelia*.

172

Appendix 10

Two Recent Views of Aeschines' Prosecution of Ctesiphon in 330

In recent years, Cawkwell and Burke have offered two different explanations for the reason why the case against Ctesiphon finally came to trial in the summer of 330. Cawkwell believes that Aeschines brought his case to court in that year because of Demosthenes' recent failure to support Agis' campaign.[1] Burke holds that it was not Aeschines, but Demosthenes, who was responsible for having the case finally heard in 330.[2] Burke further argues that Demosthenes was working in concert with Lycurgus, who shortly before had brought a charge against Leocrates. I will examine each view separately, beginning with Cawkwell's.

Cawkwell argues that Demosthenes missed a golden opportunity in 331 to persuade the Athenians to join Agis in his war against Macedonian hegemony. According to Cawkwell, this is the reason why Demosthenes in his defense of Ctesiphon does not comment on the subject of Agis' recent defeat.[3] It also explains why Aeschines "resurrected his charge against Demosthenes after the failure of Agis' revolt." But nowhere in his speech against Ctesiphon does Aeschines say that Demosthenes miscalculated in opposing support for Agis. On the contrary, Aeschines (3.166–67) criticizes him for his vague rhetoric about unnamed politicians who wished to weaken Athens and for his false boast that he had brought about the revolt of Sparta, Thessaly, and the Perrhaibi. His attack is on Demosthenes' cowardice and boastfulness, not his mistaken advice. Furthermore, Cawkwell is wrong to dismiss the sound reasons for Athens staying out of the war.[4] Even with Athenian assistance, Agis would have had a difficult time prevailing over Antipater. Cawkwell cites Athenian naval strength at the time, but this would have had no effect on the outcome of the revolt, which was decided in a land battle. One should recall the situation in 338: although Athens enjoyed control of the sea, Philip was still able to win his victory at Chaeronea. In 323 the Athenians also had naval superiority in the Aegean as well as the backing of Aetolia, Thessaly, and much of the Peloponnese, yet were still unable to defeat the forces of Antipater and Craterus (D.S. 18.11–12, 14.4–15.9, 16.4–17.5).

Burke holds that Demosthenes was responsible for Ctesiphon's case coming to trial in 330. First, he argues that Aeschines had no incentive for "reopening his suit" and that his motives for bringing his charge were to deprive "Demosthenes of the popular vote of confidence with which an uncontested proposal would have provided him" and to deter "others from proposing additional crowns for Demosthenes." But that is surely because Demosthenes did nothing between 336 and 330 to make himself worthy of a crown. As we noted in chapter 7, these years were a period of relative inactivity for both Aeschines and Demosthenes. If this were one of Aeschines' motives, why did no one propose a crown for Demosthenes between 330 and 323 after Aeschines lost his case? Just as we do not need the threat of prosecution to explain the absence of honors for Demosthenes between 330 and 323, we likewise do not need it to explain his lack of honors in the period 336 to 330. As for the claim that Aeschines' charge by itself would have tarnished Demosthenes' honors, that is unlikely. Aristophon had dozens of his proposals challenged by the same legal means Aeschines employed against Ctesiphon, yet he was acquitted each time without any cumulative loss of prestige (Aeschin. 3.194).

Burke then claims that Aeschines "could have caused only minimal discomfort by reopening the suit." To begin with, Aeschines did not reopen the suit. Technically speaking, the case had never gone to trial and so was not yet closed. Next, Aeschines stood to gain a great deal of satisfaction from a conviction that would have damaged his opponent's reputation. A verdict against Ctesiphon could have been construed as a declaration that Demosthenes did not deserve the honors proposed by his friend and thereby as a partial vindication for Aeschines' opposition to his policies. Finally, Burke assumes that "whatever political support he (i.e., Aeschines) may have been able to muster earlier in the decade on behalf of his cause was by 330 seriously diminished. And without strong partisan support, Aeschines' chances of gaining a political victory in the courts were not great at all." This assessment of Aeschines' political strength in 330 is based on nothing more than speculation. We simply do not know anything about Aeschines' political allies at this time. We do know, however, that two men who had been closely associated with him earlier, Phocion and Nausicles, were still both prominent.[5] Furthermore, it is difficult to tell what impact that political support (or lack thereof) would have had on a verdict. After all, the members of the court were sworn to judge in accordance with the laws, not on the basis of political influence. We should also recall that in 343 Aeschines had considerable support at his trial, yet came within an ace of losing his case. Burke also notes that Aeschines had passed up earlier opportunities to attack honorary decrees for Demosthenes and takes this as an indication that he had no desire to bring his case to trial. But a failure to prosecute before 336 had nothing to do with a decision to delay prosecution until 330. Nor does Burke take into account the reasons that made 330 a propitious year for bringing the case to trial.

Burke next turns to the advantages Demosthenes had for forcing Aeschines to bring his suit in 330. He cites Aeschines' alleged "inability to secure strong partisan support for his cause" and "the harm done to his procedural case by the six years delay." According to Burke, Demosthenes' aim was the same as that of Lycurgus in bringing his suit against Leocrates: "to invigorate popular opposition to Macedon but do so in such a way as to avoid the risk of an inopportune military commitment." The major weakness in Burke's analysis is his inability to explain how Demosthenes could have forced Aeschines to bring his case to court. The person who initiated a prosecution, then failed to bring it to trial, suffered a form of automatic *atimia:* until he brought his case to court, he was barred from bringing any other public charges.[6] But he could only be prosecuted for defying this ban. To our knowledge, however, Aeschines brought no further public charges after 336 and thus could not be threatened with prosecution by Demosthenes. There was no other way a defendant could proceed against a prosecutor who did not wish to follow through on his prosecution. And Demosthenes certainly does not allude to any threat on his part to coerce Aeschines into proceeding. In fact, Demosthenes (18.308) speaks as if it was Aeschines who was responsible for bringing the case to trial in 330.

Burke thinks that in forcing Aeschines to proceed, Demosthenes was cooperating with Lycurgus, who shortly before had prosecuted Leocrates for deserting Athens during the crisis after Chaeronea. He cites three cases where "Lycurgus and Demosthenes worked in consort during the third quarter of the fourth century," noting how they opposed Macedon, helped build Athenian defenses, and "possessed a similar desire to return Athens to her former postion of Greatness." But similar aims and views need not betoken active cooperation. True, there were similarities "in the tone, in the circumstances, in the mood and in the occasions" between the trials of Ctesiphon and Leocrates, but they do not constitute an argument for collaboration, especially in the absence of other evidence.

Appendix 11

Philip's Relationship with the Thessalians

Ever since the late nineteenth century, scholars have believed that the Thessalians elected Philip II to the position of *archon* in their league sometime in the 350s.[1] Despite its widespread acceptance, this belief lacks firm support in the ancient sources and should be rejected.

The view that Philip was *archon* of the Thessalian League rests on a misinterpretation of a passage in Justin's epitome of Pompeius Trogus' *Philippic History* (11.3.1–2). According to Justin, Alexander, soon after his accession to the Macedonian throne, marched to Thessaly and asked them to renew the ties they had maintained with his father. After hearing his appeal, the Thessalians voted to make him *exemplo patris dux universae gentis* and to entrust to him their taxes and revenues. It is assumed that the *gentis* referred to must be the Thessalian race, but it could equally well apply to the Greek race. Indeed, the adjective *universae* appears to point to some larger entity than a local confederation. Note in particular the phrase *universae Graeciae* where Justin (9.5.2) describes the Common Peace imposed by Philip after Chaeronea.[2] The phrase *exemplo patris* also indicates that the position of *dux* should be a position held previously by Philip that Justin had mentioned earlier in his narrative. Justin (9.4.2; 5.4) twice calls Philip "leader" (*dux*) of Greece in his account of events after Chaeronea. Justin is here clearly referring to Philip's position as leader of the League of Corinth, whose members included most of the poleis on the Greek mainland. This should therefore be the same position that Justin says the Thessalians voted that Alexander should hold *exemplo patris*. Furthermore, Justin (11.2.5) states shortly before his account of the Alexander's appeal to the Thessalians that Alexander was elected "leader" (*dux*) by the cities that had been summoned to Corinth just as his father had been (*exemplo patris*). The close similarities in wording strongly indicates that the adjoining passages refer to the same position.

In one passage, Justin (8.2.1) states that the Thebans and the Thessalians chose (*eligunt*) Philip, king of Macedon, as their leader (*ducem*) against Onomarchus, but this must refer to Philip's position as leader of the Amphictyons who were attempting to regain control of the temple at Delphi from the Phocians. It cannot refer to Philip's election as *archon* of the Thessalian League since the position was awarded not by the Thessalians alone, but by the Thessalians and the Thebans acting together. If one interprets the passage to mean that Philip was elected *archon* of the Thessalian League, one is forced to conclude as well that Philip was also elected *archon* of the Theban League, but that is a conclusion that clashes with everything we know about Thebes during the period.

One might object to this interpretation of the Thessalian vote for Alexander by pointing out that the Thessalians did not have the power to confer the leadership of the League of

Corinth on the king.[3] Although they could not dictate to the rest of the Greeks who should hold this position, the Thessalians could still express their approval of Alexander's bid to gain the leadership by a vote of support. In fact, Diodorus (17.4.1) reveals that this is precisely what took place when he says that Alexander persuaded the Thessalians that "the leadership of Greece, which had been given to his father, ought to be conferred on him." The support of the Thessalians was expressed in a resolution voted by all of Thessaly (κοινῷ τῆς Θετ-ταλίας δόγματι). Justin and Diodorus are obviously describing the same event here. On the other hand, if Justin is referring to Alexander's election as *archon* of the Thessalian League while Diodorus is describing a resolution voted by the Thessalians that Alexander be made leader of the Corinthian League, one would have to explain why Justin refers to the archon-ship of Thessaly but not the leadership of Greece, and why Diodorus, when describing the same event, mentions the leadership of Greece but not the archonship of Thessaly.[4]

There is no contemporary evidence that Philip or Alexander was *archon* of Thessaly. Isocrates (5.20) attributes Philip's control of the region to his policy of winning over some communities to his alliance by benefactions and destroying those who opposed him. Satyrus (Ath. *Deipn.* 557b–e) attributes Philip's influence in Thessaly to his marriages to Nicesipolis of Pherai and Philinna of Larisa.[5] Demosthenes (9.12) says that Philip entered Thessaly as an ally and friend of Pherai, but never calls him *archon* of the league (cf. 18.211 where the Thessalians are on the same footing as Philip's other allies). Elsewhere Demosthenes (1.21–22) talks of the Thessalians voting to demand back Pagasai and to forbid Philip to fortify Magnesia and reports a rumor that they will no longer allow him to collect harbor and market duties (cf. Justin 11.3.2: *vectigalia omnia* voted to Alexander). This right granted to Philip does not show that he held the position of *archon* of the Thessalian League since it was not unusual for one member of an alliance to pay some contribution to the dominant member in return for protection. One need only compare the Athenians collecting harbor dues from their allies in the later years of the Peloponnesian War (Th. 7.28.4).[6]

In short, there is no evidence showing that Philip was *archon* of Thessaly. Philip had alliances with the Thessalian cities and held no special constitutional position in a federal government. He gained his position of influence in the region in his customary way, that is, by distributing favors to his friends, by marriage alliances with powerful families, and by keeping his enemies few and isolated so they could be easily crushed.

Notes

For the names of ancient authors and the titles of their works, I employ the abbreviations used in H. G. Liddell and R. Scott, *A Greek-English Lexicon,* 9th ed., revised by Sir H. Stuart Jones, Oxford, 1940. For the fragments of the Greek historians I use the numbers assigned by F. Jacoby, *Die Fragmente der griechischen Historiker* (Leiden, 1923–). When referring to the works of modern scholars, I use the Harvard system. Full bibliographical details for modern works can be found in the References. For the scholia I have used M. R. Dilts, ed., *Scholia in Aeschinem* (Leipzig 1992) and M. R. Dilts, ed., *Scholia Demosthenica* 2 vols. (Leipzig 1983–86).

Chapter 1

1. Aeschines is not mentioned in Justin's epitome of Trogus' history nor in the extant fragments of the works of Anaximenes, Androtion, Demetrius of Phaleron, Duris of Samos, Hermippus, Marsyas, Philochorus, and Theopompus. Nor is his name found on any surviving Attic inscriptions. Some have thought that the Aeschines listed on *IG* iv² 255 is identical with the Athenian politician, but this is unlikely. Diodorus (17.4.8) mentions Aeschines only once, when quoting (with slightly different word order) from his speech against Ctesiphon (3.173).

Plutarch drew extensively on Aeschines' speech against Ctesiphon in his *Life of Demosthenes:* 4.2 draws on Aeschin. 3.171; 9.1 draws on Aeschin. 3.152; 12.3–6 on Aeschin. 3.52; 17.1 on Aeschin. 3.85; 18 on Aeschin. 3.137–40; 20.2 on Aeschin. 3.253; 22 on Aeschin. 3.77, 160, 219; 23.3 on Aeschin. 3.161. For Plutarch's use of Aeschin. 3.159 at 21.3 see chapter 7. Although 16.4 derived in part from Aeschin. 2.47–52, Plutarch does not appear to have made much use of the speech of 343. In fact, his brief description of Demosthenes' speech to Philip on the First Embassy (16.1–2) contradicts Aeschin. 2.34–35. For Plutarch's mistaken belief (shared by Photius *Bibl.* 491ᵃᵇ) that Aeschines and Demosthenes did not deliver their speeches about the false embassy of 346, see Schaefer (1885–87) 2: 413–16.

For the ancient biographies of Aeschines see chapter 2, note 1, and Harris (1988b).

The only piece of evidence about Aeschines' life that does not derive from his speeches and those of Demosthenes is the statement of Idomeneus (*FGrHist* 338 F 10 = Plu. *Dem.* 15.5) that Aeschines escaped conviction on the charge of false embassy by a mere thirty votes. On this see Schaefer (1885–87) 2: 413, note 2.

2. The penalties for failure to gain one fifth of the votes were the same as those for failing to follow through on a public prosecution. See the evidence set forth in Harrison (1971)

83, note 2, with the discussion in Harris (1989b) 133, note 40, and Harris (1992b) 79–80. Magistrates presiding at trials: Harrison (1971) 4–36. Absence of rules of evidence enforced by presiding magistrate: Bonner (1905) 20. There was a law against hearsay (Dem. 44.55; 57.4), but it never appears to have been enforced by a magistrate during a trial. On this law see Wyse (1904) 541.

3. Schaefer's use of consistency: Schaefer (1885–87) 2: 197–99. Aeschines' statements about his relationship with Philocrates: Aeschin. 1.174; 2.14, 19, 20. Demosthenes' statements about the Greek ambassadors: Dem. 18.23; 19.16.

4. Men condemned without good reason: Th. 2.65; 4.65. Trials conducted within the space of one day: Harrison (1971) 161. Aristotle's anecdote: Arist. *Rh.* 2.3.13.1380b. One could also point to the case of the Hellanotamiai who were condemned and executed, but later found to be innocent of the crimes they were accused of (Antiphon 5.69–71). Though there were many miscarriages of justice, one should not exaggerate the deficiencies of the Athenian legal system. For a healthy corrective to pessimistic estimates of the Athenian system, see Meyer-Laurin (1965).

5. There is much evidence that indicates the delivered and written versions of the speeches corresponded very closely: Schaefer (1858) 68–9, 72–77. Worthington (1991) argues that the presence of ring-composition in the speeches of Dinarchus shows that he revised his speeches extensively after their oral delivery, but I am not sure the argument is sound. Certainly no one would argue that the presence of ring-composition in Homer and Pindar indicates that the versions of their poems found in the manuscripts differed greatly from the oral versions.

6. Dover (1968) 168–69 does not consider the possibility of explaining the discrepancies in this way and consequently exaggerates the extent of the differences between the orally delivered and written versions of the speeches. His views are endorsed by Todd (1990a) 167. Schaefer (1858) 69–72 also did not consider this kind of explanation.

Such an explanation probably accounts for the differences between Dem. 19.175–77 (Demosthenes accuses Aeschines of having met secretly with Philip at Pherai during the night, but does not say how he traveled to meet him) and Aeschin. 2.124 (Aeschines states that Demosthenes accused him of crossing the river Loidias at night in a small boat to meet with Philip) and those between Dem. 19.193–96 (Demosthenes praises Satyrus for asking Philip to release the daughters of Apollophanes of Pydna) and Aeschin. 2.156 (Aeschines recalls how Demosthenes praised Satyrus, but says that Satyrus' friends were chained and working in Philip's orchard, a detail missing in Demosthenes). In the first case, Aeschines probably added the detail about crossing the river in a small boat to stress how implausible Demosthenes' charge was. In the second, Aeschines may have added the pathetic detail to make fun of his opponent's exaggerated attempt to arouse pity for the daughters of Apollophanes. Schaefer also found a discrepancy between the remarks made by Demosthenes (19.287) and Aeschines (2.150–52) about the sons of Philodemus, but there is no actual discrepancy: see Harris (1986a).

7. Comparison with Dionysius and description of priestess's dream: Aeschin. 2.10. A *scholion ad loc.* claims that Demosthenes made these remarks before the *diaitetai*. But proceedings before the *diaitetai* were confined to *dikai* or private suits and never took place as part of *graphai* or public prosecutions: see Arist. *Ath.* 53 with Rhodes (1981) 587–96. Another *scholion* on the same passage says the dream is described in Book 6 of Timaeus' history (= *FGrH* 566 F 29) and gives a short description. Whatever Demosthenes said about the dream in court, it probably struck him as likely to look ψυχρόν in a written version, so he deleted it. Note that Plutarch (*Dem.* 10) says Demosthenes showed far more boldness and daring in his spoken speeches than in his written ones. Charge about driving away Critobulus: Aeschin. 2.86.

8. Demosthenes says Aeschines spoke on Elaphebolion 19: Dem. 19.15–16. Aeschines refutes with evidence: Aeschin. 2.63–66. Aeschines says Demosthenes carried only one talent: Aeschin. 2.100. Demosthenes disproves with witnesses: Dem. 19.169–71. Decree of Council cited by both orators: Aeschin. 2.91–92; Dem. 19.154. Note also the general conclusion of Schaefer (1858) 81: "Demnach geht meine Ansicht dahin dass Aeschines in seiner Rede wider Ktesiphon nachträglich zum Zwecke der Herausgabe einige Änderungen vornahm, hier auslassend, dort hinzusetzend; dass Demosthenes seine Gegenrede hinterdrein niederschrieb, ebenfalls mit einigen Änderungen letzter Hand; dass aber beide Reden in der Hauptsache so wie sie gehalten sind uns vorliegen" (*in general both speeches have been preserved just as they were delivered*). Lavency (1964) 190 arrived at a similar conclusion by a different route: "les recherches dont nous avons exposé le résultat accréditent la thèse de la conformité du discours publié au texte preparé" (*our investigations . . . support the view that the published speech conformed to the text prepared [for delivery in court]*).

Two inscriptions found in Attica record decrees quoted or paraphrased in a speech of an Athenian orator. The first is a decree of honors granted to Epicerdes of Cyrene (*IG* ii^2 174 with Meritt [1970]), which is discussed at Dem. 20.42. As Meritt notes, Demosthenes' "quotation is remarkably close." Lycurgus' paraphrase of the Ephebic Oath (*Leocr.* 76–77) is also very close to the text of the oath found in a contemporary decree from the deme of Acharnai—see Tod (1948) 303–7. At first glance, Lysias' quotation (13.70–72) from the decree granting rewards for Phrynichus' assassins appears to be at odds with *IG* ii^2 110 + , but see Meiggs and Lewis (1969) 263. Aeschines occasionally places parenthetical phrases in his quotations of laws (see Harris [1992b] 77) or slightly alters the wording (see chapter 7), but this is a different matter.

9. For bibliography and discussion of the Athenian archives, see Thomas (1989) 68–83. Thomas may exaggerate the chaotic state of record-keeping in the Metroon—see West (1989). One should distinguish between private documents, which were not kept in the Metroon and thus were less reliable, and public documents. (The anecdote recounted by Athenaeus [*Deipn.* 407b–c) about Alcibiades walking into the Metroon and erasing an indictment need not be believed.) On private documents see Calhoun (1914).

10. Widespread bribery of witnesses: Dem. 29.28; Isoc. 18.51f; Lys. 29.7. On bribery in general in Greek politics, see Harvey (1985). Political clubs in 411: Thuc. 8.54.4. Activities of the clubs: Calhoun (1913) 77ff. *Dike pseudomartyrion:* Harrison (1971) 192–98. Penalty for conviction: Andoc. 1.74. The man who prosecuted on this charge and failed to obtain a conviction suffered only a slight penalty—see Dem. 47.2. Todd in Cartledge, Millett, and Todd (1990) 27 argues that Athenian witnesses had two functions, first, "to tell the truth," and second, "to support the litigant for whom he appears." It is more accurate to state that the interests of litigants were different from those of the court in respect to witnesses. Litigants called on witnesses to provide support for their cases, and courts listened to them to find out the truth (see Ar. *Rhet.* 1.1.8.1354b for the role of the court). In this regard the Athenian courts were no different than modern courts.

11. For instance, all the documents found in Dem. 18 are forgeries. See Wankel (1976) 79–82 for discussion and bibliography. MacDowell (1990) 43–47 believes some of the documents in Dem. 21 are genuine, but see Harris (1992b) 75–78. The authenticity of these documents requires a comprehensive study since the earlier works written about the issue are now outdated. Demosthenes charges bribery: Dem. 19.166–68. For discussion of the charge, see chapter 5.

12. Aeschines claims Demosthenes was nominated by Philocrates: Aeschin. 2.18–19. For discussion see chapter 3.

13. Council's failure to vote honors: Dem. 19.32. For discussion see chapter 5.

14. Decrees kept by the Secretary of the Council: *Ath. Pol.* 54.3 with Rhodes (1972)

136–37. Letters from foreign states: Dem. 19.38, 51. Records of trials: trials: Harrison (1971) 91. Aeschines calls on *proedroi* to testify: Aeschin. 2.85. Members of First Embassy testify about their reports: Aeschin. 2.46.

15. Representatives from Phocis testify: Aeschin. 2.143. Jason of Pherai testifies: [Dem.] 49.22. Sworn statements left by men going abroad: Aeschin. 2.19; Dem. 46.7; Is. 3.18. Summons to testify: Aeschin: 2.68; [Dem.] 59.28. Todd in Cartledge, Millett, and Todd (1990) 24–25 claims the procedure was only available against reluctant witnesses actually in court, but Dem. 32.30 proves his view incorrect (Carey [1992] 25). Fine for refusing to obey summons: Aeschin. 1.46. Disenfranchised and exiles unable to testify: Dem. 21.95; [Dem.] 59.26–27. Male children of Athenian citizens were also able to testify—see Harris (1988). The unconvincing attempt of Trevett (1991) to deny male minors could testify is based on the false view that the loans to Timotheus made by Pasion did not come from his bank.

16. Time limit on speeches: Rhodes (1981) 719–23. Clepsydra measures speeches: Young (1939). Need to refute only most serious charges: Lys. 24.21; Hyp. *Lyc.* 8–10. Aeschines charges Demosthenes entered Council by means of bribery: Aeschin. 3.62.

17. Aeschines accused of being *tritagonistes:* Dem. 18.262; 19.246. Aeschines alludes to charge: Aerschin. 2.157. Demosthenes charged with being *logographos:* Aeschin. 2.165, 180; 3.173. Demosthenes as *logographos:* Dem. 22. *hyp.* 2.13; Dem. 23. *hyp.* 2.4.

18. Aeschines boasts in 346 about cooperating with Philocrates: Aeschin. 1.174. Aeschines denies in 343 working with Philocrates: Aeschin. 2.14, 19, 20.

19. Two accounts of outbreak of Fourth Sacred War: Aeschin. 3.113–24; Dem. 18.143–59. For discussion see Chapter 7.

20. The method developed here for evaluating the evidence found in the orators' speeches applies only to the use of their statements as historical evidence for contemporary events. For the Attic orators as sources for events of earlier periods, see Pearson (1941) and the more extensive treatment of Nouhaud (1982). For the use of the orators as sources for Athenian law see Wolff (1974) 27–39. As sources for religious beliefs see Mikalson (1983) 7–8. As sources for popular morality see Dover (1974) with the cautionary note of Harris (1990).

Chapter 2

1. Unreliability of anecdotes: Vansina (1985) 95–96, 106, 132–33, 165–66, 169–70, 172. Interests of ancient biographers: Momigliano (1971) 71ff. Information found in lives of poets derived from statements in their works and inferences therefrom: Lefkowitz (1981). Information in lives of Aeschines derived mostly from statements found in his speeches and those of Demosthenes: Blass (1887–98) 3.2.154. Kindstrand (1982) 68–84 has examined the evidence furnished by the lives of Aeschines about his teachers and his teaching on Rhodes. While he rejects the statements about the former as "historically false," he is inclined to trust in the information about his teaching on Rhodes. But see Harris (1988b).

2. I am thus not concerned with the Solonian orders, which had fallen into desuetude by the fourth century: *Ath. Pol.* 7.4; 47.1 with Rhodes (1981) 145–46, 551. For the term "status-group" see Weber (1946) 186–88.

Davies (1981) 13–14 mistakenly conflates the two kinds of groups when he states that "the selection of the men who perform liturgies to embody the Athenian propertied class is the selection, not of an amorphous arbitrarily defined group of men at the top of the economic scale, but that of a group which with its special burdens, responsibilities and privileges formed a recognized social class." Davies bases his view primarily on [X.] *Ath.* 1.13, but ignores other passages in the work where the author stresses birth and education, rather than wealth, in the determination of social class (cf. 1.2, 5, 13; 2.15). To borrow the terminology of R. Centers (1949) 12–29, the liturgical class formed a "social stratum" in which membership was determined by one criterion, in this case wealth, and not a "social class" in which membership is determined by class consciousness. Cf. the distinction made by Cantril (1943) between "social class" and "economic class." For a useful set of criteria to establish the existence of a "social class," see Ossowski (1963) 135–36. Whereas the liturgical class could be termed a "social stratum" (Centers) or "economic class" (Cantril), it exhibited little evidence of class consciousness; the *kaloi kagathoi* did possess the requisite qualities of a "social class" by their strong sense of class consciousness and shared life-style. Because it was difficult to maintain the life-style of a *kalos kagathos* without a certain amount of property, many members of the liturgical class were considered to be *kaloi kagathoi* and vice versa, but the two groups were not identical in their membership, which was defined in different ways. These fundamental methodological issues are passed over by Ober (1989).

3. On the cavalry in general see Bugh (1988). Recruiting of the cavalry: X. *Hipparch.* 1.9, 12 (Hipparchs enroll); *Ath. Pol.* 49.2 (*katalogeis* enroll). For the date of the change, see Bugh (1982). (I find Bugh's explanation for the change unconvincing.) The community provided the recruit with a loan toward the purchase of a horse (see Lys. 16.6–7 with Kroll [1977] 97–100) and with fodder (*Ath. Pol.* 49.1; Meiggs and Lewis [1969] #84, line 4; *IG* ii^2 1264, lines 5–8; *scholia ad* Dem. 24.101), but the rest of the expenses were paid by the recruit and must have been substantial. For *hippotrophia* as a luxury affordable only by the wealthy, see Davies (1981) 97–105. It would thus have been natural for the Hipparchs or *katalogeis* to look for recruits in the houses of those who performed liturgies. Note that someone who served in the cavalry as a young man was expected to perform liturgies when older (Dem. 42.21–25) and that the size of the cavalry was roughly the same as that of the liturgical class (Ar. *Eq.* 225; X. *Hipparch.* 9.3 and Dem. 14.13 place it at 1,000; *Ath. Pol.* 24.3 and Th. 2.13 place it at 1,200).

Number of liturgies: Davies (1967). Selection of *choregoi: Ath. Pol.* 56.3 with Rhodes (1981) 622–23. Duties of *choregos:* Pickard-Cambridge (1968) 75–78, 86–93. Cost of putting on a performance: Lys. 21.1. Costs of liturgies: Amit (1965) 103–15. The trierarchical system was reformed about 357: MacDowell (1986). Size of the liturgical class in the fourth century: Rhodes (1982) 2–5. Property required for inclusion in the liturgical class: Davies (1971) xxiv.

4. On the *eisphora* symmories see MacDowell (1986). On the question of the *pro-eisphorontes* see Wallace (1989b).

5. On the ephebeia in general see Pélékidis (1962). Age-classes: *Ath. Pol.* 53.4. Service as ephebes: Aeschin. 2.167; *Ath. Pol.* 42.3–4. Calling up by age-class: *Ath. Pol.* 53.7. Service until age fifty-nine: *Ath. Pol.* 53.4. Older men called up only in emergencies: Dem. 3.4; Aeschin. 2.133 (reading τετταράκοντα). There may have been an alternate method of calling up hoplites: Rhodes (1981) 327. For a summary of recent work on the population of Athens see Rhodes (1988) 271–77. For a different view see Hansen (1982), (1985), (1988).

6. For the distinction between the liturgical class and the *kaloi kagathoi* see note 2.

7. For the absence of an aristocracy of birth in Classical Greece see Veyne (1990) 120–22. This important work, which was originally published in French in 1976, is completely ignored by Ober (1989), whose own account of status places too much emphasis on birth and neglects other criteria. Finley (1985) 35–61 discusses social status, but his analysis is marred by his unwillingness to identify the specific criteria for social respectability. For an attempt to classify the various meanings of the term *kalos kagathos* see Wankel (1961). This work contains good discussions of individual passages, but the attempt to classify all uses of the term is too rigid. Nor am I convinced by his argument that the term changes its meaning during the fourth century.

8. "Being a *kalos kagathos* was a matter of what is nowadays called 'life-style'." (de Ste. Croix [1972] 372). Ideal of self-sufficiency: Aymard (1943). Misfortune of having to work for another: X. *Mem.* 2.1.8.3–4; Arist. *Rh.* 1.9.1367a27; *Pol.* 1.5.1260a36–b6. Manual work undertaken only under the constraint of poverty and considered slavish: [Dem.] 57.45; Aymard (1948). Attitudes to hired labor: de Ste. Croix (1981) 179–204. Physical work considered demeaning: X. *Oec.* 4.2–3; Pl. *R.* 2.371c. Importance of leisure: Arist. *Pol.* 2.5.1269a34–36; 4.4.1291b25–26; 7.8.1329a1–2; 7.13.1333a33–36; 7.13.1334a14–16. On the symposium in general see Murray (1983). Hunting and exercising in the gymnasium: Ar. *Eq.* 1383; *Nub.* 1,002–23; *Ran.* 727–29; Isoc. 7.45 (note how he surreptitiously slips in philosophy at the end of his list of respectable activities—one wonders if his opinion was shared by other *kaloi kagathoi*). Observe how Aeschines in response to Demosthenes' aspersions on the social standing of his brother Philochares asserts he frequented the gymnasia: Aeschin. 2.149.

9. *Kalos kagathos* as *plousios:* Pl. *R.* 8.569a; [X.] *Ath.* 1.2, 14; 2.15. Hoplites linked with *gennaioi* and *chrestoi:* [X.] *Ath.* 1.2; X. *Mem.* 3.5.19. Hoplites as *gnorimoi:* Arist. *Pol.* 5.2.1303a8–10. Cavalrymen as *kaloi kagathoi:* Ar. *Eq.* 225–27; Din. 3.12. The word *gennaioi* used to describe upper class: [X.] *Ath.* 1.2.4–5, 13–4; Isoc. 16.25, 31, 33; 19.7, 33. *Eugeneia* as the product of old wealth: Arist. *Pol.* 4.6.1294a21–22; 5.1.1301b3–4. Note that when the Sausage-Seller is questioned to see if he is really a *poneros,* he is asked about his parents (Ar. *Eq.* 185–86).

Although a few sophists began in the later fifth century to question the importance of good birth, it is clear from the remarks of Antiphon fr. 44B (Diels-Kranz) that the prejudice in favor of it was still widespread. For skepticism about its value, see Eur. *Dictys* fr. 336, *Alex.* fr. 52; *El.* 367–85 (life-style and the kind of company one keeps are better indications of respectability than wealth and birth).

Boasting about ancestors: Lys. 6.54; 10.27–28; Isoc. 16.25. Aristotle's advice: Arist. *Rh.* 2.9.1387a18–31. Cratinus on *nouveaux riches:* Cratin. fr. 201 (Kock). Taunt directed at Iphicrates: Plu. *Mor.* 187b; Arist. *Rh.* 1.9.1367b18. Compare the insult cast at Apollodorus for his father's servile birth: [Dem.] 50.26. Insults to Phormio and Pasion: [Dem.] 45.73–76, 81–82, 86. Other disparaging allusions to servile birth: Lys. 13.18, 64, 73, 76; 30.2, 5, 27; Dem. 21.149–50.

Davies (1981) 71 believes that expressions of hostility against parvenus were less frequent in the period after 386 and attributes this phenomenon to a change in social attitudes. But if attitudes had changed so much, why does Aristotle, writing after 386, advise those speaking in court to appeal to the prejudice against parvenus?

10. For an exposition of the content and ideals of the traditional education, see Pl. *Men.* 94b1–4; *Prt.* 325a8–326c1; Ar. *Nub.* 961–1023 (albeit with a satiric twist). Marrou (1967) 76–77 argues that there was a "démocratisation" of the traditional education in Athens during the fifth century, but still recognizes that it remained "more or less . . . the privilege of an elite" (*de fait, elle restera toujours plus ou moins, comme le souligne Platon, le privilège d'une élite, qui seule la poussera jusqu'au bout, étant plus à même de consentir les sacrifices qu'elle exige et mieux placé pour en apprécier les avantages*). Connection between education and social status: Isoc. 13.6; 15.220; 16.33; Lys. 20.11–12; Ar. *Eq.* 191–92; *Ran.* 728–29; [X.] *Ath.* 1.13; X. *Symp.* 3.4. Physical deformity of the *banausos:* X. *Oec.* 4.2–3. Note also that at Ar. *Ec.* 385–87 Chremes explains the paleness of the women disguised as men by assuming that they are cobblers. The physique of the thetes was also disfigured by rowing in the fleet (Ar. *Eq.* 1368). For the ignorance of the *poneros* see Ar. *Eq.* 188–89; [X.] *Ath.* 1.5, 7. Cf. lack of education as an insult: Aeschin. 1.166; 2.113; 3.130 (all directed at Demosthenes and all untrue); Eup. fr. 183 (Kock).

11. Praise of farming: X. *Oec.* 5. We must not think of Attic farmers as a homogeneous

mass of poor peasants existing at the level of bare subsistence. Many served as hoplites, and a few like Strepsiades were successful enough to marry into older, more respectable families. Absence of leisure for farmers: Arist. *Pol.* 6.2.1318b10–15; 7.8.1329a1–2. Farmers set apart from *demos:* [X.] *Ath.* 2.14. The social ambivalence toward farmers is reflected in Aristotle's *Politics.* In his eyes a democracy that includes farmers, but bars other members of the lower classes will be better governed than a state that does not thus discriminate (*Pol.* 6.2.1318b6–17; 4.5.1292b26–35). Yet when constructing his ideal state, Aristotle excludes farmers completely and assigns their tasks to slaves and *perioikoi* (*Pol.* 1329a1–2, 25–26). Vast majority of Athenian citizens hold land: Lys. 34 *hyp.* (If Phormisius' proposal to limit citizenship to those who held land had passed, only 5,000 would have been disenfranchised. I do not share the skepticism of Gomme (1933) 26–27 about the figure.)

12. The most thorough treatment of Aeschines' family background and early career is Schaefer (1885–87) 1:215–28. Although Schaefer has many useful observations about the sources, he is overly inclined to accept Demosthenes' slanders. Blass (1887–98) 3.2: 154–59 for the most part follows Schaefer, as does Thalheim (1894) 1050–51. Ramming (1965) 24–25 merely summarizes the statements found in the speeches without analyzing them.

13. Dem. 19.249, 281. Cf. 199.

14. Defendants boast of services to Athens: Davies (1971) xviii, notes 3 and 4. "Forensic *charis"*: Davies (1981) 92–95. A challenge to list services to the city is not found in the following speeches made by prosecutors: Lys. 26, 27, 28, 29, 30; Aeschin. 1, 3. On the psychology of "euergetism" in the Classical Greek *polis* and later see Veyne (1990) 70–200.

15. Atrometus' year of birth: Aeschin. 2.147. Problem involved in determining year of birth from information about age in a given year: Davies (1971) 125–26. Atrometus spends his youth exercising in the gymnasium: Aeschin. 2.147. Atrometus' membership in the same phratry as the Eteobutadai insignificant: Blass (1887–98) 3.2: 156, note 3. Role of *gene* within phratries: Andrewes (1961); Lambert (1993) 59–74.

16. Spartan raids in early part of war: Th. 2.19; 3.1.26. Damage resulting from occupation of Dekeleia: Th. 7.27.5. While the occupation of Dekeleia caused much harm, it is unlikely to have done lasting damage to Athenian agriculture: Hanson (1983). Kothokidai as Aeschines' deme: Dem. 18.180. Location of Kothokidai: Traill (1975) 44.

17. Atrometus' service during the reign of the Thirty: Aeschin. 2.147.

18. Date of appointment of Thirty: Rhodes (1981) 436–37. Date of the restoration of the democracy: Rhodes (1981) 462–63. Suggestion that Aeschines fought for a satrap: *scholion ad* Aeschin. 2.147. Clearchus recruits mercenaries for Cyrus: D.S. 14.12.9.

19. Mercenary service as a sign of poverty: Is. 2.6. Cf. Demosthenes' statement that Aeschines' brother-in-law hired himself out to Chabrias, probably meant as an insult (Dem. 19.287). For the problem involved with the name of the brother-in-law, see Harris (1986a). Greek mercenaries in Asia during the 390s: D. S. 14.37.1; X. *HG* 3.2.15; Parke (1933) 43–48. Davies (1971) 545 does not discuss the chronological problems posed by Aeschines' account of his father's activities, but nevertheless places his mercenary service in the 390s.

Although Atrometus may have helped to overthrow the Thirty in 403, he was probably not one of the men of Phyle. These men received rewards for their actions (Aristophon of Azenia, for example, received *ateleia* [Dem. 20.148]) and had their names on a stele honoring their deeds. Fragments of this stele have been identified by Raubitschek (1941), but they are too few to allow us to determine whether Atrometus' name stood on it. Nonetheless, Aeschines was aware of the decree for he had it read out in court in 330 (Aeschin. 3.187–90). If Atrometus had in fact been one of those honored, we would expect Aeschines to have cited the fact or to have mentioned any award made to his father.

20. Aeschines' references to his mother: Aeschin. 2.78, 148. Athenian customs about using a woman's name: Schaps (1977).

21. Demaenetus' exploit: *Hell. Oxy.* 1.1–3; 3.1–2 with Bruce (1967) 50–51.

22. For Aeschines' carelessness about historical facts, see for example, Aeschin. 3.139 where he claims Pyrrhander of Anaphlystos never was able to convince the Thebans to conclude an alliance with Athens. In point of fact Pyrrhander was one of the ambassadors who helped to bring Thebes into the Second Athenian Confederacy (*IG* ii² 43, lines 76–77). Compare also the numerous errors in his account of fifth-century history: Aeschin. 2.172–76. A similar account is found in And. 3.3–12. It is generally believed that Aeschines drew upon Andocides (e.g. Thomas (1989) 119), but I find it difficult to believe Andocides would have made such egregious errors about events shortly before his birth. Is it not more likely that Aeschines made these mistakes, which were then copied by the person who composed the forgery *De Pace,* which was preserved alongside another forgery, *Against Alcibiades,* in the corpus of Andocides' works? This would make the theory of Thompson (1967) that Hellanicus was the ultimate source of both Andocides and Aeschines unnecessary.

23. Demosthenes' slanders in 330: Dem. 18.129–30, 258–60.

24. Glaucothea's rites as those of Dionysus Sabazius: Wankel (1976) 1133ff. Burkert (1987) 19, 33, 43, 70, 96–97. Dionysiac elements: Cole (1980). Orphic influence: Parker (1983) 303. Elements reminiscent of the Eleusinian Mysteries: Roussel (1930) 58–65 (*liknon*).

25. Aeschines' service as hoplite: Aeschin. 2.167–70. Cost of armor and weapons: Connor (1988) 10, note 30. Inability of hoplite to afford expenses of campaign: Lys. 16.14.

26. Epicurus insulted for being the son of a schoolteacher: D. L. 10.4. Although the source for this information is not contemporary, it probably derives ultimately from remarks made by Epicurus' rivals. Aeschines' brothers frequent the gymnasia: Aeschin. 2.149. Aeschines frequents the gymnasia: Aeschin. 1.135; 3.216. Cf. [Plu.] *Mor.* 840a.

27. Cleobulus' tombstone: Papademetriou (1957). Costs of stelai: *IG* ii² 133, lines 17–20 (twenty drachmai); 148, lines 6–10 (twenty drachmai); 212, lines 47–49 (thirty drachmai); 226, lines 21–26 (thirty drachmai). The fact that the stele made for Cleobulus contained a relief would not have made it more expensive. Compare the stele bearing the decree against tyranny (Meritt [1952] 355–59). This stele is adorned with a relief depicting Democracy placing a wreath on the head of a figure representing the People of Athens and is inscribed with a decree containing far more letters than the couplet on Cleobulus' tombstone, yet its cost was only twenty drachmai. For more lavish tombstones see Diepolder (1931) plates 23, 26, 27, 30, 31, 37, 40, 41, 46, 47, 54. Custom of honoring the dead not confined to a small elite: Humphreys (1980) 123.

28. Claim that Aeschines came from an old priestly family: Papademetriou (1957) 163. Priests classified as magistrates: Pl. *Lg.* 758e1–759e3; Arist. *Pol.* 4.12.1299a15–19. Priests undergo *euthynai* just as magistrates do: Aeschin. 3.18. Distinction made between priest and seer: Pl. *Plt.* 290c–d. On seers in general see Bouché-Leclerc (1879–82) 1–226. For a list of all known *manteis* in the Archaic and Classical periods see Kett (1966). *Loci classici* for the right of anyone to prophesy: Hom. *Il.* 12.200–50 (Hector challenges the interpretation made by Polydamas of the omen of the eagle); *Od.* 2.146–207 (Eurymachus challenges the interpretation made by Halitherses); Hdt.7.143 (Themistocles offers different interpretation of Delphic oracle). Practice of divination: Halliday (1913). Importance of flight of birds in *mantike:* Aesch. *Pr.* 488–92; X. *Mem.* 1.1.3. Seers offer advice at public meetings: Th. 8.1.1; *Ath. Pol.* 54.6. Advice of seer given to Xenophon: X. *An.* 7.8.1–6. Certain seers regarded as quacks and charlatans: Pl. *R.* 364b–c; *Lg.* 909b–d; Ar. *Av.* 959–91; *Nub.* 332. By contrast the seers of tragedy, such as Teiresias in Sophocles' *Oedipus the King* and *Antigone* and in Euripides' *Bacchae* and Calchas in Sophocles' *Ajax,* are quite trustworthy and respectable. Lampon: Th. 5.19.2; 24.1; *IG* i² 76, line 47; Plu. *Per.* 6.2. Sthorys granted citizenship for accurate prophecy: Osborne (1970). Thrasyllus: Isoc. 19.5–7.

29. Aeschines recites poetry: Aeschin. 1.128–29, 144, 148–52; 2.158; 3.135, 184–85, 190. Role of poetry in training of orator: North (1952). Use of poetry in Attic oratory: Perlman (1964). Aeschines criticizes enemies for lack of knowledge and refinement: Aeschin. 1.137, 166; 2.39, 151; 3.117, 130, 238, 241. Cf. Blass (1887–98) 2:181, note 5. Note his frequent use of words denoting lack of refinement: *apaideusia* (Aeschin. 1.132; 2.113, 153; 3.241), *apaideutos* (Aeschin. 1.45, 137, 166, 185; 3.130); *apaideutos* (adv.) (Aeschin. 3.238); *aschemoneo* (2.39, 151, 246); *aschemon* (2.152); *aschemosyne* (3.76). By contrast only two of these words are found in Demosthenes' entire oeuvre: *apaideutos* (20.119), *aschemoneo* (22.53). The words are not found at all in Andocides, Dinarchus, Lycurgus, Isaeus, Antiphon, and Lysias. On Aeschines' education in general, see Blass (1887–98) 2:181–85. Aeschines receives education from his father: Quint. *Inst.* 2.17.12.

30. Aeschines' lack of rhetorical training: Phld. *Rh.* 1.14; 2.97 (Sudhaus). Isocrates' fees: Dem. 35.42; Plu. *Dem.* 5.6; [Plu.] *Mor.* 873d; 838e. [Plu.] *Mor.* 838f claims Isocrates never asked for fees from Athenians. This is accepted by Davies (1971) 246, but the information found in Demosthenes disproves it. Hostility of Pheidippides: Ar. *Nub.* 100–25. Anytus' attitude toward Sophists: Pl. *Men.* 91c. Social status of Anytus: Lys. 13.78; Pl. *Men.* 90b; X. *Ap.* 29. Callicles' contempt: Pl. *Grg.* 520a. Laches' attitude: Pl. *La.* 197d. Other evidence of upper-class attitudes toward the Sophists: Pl. *Phdr.* 257d; *Prt.* 312a–b. One cannot claim that the statements made about the Sophists by the young *kaloi kagathoi* in the dialogues are the product of Platonic malice and cannot therefore be cited as evidence of upper-class attitudes, since Socrates, who acts to some extent as Plato's mouthpiece, is far more gentle in his criticisms. Xenophon appears to be more harsh (Guthrie [1971] 37). Cleon's appeal to prejudice against Sophists: Th. 3.38.7. Connor (1971) 163ff. fails to draw a distinction between attitudes toward the traditional education and toward the Sophists and as a result misinterprets Cleon's remarks. A similar mistake is made by Ober (1989) 156–91, who also fails to understand Aeschines' use of poetry.

31. Demosthenes on social status of Aeschines' family: Dem. 19.237.

32. Aeschines' military career: Aeschin. 2.168–70.

33. Aeschines and Aphobetus serve as undersecretaries: Dem. 19.237. Demosthenes reminds Aeschines of the herald's curse: Dem. 19.70. Cf. 200, 237, 314. Aeschines as secretary: Dem. 18.261. Aeschines' younger brother Aphobetus (Aeschin. 2.149) may have been Secretary of the Council in 319/18 if he is identical with the Aphobetus found in *IG* ii² 387, line 3. However, the inscription is fragmentary and the demotic is missing, making it risky to posit an identification on the basis of the name alone—see Thompson (1974). Furthermore, Aeschines held the post of secretary when he was younger and before moving on to the higher post of ambassador. It is thus unlikely that Aphobetus would have taken the position of secretary when he was around sixty after having held more prestigious positions.

34. Public secretaries: *Ath. Pol.* 54.3–5 with Rhodes (1972) 135–41.

35. Aeschines' voice: Dem. 19.126, 199, 206, 337–40. Aeschines' familiarity with laws and decrees: Aeschin. 1.9–35; 3.9–48. Cf. [Plu.] *Mor.* 840f. Privileges of secretaries: *Ath. Pol.* 54.3–4 with Rhodes (1981) 520.

36. Aeschines becomes actor after public secretary: Dem. 18.261–62. Aeschines' acting career: Dem. 18.262; 19.246, 337. Meaning of the term *tritagonistes:* Pickard-Cambridge (1968) 133.

37. Aeschines alludes to Demosthenes' remarks about his acting: Aeschin. 2.157.

38. Low opinion of actors: [Arist.] *Pr.* 30.10. This evidence was accepted by Schaefer (1887–89) 1:251. Neoptolemus as Athenian ambassador: Dem. 5.6; 19.12, 315. Aristodemus as Athenian ambassador: Aeschin. 2.15–17, 52; 3.83; Dem. 19.315.

39. An anecdote of Critolaus reported by Aulus Gellius (11.9.2) records that Aristodemus received a talent for a performance. On actors in general, see Ghiron-Bistagne (1976).

40. Aeschines brings family into court: Aeschin. 2.152, 179. Custom of defendant using his family to arouse pity: Hyp. *Eux.* 41. X. *Mem.* 4.4.4 incorrectly implies the practice was illegal.

41. Aeschines marries daughter of Philodemus: Aeschin. 2.152. Aeschines inherits five talents from Philon: Dem. 18.312. Philodemus' uncle a member of the Thousand: *IG* ii² 1929, line 18. Stemma of Aeschines' family: Davies (1971) 543, 546. Function of the Thousand: Rhodes (1982) 11–14.

42. Evidence for the size of dowries in Classical Athens: Casson (1976) 53–56. Defendants list services to state: note 14 above. It is perhaps no coincidence that none of the men known to have challenged to an *antidosis* procedure is known to have been active in politics at the time of the challenge. Isocrates is the only prominent person known to have been challenged, but he never aspired to public office (Isoc. 15). The unknown defendant of Lys. 3 was challenged and lost, but he does not appear to have been a politician. Nor were Phaenippus (Dem. 42) and Megacleides (D. H. *Din.* 13), who were also challenged to an *antidosis*. Pasicles, the son of Pasion, was involved in a suit concerning an *antidosis,* but he too never pursued a career in politics as far as we can tell (Hyp. fr. 134 [Kenyon] = Harpocration *s.v. symmoria*). Demosthenes charges that Meidias had to be challenged to an *antidosis* before he performed any liturgies (Dem. 21.156), but this is the testimony of a hostile source, who fails to specify the date, challenger, and circumstances. Even if the charge were true, the incident might have occurred before Meidias entered politics. Demosthenes himself was challenged to an *antidosis* by Meidias' brother Thrasylochus (Dem. 21.78–9; 28.17). In this case, however, the circumstances were unusual, for the challenge was initiated not to force Demosthenes to undertake duties he was attempting to shirk, but as part of the legal maneuvers employed by his guardians. Despite the burden the liturgy placed on his troubled estate, Demosthenes responded by performing the duty.

43. Demosthenes as *hegemon* of his symmory: Dem. 21.157. Demosthenes' property: Davies (1971) 126–36 with the correction of Harris (1988c) 361–62. Demosthenes' troubles with his guardians: Dem. 27–31. Training with Isaeus: [Plu.] *Mor.* 839e; 844b–c. Demosthenes' liturgies: Davies (1971) 135–37. Prosecution of Cephisodotus: Aeschin. 3.51. Demosthenes as *logographos:* Chapter 1, note 17. Demosthenes delivers first speech in 354/53: D.H. *Amm.* 1.4. Date of Demosthenes' birth: Harris (1989b) 121–25.

44. Date of Timarchus' birth: Aeschin. 1.49 with Harris (1988a). Timarchus as member of Council and as magistrate on Andros: Aeschin. 1.107–8. Timarchus serves on embassies: Aeschin. 1. 120. Nausicles as contemporary of Aeschines: Aeschin. 2.184. Nausicles' victory at Thermopylai: D.S. 16.37.3. Aeschines' date of birth: Aeschin. 1.49 with Harris (1988a). Aeschines' first speech in the Assembly: Chapter 3.

45. On the powers of the Athenian Assembly see Hansen (1987) 94–124. For the right of anyone to address the Assembly see Aeschin. 1.27; Eur. *Suppl.* 438–41.

46. For the small number of citizens who regularly spoke see Perlman (1963) 328–30. Although the number of those who spoke frequently was small, the total number of those who spoke and moved decrees at least once must have been surprisingly large: Hansen (1989) 93–127. On the term *rhetores* see Hansen (1989) 1–24. For the offices held by Athenian politicians see Roberts (1982a).

47. On ambassadors in Athens and other Greek states see Mosley (1973).

48. Annual election of generals: *Ath. Pol.* 61.1 with Rhodes (1981) 677–78. Absence of special privileges for generals: Rhodes (1972) 43–46. It is possible that in the fifth century "convening the ecclesia and arranging its agenda at this time may have been the joint prerogative of the *prytanes* (acting on behalf of the *boule*) and the generals" (Rhodes), but otherwise the generals do not appear to have possessed privileged access to the Council.

49. Importance of spending money to win *charis:* Davies (1981) 91–101. Financing

feast for tribe at festival: Dem. 21.156. Alcibiades' *epidosis:* Plu. *Alc.* 10. On the *epidosis* in general see Migeotte (1992). Cimon's largesse: Plu. *Cim.* 10; *Ath. Pol.* 27.3. Mantitheus' boast: Lys. 16.14. Demosthenes ransoms prisoners: Dem. 19.166–71. Aeschin. 2.100; [Plu.] *Mor.* 851a. Chabrias celebrates victory at Colias: [Dem.] 59.33.

50. Nicomachides' complaint: X. *Mem.* 3.4.1–3. Pericles' victory as *choregos: IG* ii^2 2318, lines 9–11. Nicias' generosity: Plu. *Nic.* 3. Meidias cites his liturgies: Dem. 21.153.

51. Size of courts: *Ath. Pol.* 68.1 with Rhodes (1981) 728–29. Audience at trials: Dem. 20.165; 54.41. Prosecutions by Lycurgus: D.S. 16.88.1; Lycurg. 1; frr. 75, 77, 91 (Sauppe). Prosecutions by Hyperides: Hyp. *Phil.; Dem.; Eux.* 29. Prosecutions by Aristophon: Din. 3.17; [Dem.] 51.9, 16. Prosecutions by Aristogeiton: Dem. 25.37–38, 87, 94. Trial of Timarchus: chapter 5.

It is significant that we never hear of Miltiades, Cimon, Themistocles, Aristides, Nicias, or Alcibiades acting as prosecutors on public charges. Pericles acted as prosecutor once, but that was only after he was elected to the position by the Assembly. According to Plutarch, he performed the task with conspicuous distaste (Plu. *Cim.* 14.3–5; *Per.* 10.6. But see also *Ath. Pol.* 27.1). The only one before Cleon to make a career of prosecuting public officials appears to have been Ephialtes (*Ath. Pol.* 25.1–2). His unusual career won him an unusual end: he was the only Athenian politician known to have been assassinated in the fifth century before the Revolution of 411. Did his fate deter others from following the same path for the next three decades?

52. Tendency to elect as ambassadors men who have ties to foreign city: Mosley (1973) 44. Family of Alcibiades: Davies (1971) 9–22. Family of Cimon and Miltiades: Davies (1971) 294–312. Family of Thucydides: Davies (1971) 230–37. Family of Pericles: Davies (1971) 455–60. Family of Callistratus: Davies (1971) 277–82. Family of Timotheus: Davies (1971) 506–12. For a complete list of all Athenians known to have been *rhetores* and generals in the years 403–322, see Hansen (1989) 25–72. Very few of these men had fathers or other ancestors who achieved renown in politics. This is true not only for the numerous obscure figures, but also for some of the most prominent politicians in the period including Demosthenes, Eubulus, Demades, Aristophon, Apollodorus, Iphicrates, Hyperides, and Chares. But see Davies (1981) 117–30. Phocion as Chabrias' *protégé:* Plu. *Phoc.* 6–7.

53. For the trial of Timarchus see chapter 5.

54. Habitual prosecutors as *poneroi:* Isoc. 15.99–100; Lys. 7.1. Term "sycophant" used as an insult: Aeschin. 3.172. Note that the most popular thing done by the Thirty Tyrants was the execution of the sycophants: X. *HG.* 2.3.12, 38; Lys. 25.19; *Ath. Pol.* 35.3. Osborne (1990) attempts to whitewash the sycophants, but his arguments are demolished by Harvey (1990). Harvey gives a complete list of *testimonia* for sycophants. Many of those who brought *graphai* against politicians tried to justify their prosecutions by claiming they were only pursuing a private feud (Aeschin. 1.1–3; [Dem.] 58.1–4; 59. 1–16). Courts unworthy of a *gennaios:* Ar. *V.* 503–7. Note also how speakers often tried to win the good will of a court by pleading inexperience in legal proceedings: Aeschin. 1.1; Pl. *Ap.* 17d; Lys. 7.1. Cf. Aeschin. 2.182.

55. Lycurgus as member of Eteobutadai: [Plu.] *Mor.* 842b. Philochares as general: Aeschin. 2.149. Iphicrates is referred to in the past tense in Dem. 23.129–36. This speech was delivered in 352/51 (D.H. *Amm.* 1.4). Marriage of Menestheus to Timotheus' daughter: [Dem.] 49.66. Exile of Timotheus: Nep. *Tim.* 3.5. Career of Conon: Davies (1971) 511–12.

56. Nausicles nominates Aeschines: Aeschin. 2.18. Nausicles as ambassador: Chapter 3. Nausicles testifies for Aeschines: Aeschin. 2.184. Nausicles gains fame at Thermopylai: D.S. 16.37.3; 38.2; Justin 8.2.8. Gold crown for Nausicles: *IG* ii^2 1496, lines 49–51; Dem. 18.114; Davies (1971) 396. Importance of ties between contemporaries: Rhodes (1986) 135–36.

57. Aeschines' honors: Aeschin. 2.168–70. Phocion's campaign on Euboea: Plu. *Phoc.*
12–14; Aeschin. 3.86–88; Dem. 21.161–67; 39.16; [Dem.] 59.4 with Cawkwell (1962a)
127–30, Brunt (1969) 245–48, and Griffith (1979) 318, note 2. For the correct name of the
taxiarch, see von Wilamowitz (1909). The speculative attempt of Knoepfler (1981) to recon-
struct Phocion's strategy is flawed by his mistaken belief that the cavalry Demosthenes
(21.163) states landed at Argura was part of the original expedition. But the words of
Demosthenes make it clear that this force was sent much later to relieve (διαδόχην) the
cavalry that originally went with Phocion to Euboea. For a criticism of the analysis of the
campaign made by Tritle (1988) 76–86 see Cartledge (1989) 79.

58. Phocion and Eubulus appear on behalf of Aeschines: Aeschin. 2.170, 184. Aeschines sent as ambassador under the decree of Eubulus: Dem. 19.304. Aeschines attacked for
supporting policy of Eubulus: Aeschin. 2.8. Aeschines and Eubulus advocate peace with
Philip in 346: Chapter 4. Aeschines and Phocion negotiate with Philip after Chaeronea:
Aeschin. 3.227; Dem. 18.282; Nepos *Phocion* 1.3; Plu. *Phoc.* 17. Meidias as associate of
Eubulus: Dem. 21.205–7. Aeschines' praise for Meidias: Aeschin. 3.115. Stephanus as an
associate of Eubulus: [Dem.] 59.48. Stephanus and Aeschines on Third Embassy: Aeschin.
2.140. Phaedrus provides testimony for Aeschines: Aeschin. 1.43–50. Association of Stephanus and Phaedrus: *IG* ii² 213.

59. Philon serves with Chabrias in Egypt: Dem. 19.287. For the problem involved with
Philon's name see Harris (1986a). Phocion and Chabrias: Plu. *Phoc.* 6–7.

60. Eubulus and the Theoric Fund: Cawkwell (1963a). Increase in Athenian revenues:
Dem. 10.37–38. Eubulus' building projects: Aeschin. 3.25. Aeschines may exaggerate Eubulus' power—see de Ste. Croix (1964). Aphobetus' position: Aeschin. 2.149.

61. Phocion's role in battles near Naxos and Chios: Plu. *Phoc.* 6. Phocion elected
general forty-five times: Plu. *Phoc.* 8.2 with Tritle (1992). Gehrke (1976) 5–17 analyzes
Phocion's leadership at Tamynai and on Cyprus in 344 and concludes "er keineswegs ein
Feldherr mit überragenden militärischen Fähigkeiten war" (*he was in no way a commander
with outstanding military abilities*). He criticizes him for allowing part of his army to be
drawn into battle too early and for failing to remain close to his troops while busy with the
sacrifices at Tamynai. He does credit the general with "eine bemerkenswerte Tapferkeit im
Gefecht" (*a noteworthy bravery in battle*) and with good judgment, but finds this latter virtue
"eine politische, nicht eine militärische Qualität" (*a political, not a military quality*). This is
unfair. It is unreasonable to blame Phocion for the lack of discipline among his troops, who
may well have been trained by others. Furthermore, we should note that it was actually
Plutarch who allowed his troops to be drawn into battle prematurely and that Phocion's
infantry remained in position until he gave his order. And Phocion's attention to the sacrifices
was part of his duty as a commanding officer (e.g., Hdt. 6.1121; 9.36–37). Indeed, had he
not waited for a good omen, his haste might have had a disastrous effect on the morale of his
troops. Gehrke also ignores Plutarch's attractive suggestion that Phocion's delay might have
been deliberate, aimed at drawing the enemy closer to his camp before opening battle. Since
his camp was located in a strong position atop a ridge, this tactic made good sense. Nor can
Phocion's presence of mind in the face of an initial setback and good judgment be dismissed
as merely "political qualities." Both are certainly the mark of a good field commander.
Gehrke further takes Phocion to task for allowing his troops to plunder while on Cyprus. This
criticism is also unfair; the soldiers were following the traditional practice of gathering
supplies in enemy territory. Diodorus, for one, saw nothing untoward in their behavior. In
fact, news of the rich plunder had one very beneficial effect: it attracted more mercenaries. For
a more positive estimate of Phocion's military abilities, see Tritle (1988) 76–96.

62. Phocion as a speaker in the Assembly: Plu. *Phoc.* 7. Unpopularity as a speaker: Plu.
Phoc. 3. Tritle (1988) 97–100 adduces evidence to show that Phocion advised the Assembly

on several occasions, but his attested political activity is rather meager for someone whose career lasted as long as his did.

63. On the nature of political groups in Athens see the sensible summary in Hansen (1991) 277–87.

64. Pericles' boast: Th. 2.37.2 with the analysis of Harris (1992a). Lack of wealth as impediment to political career: Rhodes (1986) 144. Aeschines' career shows how simplistic it is to analyze Athenian politics in terms of a rigid divide between a privileged elite and a passive mass of citizens. For this mistaken approach, see Ober (1989) 112–18. Compare Aeschin. 1.27.

Davies (1971) 547 thinks there "is just enough information about Aeschines' property . . . to allow the suspicion that he could have joined his wife's family in the liturgical class, had he wished to do so," yet recognizes that most of the information is unreliable since it comes from Demosthenes. We have already discussed the alleged legacy from Philon; for the bribes from Philip (Dem. 19.167), see chapter 5.1; for the "loan" from the Three Hundred, see chapter 7. Demosthenes' charges about a farm at Pydna (Dem. 19.145, 312; cf. *scholia ad* Aeschin. 1.3) and a farm in Boeotia (Dem. 18.41; cf. Philodemus *Rh.* 2.172) are not supported by evidence. Davies attributes "his failure to contribute to *epidoseis* or to perform liturgies" to the fact that "the bulk of his property lay abroad and was therefore out of the reach of an *antidosis* challenge or of an *apographe* of unregistered property." Even if this property in foreign territory existed, why does Demosthenes nowhere furnish any evidence at all about it?

Chapter 3

1. Original rationale for the Confederacy: D.S. 15.28.2–4. Athens poses as liberator of the Greeks: *IG* ii² 43, lines 9–11. Failure of the Confederacy: Cawkwell (1981). Cargill (1981) demonstrates that in general the Athenians observed the guarantees promised to the members in the charter of the confederacy, but pays less attention to other sources of discontent.

2. Mausolus' role in the Social War: Dem. 15.3. Social War: D.S. 16.7.3–4; 21.1–22.2. Causes of Social War: Hornblower (1982) 205–11.

3. Isoc. 8; Aeschin. 2.74–77. In fact, Aeschines takes up several of the same points made by Isocrates. Compare Isoc. 8.37 with Aeschin. 2.74–77; Isoc. 8.29, 46 with Aeschin. 2.71; Isoc. 8.44–45 with Aeschin. 2.71–72. For these and other "echoes" in the works of Isocrates, Aeschines, and Xenophon, see de Romilly (1954), who sees in them the traces of a common doctrine held by a set of moderates. But Aeschines' views differed from those of Isocrates in significant regards: chapter 5.

4. Eubulus' role in the financial recovery: Cawkwell (1963a) 54–61. Date of Xenophon's *Poroi:* Sealey (1965) 168–69. Demosthenes' proposal: Dem. 14.14–30. Collection of arrears to *eisphora:* Dem. 22.48–49. Abolition of exemptions from liturgies: Dem. 20.127. Rise in public revenues: Dem. 10.38; Theopompus *FGrHist* 115 F 166.

5. Foundation of Amphipolis: Th. 1.100; 4.102; D.S. 12.35. Natural resources of surrounding area: Th. 4.105, 108. Capture by Brasidas: Th. 4.105–6. Subsequent attempts to regain: Th. 5.18.5, 21, 35, 83.4; 7.9. Basis of Athenian claims to Amphipolis: Graham (1964) 199–206, 245–48. Macedonian garrison: D.S. 16.3.3.

Aeschines (2.32) says that King Amyntas of Macedon sent a representative to a conference of the alliance of the Spartans and the other Greeks and that this representative voted with the other Greeks to recognize Athenian ownership of Amphipolis. For a critique of previous attempts to identify the conference, see Jehne (1992) 277, note 29. Demosthenes (19.137) states that the Great King made a similar declaration in 367/66–for the date, see Buckler (1980) 249. Hegesippus alludes to these declarations ([Dem.] 7.29). As Jehne (1992) has shown, the Athenian claim to Amphipolis rested not on any explicit statement, but to a clause in the Common Peace treaties that granted all parties the right to ''hold their own territories.''

6. Defeat of Perdiccas and accession of Philip: D.S. 16.2.1–3.2. Beloch (1922) 2:49–61 and Griffith (1979) 208–9 place the defeat of Perdiccas and the accession of Philip in the early summer of 359. Hatzopoulos (1982) prefers the autumn of 360 but see Hammond (1989) 137, note 1. Justin 7.5.6–10 appears to imply that at first Philip was only appointed regent for Amyntas, son of Perdiccas. For arguments in favor of Diodorus' account, see Ellis (1971) and Griffith (1979) 702–4. Numismatic evidence has now confirmed Diodorus—see Hersh (1990).

7. Defeat of Pausanias and Argaeus: D.S. 16.3.3–6. Schaefer (1885–87) 2:18 suggests on the basis of Polyaen. 4.2.17 that the withdrawal of the garrison from Amphipolis may have also been aimed at winning over the Thracian kings. Secret negotiations about Amphipolis: Theopompus *FGrHist* 115 F 30; *schol. ad* Dem. 2.6. Since these secret negotiations with the Council took place in the context of Philip's peace talks with Athens, they should be dated to 359. Philip later alluded to these secret negotiations while besieging Amphipolis in 357, by which time they had become an ''open secret''—see Dem. 2.6–7. The inability of the members of the Council to keep a secret was evidently something of a joke: Ar. *Ec.* 441–44. But no formal secret agreement could have been ratified by the Council—see de Ste. Croix (1963) with references to earlier treatments of the negotiations.

8. Philip's victory over the Illyrians and Paeonians: D.S. 16.4.2–7. Philip's attack on Amphipolis: D.S. 16.8.2–3. Chronology of Amphipolis campaign: Heskel (1987) 104–5. Olynthian attempt to conclude alliance with Athens: Dem. 2.6. Philip's promise to hand over Amphipolis: Dem. 2.6; [Dem.] 7.27. Capture of Pydna: D.S. 16.8.3.

9. Philip's promise to the Olynthians and the siege of Potidaia: D.S. 16.8.3–5; Dem. 2.7; 6.20; 23.107, 116. Treaty between Philip and Chalcidians: Tod (1948) #158. Fall of Methone: D.S. 16.31.6; 34.5; Dem. 1.9; 4.35. Since Diodorus recounts the siege under the years 354/53 and 353/52, this would place the fall of Methone in the campaigning season of 353. Griffith (1979) 255, following Kahrstedt (1910) 42, takes *IG* ii² 130 as evidence that the siege had begun in 355, but this reads too much into the decree.

Plutarch (*Alexander* 3.4–5) places the fall of Potidaia around the same time as the Olympia of 356. According to Miller (1975) 215–31, the festival began on July 29 that year. Diodorus (16.8.2–3), who mistakenly places the fall of Potidaia in 358/57, states that Philip answered the call from the citizens of Crenides after he had taken Potidaia. Since the alliance that the Athenians concluded with Cetriporus, Lyppeius, and Grabus in July 356 belongs to the period after the capture of Crenides (*IG* ii² 127, line 45), however, Griffith (1979) 248–51 may be correct in placing this appeal before the final capitulation of Potidaia.

10. Foundation of Crenides: D.S. 16.3.7. Date of the death of Cotys: Badian (1980) 54. Treaty dividing Thrace among three sons of Cotys: Dem. 23.8, 170. Appeal of Crenides to Philip: St. Byz. *s.v.* Philippoi. Berisades as ruler of western Thrace: Dem. 23.8–10, 170. Philip's take-over of Crenides: D.S. 16.8.6–7. Alliance between Athens, Cetriporus, Lyppeius, and Grabus: *IG.* ii² 127. Philip's victory over the alliance: D.S. 16.22.3.

The idea put forward by Griffith (1979) 247–48, that Berisades allowed the Thasian colonists to found the city in return for the payment of tribute is implausible. It is hard to believe that the king would have allowed a foreign power to set up a colony in the most valuable part of his kingdom, tribute or no tribute. Besides, Diodorus makes it clear that Crenides was a colony of Thasos, not a concession granted by Berisades. Collart (1937) 137–38, thought that Cersebleptes was the king who threatened Crenides. This is unlikely. Cersebleptes' territory lay far to the east; he would have had to march his army through the kingdoms of his brothers Amadocus and Berisades to strike at Crenides. Furthermore, there is no evidence Berisades and Cersebleptes were at odds during this time. Far otherwise; they had just made peace with each other.

11. Request of Byzantium, Perinthos, and Amadocus: *scholia ad* Aeschin. 2.81. Cf. Theopompus *FGrHist* 328 F 101. Philip's illness and withdrawal: Dem. 1.13; 3.4–5. Dem. 1.13 places the expedition to Thrace right after Philip's victory in Thessaly, which Diodorus places in 353/52 and 352/51, that is, the campaigning season of 352 (D.S. 16.35.4–6; 38.1–2). Dionysius of Halicarnassus (*Dinarchus* 13) dates the Athenian expedition to Thermopylai, which followed Philip's victory in Thessaly, to 353/52, while Demosthenes 3.4–5 (delivered in 349/48—see D.H. *Amm.* 1.9) places Philip's campaign in Thrace "two or three years ago," that is 35 2/51 or 351/50. All this evidence puts Philip's Thracian campaign in 352. Martin (1981) places the campaign in 353 on basis of a mistranslation of Dem. 3.4–5, as does Buckler (1989) 181–86. See Harris (1989c) 268, note 18. Ellis (1976) 82–87 and Griffith (1979) 224 follow Hammond (1937) in placing these campaigns in 352, with the Thracian campaign extending into 351.

Spartan victory at Aigospotamoi and its effects: D.S. 13.107.4; X. *HG.* 2.2.10–12. Spartan seizure of the Hellespont in 386: X. *HG.* 5.1.28–29. Importance of area for Athens: Dem. 20.31–32; Arist. *Rh.* 3.10.1411a14; Garnsey (1988) 134–49.

Aeschines (2.81) states that he saw the son of Cersebleptes as a hostage in Pella in 346. Aeschines clearly implies this was during the Second Embassy. Aeschines asserts that he reported everything he had seen or heard on both the First and Second Embassies. Then he states that he saw Cersebleptes' son as a hostage in Philip's court. In the next sentence he contrasts this occasion with another occasion during the First Embassy (note the *men . . . de . . .* construction), indicating that the previous sentence must refer to the Second Embassy. Furthermore, Dem. 3.4–5 implies Philip was not successful in 351. Finally, it is hard to understand how Cersebleptes could have acted so independently in the following years if his son was held hostage in Macedon. And if the first campaign was successful, why was another one necessary? Ellis (1976) 87–88 and Griffith (1979) 282–83 do not discuss the issue, but assume Philip defeated Cersebleptes and took his son hostage in 351.

12. Thracian attempts to take Chersonese: Dem. 23.114–15, 130, 153–55, 158. Charidemus under Cotys and Cersebleptes: Dem. 23.149, 163–65. Treaty of 357 between Athens and Thracian Kings: Tod (1948) # 151. Cersebleptes ignores treaty: Isoc. 8.22. Cersebleptes' appeal to Athens: Dem. 3.4. Cersebleptes' offer to hand over cities in Chersonese: D.S. 16.34.4. Location of Thracian forts: appendix 5. According to Demosthenes (3.5), Charidemus was sent with ten empty ships and five talents of silver. These talents must have been given to hire mercenaries since by 349/48 he was still in the Hellespont with at least eighteen ships and 4,000 peltasts (Theopompus *FGrHist* 328 F 50)—see Badian (1980). Ellis (1977) claims the ships were sent for reconnaissance, but only one ship would have sufficed for this purpose. This would also not explain why Charidemus was given five talents.

13. Olynthian overtures to Athens: Dem. 23.109. Dem. 1. *hypoth.* 2 places these negotiations at a time when Philip was absent. Philip's demonstration against Olynthus: Dem. 4.17; Griffith (1979) 296–304. Date of Dem. 4: Cawkwell (1962a) 122–27. The banishment of the pro-Athenian Apollonides may have taken place in response to Philip's demonstration, but the incident is not dated (Dem. 9.56, 66; [Dem.] 59.91).

14. Philip's demand to the Olynthians: Justin 8.3.10. Ellis (1973) places the flight of Arrhidaeus and Menelaus around 352, Griffith (1979) 699–701 in 359. Philip's attack on cities of Chalcidice: D.S. 16.52.9. Chares' expedition to Olynthus: Philochorus *FGrHist* 328 F 49. Charidemus' expedition to Olynthus: Philochorus *FGrHist* 328 F 50. Chronology of Athenian expeditions to Olynthus: appendix 2.

15. Philip's offer carried by Euboean ambassadors: Aeschin. 2.12.

16. Phrynon's capture and Ctesiphon's mission: Aeschin. 2.12–13.

17. Ctesiphon's report and Philocrates' decree and trial: Aeschin 2.13–14.

18. Later version of Philocrates' decree and trial: Aeschin. 3.62. Demosthenes on the role of Ctesiphon and Aristodemus: Dem. 19.12,18, 94, 315. Demosthenes also mentions Neoptolemus' role during the negotiations, but Aeschines says nothing about him.

19. Heskel and Badian (1987) do not understand "how, at just this time, Phrynon could get the idea that Philip might be persuaded . . . to return to him some money which he had either just calmly pocketed or not received at all" and "how, at this same time (i.e., before the fall of Olynthus), the Athenians could enthusiastically receive a peace offer by Philip" and prefer to place the embassy of Ctesiphon after the fall of Olynthus. As I have pointed out, however, Phrynon could have been encouraged by the Macedonian invitation to talk about peace carried by the Euboeans. By placing the embassy of Ctesiphon after the fall of Olynthus, they also create a very awkward problem: why were negotiations not begun after the acquittal of Philocrates when the *hypomosia* on his decree was lifted? Why was it necessary for him to pass another decree later on for negotiations to begin? On the other hand, if we place his first proposal to begin negotiations before the fall of Olynthus, it is possible to explain why it was never acted on. Philip's championing of the god of Delphi: D.S. 16.35.6; 60.4. Griffith (1979) 274–75 underestimates the importance of religion in the policies of the Greek states. For Athenian popular religion at the time see Mikalson (1983).

20. For the evidence and chronology for these events see appendix 2.

21. Compare Demosthenes' criticism of Athenian strategy: Dem. 4.40–41.

22. Aeschines as champion of a coalition against Macedon: Dem. 19.10–12, 302–6. Aeschines alludes to these activities: Aeschin. 2.79.

23. Atrestidas held the position of *demiourgos* in Megalopolis: *SIG*³ 183, line 10.

24. Stalemate in the Peloponnese: Dem. 18.18. Chios and Rhodes: Dem. 5.25: 15.3, 15, 27. Byzantion: *schol. ad* Aeschin. 2.86. Sacred War in Central Greece: Dem. 18.18 and chapter 5.

25. Aristodemus' embassy and the decision to send the First Embassy: Aeschin. 2.15–19. In his speech of 330, Aeschines (3.62–63) mentions only the decree of Philocrates to send the First Embassy and Demosthenes' collaboration with Philocrates. For the date of the departure of the First Embassy see appendix 4.

26. Honorary decrees listing the reasons for the award: *IG* ii² 29, lines 13–17; 103, lines 21–27; 116, lines 35–37; 212, lines 39–41. See also Henry (1983).

27. Inscriptions listing the names of ambassadors elected: *IG* ii² 34, lines 35–37; 41, lines 16–21; 43, lines 73–77.

28. Phocian change of policy: Aeschin. 2.132–33. Traditional view of change in Athenian policy: Schaefer (1885–87) 2:188–90; Grote (1869) 9:365–69; Beloch (1922–23) 3.1:510; Cawkwell (1960) 420–21; Markle (1970) 59; Ellis (1976) 106–7, 109; Cloché (1934) 223–24.

29. Analysis of situation in Greece: Aeschin. 2.79; Dem. 18.18–21. Demosthenes claims that the Thebans were about to turn to Athens in 346, but this cannot be correct. See Wankel (1976) 207. In 343 Demosthenes said that Philip began negotiations with Athens with the intention of tricking the Phocians and convinced Aeschines and Philocrates to participate in his scheme. For this charge, see chapter 5.

30. Theopompus *FGrHist* 115 F 164. For the date of the speech see appendix 6.

31. Phalaecus trusts in Philip: Aeschin 2.135; Dem. 9.11. Situation in central Greece: chapter 5.

32. Members of the First Embassy: Philocrates (Aeschin. 2.18; Dem. 19.13); Demosthenes (Aeschin. 2.18; Dem. 19.13); Aeschines (Aeschin. 2.18); Aristodemus (Aeschin.

2.19, 52); Iatrocles (Aeschin. 2.20); Dercylus (Aeschin. 2.47); Aglaocreon (Aeschin. 2.20); Cimon (Aeschin. 2.21); Ctesiphon (Aeschin. 2.42–43; 47, 52). The Ctesiphon who served on the First Embassy may be identical with the man of the same name found at *IG* ii^2 2409, line 36, and the man whom Aeschines accused in 330—see Lewis (1955) 31. Phrynon is mentioned as an ambassador by Demosthenes (19.189, 197, 229) and by Aeschines (2.8), but it is not clear in these passages whether the speakers are referring to the First or Second Embassies. But since Aeschines, Demosthenes, Iatrocles, Dercylus, and Aglaocreon all served on both the First and the Second Embassies, it is probably safe to assume Phrynon also served on both. Dem. 19. *hypoth.* 2.4 lists all the members of the First Embassy, naming all those mentioned in the speeches of Aeschines and Demosthenes with the exception of Aglaocreon and the addition of Nausicles, whom neither orator says was on the First Embassy. The author of the hypothesis may have had access to a lost historical work, but it is more likely that he relied on an inference from Aeschines' speech. Reading that Demosthenes was nominated by Philocrates, who also served on the embassy, he might have inferred that Nausicles, who nominated Aeschines (Aeschin. 2.18), must likewise have gone on the First Embassy. But if the information found in the hypothesis is correct, Aglaocreon was not considered one of the ten ambassadors, but was an additional member of the embassy. This was indeed the case on the Second Embassy (Aeschin. 2.97). On the size of embassies see Mosley (1965).

33. For the embassy sent out to rally the Greeks, see appendix 3.

34. Demosthenes' concern in 343 with the Second Embassy: Dem. 19.8 (all charges relate to the Second Embassy); Aeschin. 2.123.

35. Demosthenes mentions First Embassy: Dem. 19.13. Aeschines' reply to the charge and account of journey to Macedon: Aeschin. 2.20–22.

36. Aeschines' account of the speeches: Aeschin. 2.22–35.

37. Criticism of Aeschines' account: Schaefer (1887–89) 2:202–4. Demosthenes has no difficulty addressing Philip during the Second Embassy: Aeschin. 2.108 (note, however, that Aeschines [2.112] says his speech was met with howls of laughter). Aeschines fails to mention Amphipolis: Dem. 19.253–54. Aeschines reports Demosthenes' promise to speak about Amphipolis: Aeschin. 2.21. Demosthenes plans to speak about topics relating to Amphipolis omitted by others: Aeschin. 2.48. Plutarch's account: Plu. *Dem.* 16.1.

38. Aeschines has ambassadors testify: Aeschin. 2.54. Extent of testimony: Aeschin. 2.44. Demosthenes has verses read out: Dem. 19.255.

Of the eleven men on the First Embassy, there were eight whom Aeschines could have called on to testify. This number excludes Philocrates, who had fled from Athens before his trial and condemnation (Aeschin. 2.6; 3.79, 81; Din. 1.28; Hyp. 4.29), Aeschines himself, and Demosthenes. Of these eight, at least four were present and testified on Aeschines' behalf: Dercylus (Aeschin. 2.155), Iatrocles (Aeschin. 2.126), Nausicles (Aeschin. 2.184— but see note 32 above), and Aglaocreon (Aeschin. 2.126). Aristodemus was not present in court—being an actor, he was probably abroad performing at a foreign dramatic festival—but left a sworn statement witnessed by several citizens to be read out by Aeschines (Aeschin. 2.19). Thus out of the eight who could have testified, five actually submitted testimony on Aeschines' behalf. The other three, Cimon, Ctesiphon, and Phrynon, are not referred to as present, but may also have been in court that day. Demosthenes (19.233) calls witnesses to prove that Phrynon sent his son to Macedon, but his statements reveal nothing about his whereabouts that day. Furthermore, it is clear that none of the ambassadors testified for Demosthenes.

39. Speeches of Athenian ambassadors at Sparta: X. *HG* 6.3.4–17 with Ryder (1963).

40. Demosthenes' sarcastic comments recounted by Plutarch: Plu. *Dem.* 16. Aeschines

as Plutarch's source for these comments: Aeschin. 2.51–52. Cf. 112. Plutarch uses Theopompus as a source: Plu. *Dem.* 4.1; 13.1; 14.3; 18.3–4; 21.2. Theopompus' hostility to Demosthenes: Plu. *Dem.* 13.1; 14.3. But see Plu. *Dem.* 18.4.

41. Aeschines speaks about Amphipolis: Aeschin. 2.28–33. Chersonese discussed during First Embassy: Aeschin. 2.82. Cf. Dem. 19.78–79.

42. Fifty ships mentioned by Demosthenes: Aeschin. 2.36–37. Ships voted to go to Thermopylai: Aeschin. 2.133.

Markel (1970) 73, Ellis (1976) 109, and Sealey (1955) all assume that the situation in central Greece was discussed by the First Embassy during their talks with Philip. Ramming (1965) 51 also thinks the subject came up, but argues implausibly that Philip did not yet know about Phalaecus' return to power. Buckler (1989) 118–27 does not appear to distinguish between the different aims of the First and Second Embassies.

There is no reason to think that the fifty ships voted by the Athenians in early 346 were the same as those later said to be with Proxenus (Dem. 19.322). That is impossible since it would have meant Proxenus had no ships at all before the fifty ships voted by the Assembly arrived. Moreover, it is difficult to understand how Proxenus could have been ordered to proceed to Thermopylai from Oreos, where he was stationed (Dem. 19.155) unless he had some ships with him already. As Demosthenes' remark reveals, the fifty ships were still not available by the time the First Embassy left for Macedon. Thus the fifty ships mentioned by Demosthenes (19.322) were probably Proxenus' original force. It would therefore appear that Demosthenes' prediction that the fifty additional ships called for by the Assembly would never be equipped was an accurate one.

43. Ambassadors meet again with Philip: Aeschin. 2.38–39. Philip's conditions: [Dem.] 7.26; *scholia ad* [Dem.] 7.18 and 23; Isoc. 5.1–2; Dem. 5.25; 19.22, 253–54; Theopompus *FGrHist* 115 F 166. Demosthenes recognizes the importance of Amphipolis to Philip: Dem. 6.17.

44. Philip's promise about the Chersonese: Aeschin. 2.82. Cf. Dem. 19.78–79. Demosthenes attempts to exclude Cersebleptes: Aeschin. 2.84–85. Assembly turns down Cersebleptes: chapter 4.

Cersebleptes must have been excluded from the Peace of Philocrates since he was not a member of the *synedrion* and thus not eligible for inclusion in the treaty. For the Athenian allies eligible for the treaty, see note 46. The fact that Cersebleptes was not a member of the *synedrion* is clearly indicated by the request of his representative Critobulus to have him made a member in Elaphebolion of 346 (Aeschin. 2.83 with the discussion in chapter 4. Cf. Aeschin. 3.74). Furthermore, Cersebleptes is not listed among the members of the Confederacy in its charter (*IG* ii² 43), and the treaty that he and his brothers made with Athens (*IG* ii² 126) differs in form and content from those of states that entered the *synedrion* (*IG* ii² 42, 44, 96, 97). In fact, Demosthenes (23.173) calls this treaty συνθῆκαι, not a συμμαχία. Diodorus (16.34.4) speaks only of φιλία. The treaty itself appears to have been concerned only with the payment of tribute by cities in Thrace and did not contain more extensive terms of alliance. See also Cargill (1981) 90–92.

45. Philip's letter: Dem. 19.40–41. Cf. [Dem.] 7.33.

46. Aglaocreon could only have represented the members of the *synedrion,* and not the independent allies of Athens. These independent allies would have sent their own ambassadors to Philip, as for instance, the Spartans did just a few months later (Aeschin. 2.136). Moreover, Aeschines (2.86) says that the allies were present when the oaths were sworn to the treaty, then calls on the *synedroi* to testify to his statement. This indicates that only the allies who belonged to the *synedrion* swore the oaths to the treaty (Aeschin. 3.74). I do not share the idea of Markle (1970) 78, 117–18 that it was left unclear which Athenian allies were meant. It is impossible to believe that such a crucial issue would have been left ambiguous in this way.

There is certainly no other case in Greek history where it was left unclear during diplomatic negotiations who was actually qualified to be included in a treaty.

Chapter 4

1. Aeschines' account of events before Elaphebolion 18: Aeschin. 2.45–62. The account given in the later speech (Aeschin. 3.63–68) is essentially an abridged version of the earlier one and contains nothing new aside from the allegation that Demosthenes proposed to have the Assembly meet on Elaphebolion 8. Hansen (1983) 70 accepts the charge as fact and inserts a meeting on that day in his calendar of events for the month. But the charge is unlikely to be true: Harris (1986b) 371–73. Hansen (1989) 186–87 attempts to defend his position, but his argument is not convincing—see Harris (1991) 337.

There are several treatments of the events leading up to the meeting of Elaphebolion 18, but they tend to be either superficial or uncritical in their use of sources. The discussion of Schaefer (1885–87) 2:207–22 is marred by his bias against Aeschines. Markle (1967) 81–91 believes that Demosthenes' wish to speed the ratification of the treaty was motivated by his desire to create a situation where Athens could protest the seizure of the Thracian forts. Yet if this were his aim, it is odd that Demosthenes never says it was. Ramming (1965) 51–52, Ellis (1976) 111, and Buckler (1989) 129 each devote less than a page to these crucial events. For the shortcomings of Cawkwell (1960), see appendix 3.

2. Antipater and Parmenion as Macedonian ambassadors: Dem. 19.69. For their careers see Berve (1926) *s.v. Antipatros* and *Parmenion*. The second hypothesis to Dem. 19 also lists Eurylochus, but he is not mentioned by either orator.

The First Embassy left Athens after the *spondophoroi* returned there in early Anthesterion (see appendix 4). This embassy traveled to Macedon far more quickly than the Second Embassy, which took twenty-three days to reach Pella (Dem. 19.155, 163). The negotiations with Philip during the First Embassy appear to have lasted only a day (Aeschin. 2.22–29). The First Embassy thus should have returned to Athens in late Anthesterion and reported to the Assembly around Anthesterion 30. It could not have reported in early Elaphebolion, since the Assembly did not meet until the ninth of the month—see Harris (1991). Meetings often took place on Elaphebolion 9, but we know that between the meeting at which the First Embassy reported and the Dionysia, which began on Elaphebolion 10 (see Mikalson [1975] 124–27) news was carried to the Macedonian ambassadors waiting outside of Attica that they could come to Athens and that they arrived in time to see the Dionysia (see note 4). This rules out the possibility the First Embassy reported on Elaphebolion 8 or 9.

3. Situation in Elaphebolion 346: Aeschin. 2.70–74. Aeschines' comments about Chares are probably exaggerated, but the Assembly's uncertainty in regard to his whereabouts is proven by the decree of Cephisophon. Chares' letter about the capitulation of Cersebleptes on Elaphebolion 24 (Aeschin. 2.90) may have been sent in response to Antiochus' mission. For Athenian concern about the grain supply at this time see *IG* ii² 212. The decision to renew the alliance with Mytilene, also dated to this month (*IG* ii² 213), may also have been motivated by concern over the security of the grain route.

4. Meeting of the Council: Aeschin. 2.45–46. The account Aeschines (3.63) gave in 330 is virtually the same except that he adds that Demosthenes proposed a truce with the Macedonian herald and ambassadors at this meeting. Aeschines (2.53) mentions this decree in his speech of 343, but places it at the subsequent meeting of the Assembly. There is no inconsistency between the two accounts: Demosthenes first proposed the truce in the Council, which then included it as part of the *probouleuma* submitted to the next meeting of the Assembly. Nor is there any inconsistency between the two versions of this proposal given by Aeschines

(2.53: truce with the herald who has already arrived and the ambassadors, who are about to arrive. 3.63: truce with the herald and ambassadors). The former is the fuller, official wording, the latter Aeschines' abbreviated version. Since Athens was still at war with Philip, the ambassadors had to remain outside Attica until the truce was concluded. The herald, however, enjoyed inviolability and could enter Attica without a truce. Compare the similar procedure employed by the Athenians entering Macedon: Dem. 19.163. On the procedure see Mosley (1973) 84.

5. Resolution of the Allies: Aeschin. 2.60. This resolution should not be confused with the one submitted by the Allies to the Assembly on Elaphebolion 18 (Aeschin. 3.69–71). That resolution was a proposal to conclude peace with Philip and to allow any other Greek state that wished to swear the oaths to the treaty within three months. The resolution quoted by Aeschines in 343 was concerned only with setting the dates for the debate about the treaty in the Assembly. Schaefer (1885–87) 2:216–18 mistakenly identifies the two resolutions, but see Marshall (1905) 33–34 and Cawkwell (1960) 420, note 1. Markle (1970) 95, note 1, arbitrarily rejects Cawkwell's argument and returns to Schaefer's view. Aeschines' support for the Resolution of the Allies: Aeschin. 2.61. Aglaocreon of Tenedos shares lodgings with Aeschines and testifies for him: Aeschin. 2.20, 126–27.

6. Report of the First Embassy to the Assembly: Aeschin. 2.47–54.

7. Demosthenes' proposals: Aeschin. 2.53. For the *probouleuma,* see Rhodes (1927) 52–81.

8. Aeschines' refutation of Demosthenes' charge: Aeschin. 2.57–60.

9. Aeschines' charge: Aeschin. 2.61–62. Hansen (1983) 37 misinterprets the charge—see Harris (1986b) 368. Cf. Hansen (1989) 181.

10. For the procedure see, e.g., *IG* ii² 96, 103, 128, 208; and Aeschin. 2.58. For access to the Assembly granted by the Council see *IG* ii² index *s.v.* προσάγειν with Rhodes (1972) 20, 43. Aeschines repeats the charge in 330: Aeschin. 3.64, 68. Demosthenes' reply to the charge in 330: Dem. 18.23–24, 28. Note Demosthenes' use of the word προσάγειν at 28. (He is not using the term to refer to his proposal to grant *proedria* to Philip's ambassadors *pace* Wankel [1976] 256.) Hansen (1983) 64–67 does not realize that the decree of Demosthenes referred to at Aeschin. 2.61 and 3.68 was passed in the Council and mistakenly identifies it with the one referred to at Aeschin. 2.53.

The language of the decree passed by Demosthenes in the Council departs in one respect from the standard formula found in these decrees. Normally the Council called on the *proedroi* to introduce the ambassadors "into the first (i.e. next) meeting of the Assembly (e.g., *IG* ii² 107, lines 10–11; 44, lines 8–9). However, the next meeting of the Assembly was devoted to a discussion of business relating to the Dionysia (Aeschin. 2.61; Dem. 21.9 with Pickard-Cambridge [1968] 64, 6). MacDowell (1990) 227–28 believes this meeting took place on Elaphebolion 17, but see Harris (1992b) 76. The large amount of business already scheduled for that meeting would have precluded any lengthy debate about the treaty on that day so another meeting on Elaphebolion 18 had to be scheduled for that business. But a minor item of business such as the honors for the sons of Leucon could easily have been fitted on the agenda for the meeting that discussed the Dionysia *pace* Lewis (1955) 25–26 (*IG* ii² 212), just as the matter of money to be paid to the sons of Leucon was added to the meeting that discussed the treaty with Philip (*IG* ii² 212, lines 53–59).

11. Demosthenes' reply in 330: Dem. 18.23. Aeschines must have realized that any mention of the failure of the embassies sent in 348 would have undermined his point here. Hence he postpones his allusion to their lack of success until later in his narrative and omits it in his account of events leading up to the Peace of Philocrates.

12. For the Greek embassies to Philip, see chapter 5.

13. Regulations for the debate: Aeschin. 2.65. Previous scholarly treatments of the

meetings on Elaphebolion 18 and 19 do not take account of the implications of this decree and do not approach the evidence for the meetings in a critical and systematic fashion.

14. Demosthenes' charges in 343: Dem. 19.13–16, 144, 159, 291, 321.

15. Only members of the *synedrion* included in Philip's version of the treaty: Aeschin. 2.86; 3.74. Treaty between Athens and Phocis: D.S. 16.27.5. Buckler (1989) 134 contains good criticisms of Demosthenes' charge about the Phocians.

Phocis is not listed on the stele that recorded the names of the members of the *synedrion* (*IG* ii² 43). This would prima facie imply that the Phocians were never members but this argument should not be pressed since the list was clearly not kept up to date after a certain period. If it had been kept up to date, the names of those states that revolted such as Chios, Byzantion, and Rhodes (D.S. 16.7.3) would have been erased, but that is not the case. And the names of states that left the confederacy and later rejoined such as Mytilene (*IG* ii² 213; cf. Dem. 15.19; [Dem.] 40.37) would have been erased, then later reinscribed, but there is no evidence for this either. Note also that there are only about sixty names on the stele, while Diodorus (15.30.2) states that the total membership of the confederacy reached seventy. (The attempt of Cargill [1981] 46–47 to emend the text of Diodorus on the basis of the inscription should therefore be rejected.) Marshall (1905) 94 and Cargill (1981) 67 believe that admission to the Confederacy was closed in around 369. Despite the absence of evidence for the admission of new members after this time, it is clear from Aeschin. 3.83–84 that new members could still apply for admission in 346. In fact, there is a case of a former member, Mytilene, being readmitted.

16. Foreign ambassadors introduced into the Assembly: note 10 above. Foreign ambassadors speaking in the Assembly before the debate about their request: Th. 1.31–44; 4.16–22; 5.44.3–46; X. *HG* 6.5.33–36; 7.1.1–14. In three of these passages the foreign ambassadors remain in the Assembly during the debate and answer questions posed by the Athenians.

17. Aeschines' reply to the charge about the Phocians: Aeschin. 2.133ff. Aeschines' reply to the second charge: Aeschin. 2.65 (there is no indication that these orders were ever rescinded). Aeschines' lukewarm support for the treaty: Aeschin. 2.75–77. Amyntor's testimony: Aeschin. 2.64, 67–68. Demosthenes may not have submitted his proposal to the *proedroi*. Had he done so, Aeschines would probably have summoned these officials to testify, as he does elsewhere (Aeschin. 2.85).

18. Aeschines' boast in 346: Aeschin. 1.174.

19. Aeschines' account in 330: Aeschin. 3.69–72.

20. Resolution of the Allies: Aeschin. 3.69–70.

21. Aeschines' reluctant support for Philocrates' version of the treaty: Aeschin. 2.75–77. Eubulus' speech: Dem. 19.291. Support for continuing the war: Aeschin. 2.74. Aristophon's speech: Theopompus *FGrHist* 115 F 166. Philocrates' version of the treaty: Aeschin. 3.54. Treaty ratified on Elaphebolion 19: Dem. 19.57.

22. No mention of Cersebleptes during the meetings of Elaphebolion 18 and 19: Aeschin. 3.82. Demosthenes' charges about Cersebleptes belong to a later period: Dem. 19.174–81.

23. Aeschines charge in 343: Aeschin. 2.81–86. The word συναναγραφῆναι must refer to having Cersebleptes' name inscribed on the list of members of the *synedrion*. It cannot refer to inscribing the name of Cersebleptes on the stele recording the terms of the treaty between Philip and Athens since on none of the preserved inscriptions that record treaties made by Athens and her allies with a foreign power are the names of the members of the *synedrion* listed (e.g., *IG* ii² 105, 112).

24. Aeschines' charge of 330: Aeschin. 3.73–75. Philip's letter: [Dem.] 12.8. Scholarly opinion about the letter's authenticity: Griffith (1979) 714–16. The letter does distort the reply of the Athenians to the Persian embassy of 344/43, but does not tend to invent facts—see Harris (1989a).

Chapter 5

1. Common Peace: Ryder (1965). Reelection of ambassadors: Aeschin. 2.97 with chapter 3, note 32.

2. Instruction to receive oaths: Aeschin. 2.91, 98, 103; Dem. 19.161. Prisoners: Aeschin. 2.103. "Anything of benefit to Athens": Aeschin. 2.104. Other examples of this clause: Thuc. 6.8.2; Mosley (1973) 25. Demosthenes' objection: Aeschin. 2.104.

3. Assembly's order to Council and Demosthenes' decree: Dem. 19.154. Demosthenes' charge about delay: Dem. 19.150–62. Cf. 18.25–27. Discussion of Dem. 19.154: Harris (1986b) 366–67.

4. Cersebleptes' position in the treaty: chapter 3. Thracian fortresses: appendix 5. Aeschines chooses to refute Demosthenes' charge by reading out a letter from the general Chares stating that Cersebleptes had surrendered to Philip on Elaphebolion 24, many days before the Second Embassy was instructed to leave on its journey to Philip. His decision to refute Demosthenes' charge in this way is quite understandable: he obviously did not wish to admit that the terms of the treaty that he, as one of the members of the First Embassy, brought back from Philip, did not include Cersebleptes. Ellis (1976) 113 claims that it would have been pointless for the embassy to have gone straight to Philip in Thrace and "quite possibly (had they attempted to hinder his campaign) destructive of the peace," but does not explain how the ambassadors could have prevented Philip from completing his conquest of Thrace.

5. Arrival in Pella in late Munichion: Aeschin. 2.92 (ambassadors depart after Munichion 3); Dem. 19.155 (journey takes twenty-three days). Greek embassies in Pella: Aeschin. 2.104, 108, 112, 136; Dem. 19. *hypoth.*, 139; D.S. 16.59.2.

6. Causes and outbreak of the Third Sacred War: D.S. 16.23.2–6; 24.4–25; 27.3–5; 29.1–4 with Buckler (1989) 9–29. Diodorus (16.23.3), Pausanias (10.2.1), and Justin (8.1) all give different reasons for the fine imposed on the Phocians.

7. Philip's campaign in Thessaly: D.S. 16.35.1–6; 38.1–2; Griffith (1979) 267–81; Buckler (1989) 58–81.

8. Phalaecus supports Callias of Chalcis: *schol. ad* Aeschin. 3.87. On the proposal of Cawkwell (1962a) 129–30 to emend the text of Aeschin. 3.87 see Brunt (1969) 289–90. Phayllus succeeds Onomarchus: D.S. 16.36.1; 37.1–6; 38.3–5. Phalaecus succeeds Phayllus: D.S. 16.38.6. Investigation and trial of Philon: D.S. 16.56.2–8; Paus. 10.2.5. Renewal of ties with Athens: Aeschin. 2.132.

9. Philip's aid to Thebes: D.S. 16.58.2–4. The small size of the contingent may have been dictated by Philip's military needs at the time.

10. Phalaecus' rebuff to Athens: Aeschin. 2.132–35. Embassies in Pella: note 5 this chapter.

11. Thessalians desire to regain position: Dem. 2.7. Griffith (1979) 274–77 does not take the religious factor seriously enough.

12. Date of Philip's return: Dem. 19.155. Aeschines' account of the conference: Aeschin. 2.101–7.

13. Phalaecus' volte-face: Aeschin. 2.132–35.

14. Boeotian cities lost to the Phocians: D.S. 16.58.1. Spartan attempts to weaken Theban power in Boeotia: X. *HG* 4.8.15; D.S. 15.51.3. Isocrates' proposals: Isoc. 5; Perlman (1957). Philip's promise: Dem. 19.40–41.

15. Demosthenes' appeals to anti-Theban sentiment: Dem. 1.26; 6.7, 11, 19; 9.11; 19.60, 66, 83, 325. Demosthenes' concessions to Thebes in 339: Aeschin. 3.142–43. Demosthenes unlikely to have foreseen in 346 the later treaty with Thebes: Errington (1981) 74.

The passages cited by Markle (1974) 259–60 do not show that Demosthenes held a pro-

Theban policy prior to 340. Twice in his speech of 343 Aeschines (2.141, 143) accuses Demosthenes of being a *proxenos* of Thebes, but does not provide proof for his charge. Nor is there any evidence in other sources for Demosthenes' life about such a *proxenia*. Furthermore, Demosthenes is unlikely to have been a *proxenos* of Thebes at this time, either by inheriting the honor from his father or by gaining it by himself. The first possibility can be ruled out since neither Demosthenes' father nor any of his ancestors appear to have been active in politics or to have had any special connection with Thebes. On the other hand, we can exclude the possibility that the Thebans granted Demosthenes the honor. We certainly never hear of Demosthenes performing any favors for Thebans visiting Athens or promoting Theban interests in the Assembly prior to 346. Such a policy would have been especially foolish at the time since Athenian relations with Thebes had been hostile from the 360s when Athens renewed her ties with Sparta (see Buckler [1980] 87–92). And even if Demosthenes was a *proxenos* of Thebes, we could still not assume that his policy was consistently pro-Theban. Pericles, after all, was a *proxenos* of Sparta, but that did not stop him from pursing a hard line against Sparta in 431 (Cawkwell [1963b] 207, note 4).

16. Demosthenes' charge of bribery: Dem. 19.166–68.

17. Absence of a Macedonian constitution: Errington (1978). Athenian law about gifts: *Ath. Pol.* 54.2 with MacDowell (1983). Athenian attitudes about foreign gift-giving: Perlman (1976). Impolite to refuse a gift: Harvey (1985) 105–6.

Ellis (1976) 114 argues that Philip did not wish to release the Athenian prisoners immediately because he wanted to use them as a "means of persuading the Athenian *demos* to comply with his requests." Ellis also claims that Philip realized that "if he were to refuse, he would provide his opponents with ammunition for a charge of bad faith." But none of our sources suggests that Philip intended to use the prisoners as pawns in his diplomatic maneuvers. In fact, after the Athenians failed to comply with Philip's request to send troops, he still released the prisoners ([Dem.] 7.38). Nor is there any evidence to show that Philip's enemies in Athens ever used his delay in releasing the prisoners as a charge against him in 346. Philip's reason for releasing the prisoners so that they would return to Athens at the time of the Panathenaea is better explained by Schaefer (1885–87) 2.260: "bei diesem herrlichstem aller athenischen Feste sollten sie erscheinen um die Grossmut des Königs recht glänzend ans Licht zu stellen" (*to highlight the generosity of the king in a very splendid way*).

18. Aeschines' account of the speeches to Philip: Aeschin. 2.108–17. Testimony about the First Embassy: Aeschin. 2.46, 55. Testimony about the meeting of the ambassadors: Aeschin. 2.107. Aeschines' report of the speech consistent with report to the Assembly: Aeschin. 2.119.

19. Proposal to Thebans in 479: Hdt. 9.86–88. Phalaecus contrasted with the innocent: Aeschin. 2.142. Blame for theft of sacred money on Philon: D.S. 16.56.3–8.

20. Aeschines' advice about Thebes: Aeschin. 2.119.

21. Philip's letter: Dem. 19.36–41. Companions say that Philip will punish Thebes: Aeschin. 2.137.

22. Philip intends to liberate Boeotia: Markle (1974), Ellis (1976) 107–20. Decree of Assembly calling for expedition against those preventing meeting of the Amphictyons: Dem. 19.47–51.

Demosthenes (19.20) claims that Aeschines told the Assembly that the Athenians would hear within a few days that Thebes was cut off from the rest of Boeotia and under siege, that Thespiai and Plataia had been refounded, and that all this would be accomplished without the Athenians leaving their homes. Aeschines (2.119) never says he told the Athenians that Philip would liberate Boeotia. All Aeschines states is that he told Philip that Thebes should be a part of Boeotia, not Boeotia subject to Thebes. In the passages cited by Markle (e.g., Aeschin. 1.169; Dem. 5.9–10) much is said about Philip's promises but nowhere is there talk of a specific promise to liberate the cities of Boeotia. Finally, we should note that a few years later the ambassadors sent by Philip were able to deny that the king ever made any promises at all (Dem. 6 *hypoth.*).

23. Philip's promise to the Thessalians: Aeschin. 2.136. Philip's assurance to the Phocians: Dem. 9.11. Cf. Dem. 19. *hypoth.* 2.7.

24. Philip swears oaths: Dem. 18.32. The statement in Dem. 19. *hypoth.* 2.7 that Philip swore the oaths at Pherai should be rejected—see Griffith (1979) 344, note 4. Thessalians swear oaths: Dem. 19.158. Contrary to Demosthenes' insinuations, there is nothing suspicious about the manner in which the Thessalians swore the oaths—see Mosley (1971). Aeschines and Philocrates have Phocians and Halians excluded from treaty: Dem. 19.44, 174. Dispute about Halus: Dem. 19.36, 39.

25. Philip's letter: Dem. 19.38–41. Date of the Panathenaea: Mikalson (1975) 34. Ransom for prisoners: Dem. 19.168–72 (supported by the testimony of witnesses). Demosthenes' charge about Philip's letter: Dem. 19.174–78. Aeschines' defense: Aeschin. 2.124–29.

Schaefer (1885–87) 2:266 claims that although Aeschines proves that he did not meet Philip at night, he does not refute the charge that he met the king alone during the day. Schaefer was therefore inclined to accept Demosthenes' charge about the letter. But Demosthenes never proves that Aeschines met privately with Philip during the day. Besides, it is absurd to think that Philip needed any help composing the letter, as Aeschines (2.129) rightly points out.

26. Cawkwell (1962b) 453–59 and (1978) 129–30, Markle (1974) 265, and Ellis (1976) 116–17 all state that Philip was in control of the pass at Thermopylai by Skirophorion 13. Wankel (1980) correctly observes, however, that D.S. 16.59.2 states that Phalaecus held Nikaia, one of the three fortresses that controlled the pass when he entered into negotiations with Philip. But, *pace* Wankel, the Athenians were in no position to come to Phalaecus' assistance at this juncture. Although Philip did not have complete control of the pass, Phalaecus was surrounded by Macedonians and Thessalians on one side and Thebans on the other. Furthermore, the Athenians could not have mounted an expedition quickly enough to affect the outcome of events. One must recall that in 352 they were able to stop Philip only because they already had a major force in the vicinity. Finally, there is no indication that Proxenus had many hoplites with him at Oreos.

27. Demosthenes' charges: Dem. 19.17–18, 35.

28. Demosthenes cites *probouleuma:* Dem. 19.32.

29. Cf. Markle (1974) 262, note 1.

30. Schaefer (1885–87) 2:267–68 accepts without question Demosthenes' interpretation of the *probouleuma.* The explanation Demosthenes (19.32) gives for his failure to receive a vote of honors at the time is unconvincing.

31. Illegal for the Council to award honors before *euthynai:* Aeschin. 3.9–12. Cf. Wüst (1938) 7–9. Clause inserted in honorary decrees: Harris (1994a) 147, 150, note 26. Cawkwell (1960) 98–101 and (1978a) 104–5 claims that another *probouleuma*, this one containing honors, was passed before the meeting of Skirophorion 16. But if this were true, why did Aeschines not have it read out at his trial in 343? Honors for the First Embassy: Aeschin. 2.46, 53.

32. Open *probouleuma:* Rhodes (1972) 58.

33. Aeschines' speech to the Assembly: Dem. 19.36–50.

34. Aeschines' account: Aeschin. 2.119–35. Demosthenes' remarks in 346: Dem. 5.9–10. Aeschines' explanation for Philip's failure to attack Thebes: Dem. 6.14; Aeschin. 2.141.

35. Euboea in Philip's sphere of influence: Dem. 19.22, 220, 326 with Brunt (1969) 289–91. Philip in communication with the Euboeans: Aeschin. 2.12.

36. Aeschines claims Demosthenes proposed honors for the embassy: Aeschin. 2.121. Aeschines has Demosthenes' earlier decree of honors read out: Aeschin. 2.46, 54. Demosthenes expresses doubts about Philip's intentions: Dem. 5.10.

37. Philocrates' decree: Dem. 19.47–50.

38. Reelection of ambassadors and resignation of Demosthenes: Dem. 19.121–22.

39. Duties of the *logistai: Ath. Pol.* 54.2. The ambassadors must have submitted their accounts before Skirophorion 21 when Dercylus left Athens on the Third Embassy (see note 43 below). Since magistrates could not leave Attica before they submitted their accounts (Aeschin. 3.21), Dercylus must have submitted his accounts before this date. Traveling expenses of ambassadors: Dem. 19.158 with Mosley (1973) 74–77. All magistrates must submit accounts: Aeschin. 3.17–22. *Euthynoi* receive accusations: *Ath. Pol.* 48.4. Procedure used by Timarchus and Demosthenes: MacDowell (1978) 171. The *logistai* could also receive accusations (Aeschin. 3.23), but these were probably confined to matters concerning financial accounts. Until a magistrate submitted his account to the *logistai,* he was considered ὑπεύθυνος and could not receive honors from the Council or Assembly and or leave Attica (Aeschin. 3.21). After the *logistai* had received his accounts, the magistrate was apparently free to leave Attica, even if someone subsequently accused him before the *euthynoi* and his case had not yet come to court. This is shown by the fact that Aeschines was able to serve on the Third Embassy to Delphi after being accused by Demosthenes and Timarchus. If Aeschines had done this illegally, Demosthenes would have made an issue of it in his speech of 343.

40. Aeschines' attempt to thwart the prosecution: Dem. 19.211–13.

41. Timarchus charges Aeschines: Aeschin. 1. *hypoth.;* 1–2; Dem. 19. *hypoth.* 2.10. Timarchus as a member of the Council: Aeschin. 1.80. Blass (1887–98) 2:193 suggests that Demosthenes and Timarchus began to work together when they served in the Council together in 347/46. Timarchus' decree: Dem. 19.286: Hegesander and Hegesippus as associates of Timarchus: Aeschin. 1.55–71, 95–96, 110–11, 154. Hegesippus proposes alliance with the Phocians: Aeschin. 3.118. Hegesippus accompanies Demosthenes to the Peloponnese: Dem. 9.72. Hegesippus opposes Philip's proposals for revision: [Dem.] 7.

42. Aeschines' illness: appendix 7.

43. Dercylus reported to the Assembly on Skirophorion 27 that the Phocians had surrendered on Skirophorion 23 (Dem. 19.60). Dercylus heard the news of the surrender at Chalcis probably the day after it occurred. This means that the trip from Chalcis to Athens took him two or three days. If his trip from Athens to Chalcis took the same amount of time, he should have left Athens about Skirophorion 21. Demosthenes blames Aeschines for causing the defeat of the Phocians: Dem. 19.47–63 (esp. 53), 72–77, 321–24. Both Aeschines and Demosthenes say that there were Phocians in Athens at the time, but differ about their functions. Demosthenes (19.59) calls them πρέσβεις while Aeschines (2.130) describes them as δρομοκήρυκες . View that the Athenian failure to send troops was responsible for the Phocian surrender: Markle (1974) 265; Ellis (1976) 119–20.

44. Phalaecus comes to terms with Philip: Aeschin. 2.140; D.S. 16.59.3.

45. Dercylus hears news of Phocian surrender: Dem. 19.60. Decree of Callisthenes: Dem. 18.36–38; 19.86, 125; Aeschin. 2.139; 3.80.

46. Philip requests troops: Dem. 19.51–52; Aeschin. 2.137. Demosthenes claims Philip will take troops hostage: Aeschin. 2.137.

47. Aeschines blames ruin of Phocis on Athenian failure to send troops: Aeschin. 2.140–41.

48. Philip convenes Amphictyons: D.S. 16.59.4. Aeschines defeats proposal of Oetaeans: Aeschin. 2.142–43 (supported by testimony of Phocians). Settlement imposed on Phocis: D.S. 16.60.1–3; Buckler (1989) 141–42. The three cities referred to by Diodorus must

be the cities the Phocians captured in Boeotia: Orchomenos, Coroneia, and either Corsiai or Tilphosaion (D.S. 16.56.2; 58.1; Dem. 19.112, 141, 325). Griffith (1939) discusses whether or not the settlement of 346 was a *koine eirene* or not and takes full account of earlier views. I do not share Griffith's view that Philip did not wish to stabilize the situation in 346 nor his assumption that Philip proposed to expand the settlement into a *koine eirene* in 343—see chapter 6.

49. Causes of the Fourth Sacred War: chapter 7.

50. Athens refuses to send delegation to Pythian games: Dem. 19.128. Philip presides over games: D.S. 16.60.2. Phocian seats on the council awarded to Philip: Dem. 5. *hypoth.* Demosthenes opposes protest: Dem. 5.14–23. Aeschines supports request of ambassadors: Dem. 19.111–13.

51. Homosexual prostitution not illegal: Dover (1978) 29–30. Law about *rhetores:* Aeschin. 1.24–32; Dover (1978) 23–31. For a discussion the social issues raised by the speech see Winkler (1990) 45–70 and Cohen (1991) 171–202. Aeschines' inexperience and motive: Aeschin. 1.1–3.

52. Date of Timarchus' trial: Harris (1985). Wankel (1988) questions this dating, drawing attention to Aeschines' statement (1.77) that the revision of the citizen-list was completed before the trial. Wankel assumes that this process would have consumed several months ("Diese Gesamtrevision muss in der Tat ein längerer Vorgang gewesen sein.") and concludes that the trial could not have taken place until early 345. Wankel appears to think that the revision was a lengthy process like a modern census, but his anachronistic assumption is refuted by the account of the process given at Dem. 57.9–13 where the plaintiff describes how the qualifications of sixty men were reviewed in a few hours in one deme. This means that each deme would have taken only a day or two to complete the process of revision. Since there is no reason to think that the process was not carried out at roughly the same time in all the demes, the "Gesamtrevision" need not have taken more than several weeks at the most. Wankel also compares the delay between Aeschines' accusation of Ctesiphon in 336 and the resulting trial in 330 and claims that trials were often delayed for no apparent reason. But the two situations were completely different. In 346 Aeschines had to act quickly to fend off an impending prosecution. In 336 Aeschines was under no such pressure and was at leisure to wait for circumstances to provide him with a more favorable atmosphere, which did not occur until 330. For a discussion of the reasons for Aeschines' delaying his prosecution of Ctesiphon see chapter 7.

53. Aeschines' civics lesson: Aeschin. 1.4–38.

54. Liaison with Misgolas: Aeschin. 1.41–53.

55. Business with Pittalacus and Hegesander: Aeschin. 1.53–69. Pittalacus must have been a freedman since he later brought legal proceedings against Hegesander. Furthermore, if he had been a public slave, why did not a magistrate step forward and claim him as state property when Hegesander asserted he belonged to him? See Jacob (1979) 158–62.

56. Autolycus' report: Aeschin. 1.81–85.

57. Timarchus squanders his patrimony: Aeschin. 1.95–105.

58. Venality in public office: Aeschin. 1.106–13.

59. Defense of rumor and hearsay: Aeschin. 1.77–81. Areopagus draws on personal knowledge: Aeschin. 1.92–93. Ridicule of demand for evidence of contract: Aeschin. 1.160–65.

60. Timarchus not in a registered house of prostitution: Aeschin. 1.119–24. Demosthenes says rumor is unreliable: Aeschin. 1.125–26. Hesiod and Homer on rumor: Aeschin. 1.127–30.

61. Demosthenes brings up Phocians: Aeschin. 1.166–69.

62. General accuses Aeschines of hypocrisy: Aeschin. 1.132–35. Aeschines' reply:

Aeschin. 1.136–47. For a discussion of Aeschines' treatment of this topic see Dover (1978) 41–59. Demosthenes' quotation of poetry in his speech of 343 is unusual for him and is no doubt done in response to Aeschines' extensive quotations in his speech against Timarchus— see North (1952) 24–25.

    63. Timarchus' punishment: Dem. 19.2, 257, 284–85, 287.

Chapter 6

    1. These assumptions have influenced several recent works including Markle (1970), Cawkwell (1963b) and (1978b), Ellis (1976), and to a lesser extent Griffith (1979). For a critique of these assumptions, see Errington (1981) 76–82. Cf. Buckler (1989) 121–25, 147.

    2. Sources for Persian appeal: Did. *In D.* 7.5–32, Philochorus *FGrHist* 328 F 157; D.S. 16.44.1. Diodorus dates the Persian appeal to 351/50, but see Beloch (1922) 285–87. Pytho's embassy: [Dem.] 7.18–23; Dem. 18.136. Demosthenes alludes to Persian offer in 341: Dem. 10.34. Identification of Macedonian embassy and interpretation: Wüst (1938) 64–67.

    3. For a detailed discussion of Didymus' mistake and of the Persian appeal of 344/43 see Harris (1989a). I leave out of the discussion the alliance between Philip and Artaxerxes mentioned at Arr. *An.* 2.14.2. For a summary of the debate about the treaty, see Bosworth (1980) 229–30. Bosworth himself is skeptical about its existence as is Griffith (1979) 485–86.

    4. Isocrates proposes invasion of Asia: Isoc. 5. Philip plans invasion: D.S. 16.89.2–3; 91.2; Justin 9.5.8–9.

    5. Philip fights Illyrians: D.S. 16.69.7. For a discussion of this campaign see Griffith (1979) 469–74. Philip hands over cities of Cassopia to Alexander: [Dem.] 7.32. Griffith (1979) 308, note 3, 504–9, places Philip's removal of Arrybas from the throne of Epirus shortly before 342/41, but see Errington (1975) and Heskel (1988). Philip's aid to Argos and Messene: Dem. 6.15. There is no reason to doubt Demosthenes here: Griffith (1979) 474–78. Philip intervenes in Thessaly: Griffith (1979) 522–44.

    6. Demosthenes' embassy to the Peloponnese: Dem. *hypoth.* 6. Date of Dem. 6: appendix 8.

    7. Demosthenes alludes to Aeschines and Philocrates: Dem. 6.30 (cf. Dem. 19.46). Rumors about Philip: Dem. 6.14–15.

    8. Demosthenes replies to criticisms: Dem. 6.16–17.

    9. Pytho's embassy: [Dem.] 7.18–23. Date of Pytho's embassy: appendix 8. Philip does not promise to accede to all demands: Ellis (1976) 145.

    10. Hegesippus proposes to amend clause about territory: [Dem.] 7.24–29. Hegesippus claims Pytho assented to Athenian demand: [Dem.] 7.20.

    11. Demand to return Halonnesos: [Dem.] 7.2. Athenian proposal to defend freedom of the Greeks: [Dem.] 7.30. The proposal to defend the freedom of the Greeks has been misunderstood by modern scholars who think it was a proposal to transform the Peace of Philocrates into a Common Peace. This includes Cawkwell (1963b) 132, Ellis (1976) 144–45, Griffith (1979) 490–91. If this had been so, the Athenians would have proposed that all the Greek cities that had not sworn the oaths to the peace be permitted to do so. But the Athenians proposed nothing of the sort. Their proposal is that both they and Philip swear an oath to preserve the freedom of the Greeks who had not been parties to the Peace of Philocrates. It is also clear that it was the Athenians, not Philip, who made the proposal, and [Dem.] 7.18 and 26 do not prove the contrary (*pace* Cawkwell). Cf. Brunt (1969) 262, note 2: "In defiance of all the evidence Cawkwell makes the proposal for a *koine eirene* emanate from Philip."

    12. Philip rejects amendment about territory: [Dem.] 7.26. Offer to submit disputes to arbitration: [Dem.] 7.7–8. Offer to "give" Halonnesos: [Dem.] 7.2, 4–6. Proposal to sup-

press piracy: [Dem.] 7.14–16. Agreements about legal procedure: [Dem.] 7.9–13. Nature of *symbola:* Gauthier (1972). Dispute about Cardia: [Dem.] 7.39–45. Philip's letter: [Dem.] 7.1, 46.

13. Hegesippus' reply: [Dem.] 7.

14. One should not interpret Hegesippus' words about Philip's benefits ([Dem.] 7.35) as an allusion to a gift of lands in Persia. See Errington (1981) 80–81.

15. Aeschines supports Pytho: Dem. 18.136. Aeschines criticizes Hegesippus' objection: Aeschin. 3.83. Cf. [Dem.] 7.23 where one of the "instructors" may be Aeschines. Dem. 19.209 may refer to Aeschines' failure to be elected to serve on this embassy, but there is no way to achieve certainty on the matter.

16. Flight and conviction of Philocrates: Hyp. *Eux.* 29; Aeschin. 3.79; Dem. 19.116; Din. 1.28; *Hesperia* 5 (1936) 399–400, lines 45–50, 111–15. The general Proxenus may also have been convicted in 343 for failing to help the Phocians—see Dem. 19.280–81 with *schol. ad loc. Eisangelia* procedure: Hansen (1975). Demosthenes challenges other ambassadors: Dem. 19.116–17.

17. Aeschines and Demosthenes view Philocrates' flight as an admission of guilt: Aeschin. 2.6; Dem. 19.116.

18. Philip helps friends in Megara: Dem. 19.87, 204, 294–95, 334. Phocion's expedition to Megara: Plu. *Phoc.* 15. Griffith (1979) 498 connects Phocion's expedition with the manning of Panacton described in Dem. 54.3. Griffith does not consider the possibility that the latter incident is also alluded to at Dem. 19.326, but see Carey and Reid (1985) 69 for another possibility.

19. Stasis in Elis: Dem. 9.27; 10.10; 18.295; 19.260–61, 294; Paus. 4.28.5; 5.4.9. Philip helps supporters in Euboea: Dem. 9.57–68; 19.87, 204, 326, 334.

20. Dem. 19.25–28 makes it clear that the following section is aimed at proving the first two charges. The third and fourth are dealt with in 150–65, and the fifth at 106–20 and 166–68. At 178 Demosthenes accordingly states that he has proven all his charges. Weakness of Demosthenes' charge of bribery: Chapter 5. Report of Aeschines and Philocrates leads to defeat of Phocis: Dem. 19.17–101. Contrast with saving of Thermopylai in 352: Dem. 19.83–87. Security of Chersonese does not compensate for loss of Phocis: Dem. 19.78–79. Gains made by Philip: Dem. 19.78, 81, 85, 90f., 128, 141–42, 148f., 178f., 325, 334–35.

21. Loss of Thracian fortresses: Dem. 19.155–61.

22. Demosthenes denies supporting treaty: Dem. 19.144. Honors to Macedonian ambassadors: Dem. 19.234–36. Demosthenes tries to speed up Second Embassy: Dem. 19.154. Demosthenes claims to have denounced Aeschines and Philocrates: Dem. 19.25.

23. Demosthenes supports Philocrates: Aeschin. 2.61. Demosthenes honors Macedonian ambassadors: Aeschin. 2.55, 108–13. Demosthenes prevents other Greeks from sharing in the peace: Aeschin. 2.58–62. Demosthenes opposes inclusion of Cersebleptes: Aeschin. 2.83–84. Demosthenes flatters Philip: Aeschin. 2.106–12.

24. Aeschines cites decree about procedure on Elaphebolion 19: Aeschin. 2.65. Aeschines explains his support for the treaty: Aeschin. 2.70–77. Phalaecus responsible for defeat of Phocis: Aeschin. 2.131–32.

25. Aeschines defends peace: Aeschin. 2.172–77.

26. Aeschines acquitted: Aeschin. 2. *hypoth.* Help of friends: Aeschin. 2.170, 184.

27. Dispute over Cardia: Dem. 8. *hypoth.*

28. Demosthenes' opponents criticize Diopeithes and Chares: Dem. 8.30. Aeschines criticizes Chares: Aeschin. 2.71–73. Proposal to recall Diopeithes: Dem. 8.17. Philip has no hostile designs: Dem. 8.17, 56. Athens should observe the peace: Dem. 8.52. Athens should follow Philip in keeping the peace: Dem. 8.4–8.

29. Campaign in Thrace aimed at Athens: Dem. 8.44–45. Need for allies: Dem. 8.46–47.

30. Athenian alliance with Achaea, Arcadia, Argos, and Megalopolis: Dem. 9.92; *schol. ad* Aeschin. 3.83; *IG* ii² 225. Cf. Wüst (1938) 93–94 with references to earlier literature, and Ellis (1976) 158.

31. Aeschines criticizes alliance with Euboea: Aeschin. 3.85–105. Expedition to Eretria: *schol. ad* Aeschin. 3.103. Cf. *IG* ii² 230.

32. Antiphon affair: Dem. 18.132; Dinarchus 1.63; Plu. *Dem.* 14. Plutarch's account differs from that of Demosthenes and Dinarchus. He says that Demosthenes arrested Antiphon after the Assembly had released him and brought him before the Areopagus and implies that Demosthenes proved him to be a traitor in front of the Areopagus, which then handed him over for execution. Plutarch has obviously misread his sources here or altered the story to fit his portrait of Demosthenes as a man who braved the opposition of the Assembly. Wallace (1989a) 113–15 attempts to reconcile Plutarch's version with the information found in Demosthenes and Dinarchus. According to Wallace, Antiphon was tried twice for the same offense, but that was strictly impossible in Athenian law (Dem. 24.54–55). For the legal grounds to Aeschines' objection to Antiphon's arrest, see appendix 9.

33. Delos affair: Dem. 18.134–36. Ellis (1976) 131–32 rejects Demosthenes' explanation of the decision of the Areopagus and substitutes his own. He argues that the Areopagus felt that it was inappropriate to appoint a man who "had associated himself with the attempts to confine the Phokian punishment to the leaders alone." Yet Ellis does not note that Aeschines' defense of the Phocians after their surrender in 346 did not offend the Amphictyons. In fact, it was his speech that convinced them to reject the extremely harsh punishment proposed by the Oetaeans (Aeschin. 2.142–43). Ellis also does not explain why the Areopagus considered Hyperides a suitable replacement. His main argument against Demosthenes' explanation is that "the Council would not have allowed important international issues to be decided by childish petulance." But their decision not to allow Aeschines to represent Athens because he was suspected of treason hardly qualifies as "childish petulance."

34. Those who attribute the breakdown in relations between Athens and Philip primarily to the demagoguery of Demosthenes include Cawkwell (1963b), Wüst (1938) 72ff., and Ellis (1976) 146ff.

Chapter 7

1. Perinthos turns to Athens: D.S. 16.74.2. Philip's siege of Perinthos: D.S. 16.74.2–76.4; Philochorus *FGrHist* 328 F 53–54. Philip seizes grain ships and sends letter: Dem. 18.73 with *scholia ad loc.;* Philochorus *FGrHist* 328 F 162; Theopompus *FGrHist* 115 F 292. Philip attacks Byzantium: D.S. 16.76.3; 77.2. Athens votes for war and destroys stele: Philochorus *FGrHist* 328 F 55A and 55B. Cf. D.S. 16.77.2.

2. Demosthenes' naval reform: Dem. 18.102–7 with Wankel (1976) 554–79; Din. 1.42; Hyp. fr. 134 (Blass). Demosthenes may have held the position of *epistates* of the navy when he made his proposal: see Develin (1989) 339. For a different interpretation of the reform, see Gabrielsen (1989). Aeschines criticizes proposal: Aeschin. 3.222. Meidias abuses system: Dem. 21.155. Aeschines damages proposal: Dem. 18.312. Nature of *eranos* loan: Maier (1969). Nature of trierarchic symmories: MacDowell (1986).

Demosthenes first passed a *psephisma* (decree) to have a *nomos* (law) about the trierarchy discussed. The *psephisma* was attacked by a *graphe paranomon*. After Demosthenes was acquitted on this charge, the *nomos* was discussed and amended. For the procedure see Hansen (1983) 173–75.

3. Phocion leads troops against Eretria: Philochorus *FGrHist* 328 F 160–61. Phocion commands fleet: Plu. *Phoc.* 14; Nepos *Phocion; IG* ii² 1628, lines 436–38; 1629, lines 957–60. Eubulus' decree: Dem. 18.70, 73. For the context of this decree see appendix 5.

4. Philip's campaign against Atheas: Justin 9.2.1–16. Wüst (1938) 145 claims that the campaign was undertaken to impress the Greeks, but the Greeks were not impressed by victories over barbarian tribes. Wüst does not take into account Philip's need to punish the disloyal Atheas, to maintain his reputation among the northern tribes, and to provide his troops with booty after the setbacks in the Hellespont. Griffith (1979) 581–84 gives a better analysis of Philip's aims during the campaign.

5. Date of the Amphictyonic meeting: Aeschin. 3.115 with Wankel (1981) 159–66. Philip away in the north: Aeschin. 3.128; Justin 9.2.1–16. Aeschines may have been able to provide witnesses to support his account, but he did not do so for some reason. He says that he was accompanied to Delphi by the *hieromnemon* Diognetus, his friend Meidias, and Thrasycles. Diognetus was ill on the day of the meeting and thus unable to attend; Meidias appears to have attended, but died before the trial of Ctesiphon (Aeschin. 3.115). Yet, Thrasycles could have testified. He may be identical with the man of the same name who prosecuted the children of Lycurgus ([Plu.] *Mor.* 842d).

6. Aeschines' reply to the Locrian charge: Aeschin. 3.115–22.

7. Declaration of sacred war and Philip's later intervention: Aeschin. 3.123–29.

8. Demosthenes' criticism of Aeschines' account: Dem. 18.150. Earlier skepticism about Demosthenes' criticisms: Schaefer (1885–87) 2:535; Beloch (1922) 2:556, note 3. It is important to observe Demosthenes' misleading use of legal language in the passage. First, there is the verb προκαλέσασθαι, which refers to the action of the prosecutor when summoning the defendant to appear before a magistrate (see Harrison [1971] 85). Second, there is the phrase τίς οὖν ἐκλήτευσεν ἡμᾶς. The verb κλητεύειν is found only in the Demosthenic corpus, Isaeus, and Aristophanes. In all the passages where it is found, the verb has one of two possible meanings, the first is "to be a witness to a summons" (Dem. 47.27; 53.15, 17; Is. fr. 88 and fr. 108; Ar. *Vesp.* 1413; *Nub.* 1218). The second is "to summon to testify as a witness" (Is. fr. 118; Dem. 32.30; 59.28). The compound ἐκκλητεύειν appears twice in Aeschines (1.46; 2.68) and once in Isaeus (fr. 119) and always has the second meaning. For the legal procedure associated with the first meaning, see Harrison (1971) 85; for that associated with the second, see Harrison (1971) 139–40. Demosthenes is clearly challenging Aeschines to provide a witness to prove that an actual summons was made to the Athenians. But the procedure was obviously inapplicable at a meeting of the Amphictyons. Wankel (1976) 806–7 thinks that Demosthenes is referring to a procedure involving "offizielle κλητῆρες," but there is no evidence that indicates the verb could ever refer to a summons made by a public official. A similar error is made by Bonner and Smith (1943) 10.

9. Locrians as traditional allies of Thebes: D.S. 16.27.5; 28.3; 29.1; 30.3. Philip's appeal to Thebes: Dem. 18.213; D.S. 16.84.5; D.H. *Amm.* 1.11. Demosthenes cites Philip's letter to the Peloponnesians: Dem. 18.156–58. Philip away in north during crisis: Aeschin. 3.128. See also the important insight of Sealey (1978) 313–14. One should not think that the Thessalians must have been acting on Philip's orders because he held the position of *archon* of the Thessalian League. Philip's tenure in this office is a modern fiction—see appendix 11.

10. Decree of the Amphictyons: Aeschin. 3.124.

11. Nikaia awarded to Thessalians: Dem. 5.22; Aeschin. 3.140. Didymus in *Dem.* 11.36, citing Philochorus *FGrHist* 328 F 56, informs us that after seizing Elateia, Philip asked the Thebans to surrender Nikaia to the Locrians contrary to the decree of the Amphictyons. This reveals that the Thebans had taken Nikaia sometime before. Earlier scholars either accepted Demosthenes' accusation of treason or assumed that the outbreak of the sacred war was to Philip's advantage. See, for example, Wüst (1938) 149: "Der Ausbruch des Vierten

Heiligen Krieges lag letzen Endes in Philipps Interesse und ist wohl sein Werk: darüber ist sich die Forschung zeimlich einig'' (*the outbreak of the Fourth Sacred War was in the final analysis in Philip's interest and no doubt his work; on this matter modern scholarship is fairly unanimous*). See also Glotz (1909) and de Sanctis (1897). See Wüst (1938) 149, note 1, for references to earlier literature. Griffith (1979) 586 absolves Aeschines, but still thinks Philip plotted to stir up the war. Ellis (1976) 187 believes Philip was behind the Locrian charge against Athens.

12. Amphictyons elect Philip general: Dem. 18.152. Philip seizes Elateia and appeals to Thebes: Aeschin. 3.140; Dem. 18.213; D.H. *Amm.* 1.11; D.S. 16.84.5; Plu. *Dem.* 18. The Thessalians must have been among the allies of Philip at Chaeronea: D.S. 16.85.5. Philip's compromise: see previous note.

13. News of Philip at Elateia and Demosthenes' proposals: Dem. 18.168–79; D.S. 16.84.1–85.1; Plu. *Dem.* 18. Demosthenes' negotiations at Thebes: Dem. 18.211–15. Demosthenes' concessions: Aeschin. 3.141–45 with the cogent discussion of Mosley (1971). Troops sent to Amphissa: Aeschin. 3.146.

14. Greeks join Athenians: Dem. 18.237 (Euboea, Achaea, Corinth, Thebes, Megara, Leucas, Corcyra); Paus. 7.6.3 (Achaea), 10.3.3 (Phocis); [Plu.] *Mor.* 851b (Locris); Aeschin. 3.97 (Acarnania); *IG* ii² 237 with the discussion of Schwenk (1985) 1–12 (Acarnania). Philip's appeal to the Peloponnesians: Dem. 18.156–58. Philip takes Amphissa: Polyaenus *Strat.* 4.2.8. Skirmishes with Philip: Dem. 18.156–58.

15. Aeschines criticizes decision to send troops to defend Amphissa: Aeschin. 3.146.

16. Philip's peace offer: Aeschin. 3.148–51; Plu. *Dem.* 18; *Phoc.* 16. Plutarch (*Dem.* 18) draws on Theopompus so there is good reason to take his statement as confirmation of Aeschines' assertions. Aeschines lays more stress on the proposals made to the Boeotians and Demosthenes' efforts to derail them and only alludes to Philip's offer to Athens. But Plutarch indicates there was a debate in the Assembly. Since Demosthenes must have won this debate and persuaded the Athenians to reject the offer, Aeschines not surprisingly neglects to mention it.

17. Diodorus (16.85.6) gives the edge in troop strength to Philip, but see Griffith (1979) 599, note 4. Demosthenes flees battlefield: Aeschin. 3.152; Plu. *Dem.* 20. Date of Chaeronea: Plu. *Cam.* 19.5. Athenian losses: D.S. 16.86.5.

18. Panic in Athens: Dem. 18.230, 295. Evacuation of women and children: Lyc. *Leocr.* 16. Council to secure harbor: Lyc. *Leocr.* 37. Men over fifty called up: Lyc. *Leocr.* 39; Din. 1.79. Demosthenes' motions and appointment: Dem. 18.248. Aeschin. 3.159 and Din. 1.79 probably refer to this appointment in unflattering terms. Appeal to Andros, Ceos, Troizen, and Epidauros: Lyc. *Leocr.* 42. These cities were probably solicited since they were nearby and could send troops quickly. They could also help to block access to the Piraeus. Power of the Areopagus: Lyc. *Leocr.* 52; Din. 1.82–83 with Harris (1994c) 177–78. Cf. Aeschin. 3.252. Voluntary contributions: Din. 1.80. Nature of the *epidosis:* Migeotte (1992). Proposal to free slaves: Schaefer (1885–87) 3:9, note 3. Schaefer (1885–87) 3:4–18 remains the most thorough treatment of Athenian measures after Chaeronea. For a more recent account see Will (1983) 8–11.

19. Philip releases prisoners and offers treaty: D.S. 16.87.3; Justin 9.4.4–5. Cf. [Demades] 9. Gift of Oropos: Paus. 1.34.1; *scholia ad* Dem. 18.99. Loss of Confederacy: Paus. 1.25.3. Lemnos, Imbros, and Skyros retaincd: Arist. *Ath. Pol.* 61.6; 62.2. Samos: D.S. 18.56.7–8; Arist. *Ath. Pol.* 62.2 with Rhodes (1981) 694–95. Delos: *Ath. Pol.* 54.7; 56.3; 62.2 with Rhodes (1981) 693–94; *IG* ii² 1652, lines 20–28.

20. Ransom of prisoners and dead and recall of exiles: Justin 9.4.5–10; Paus. 9.1.3. Garrison in Thebes: D.S. 16.87.3. Plataea restored: Paus. 9.1.3; 4.27.10. Orchomenos: Paus. 4.27.10; 9.37.3. Cf. Arr. *An.* 1.9.10. Thespiai: Dio Chrys. 37.42 with Schaefer (1885–87)

3:19, note 1. All these cities joined in the destruction of Thebes in 335. See D.S. 17.13.5; Arr. *An.* 1.8.8; Justin 11.3.8. On the settlement see Roebuck (1948) 137–38.

21. Aeschines, Phocion, and Demades negotiate with Philip: Aeschin. 3.227; Dem. 18.282, 287; [Demades] 9; Nep. *Phoc.* 1.

22. Philip's settlement in the Peloponnese: Roebuck (1948) 141–47.

23. Philip summons Greeks to Corinth: Justin 9.5.1; Plu. *Phoc.* 16.5. Guarantee of freedom and autonomy: [Dem.] 17.8. Security of Macedonian throne: Tod (1948), #177, lines 10–11. Revolutionary measures banned: [Dem.] 17.15. No support for exiles: [Dem.] 17.16. Punishment of offenders: [Dem.] 17.6; Tod (1948), #177, lines 15–25. *Synedrion* resolves disputes: Tod (1948), #179. Philip elected to lead expedition: D.S. 16.89.2–3.

24. Earlier scholars thought that the League of Corinth was inspired by the Panhellenic ideas espoused by Isocrates, but Wilcken (1929) has shown that the actual form of the organization owed little, if anything, to his ideas.

25. Cooperation of the *synedrion* during Agis' revolt: Curt. 6.1.20; D.S. 17.73.5–6.

26. Demosthenes was elected to go as ambassador to Alexander during the revolt of Thebes, but backed out of the mission (Aeschin. 3.161; Plu. *Dem.* 23). Otherwise we know of no diplomatic activity by Demosthenes until his embassy to Arcadia in 323/22 (Plu. *Dem.* 27.4–5) with the possible exception of a sacred embassy to Olympia in 324 (Din. 1.81 with Worthington [1992] 250–51).

Demades convinces the Assembly to make peace: Dem. 18.285; [Demades] 9. Honors for Philip: D.S. 16.92.1–2; [Demades] 9. Demades persuades Athens to join Common Peace and League of Corinth: Plu. *Phoc.* 16.5. Proxeny for Euthycrates: Hyp. fr. 1 (Blass). Honors for Alcimachus and Antipater: Harpocration *s.v.* Alcimachus and *s.v.* Antipater; *IG* ii² 239 with the full discussion of Schwenk (1985) 27–30. Other honorary decrees passed by Demades: *IG* ii² 346, 353, 399, 405.

27. Revolt of Thebes and Alexander's demand to surrender opponents: Arr. *An.* 1.7.1– 10.6; Plu. *Dem.* 23; *Phoc.* 17. Bosworth (1980) 92–95 follows Schaefer (1885–87) 3:137, note 2, and argues that the list of men demanded by Alexander found at Plu. *Dem.* 23.4 is the most reliable list in our sources, but Harris (1994a) argues that Arrian's list is probably better. Demades' liturgies: Plu. *Phoc.* 30.6. Election to Treasurer of Military Fund: Mitchel (1962).

28. Aeschines expressed distaste for new style of diplomacy: Aeschin. 3.250–51. Phocion rejects Alexander's gifts: Plu. *Phoc.* 18.

29. Prosecution of Lysicles: D.S. 16.88.1; Dem. 18.300 with Wankel (1976) *ad loc.* Roberts (1982b) argues that Chares was behind the prosecution of Lysicles, but her idea is questioned by Wankel (1984). Demosthenes delivers funeral oration: Dem. 18.285–88; Plu. *Dem.* 21. Demosthenes prosecuted: Dem. 18.222, 249, 285.

30. Demosthenes' failure to be elected: Aeschin. 3.159. For the post referred to by Aeschines, see Ryder (1976). The demonstrative τοῦτο in the phrase ἀλλὰ τοῦτο Ναυσικλεῖ προσετάττετε must refer to this position—see Harris (1994a). There is no reason to disbelieve Aeschines' statement that Nausicles was elected. It adds nothing to his case, was a recent event, and a matter of public knowledge.

31. Demosthenes' decree: Aeschin. 3.27. Demosthenes' election: Aeschin. 3.31. Demosthenes as Commissioner of the Theoric Fund: Aeschin. 3.24; Dem. 18.113.

32. For Lycurgus' career see Davies (1971) 348–53. Lycurgus' building program: Will (1983) 77–100. Colony to Adriatic: *IG* ii² 1629, lines 170–77. Grain shortage: Will (1983) 107–13, Garnsey (1988) 154–62. Aeschines' intermittent political activity: Aeschin. 3.217– 18; Dem. 18.308–11. Demosthenes contributes 100 *minai:* Aeschin. 3.17; Dem. 18.111–17.

33. Ctesiphon's decree: Aeschin. 3.17–23, 49, 236–37; Dem. 18.57. Aeschines' legal case: Aeschin. 3.4–50. On the identity of Ctesiphon see Wankel (1976) 13, note 19.

34. Dates of indictment and trial: Wankel (1976) 13–37.

35. Assassination of Philip: D.S. 16.93–95; Arr. *An.* 1.1.1. Reaction of Demosthenes: Aeschin. 3.160; Plu. *Dem.* 21–22.

36. Alexander seizes control: Arr. *An.* 1.1.1–3; Plu. *Alex.* 11; D.S. 17.2.1–49. Theban revolt and punishment: D.S. 17.8.3–14; Arr. *An.* 1.7–8; Plu. *Alex.* 11–12; *Dem.* 23. Aeschines (3.240) charges that the Arcadians would have supported Thebes if Demosthenes had supplied them with the money he received from the Great King. The charge is repeated with more details by Dinarchus (1.10–11, 19–21), but neither orator provides any evidence.

37. Alexander invades Asia: Arr. *An.* 1.11.3–8; D.S. 17.16.1–17.7. Demosthenes confident before Issos: Aeschin. 3.164.

38. Agis' revolt: Arr. *An.* 2.13.4; 3.6.3, 16.10; D.S. 17.48.1–2; 62.6–63.4; 73.5–6; Curtius 6.1; Justin. 21.1. Modern discussions: Badian (1967), Cawkwell (1969) 170–73. For a convenient summary of the evidence with a discussion of the issues, see Bosworth (1988) 198–204. For criticisms of attempts to link Aeschines' prosecution with the defeat of Agis, see appendix 10.

39. Demosthenes' hypocrisy: Aeschin. 3.163–67. Dinarchus (1.34–36) is very vague about Demosthenes' activity at the time of Agis' revolt, adding virtually nothing to Aeschines' comments. Cf. Plu. *Dem.* 24.1. Far from criticizing Demosthenes for failing to support Agis, Aeschines (3.254) urges the court not to crown his opponent so as to demonstrate to Alexander that Athens does not sympathize with those who violate the Common Peace.

40. Aeschines aware of Alexander's victory at Gaugamela: Aeschin. 3.132. Aeschines accuses Demosthenes of accepting Persian gold: Aeschin. 3.156, 173, 239–40, 257–59.

41. Aeschines bewildered by contemporary events: Aeschin. 3.132–33.

42. Aeschines' arrangement of topics: Aeschin. 3.9, 54–55.

43. Aeschines' first charge: Aeschin. 3.9–31.

44. Aeschines paraphrases law about crowns: Aeschin. 3.11, 26. Aeschines quotes law: Aeschin. 3.30.

45. Aeschines quotes Ctesiphon's decree: Aeschin. 3.49–50, 236–37. Public burial grounds torn up before Chaeronea: Lyc. *Leocr.* 44. Cf. Dem. 19.248. Demosthenes quotes decree: Dem. 18.118.

46. Demosthenes' reply: Dem. 18.113–17.

47. Intent of law about crowns: Aeschin. 3.9–12. Phocion reelected forty-five times: Tritle (1992). Nausicles, Diotimus, Charidemus, and Neoptolemus receive crowns: Dem. 18.114–16. For a fuller discussion of this legal issue in the case, see Harris (1994b) 142–48.

48. Aeschines cites laws about announcement of crowns: Aeschin. 3.32–36.

49. Aeschines justifies his interpretation of the laws about announcing honors: Aeschin. 3.37–48.

50. Demosthenes replies to Aeschines arguments about announcement of crowns: Dem. 18.120–22. Epigraphical evidence supporting Demosthenes: Gwatkin (1957) 138, note 57.

51. Earlier scholars, both ancient and modern, have thought that Aeschines has the stronger legal case. See, for example, Libanius in Dem. 18. *hypoth.* 1; Quint. *Inst.* 7.1.2; Gwatkin (1957); Meyer-Laurin (1965) 32; Wankel (1976) 32. Note that most of the speech is devoted to a denunciation of Demosthenes' career (Aeschin. 3.49–167) and that the discussion of legal issues occupies less than one fifth of the speech.

52. Aeschines refers to law about false statements: Aeschin. 3.50.

53. Aeschines attacks Demosthenes again for Peace of Philocrates: Aeschin. 3.58–81. For a discussion of the new charges see Harris (1986b) 371–73 with chapter 4.

54. Aeschines attacks Demosthenes' policy toward Euboea: Aeschin. 3.84–105. On the loan from Oreos, see Brunt (1969) 254–55.

55. Aeschines attacks third and fourth periods of Demosthenes' career: Aeschin. 3.106–67.

56. Court should apply letter of the law: Aeschin. 3.194–206. Demosthenes and the desire for honors: Aeschin. 3.176–90. Moderate life-style: Aeschin. 3.217–18.

57. Aeschines anticipates charge: Aeschin. 3.216. Demosthenes accuses Aeschines of being hireling of Philip: Dem. 18.51–52, 284.

58. Private hatreds motivate public charges: Aeschin. 1.2. Repaying enemies: Pl. *Meno* 71e; Hesiod *Op.* 709–11; Dover (1974) 180–84.

59. Demosthenes' reluctance to boast: Dem. 18.3–4. Plutarch (*Mor.* 542b, 543b) admired the speech for Demosthenes' ability to praise his own achievements without causing offense. Victory on Euboea: Dem. 18.81–86, 95. Law on trierarchy: Dem. 18.102–10. Allies gained: Dem. 18.233–41, 244. Rowe (1966) believes that Demosthenes portrays Aeschines as an *alazon*, a person who claims qualities he does not possess (Arist. *EN* 4.7.1127a, 21), but see Wankel (1976) 60, note 139, and Dyck (1985).

60. Chaeronea explained away: Dem. 18.197–230.

61. Acquittal of Ctesiphon and exile of Aeschines: Schaefer (1885–87) 3:292. Aeschines offers no advice: Dem. 18.242–43, 273. Demosthenes compares contributions: Dem. 18.257, 267.

Appendix 1

1. For the ties between Chares and Aristophon see Sealey (1967) 165.
2. See chapter 4.

Appendix 2

1. Arrian (*An.* 1.10.2; 11.1) indicates that the Macedonian Olympia occurred soon after the Eleusinian Mysteries, which were celebrated in Metageitnion (see Mikalson [1975] 46), that is, in Boedromion at the earliest and possibly later. Cawkwell (1962a) 130 thinks that Olynthus fell during the Macedonian Olympia, but Ellis (1976) 264, note 45 observes that D.S. 16.55.1 and Dem. 19.192 show that the celebration followed the victory (cf. Carter [1971] 427).

2. Cawkwell (1962a) 130 dates the first expedition to Boedromion. He notices that Demothenes (19.266) states that all the Chalcidian cities were taken within a year. Since Olynthus fell according to Cawkwell in Boedromion of 348, that would put the opening of Philip's attack in Boedromion of 349 and the first Olynthian appeal to Athens soon afterward. But Demosthenes only says that the Chalcidian cities fell before a year had elapsed; his words are vague, and the period might be several months less than a year. Furthermore, Cawkwell's date for the fall of Olynthus is probably too early. Cawkwell's second argument is that the first expedition must have occurred early in the archonship of 349/48 since it is recorded right after the archon's name in the fragment of Philochorus. This argument, borrowed from Jacoby, has been rightly questioned by Brunt (1969) 256, who shows that it is inadvisable to build any conclusions about chronology on this theory of citations. Cawkwell is followed by Carter (1971) 420–21.

3. Cf. Cawkwell (1962a) 131.

4. Cf. Carter (1971) 422. Cawkwell (1962a) 129 thinks the cavalry went to Olynthus "probably late in Elaphebolion."

5. Carter (1971) 425 places the cavalry from Euboea in the third expedition, but does not take account of these objections.

6. The delay caused by the Etesian winds, which can blow for many days, but are unlikely to have made sailing impossible for more than a few weeks. See Casson (1971) 272–74. One must also remember that oared ships would be less impeded by adverse winds.

7. Miller (1975).

8. Schaefer (1885–87) 2:167.

9. Markle (1970) 33–36. Markle is followed by Ellis (1976) 100, and 264, note 45.

Appendix 3

1. Schaefer (1885–87) 2:171–73. Schaefer was followed by Pokorny (1913) 136 and by Kahrstedt (1910) 65–66.

2. Cawkwell (1960) 421.

3. Markle (1974) 257, note 1. Markle (1970) 309–23 contains more arguments against Cawkwell's view, but the argument repeated in the footnote to his article is the decisive one. Ramming (1965) 30–31 also rejected Cawkwell's dating of Eubulus' decree. He argued that Philip would have been more likely to have given captives away soon after the fall of Olynthus and that the decree of Eubulus was passed in response to the fall of Olynthus. Ramming was followed by Wankel (1976) 233–35.

4. Cawkwell (1978a) 93–98.

5. Markle (1970) 319 draws attention to the fact that Demosthenes (19.304) says Aeschines was sent as an ambassador to the Peloponnese and argues that this implies Aeschines was not sent just to speak to the Arcadians, but also to many other cities in the region, a task that would have required a considerable period of time. But Aeschines could still have been called an ambassador to the Peloponnese even if he had only been sent to the Arcadians.

6. Cawkwell (1978a) 94.

7. Cawkwell's error is repeated by Hansen (1989) 182–83, who misrepresents the arguments of Harris (1986b) 371–73 and does not reply to the objections stated there to his interpretation of Aeschin. 2.72.

8. For questioning in court, see Carawan (1983).

9. Schaefer (1885–87) 2:171–73.

10. The Olynthian woman mentioned at Dem. 19.196 was not still waiting to be given away, but had already been given away by Philip, who, as conqueror, had the sole right to distribute booty, to Xenophon. For the traditional practice see Hdt. 8.121–22; 9.80–81 (cf. 85); Th. 3.114; X. *An.* 7.4.2; *HG* 7.4.27; D.S. 11.33.1; 13.34.4–5; 15.21.2; Arr. *An.* 1.16.5–6.

Appendix 4

1. Pickard-Cambridge (1914) 237–38, 259, note 3.

2. Dates of the truce: *IG* i³ 6, lines 45–89. On sacred truces in general, see Parker (1983) 154–58. Dates of the Mysteries: Mikalson (1975) 65 (Greater Mysteries last from Boedromion 15 to 23), 120–21 (Lesser Mysteries occur in the period Anthesterion 20–26). Rougemont (1973) 98–100 holds that two different sets of truces are referred to in *IG* i³ 6, one for Athens and the other for those areas outside of Athens. Only the former was limited to fifty-five days, while the other was of indefinite duration. I do not think that the text of the inscription can bear such an interpretation. First, there do not appear to be two different truces

for the Lesser Mysteries mentioned in the text. There is only one truce for the Lesser Mysteries, lasting fifty-five days. Second, the part of the text that concerns the Greater Mysteries makes no such distinction. If such a distinction were present, we should expect the words to show it (*e.g.*, τὰς μὲν σπονδὰς . . . τὰς δὲ σπονδὰς . . .). Instead the text reads σπονδὰς . . . τὰς δε σπονδὰς. The δέ is merely continuative—see Denniston (1950) 162–63. The definite article is used to show that the truce is the same as the one referred to in the previous clause, "the (one, specific) truce"—for the use of the article see Renehan (1976) 69–74. Third, I find it odd that the period of the truce for the area outside Athens should be left indefinite. This goes against Rougemont's own findings for the Pythia (see Rougemont [1973] 84–85, 99).

    3. Schaefer (1885–87) 2:189, note 1.

    4. Cloché (1916) 119–20.

    5. Cawkwell (1960) 429–32. Ramming (1965) 34–41 places the announcement of the refusal in Athens on Anthesterion 8–10.

    6. Markle (1970) 328–38.

    7. Cf. Cloché (1916) 119–20; Markle (1970) 328–30.

    8. Tod (1948), #137. Sealey (1955) concludes on the basis of this inscription that "the Athenian deliberations about the rejection of the mystic truce fell in a period covering the last sixteen days of the truce and the following ten days." He uses this conclusion to support his idea that the *spondophoroi* reported the news of the Phocian refusal on the same day as the debate about the peace with Philip took place. This is improbable; as I argue below, the *spondophoroi* must have returned to Athens before, and not after, the Mysteries began, and must have made their report then. For other criticisms of Sealey's idea, see Cawkwell (1960) 430–32 and Markle (1970) 335–37.

    9. *IG* ii² 1672, lines 4, 106–7, and 227.

    10. Dates of the first prytany of 329/28: Cawkwell (1960) 429–32.

    11. Using the calculations of W. K. Pritchett and O. Neugebauer (1947) 50–51 that in 329/28 Pyanopsion 30 = Prytany IV,11 = 119th day, we get Pyanopsion 20 = Prytany IV,1 = 109th day and Maimakterion 25 = Prytany IV,36 = 114th day. The dates in this note supersede those of Cawkwell (1960) 431, note 1.

    12. Using the calculation of Meritt (1961) 44–45 that Pyanopsion 29 = Prytany IV, 11 = 118th day, we arrive at Pyanopsion 19 = Prytany IV,1 = 108th day and Maimakterion 24 = Prytany IV,35 = 142nd day.

    13. Following Meritt (1961) 44–45, with Thargelion a full month, Skirophorion a hollow month, and the tenth prytany lasting thirty-six days.

    14. Following Pritchett and Neugebauer (1947) 24–26, with the last prytany lasting thirty-five days, and Dinsmoor (1931) 428, who makes Thargelion hollow and Skirophorion a full month.

    15. Markle (1970) 330–32.

    16. Cawkwell (1960) 431, note 1. Cf. Rougemont (1973) 90, note 49: "Nous y avons lu εἰς μυστηρια. . . . A, ensuite une haste à gauche de l'axe de la file, sur le bord gauche d'un petit trou de la pierre et, sur le bord droit de cette brisure, des traces peu distinctes qui ne permettent ni de confirmer ni d'infirmer la lecture de Kirchner. E est possible, p serait tentant, rien ne semble assuré" (*the letter e is possible, the letter p would be tempting, but nothing is certain*). See also Markle (1970) 332, note 1.

    17. This is clear from Aeschin. 2.133 (ἐσπείσαντο). Cf. L.S.J. *s.v.* σπένδω Med.II.

    18. Cf. Dem. 19.159–64. Demosthenes wished to have Philip swear to the Peace of Philocrates as soon as possible so that he would immediately be bound by its conditions and thus be prevented from seizing any more Athenian territory. For the "Verbindlichkeit" of treaties deriving from the swearing of oaths, see Kussmaul (1969) 18–20.

19. Th. 5.49.1–50.4. If one can assume that the Athenians found out about the arrest of the *spondophoroi* by the Trichonians soon after it occurred, this would indicate that they were still abroad in early Boedromion, that is, during the truce not before it started.

20. Rougemont (1973) 98–100 does not think that a month would have sufficed for the journey of the *spondophoroi*. He points to the fact that in the early second century B.C. they appear to have gone to Syria (*IG* ii² 785; for the date of this inscription see Meritt [1961] 235) and to Egypt (Plb. 28.19.4 [169 B.C.]). These were, however, probably special honorific missions to Hellenistic monarchs and should not be taken as evidence for the normal route the *spondophoroi* took two centuries earlier.

21. It is clear from the inscription published by Arvanitopoullos (1914) 168, lines 41–43 that the *spondophoroi* were required to report the names of cities that had accepted the truce after their return to Athens.

22. We know that the *spondophoroi* went as far north as Gonnoi in Thessaly—see Arvanitopoullos (1914).

Appendix 5

1. Meritt, Wade-Gery, and McGregor (1939) 545–46.

2. Meritt, Wade-Gery, and McGregor (1939) 544–46.

3. Meritt, Wade-Gery, and McGregor (1939) 517–18, 545.

4. Myrtenon is called Myrtiske at Aeschin. 3.82 to make a jingle with Ergiske. For the correct form of the nominative see Wankel (1976) 254.

5. Meritt, Wade-Gery, and McGregor (1939) 475.

6. Markle (1970) 51, note 1, criticized by Ellis (1976) 265–66.

Appendix 6

1. See *FGrHist* 115 F 165 with the discussion of Wankel (1976) 256–57.

2. Fighting in Euboea described in Book 23: F 148–49. War between the Thebans and the Phocians in Book 24: F 156–57. Cf. D.S. 16.58.1 and Dem. 19.148.

3. Campaign against Olynthus in Books 23 and 24: F 147, 150–52. Cf. D.S. 16.52.9. For the locations of Assera and Skabala, both mentioned in these fragments, see Meritt, Wade-Gery, and McGregor (1939) 471, 549.

4. Markle (1970) 92, 109–10 puts the speech on Elaphebolion 19, but see chapter 4.

5. Aeschin. 2.18; 3.63.

Appendix 7

1. ἐξώμοσεν followed by indirect discourse should mean "swore that" something happened. The same verb in the middle voice followed by a direct object means to "resign" a position (Dem. 19.122, 124, 126; Aeschin. 2.94, 95; Thphr. *Char.* 24.6; Bonner and Smith [1938] 163–64). Note that Demosthenes uses the same verb to describe Aeschines' contemplated resignation and his brother's sworn statement in a deliberate attempt to mislead the court.

2. Schaefer (1885–87) 2:280, note 1, noted the claim made by Demosthenes (19.172) that he was elected twice to the Third Embassy and twice resigned. He believed the second election took place at the meeting during which Dercylus reported. But neither Demosthenes

(19.125–27) nor Aeschines (2.95–96) mention a second election at this meeting. Instead Aeschines says the Assembly instructed those originally elected to proceed to Delphi. The allusion to two resignations is probably a vague and imprecise reference to Demosthenes' resignation and subsequent refusal to go when the Assembly asked him to reconsider his initial decision (Dem. 19.121–22).

3. Dem. 19.121–22. Compare the law that awards made by the Council be announced only in the Council, and awards by the Assembly only in the Assembly (Aeschin. 3.32).

4. Aeschin. 2.142–43; Dem. 19.128–30.

5. Mosley (1973) 78.

Appendix 8

1. Dates of Demosthenes' *Second Philippic* and Aeschines' trial: D. H. *Amm.* 1.10. Date of Persian appeal to Athens: Philochorus *FGrHist* 115 F 328. Interval between Demosthenes' indictment and Aeschines' trial: Dem. 19. *hypoth.* 2.11. Cf. Schaefer (1885–87) 2:382–83.

2. Schaefer's dating of the Antiphon incident and Aeschines' removal from post as ambassador to Delphi: Schaefer (1885–87) 2:372–74. Aeschines' remarks about Areopagus: Aeschin. 1.92. Demosthenes alludes to Aeschines' failure to be elected ambassador: Dem. 19.209. Wüst's dating: Wüst (1938) 47–49. Aeschines mentions *diapsephisis:* Aeschin. 1.77, 86. Ramming's dating: Ramming (1965) 93, note 1. Wankel endorses Ramming's dating: Wankel (1976) 722. Sealey's dating: Sealey (1958).

3. Dem. 19.209 could just as easily refer to Aeschines' failure to be elected to the embassy that went to Macedon to negotiate about the revision of the Peace of Philocrates. Note also that Demosthenes says "you did not allow" which points to the Assembly, not the Areopagus. *Pace* Wankel (1976) 722, the word ἕτεϱον at Dem. 18.136 clearly dissociates the Pytho story from the others so no relationship can be postulated.

4. Demosthenes places Antiphon incident and Aeschines' removal from post before war with Philip: Dem. 18.139. This rules out the dating suggested by Sealey (1958). Outbreak of war dated to 340/39: Philochorus *FGrHist* 328 F 162; Theopompus *FGrHist* 115 F 292; D.S. 16.77.1–2. Since the grain fleet normally reached the Bosporus by Metageitnion ([Dem.] 50.4–6; Cawkwell [1978b] 186), Philip must have seized it shortly after the beginning of the year 340/39.

5. Schaefer places Hegesippus' speech after Aeschines' trial: Schaefer (1885–87) 2:382, note 2. Cf. Wüst (1938) 64–78; Ellis (1976) 143–56; Griffith (1979) 489–95, 510–16. Demosthenes alludes to Hegesippus' embassy: Dem. 19.331. Hegesippus refers to Philip's campaigns in Epirus and Ambracia: [Dem.] 7.32.

6. Demosthenes refers to incidents in Euboea, Megara, and Elis: Dem. 19.204, 294, 326. Note how elsewhere Demosthenes (10.9–10) places greater emphasis on events nearer to Attica than on more distant acts of aggression. Demosthenes refers to trial of Philocrates: Dem. 19.116.

7. For the sequence of events and chronology see chapter 3 and chapter 4 with appendix 4.

Appendix 9

1. Hansen (1976) 32–33.

2. Harrison (1971) 150.

3. Harrison (1971) 86.
4. Hansen (1975) 103.

Appendix 10

1. Cawkwell (1969).
2. Burke (1977).
3. Cawkwell (1969) 175–76.
4. Cawkwell (1969) 179.
5. Phocion still prominent: Plu. *Phoc.* 17–18, 21. Nausicles: Harris (1994a).
6. *Atimia* for failure to follow through on prosecution: Harris (1989b) 132–34, (1992b) 79–80.

Appendix 11

1. Among recent scholars, this view is accepted by Martin (1985) 91–113; Griffith (1979) 221–23, 278, 285, 294; Buckler (1989) 79–80. For references to earlier scholarship on the issue see Bosworth (1980) 50. Griffith notes: "When all is said and done, it seems right to recognize this election of Philip to the head of affairs in Thessaly as an event unique in Greek history, and very remarkable." Perhaps a little *too* remarkable.

2. Cf. the phrase *universae Graeciae* at Justin 9.3.11.

3. One should bear in mind that the verb used by Justin, *creatus est*, refers only to the procedure of voting and not to the assumption of office, which is expressed by the verb *inire* (Cic. *Agr.* 2.13; *Sest.* 72; *Att.* 2.22.5). Thus Justin only states that the Thessalians voted on the issue and does not assert that they conferred on him the position of leader of the Corinthian League.

4. The problem is noted, but not solved, by Bosworth (1980) 50.

5. For a discussion of the fragment of Satyrus, see Tronson (1984).

6. Cersebleptes may have had a similar arrangement with the Greek cities on the coast—see Dem. 23.110.

References

Abbreviations of journals follow the usage of *L'Année philologique*.

Adams, W. Lindsay and E. Borza, eds. (1982). *Philip II, Alexander the Great and the Macedonian Heritage*. Washington, D.C.

Amit, M. (1965). *Athens and the Sea: A Study in Athenian Sea-Power*. Brussels.

Andrewes, A. (1956). "Philochorus on Phratries." *JHS* 81: 1–15.

Arvanitopoullos, A. S. (1914). *Arch. Eph.*

Aymard, A. (1948). "L'idée de travail dans la Grèce antique." *Journal de psychologie* 41: 29–41.

Badian, E. (1961). "Harpalus." *JHS* 81: 16–43.

———. (1967). "Agis III." *Hermes* 95: 170–92.

———. (1980). "Philip II and Thrace." *Pupuldeva* 4: 51–71.

Beloch, K. J. (1922). *Griechische Geschichte*, 2nd ed. Vol. 3.2. Berlin and Leipzig.

Berve, H. (1926). *Das Alexanderreich auf prosopographischer Grundlage*. Munich.

Blass, F. (1887–98). *Die attische Beredsamkeit*, 2nd ed. Leipzig.

Boegehold, A. (1972). "The Establishment of a Central Archive in Athens." *AJA* 76: 24–30.

Bonner, R. J. (1905). *Evidence in Athenian Courts*. Chicago.

Bonner, R. J. and G. Smith. (1938). *The Administration of Justice from Homer to Aristotle*. Vol. 2. Chicago.

———. (1943). "Administration of Justice in the Delphic Amphictyony." *CP* 38: 1–12.

Bosworth, A. B. (1980). *A Historical Commentary on Arrian's History of Alexander*. Vol. 1. Oxford.

———. (1988). *Conquest and Empire: The Reign of Alexander the Great*. Cambridge.

Bouché-Leclercq, A. (1879–82). *Histoire de la divination dans l'antiquité*. 4 vols. Paris.

Bruce, I. A. F. (1967). *Commentary to the Hellenica Oxyrhynchia*. Cambridge.

Brunt, P. (1969). "Euboea in the Time of Philip II." *CQ* 19: 245–65.

Buckler, J. (1980). *The Theban Hegemony*. Cambridge, Mass.

———. (1989). *Philip II and the Sacred War*. Leiden.

Bugh, G. (1982). "Introduction of the *katalogeis* of the Athenian Cavalry." *TAPhA* 112: 23–32.

———. (1988). *The Horsemen of Athens*. Princeton.

Burke, E. M. (1977). "*Contra Leocratem* and *De Corona*: Political Collaboration?" *Phoenix* 31: 330–40.

Burkert, W. (1987). *Ancient Mystery Cults*. Cambridge, Mass.

Calhoun, G. M. (1913). *Athenian Clubs in Politics and Litigation*. Austin.

————. (1914). "Documentary Frauds in Litigation in Athens." *CPh* 9: 134–44.

Cantril, H. (1943). "Identification with Social and Economic Class." *Journal of Abnormal and Social Psychology* 38: 74–80.

Carawan, E. M. (1983). *"Erotesis:* Interrogation in the Courts of Fourth-century Athens." *GRBS* 24: 209–26.

Carey, C. (1992). *Greek Orators VI: Apollodorus Against Neaira [Demosthenes] 59.* Warminster.

Carey, C. and R. A. Reid. (1985). *Demosthenes: Selected Private Speeches.* Cambridge.

Cargill, J. (1981). *The Second Athenian League: Empire or Free Alliance?* Berkeley and Los Angeles.

Carter, J. M. (1971). "Athens, Euboea, and Olynthus." *Historia* 20: 418–29.

Cartledge, P. A. (1989). Review of Tritle (1988). *CR* 39: 79–80.

Cartledge, P. A. and F. D. Harvey, eds. (1985). *CRUX: Essays in Greek History Presented to G. E. M. de Ste. Croix on his 75th Birthday.* Exeter and London.

Cartledge, P. A., P. Millett, and S. Todd, eds. (1990). *NOMOS: Essays in Athenian Law, Politics and Society.* Cambridge.

Casson. L. (1971). *Ships and Seamanship in the Ancient World.* Princeton.

————. (1976). "The Athenian Upper Class and New Comedy." *TAPhA* 106: 29–59.

Cawkwell, G. L. (1960). "Aeschines and the Peace of Philocrates." *REG* 73: 416–38.

————. (1962a). "The Defence of Olynthus." *CQ* 12: 122–40.

————. (1962b). "Aeschines and the Ruin of Phocis." *REG* 75: 453–59.

————. (1962c). "Notes on the Social War." *C&M* 23: 34–49.

————. (1963a). "Eubulus." *JHS* 83: 47–67.

————. (1963b). "Demosthenes' Policy after the Peace of Philocrates." *CQ* 13: 120–38, 200–13.

————. (1969). "The Crowning of Demosthenes." *CQ* 19: 163–80.

————. (1978a). "The Peace of Philocrates Again." *CQ* 28: 93–104.

————. (1978b). *Philip of Macedon.* London.

————. (1978c). "Euboea in the Late 340s." *Phoenix* 32: 42–67.

————. (1981). "Notes on the Failure of the Second Athenian Confederacy." *JHS* 101: 40–55.

Centers, R. (1949). *The Psychology of Social Class.* Princeton.

Cloché, P. (1915). *Étude chronologique sur la troisième guerre sacrée.* Paris.

————. (1934). *La politique étrangère d'Athènes de 404 à 338 av. J.-C.* Paris.

Cohen, D. (1991). *Law, Sexuality, and Society: The Enforcement of Morals in Classical Athens.* Cambridge.

Cole, S. G. (1980). "New Evidence for the Mysteries of Dionysus." *GRBS* 21: 223–38.

Collart, P. (1937). *Philippes, ville de Macédoine.* Paris.

Connor, W. R. (1971). *The New Politicians of Fifth-century Athens.* Princeton.

————. (1988). "Early Greek Land Warfare as Symbolic Expression." *Past and Present* 119: 3–29.

Davies, J. K. (1967). "Demosthenes on Liturgies: A Note." *JHS* 87: 33–40.

————. (1971). *Athenian Propertied Families 600–300 B.C.* Oxford.

————. (1981). *Wealth and the Power of Wealth in Classical Athens.* New York.

De Sanctis, G. (1897). "Eschine e la guerra contro Anfissa." *RF* 25: 215–35.

Develin, R. (1989). *Athenian Officials 684–321 B.C.* Cambridge.

Denniston, J. D. (1950). *The Greek Particles,* 2nd ed. Oxford.

Diepolder, H. (1931). *Die attischen Grabreliefs des 5. und 4. Jahrhunderts v. Chr.* Berlin.

Dinsmoor, W. B. (1931). *The Archons of Athens.* Cambridge, Mass.

Dover, K. J. (1968). *Lysias and the Corpus Lysiacum.* Berkeley and Los Angeles.

————. (1974). *Greek Popular Morality in the Time of Plato and Aristotle.* Oxford.

————. (1978). *Greek Homosexuality.* Cambridge, Mass.

Dyck, A. R. (1985). "The Function and Persuasive Power of Demosthenes' Portrait of Aeschines in the Speech *On the Crown.*" *G&R* 32: 42–48.

Ellis, J. R. (1971). "Amyntas Perdikka, Philip II, and Alexander the Great." *JHS* 91: 15–24.

————. (1973). "The Step-Brothers of Philip II." *Historia* 22: 344–50.

————. (1976). *Philip II and Macedonian Imperialism.* London.

————. (1977). "Philip's Thracian Campaign of 352/351." *CP* 72: 32–37.

————. (1982). "Philip and the Peace of Philocrates." In Adams and Borza (1982): 43–59.

Errington, R. M. (1975). "Arrybas the Molossian." *GRBS* 16: 41–50.

————. (1978). "The Nature of the Macedonian State Under the Monarchy." *Chiron* 8: 77–133.

————. (1981). "Four Interpretations of Philip II." *AJAH* 6: 69–88.

————. (1990). *A History of Macedonia.* Berkeley and Los Angeles.

Finley, M. I. (1985). *The Ancient Economy,* 2nd ed. Berkeley and Los Angeles.

Gabrielsen, V. (1989). "The Number of Athenian Trierarchs after ca. 340 B.C." *C&M* 40: 146–59.

Garnsey, P. (1988). *Famine and Food Supply in the Graeco-Roman World: Responses to Risk and Crisis.* Cambridge.

Gauthier, P. (1972). *Symbola.* Paris.

Gehrke, H.-J. (1976). *Phocion: Studien zur Erfassung seiner historischen Gestalt.* Munich.

Ghiron-Bistagne, P. (1976). *Recherches sur les acteurs dans la Grèce antique.* Paris.

Glotz, G. (1909). "Philippe et la surprise d'Élatée." *BCH* 33: 526–46.

Gomme, A. W. (1933). *The Population of Athens in the Fifth and Fourth Centuries B.C.* Oxford.

Graham, A. J. (1964). *Colony and Mother City in Ancient Greece.* Manchester.

Griffith, G. T. (1939). "The So-called *Koine Eirene* of 346 B.C." *JHS* 59: 71–79.

————. (1979). *A History of Macedonia.* Vol. 2: 203–735. Oxford.

Grote, G. (1869). *History of Greece from the Earliest Period to the Close of the Generation Contemporary with Alexander the Great.* London.

Guthrie, W. K. C. (1971). *The Sophists.* Cambridge.

Gwatkin, W. E. (1957). "The Legal Arguments in Aeschines' *Against Ctesiphon* and Demosthenes' *On the Crown.*" *Hesperia* 26: 129–41.

Halliday, W. R. (1913). *Greek Divination.* London.

Hammond, N. G. L. (1937). "Diodorus' Narrative of the Sacred War and the Chronological Problems of 357–352 B.C." *JHS* 57: 44–78.

————. (1989). *The Macedonian State: The Origins, Institutions and History.* Oxford.

Hansen, M. H. (1974). *The Sovereignty of the People's Court in Athens in the Fourth Century B.C. and the Public Action against Unconstitutional Proposals.* Odense.

————. (1975). *Eisangelie: The Sovereignty of the People's Court in Athens in the Fourth Century B.C. and the Impeachment of Generals and Politicians.* Odense.

————. (1976). *Apagoge, Endeixis, and Ephegesis against Kakourgoi, Atimoi, and Pheugontes.* Odense.

————. (1981). "The Number of Athenian Hoplites in 431." *SO* 56: 19–32.

————. (1982). "Demographic Reflections on the Number of Athenian Citizens 451–309 B.C." *AJAH* 7: 172–89.

————. (1983). *The Athenian Ecclesia: A Collection of Articles 1976–83.* Copenhagen.

————. (1985). *Demography and Democracy. The Number of Athenian Citizens in the Fourth Century B.C.* Herning.

————. (1987). *The Athenian Assembly in the Age of Demosthenes.* Oxford.

————. (1988). *Three Studies in Athenian Demography*. Copenhagen.

————. (1989). *The Athenian Ecclesia: A Collection of Articles 1983–89*. Copenhagen.

————. (1991). *The Athenian Democracy in the Age of Demosthenes*. Oxford.

Hanson, V. D. (1983). *Warfare and Agriculture in Classical Greece*. Pisa.

Harris, E. M. (1985). "The Date of the Trial of Timarchus." *Hermes* 113: 376–80.

————. (1986a). "The Names of Aeschines' Brothers-in-Law." *AJPh* 107: 99–102.

————. (1986b). "How Often did the Athenian Assembly Meet?" *CQ* 36: 363–77.

————. (1988a). "The Date of Apollodorus' Speech Against Timotheus and Its Implications for Athenian History and Legal Procedure." *AJPh* 109: 44–52.

————. (1988b). "The Date of Aeschines' Birth." *CPh* 83: 211–14.

————. (1988c). "When Is a Sale not a Sale? The Riddle of Athenian Terminology for Real Security Revisited." *CQ* 38: 351–81.

————. (1989a). "More Chalcenteric Negligence." *CPh* 84: 36–44.

————. (1989b). "Demosthenes' Speech Against Meidias." *HSPh* 92: 117–36.

————. (1989c). "Iphicrates at the Court of Cotys." *AJPh* 110: 264–71.

————. (1990). "Did the Athenians Regard Seduction as a Worse Crime than Rape?" *CQ* 40: 370–77.

————. (1991). "When Did the Athenian Assembly Meet? Some New Evidence." *AJPh* 112: 329–45.

————. (1992a). "Pericles' Praise of Athenian Democracy." *HSPh* 94: 57–67.

————. (1992b). Review of D. M. MacDowell (1990). *CP* 87: 71–80.

————. (1994a). "Demosthenes Loses a Friend and Nausicles Gains a Position: A Prosopographical Note on Athenian Politics after Chaeronea." *Historia* 43: 378–84.

————. (1994b). "Law and Oratory." In I. Worthington, ed., *Persuasion: Greek Rhetoric in Action*. London: 130–51.

————. (1994c). Review of Worthington (1992). *BMCR* 5.2: 174–78.

Harrison, A. R. W. (1971). *The Law of Athens: Procedure*. Oxford.

Harvey, F. D. (1985). *"Dona Ferentes:* Some Aspects of Bribery in Greek Politics." In Cartledge and Harvey (1985): 76–117.

————. (1990). "The Sykophant and Sykophancy: Vexatious Redefinition?" In Cartledge, Millett, and Todd (1990): 103–21.

Hatzopoulos, M. B. (1982). "The Oleveni Inscription and the Dates of Philip II's Reign." In Adams and Borza (1982): 21–42.

Henry, A. S. (1983). *Honors and Privileges in Athenian Decrees*. Hildesheim.

Herman, G. (1987). *Ritualised Friendship and the Greek City*. Cambridge.

Hersh, C. (1990). "An Unpublished Coin of Philip of Macedonia, from His First Issue of Bronzes." *American Journal of Numismatics* 1–2: 33–36.

Heskel, J. (1987). "The Foreign Policy of Philip II down to the Peace of Philocrates." Ph.D. diss., Harvard.

————. (1988). "The Political Background of the Arrybas Decree." *GRBS* 29: 185–96.

———— and E. Badian. (1987). "Aeschines' 2.12–18: A Study in Rhetoric and Chronology." *Phoenix* 41: 264–71.

Hornblower, S. (1982). *Mausolus*. Oxford.

Humphreys, S. C. (1980). "Family Tombs and Tomb Cults in Ancient Athens: Tradition or Traditionalism?" *JHS* 100: 96–126.

Jacob, O. (1979). *Les esclaves publics à Athènes*. New York.

Jehne, M. (1992). "Die Anerkennung der athenischen Besitzansprüche auf Amphipolis und die Chersones." *Historia* 41: 272–82.

Kahrstedt, U. (1910). *Forschungen zur Geschichte des ausgehenden fünften und des vierten Jahrhunderts*. Berlin.

————. (1938). "Untersuchungen zu athenischen Behörden." *Klio* 31: 25–32.

Kett, P. (1966). "Prosopographie der historischen griechischen Manteis bis auf die Zeit Alexander des Grossen." Diss., Erlangen.

Kindstrand, J. F. (1982). *The Stylistic Evaluation of Aeschines in Antiquity.* Uppsala.

Knoepfler, D. (1981). "Argoura: Un toponyme eubéen dans la Midienne de Démosthène." *BCH* 105: 289–329.

Kroll, J. (1977). "An Archive of the Athenian Cavalry." *Hesperia* 46: 83–140.

Kussmaul, P. (1969). "Synthekai: Beiträge zur Geschichte des attischen Obligationenrechts." Diss., Basel.

Lambert, S. D. (1993). *The Phratries of Attica.* Ann Arbor.

Lavency, M. (1964). *Aspects de la logographie judiciaire attique.* Louvain.

Lefkowitz, M. R. (1981). *The Lives of the Greek Poets.* Baltimore.

Lewis, D. M. (1955). "Notes on Attic Inscriptions II." *ABSA* 50: 1–36.

MacDowell, D. M. (1976). *The Law in Classical Athens.* London.

————. (1978). *The Law in Classical Athens.* London.

————. (1983). "Athenian Laws about Bribery." *RIDA* 30: 57–78.

————. (1986). "The Law of Periandros about Symmories." *CQ* 36: 438–49.

————. (1990). *Demosthenes: Against Meidias (Oration 21).* Oxford.

Maier, G. (1969). "Eranos als Kreditinstitut." Diss., Erlangen.

Markle, M. M. (1970). "The Peace of Philocrates." Diss., Princeton.

————. (1974). "The Strategy of Philip in 346." *CQ* 24: 253–68.

————. (1976). "Support of Athenian Intellectuals for Philip: A Study of Isocrates' *Philippus* and Speusippus' *Letter to Philip.*" *JHS* 96: 80–99.

Marrou, H.-I. (1967). *Histoire de l'éducation dans l'antiquité.* Paris.

Marshall, F. H. (1905). *The Second Athenian Confederacy.* Cambridge.

Martin, T. R. (1981). "Diodorus on Philip II and Thessaly in the 350s." *CPh* 76: 188–201.

————. (1985). *Sovereignty and Coinage in Classical Greece.* Princeton.

Meiggs, R. and D. M. Lewis. (1969). *A Selection of Greek Historical Inscriptions.* Oxford.

————. (1988). *A Selection of Greek Historical Inscriptions,* 2nd ed. Oxford.

Meritt. B. D. (1952). "Greek Inscriptions." *Hesperia* 21: 340–410.

————. (1961). *The Athenian Year.* Berkeley and Los Angeles.

————. (1970). "The Ransom of the Athenians by Epikerdes." *Hesperia* 39: 111–14.

————, H. T. Wade-Gery and M. F. McGregor. (1939). *The Athenian Tribute Lists.* Vol. 1. Cambridge, Mass.

Meyer-Laurin, H. (1965). *Gesetz und Billigkeit im attischen Prozess.* Weimar.

Migeotte, L. (1983). "Souscriptions athéniennes de la periode classique." *Historia* 32: 129–48.

————. (1992). *Les souscriptions publiques dans les cités grecques.* Geneva and Quebec.

Mikalson, J. (1975). *The Sacred and Civil Calendar of the Athenian Year.* Princeton.

————. (1983). *Athenian Popular Religion.* Chapel Hill.

Miller, S. G. (1975). "The Date of the Olympic Festivals." *MDAI(A)* 90: 215–31.

Mitchel, F. (1962). "Demades of Paiania and *IG* ii² 1493, 1494, 1495." *TAPA* 93: 213–29.

Momigliano, A. (1934). *Filippo il Macedone.* Florence.

————. (1971). *The Development of Greek Biography.* Cambridge, Mass.

Montgomery, H. (1983). *The Way to Chaeronea: Foreign Policy, Decision-Making and Political Influence in Demosthenes' Speeches.* Bergen.

Mosley, D. J. (1965). "The Size of Embassies in Ancient Greek Diplomacy." *TAPhA* 96: 255–66.

————. (1971). "Athens' Alliance with Thebes, 339 B.C." *Historia* 20: 508–10.

————. (1972). "Oaths at Pherae, 346 B.C." *Philologus* 116: 145–48.

————. (1973). *Envoys and Diplomacy in Ancient Greece.* Wiesbaden.

Murray, O. (1983). "The Greek Symposium in History." In E. Gabba, ed., *Tria Corda: scritti in onore di A. Momigliano.* Como.

North, H. (1952). "The Use of Poetry in the Training of the Ancient Orator." *Traditio* 8: 1–33.

Nouhaud, M. (1982). *L'utilisation de l'histoire par les orateurs.* Paris.

Ober, J. (1989). *Mass and Elite in Democratic Athens.* Princeton.

Osborne, M. J. (1970). "Honours for Sthorys." *BSA* 65: 151–74.

Osborne, R. (1990). "Vexatious Litigation in Classical Athens: Sykophancy and the Sykophant." In Cartledge, Millett, and Todd (1990): 103–21.

Ossowski, S. (1963). *Class Structure in the Social Consciousness.* Trans. S. Patterson. New York.

Papedemetriou, G. (1957). "Aeschines" Uncle, Cleobulus the Seer (in Modern Greek)." *Platon* 9: 154–63.

Parke, H. W. (1933). *Greek Mercenary Soldiers.* Oxford.

Parker, R. (1983). *Miasma: Pollution and Purification in Early Greek Religion.* Oxford.

Pearson, L. (1941). "Historical Allusion in the Attic Orators." *CP* 36: 209–29.

Pélékidis, Ch. (1962). *Histoire de l'éphébie attique dès origines à 31 avant J.C.* Paris.

Perlman, S. (1957). "Isocrates" *Philippus*—A Reinterpretation." *Historia* 6: 306–17.

————. (1963). "The Politicians in the Athenian Democracy of the Fourth Century B.C." *Athenaeum* 41: 327–55.

————. (1964). "Quotations from Poetry in Attic Orators of the Fourth Century B.C." *AJPh* 85: 155–72.

————. (1976). "On Bribing Athenian Ambassadors." *GRBS* 17: 223–33.

Pickard-Cambridge, A. (1968). *The Dramatic Festival of Athens,* 2nd ed. Eds. J. Gould and D. M. Lewis. Oxford.

Pokorny, E. (1913). *Studien zur griechischen Geschichte im sechsten und fünften Jahrzehnt des vierten Jahrhunderts v. Chr.* Greifswald.

Pritchett, W. K. and O. Neugebauer. (1947). *The Calendars of Athens.* Cambridge, Mass.

Ramming, G. (1965). "Die politischen Ziele und Wege des Aischines." Diss., Erlangen.

Raubitschek, A. E. (1941). "The Heroes of Phyle." *Hesperia* 10: 284–95.

Renehan, R. (1976). *Studies in Greek Texts.* Gottingen.

Rhodes, P. J. (1972). *The Athenian Boule.* Oxford.

————. (1981). *A Commentary on the Aristotelian Athenaion Politeia.* Oxford.

————. (1982). "Problems in the Athenian *Eisphora* and Liturgies." *AJAH* 7: 1–19.

————. (1986). "Political Activity in Classical Athens." *JHS* 106: 132–44.

————. (1988). *Thucydides: History II.* Warminster.

Roberts, J. T. (1982a). "Athens' So-called Unofficial Politicians." *Hermes* 110: 354–62.

————. (1982b). "Chares, Lysikles, and the Battle of Chaeronea." *Klio* 64: 367–71.

Roebuck, C. (1948). "The Settlements of Philip II with the Greek States in 338 B.C." *CPh* 43: 73–91.

de Romilly, J. (1954). "Les modérés athéniens vers le milieu du ive siècle: échos et concordances." *REG* 67: 327–54.

Rougemont, G. (1973). "La hiéroménie des Pythia et les trêves sacrées d'Eleusis, de Delphes et d'Olympie." *BCH* 97: 75–106.

Roussel, P. (1930). "Initiation préalable et les symboles Eleusiniens." *BCH* 54: 58–65.

Rowe, G. O. (1966). "The Portrait of Aeschines in the *Oration on the Crown.*" *TAPhA* 97: 397–406.

Ryder, T. T. B. (1963). "Athenian Foreign Policy and the Peace Conference at Sparta in 371 B.C." *CQ* 13: 237–41.

————. (1965). *Koine Eirene. General Peace and Local Independence in Ancient Greece.* Oxford.

————. (1976). "Demosthenes and Philip's Peace of 338/7 B.C." *CQ* 26: 85–87.

de Ste. Croix, G. E. M. (1964). Review of J. J. Buchanan, *Theorika. A Study of Monetary Distributions to the Athenian Citizenry during the Fifth and Fourth Centuries B.C. CR* 14: 190–92.

————. (1963). "The Alleged Secret Pact Between Athens and Philip II Concerning Amphipolis and Pydna." *CQ* 13: 110–19.

————. (1972). *The Origins of the Peloponnesian War.* London.

————. (1981). *The Class Struggle in the Ancient Greek World.* London.

Schaefer, A. (1858). *Demosthenes und seine Zeit: Beilagen.* Leipzig.

————. (1885–87). *Demosthenes und seine Zeit,* 2nd ed. 3 vols. Leipzig.

Schaps, D. (1977). "The Woman Least Mentioned." *CQ* 27: 323–30.

Schwenk, C. (1985). *Athens in the Age of Alexander: The Dated Laws and Decrees of the 'Lycourgan Era' 338–322 B.C.* Chicago.

Sealey, R. (1955). "Proxenos and the Peace of Philocrates." *WS* 88: 145–52.

————. (1958). "On Penalizing Areopagites." *AJPh* 79: 71–73.

————. (1967). *Essays in Greek Politics.* New York.

————. (1978). "Philipp II und Athen, 344/3 und 339." *Historia* 27: 295–316.

Thalheim, T. (1894). "Aischines (15)." *RE* 1: 1,050–52.

Thomas, R. (1989). *Oral Tradition and Written Record in Classical Athens.* Cambridge.

Thompson, W. E. (1967). "Andocides and Hellanicus." *TAPhA* 98: 483–90.

————. (1974). "Tot Atheniensibus idem nomen erat." In D. W. Bradeen and M. F. McGregor, eds., *Phoros, Tribute to Benjamin Dean Meritt.* Locust Valley, N.Y.: 144–49.

Tod, M. N. (1948). *A Selection of Greek Historical Inscriptions.* Vol. 2. Oxford.

Todd, S. (1990a). "The Use and Abuse of the Attic Orators." *G&R* 37: 159–78.

————. (1990b). "The Purpose of Evidence in Athenian Courts." In Cartledge, Millett and Todd (1990): 19–39.

Traill, J. S. (1975). *The Political Organization of Attica. Hesperia* Suppl. 14. Princeton.

Trevett, J. (1991). "The Date of [Demosthenes] 49: A Re-Examination." *Phoenix* 45: 21–27.

Tritle, L. A. (1988). *Phocion the Good.* New York and Sydney.

————. (1992). "Forty-five or What? The Generalships of Phocion." *LCM* 17: 19–23.

Tronson, A. (1984). "Satyrus the Peripatetic and the Marriages of Philip II." *JHS* 104: 116–26.

Vansina, J. (1985). *Oral Tradition as History.* Madison, Wisc.

Veyne, P. (1990). *Bread and Circuses: Historical Sociology and Political Pluralism.* Trans. B. Pearce. London.

Wallace, R. W. (1989a). *The Areopagus Council to 317 B.C.* Baltimore.

————. (1989b). "The Athenian *Proeispherontes.*" *Hesperia* 58: 473–90.

Wankel, H. (1961). *Kalos kai Agathos.* Frankfurt.

————. (1976). *Demosthenes: Rede für Ktesiphon über den Kranz.* 2 vols. Heidelberg.

————. (1980). "Philipp II an der Thermopylen 346." *ZPE* 39: 57–62.

————. (1981). "Bemerkungen zur delphischen Amphiktyonie." *ZPE* 42: 153–66.

————. (1984). "Die Athenische Strategen der Schlacht bei Chaironea." *ZPE* 45: 45–53.

————. (1988). "Die Datierung des Prozesses gegen Timarchos (346/5)." *Hermes* 116: 383–86.

Weber, M. (1946). *From Max Weber: Essays in Sociology.* Trans. and ed. H. H. Gerth and C. Wright Mills. New York.

West, W. C. (1989). "The Public Archives in Fourth-century Athens." *GRBS* 30: 529–43.

Wilamowitz-Moellendorf, U. von. (1909). "Lesefrüchte." *Hermes* 44: 445–76.

Wilcken, U. (1929). "Philipp II von Makedonien und die panhellenische Idee." *Sitz. Berlin.* 291–318.

Will, W. (1983). *Athen und Alexander. Untersuchungen zur Geschichte der Stadt von 338 bis 322 v. Chr.* Munich.

Winkler, J. J. (1990). *The Constraints of Desire: The Anthropology of Sex and Gender in Ancient Greece.* London.

Wolff, H.-J. (1974). *Opuscula Dispersa.* Amsterdam.

Worthington, I. (1991). "Greek Oratory, Revision of Speeches and the Problem of Historical Reliability." *C&M* 42: 55–74.

———. (1992). *A Historical Commentary on Dinarchus: Rhetoric and Conspiracy in Fourth-Century Athens.* Ann Arbor.

Wüst, F. (1938). *Philipp II von Makedonien und Griechenland in den Jahren von 346 bis 338.* Munich.

Wyse, W. (1904). *The Speeches of Isaeus.* Cambridge.

Young, S. (1939). "An Athenian Clepsydra." *Hesperia* 8: 274–34.

Index